Developing a Legal Paradigm for Patents

DEVELOPING A LEGAL PARADIGM FOR PATENTS

Helen Gubby

eleven
international publishing

Published, sold and distributed by Eleven International Publishing
P.O. Box 85576
2508 CG The Hague
The Netherlands
Tel.: +31 70 33 070 33
Fax: +31 70 33 070 30
e-mail: sales@budh.nl
www.elevenpub.com

Sold and distributed in USA and Canada
International Specialized Book Services
920 NE 58th Avenue, Suite 300
Portland, OR 97213-3786, USA
Tel.: 1-800-944-6190 (toll-free)
Fax: +1 503 280-8832
orders@isbs.com
www.isbs.com

Eleven International Publishing is an imprint of Boom uitgevers Den Haag.

ISBN: 978-94-90947-38-5
© 2012 Helen Gubby | Eleven International Publishing

Printed in The Netherlands

PREFACE

Having studied both history and law, it is perhaps not surprising that I would be attracted to a subject which gave me the possibility to combine both these areas: the development of patent law during the earlier phase of the Industrial Revolution in England. As a young history student, one of the university courses which made the most impression on me was the course given on the Industrial Revolution. While the period evoked the spectre of the 'dark satanic mills', at the same time it was a period of invention and innovation.

I chose to examine the development of patent law during the early phase of the Industrial Revolution from the perspective of case law. As a barrister by training, I was strongly drawn to the court room argumentation, which was described in detail in some of these cases. I was deeply impressed by the quality of the advocacy shown by some of these barristers. The cut and thrust of Bearcroft in *R v. Arkwright* 1785 or the skilful submissions made by Pollock in *Cornish v. Keene* 1837 and *Crane v. Price* 1842 would still serve today as examples of how it should be done. The courts of Lord Mansfield, Lord Kenyon and Lord Tenterden have grown familiar to me over the years of this study.

Much of the research in this book was carried out as a Ph.D. I would like to thank my thesis supervisor, Professor Laurens Winkel, professor of legal history at the Erasmus University Rotterdam, the Netherlands, for his valuable advice, his kindness and support. I also appreciate the help given to me by Professor John Cairns of Edinburgh University and the comments and remarks made by Professor Vogenauer of the University of Oxford and Professor Dirk van Zijl Smit of the University of Nottingham. The suggestion to link this historical perspective to present day discussions on patents came from Professor Cohen Jehoram of the Erasmus University Rotterdam, who is also an intellectual property lawyer. On a personal note, I would like to thank my good friends and family. A huge debt of gratitude is owed to my husband, Richard. His support has been unwavering. During the time I wrote my thesis, he put together two new computers for me and provided endless technical assistance. Even more important, he was there to encourage me when the project just seemed overwhelming. I would also like to thank my daughter, Hannah, who was completing her own Ph.D. at the same time I was writing mine. Our lunches together, during which we discussed the highs and lows of the life of the Ph.D. candidate, were a great comfort. Thanks too to my boys, Bobbie and Jamie, who were prepared to tolerate this strange preoccupation of their mother's and on occasion find files that seemed to have curiously disappeared from the face of the computer or lend other technical assistance. I would also like to say thank you to my friends: you never tired of asking me how my Ph.D. was going! And thank you Nessie, who not only put me up all the times I came to London to visit the British Library, but has always been there for me. Finally, I would like to thank my parents; it is a pity that my father is not here to read this book.

TABLE OF CONTENTS

INTRODUCTION

For centuries, courts of law have been faced with the problem of determining what type of innovation is an appropriate subject matter for a patent. With each technical advance, the question of what is, and what is not, patentable must once again be determined by the courts. In more recent times, software based inventions have been the subject of considerable legal controversy and uncertainty. If a computer program is not patentable, and can only be protected by copyright, does that mean it is not possible to patent software for a program-controlled machine, or a program-controlled manufacturing process? Or should a distinction be drawn between a computer program as such and a computer program controlling a technical process? Can newly identified DNA sequences be patented or is that simply the discovery of scientific principles? The type of technology at issue may have changed since the eighteenth century, but the legal discussions these developments have engendered show some remarkable similarities to the discussions that were taking place in the courts during the Industrial Revolution.

This study traces the development of a legal structure for patents for invention during the earlier phase of the Industrial Revolution in England (1750s-1830s). In the final chapter, a jump forward is made to recent legal discussions on the patentability of software. These discussions are placed within this historical context. The study charts the development of patent law by examining judicial decision-making in patent disputes in the late eighteenth-early nineteenth century. Its focus is on the attitude of judges to patents. It examines what factors judges may have taken into account in reaching their decisions and how these factors may have affected the moulding of the legal concepts of patent law.

This emphasis is rather different from the more modern works on the patent system consulted in this study. H.I. Dutton's *The patent system and inventive activity during the industrial revolution 1750-1852* set out to assess the impact of the patent system on inventive activity. Christine MacLeod's *Inventing the Industrial Revolution: the English patent system, 1660-1800*, while providing an administrative history of the patent system, also explored the relationship between patents and inventions with particular regard to patent records. The purpose of Dirk van Zijl Smit's *The Social Creation of a Legal Reality: A Study of the Emergence and Acceptance of the British Patent System as a Legal Instrument for the Control of New Technology* was to contribute to a sociological understanding of the emergence of patent law and the way in which the patent system had been accepted by 1883 as a legal instrument to control and exploit new technology. Brad Sherman and Lionel Bentley's *The Making of Modern Intellectual Property Law: The British Experience 1760-1911* is a broader work than these three books and this study, as it is an account of the emergence of intellectual property law in general, with its categorisations of patents, copyright, design and trademarks, and analyses the way in which the law grants property status to intangibles.

In the eighteenth-early nineteenth century, the patent grant was an act of the royal prerogative, as regulated by the Statute of Monopolies 1624. Letters patent were royal proclamations which functioned as administrative instruments for granting certain powers and privileges. These powers and privileges could be various in nature, including the granting of land, titles and offices. Privileges as diverse as patents for the supervision over an industry or trade, or a patent to enforce compliance with certain statutes, allowing the patentee to levy fines if the statute in question was breached, had been granted.[1] Patents for new inventions were just one type of patent; the term 'patent' would only become specifically linked to inventions in the course of the nineteenth century. Until the late eighteenth century, patents for new inventions represented only a small minority of all the letters patent which were filed.[2]

To obtain a patent, the inventor submitted a petition requesting a patent to one of the Secretaries of State, which would be referred to the law officers of the crown (the principal law officer being the Attorney-General, assisted by his deputy the Solicitor-General). This was only the beginning of a time-consuming, bureaucratic process, which included the signing and countersigning of a warrant, a bill being drafted, signed and sealed, and a writ authorising the Chancellor to engross the patent on parchment and seal it.[3] There was, however, no system of examination and it was only rarely that an invention would be examined prior to the patent being granted. Once all the necessary fees had been paid, the patent grant was usually a formality. From the 1730s onwards, the inventor was also required to register a patent specification disclosing the nature of his invention within a certain period after the grant of patent. Under Section VI of the Statute of Monopolies, the recipient of a patent grant for a new invention had the sole right of "working or making" the invention for a term of fourteen years. This exclusive right allowed the patentee to prevent any other person from using the subject matter protected by the patent. After the enactment of the Statute of Monopolies in 1624, it was clear that an inventor could only protect his invention from piracy by patent and that patent must be in conformity with the conditions set out in the Statute. (See paragraph 4.3 and paragraph 6.4.1).

The focus of the Statute of Monopolies was on monopolies rather than patents for new inventions, as the name by which this Act has commonly come to be known implies. Section I (5) in declaring that all monopolies would be void, including letters patent, referred to grants "for the sole buying, selling, making, working or using of any thing within the

---

1   Chris Dent, "Patent Policy in Early Modern England: Jobs, Trade and Regulation", *Legal History* (2006) Vol. 10, p. 74.
2   Christine MacLeod, *Inventing the Industrial Revolution: The English patent system, 1660-1800*, Cambridge 1988, p. 2.
3   For a more detailed account see MacLeod (1988), p. 41.

realm". Section VI of the Statute provided an exception to this general prohibition on monopolies for letters patent and grants of privilege to the "true and first inventor" of "any manner of new manufactures within this realm", if that manufacture was not already in use at the time of the patent grant, and the new invention was not in some way harmful to the state. A crucial element, therefore, in determining what was the subject matter of this exclusive right granted by patent was the definition of the term 'new manufactures'. Section I of the Statute, as noted above, had referred to the buying, selling making, working or using of a "thing". Was the term 'manufacture' to be understood to be a "thing", or could the term encompass a method capable of producing a thing, the protection of the patent being applicable to the method as separate from the thing itself? The interpretation by the judiciary of the term 'manufactures', and hence the subject matter of patent protection, is one of the major elements in the development of patent law examined in this study.

In the time between the Statute of Monopolies 1624 and the Patent Law Amendment Act 1852 there were several statutes passed dealing with patents. However, the Acts of 1835, 1839 and 1844, all introduced by Lord Brougham, dealt only with certain specific details. The Act of 1835 removed the competence to extend the period of patent protection from parliament to the Judicial Committee of the Privy Council and allowed certain errors in the specification to be set right, while the Act of 1839 effected only a minor amendment regarding the granting of patent extensions (see paragraph 1.5 and chapter 3, introduction). The Act of 1844, which falls outside the period covered in this study, empowered the Judicial Committee of the Privy Council to extend patents for up to fourteen years. There was no comprehensive statutory overhauling of the patent system until the 1852 Patent Law Amendment Act. Consequently, the Statute of Monopolies remained the statutory foundation for patent law. As the interpretation of the Statute of Monopolies, and the patent specification, fell to the courts, this left the development of patent law throughout the period of this study very much in the hands of the judges of the common law courts.

Before the mid-eighteenth century, however, the common law courts had not been the primary forum to determine the validity of the royal grants of patent. At the end of the sixteenth century, Elizabeth I had resisted attempts by parliament to have cases arising out of her royal grants tried in the common law courts, rather than in her own conciliar courts. It was the crown's prerogative to grant letters patent and, as the patent was a royal privilege, any disputes were seen by the crown as a matter to be decided under her own conciliar jurisdiction, not that of the common law courts. The case of *Darcy v. Allin* 1602, tried in a common law court, marked Elizabeth's concession to parliament in this respect. Despite this apparent concession by the crown, the common law courts would hear few patent cases in the seventeenth century. Of these, perhaps the most well-known is the case of the Ipswich Cloth Makers, heard in 1614 by the Court of King's Bench. Little changed after the Statute of Monopolies came into force in 1624, even though the Statute of Monopolies had determined that all monopolies should be tried according to the common law, and not otherwise. It was the Privy Council, a body of men who were appointed and dismissed by the crown and whose function was to advise the crown on the exercise of the royal prerogative, which continued to hear patent validity cases well into the eighteenth century. The Privy Council only relinquished its competence to hear these cases in the wake of a dispute concerning Dr. James's patent in 1752 (see paragraph 1.1.1). The transfer of jurisdiction to the common law courts in the 1750s marks the starting point of this study.

The end point of the main part of this study is the 1830s. It is the decade in which an older mode of interpreting patents is clearly commuted. This discernable shift in the 1830s has been seen by several recent scholars as a watershed, marking a transition from an attitude of judicial hostility towards patents to a more favourable attitude by judges. Although Dutton acknowledged that determining the attitude of judges to patents was difficult, given that they not only seemed to be at variance with each other but also with themselves, he noted the "excessively hostile attitude of some judges". It was not until the 1830s that this period of "early prejudice" against patents gave way. Using a statistical analysis of patent cases, Dutton showed that judges were more generous to patentees after 1830 than in any previous period. This marked change in the attitudes of judges in the early 1830s was, in his opinion, because the judges now "accepted that inventions led to prosperity and economic growth".[4] His findings were endorsed by MacLeod. Pointing to Dutton's conclusion, that the attitude of common law judges was largely hostile to patents for about fifty years before 1830, she observed that in the patent litigation of the closing decades of the eighteenth century "the odds were stacked against patentees".[5]

The severity with which some judges treated the patent specification was a common cause for complaint by patentees: a patent could be set aside because of some "trifling fault" in the specification.[6] For example, a patent for an improvement to the English flute to render fingering easier and to produce notes not produced before was set aside because only one musical note had been produced, and the patent had stated a plural, 'new notes', when in fact there was just one. It was voided despite the fact that several professional flageolet players, called as witnesses, had described the patentee's instrument as "a great improvement".[7] A patent for a tapering hairbrush was set aside because, according to the judge: "Tapering means gradually converging to a point. According to the specification,

---

4   H.I. Dutton, *The patent system and inventive activity during the industrial revolution 1750-1852*, Manchester 1984, pp. 76-81.

5   MacLeod, *Inventing the Industrial Revolution: the English patent system, 1660-1800* (1988), pp. 72, 74.

6   See for example the testimony of the patent agent, William Newton, in the *Report from the Select Committee on the Law relative to Patents for Inventions 1829*, p. 76 (hereafter referred to as the *Select Committee Report 1829*).

7   *Bainbridge v. Wigley* 1810, 1 CPC 278.

the bristles would be of unequal length, but there would be no tapering to a point, which the title of the patent assumes."[8]

Should the development of patent law from the 1750s to the 1830s be read in terms of 'hostility' and 'prejudice' giving way in the 1830s to a more favourable approach because judges now thought inventions were good for the economy? Was judicial hostility and prejudice towards patents during this period a factor which affected the development of patent law? Lord Kenyon did not hide his personal distaste for patents. Lord Ellenborough was the judge who had found the two patents referred to above (the cases of *Bainbridge v. Wigley* 1810 and *R v. Metcalf* 1817) void because of grammatical irregularities. Lord Mansfield had a high rate of nonsuits and nominal damage awards in patent cases. Is this evidence of judicial 'hostility' and 'prejudice' towards patents?

By awarding the patentee the exclusive right to work or make the invention during the period of protection, a patent instituted a monopoly. The Statute of Monopolies had prohibited monopolies, as contrary to the laws of the realm. A patent for a new invention, however, was an exception to that general prohibition on monopolies, if the patent had been awarded in compliance with the conditions laid down in the Statute. Is it possible that a judge's attitude towards monopolies played a role in judicial decision-making in patent cases?

There is one other possible factor that may have affected judicial decision-making: the nature of the patent as a legal entity and the legal status of the patentee. Based on the judicial opinions expressed in copyright cases, it is apparent that neither copyright nor a patent for a new invention fitted neatly within a more traditional interpretation of property at common law. Was the patent to be seen in contractual terms, as a contract between the crown, on behalf of the public, and the individual patentee? Or was the patent a species of property? If it was a species of property, had it ever been recognised as such at common law or was it an anomalous form of property? Should the patentee's legal position best be described in terms of having a right or a privilege? Whether the attitude taken by judges to these questions had an impact on their decision-making in patent cases and the development of patent law is explored in this study.

In order to examine these factors, the case reports of the period are of vital importance and it is these case reports which form the mainstay of this study. As explained in chapter 1, from the mid-eighteenth century court reporting became more accurate and reliable. Series of reports appeared written by reporters who had specialized in reporting cases in a particular court. It was James Burrow who inaugurated this new era of court reporting with his reports on cases heard in King's Bench under Lord Mansfield (the reports were published in five volumes covering the period 1756-1772). However, not all patent cases were reported in this period and some were only partially recorded. Sometimes the only

---

8   *R v. Metcalf 1817*, 1 CPC 393.

reference to cases is to be found in the trial notebooks of the judges, in newspapers or pamphlets. These are important sources, but particularly with respect to pamphlets, it should be borne in mind that the party producing the pamphlet was not disinterested. It is to be expected that a pamphlet would highlight those statements made by a judge that were favourable to the cause of the pamphleteer.

To be consistent with the terminology of these reports, the one bringing an action is referred to as the plaintiff in this study, and not by the more modern English term 'claimant'. Quoting from these cases and legal literature of the period also entails an archaic way of referring to statutes, which was by citing the statute according to the year of the reign of a particular monarch, an abbreviation of the monarch's name, which could take a Latin form, the chapter number and section number. For example, Section VI on patents for new inventions in the Statute of Monopolies 1624 was cited as 21 Jac. 1. c. 3. s. 6: the twenty-first year of the reign of James I, chapter 3, section 6. It should also be noted that the spelling of the names of the parties was not always consistent in the case reports, for example, *Morris v. Bramson/Branson* 1776, *Harmar/Harmer v. Playne/Plane* 1807-1809 and *Macfarlane/Macfarland v. Price* 1816. The spelling in the quotations taken from eighteenth century texts has been modernised for ease of reading.

In the early years of the nineteenth century, the first of several compilations of patent cases appeared. John Davies, an official in an office where specifications were enrolled, gathered together his collection of patent cases in the period 1785 to 1816. Davies's collection of cases (DPC), which appeared in 1816, was one of the sources for later compilations. Important compilations were also made by William Carpmael and Thomas Webster. Carpmael's collection (CPC) was put together in the period 1802 to 1840. Although Carpmael had been called to the bar, he was also a trained civil engineer. Carpmael's reports were intended not just for lawyers but also for patentees, manufacturers and inventors. Like Carpmael, Thomas Webster, whose compilation was made between1802 and 1855, had also been called to the bar but he too had studied engineering. Not only did Webster's *Reports and Notes on Cases on Letters Patent* (WPC) become a standard work, he was actively involved in the campaign to reform the granting of patents, which would finally result in the legislation of 1852.[9] Although some of the reports in the compilations of Webster and Carpmael are the same, there can be variations in the reporting. For example, unlike Webster, Carpmael deals in detail with the Chancery and King's Bench hearings of *Harmar v. Playne*, respectively 1807 and 1809. These collections form a major source in the most recent compilation of patent cases by Peter Hayward. In *Hayward's Patent Cases* (HPC), all the available reports on any one particular case have been compiled. Apart from Webster and Carpmael, his sources include the English Reports (ER), Goodeve's Abridg-

---

9   William Holdsworth, *A History of English Law*, London 1964, vol. XIII, pp. 431, 442.

ment, and journals such as the London Journal of Arts and Sciences and Register of Arts (RA).[10]

It was also in the early nineteenth century that the first patent treatises appeared. John Collier's *An Essay on Patents for New Inventions* was published in 1803. Richard Godson's *A Practical Treatise on the Law of Patents for Invention and Copyright* appeared in 1823, with a supplement in 1832. On the other hand, very few lines are devoted to patents in one of the most significant general legal treatises used throughout the period under consideration here: William Blackstone's *Commentaries on the Laws of England*, the four volumes of which were first published between 1765 and 1769. Nonetheless, Blackstone's *Commentaries* are also an important source for this study. Blackstone's work, which was considered to be a classic even by contemporaries, addresses several matters of relevance to this study, such as the judicial interpretation of statutes, the object of property at common law and monopolies. The edition of the *Commentaries* used in this study is the twelfth edition, published in 1793, and the page numbers cited refer to this edition. This edition of Blackstone's *Commentaries* was edited by Edward Christian. Christian, who was the first Downing professor of the laws of England at Cambridge, would act as the editor of the 12th through to the 15th edition of Blackstone's *Commentaries*. Christian's footnotes were sometimes of a quite extensive nature. The footnotes were intended to bring Blackstone's text up to date, as well as providing Christian with a forum to make certain observations of his own. Christian's footnotes are, therefore, of interest in their own right.

Chapter 1 The Patent Courts and Court Reporting

Chapter 1 also provides a brief outline of the courts which were hearing patent cases at this time. There was no one specific court which heard patent cases in the eighteenth and early nineteenth century, as all three of the senior common law courts (King's Bench, Common Pleas and Exchequer) had jurisdiction. Patent cases in the common law courts could be heard at *nisi prius*, before a single judge and a jury. A case could, however, be considered by the full court, for example on a motion to set aside the verdict reached at *nisi prius* or on a writ of error to consider a point of law (see paragraph 1.3). The Court of Chancery, a court of equity, also had a role to play. This was primarily because only an equity court could grant an injunction.

---

10 Peter Hayward, *Hayward's Patent Cases 1600-1883*, Abingdon, Oxon. 1987.

Chapter 2 Divisions Within the Judiciary: Were Some Judges Hostile to Patentees?

In the absence of major statutory intervention in the period under consideration, the development of patent law fell largely to the judges. To contend that judges moulded the law presumes that judges have a creative function, either of an original or derivative nature. Without this creative aspect, whether judges were hostile to or prejudiced against patents, would be irrelevant. In chapter 2, a very brief overview is given of three models of judicial interpretation: the formalist, rule bound model; the creative model and the bounded creativity model. Within the judiciary a split is discernable between those judges who conceive of their role in formalist terms and those judges who adopt a teleological approach, the latter being willing to adapt the law to the perceived needs and circumstances of the day. It would seem, however, that in practice, even those judges who endorse a formalist conception of the role of the judge are more than simply a *bouche de la loi*.

The legal treatises of the eighteenth century put forward a formalist approach to the judicial role. Nonetheless, as the opinions of Lord Mansfield and some of the other judges in the Court of King's Bench make clear, the approach of some judges was teleological: not the black letter of the law but its purpose was the key to interpretation. Even a judge like Blackstone, who put forward a formalist approach to judicial decision-making in his *Commentaries*, argued for the equitable interpretation of statutes. Vogenauer, in his examination of statutory interpretation in England and on the continent, argues that the equitable interpretation of statutes was the predominant form of judicial interpretation in the period from the Year Books to 1830 (see paragraph 2.1.1 and 2.2, and paragraph 3.2). Chapter 2 explores this split within the judiciary and whether the attitude of judges to patents should be analysed in terms of difference in interpretational style rather than in terms of hostility and prejudice.

Chapter 3 Patent Law: The Interpretation of the Statute of Monopolies 1624 from the 1750s to the 1830s

In traditional areas of law, where the bounds of orthodoxy had been well established, differing interpretational styles within the judiciary were generally not particularly conspicuous. Radical attempts to push those bounds were relatively rare, but when such an attempt was made the differing approaches to the role of the judge would surface. The split between the formalist approach and the teleological approach would emerge very clearly in a new area of law virtually devoid of precedents in the common law courts: patent law. As chapter 3 will show, the different styles of judicial interpretation would affect the way in which the Statute of Monopolies was read.

In particular, it was the meaning ascribed to the term 'manufacture' in the Statute of Monopolies which brought the diversity in judicial styles of interpretation to the fore. Some judges were prepared to recognise that many patents were granted for methods of use to industry and manufacturing and, therefore, they considered that the term 'manufacture' encompassed a method. Others rejected this reading of 'manufacture'. These judges preferred a literal reading of the term or resorted to analysing the term in what they conceived to be the historical context of the Statute of Monopolies in 1624. The wording of an early seventeenth century statute would raise various interpretation issues, as the courts struggled to apply the Statute of Monopolies to the increasingly technical nature of innovative advancements in the eighteenth and early nineteenth century.

Chapter 4 Patent Law: The Interpretation of the Patent Specification 1750s to the 1830s

The interpretation of the patent specification, examined in chapter 4, would similarly split along these lines: a formalist, literal approach or a more liberal approach. The enrolment of a patent specification, describing the nature of the invention, became standard in the 1730s. Whether the patent specification had been instigated at the behest of the patentee to protect his invention, or at the will of the crown to ensure that the invention could be made by others at the expiration of the period of patent protection, is a matter of scholarly debate. It would become clear, however, that the common law courts deemed the purpose of the specification to be the instruction of the public. The wording of the specification had to reflect that purpose; it had to enable a competent, skilled workman familiar with the industry to make the invention from the specification alone. It was also required of the specification that it was apparent whether the patentee's invention was entirely new, or consisted in an improvement or addition to an older invention.

As chapter 4 will show, some judges read the specification literally, subjecting it to a strict grammatical analysis, and allowing not the slightest defect in the document. Other judges would find a specification satisfactory, even if there were minor defects, as long as an adequate and fair disclosure of the invention had been made and the instructions were clear to one skilled in the trade.

Although reading a specification in a formalist or more liberal way may have accorded with an individual judge's preferred interpretational style, chapter 4 examines other factors which could have influenced the mode of interpretation. A strict interpretation may have been prompted by the fact that a patent awarded a monopoly; it may also have arisen because of a fear of fraudulent behaviour on the part of the patentee. Those judges who construed the patent specification within a contractual context, however, were more alert to the rights as well as the obligations of the patentee. Chapter 4 examines another aspect of the judicial interpretation of the patent specification. In disclosing the nature of the invention and providing instructions to enable another to make that invention, the patent specification could contain a highly technical description and set of instructions. As a technical, scientific document, a specification could pose a challenge to those whose background was not in science and engineering. It may have prompted some judges to analyse the text of the specification primarily from a linguistic rather than a technical perspective, a perspective more familiar to the legal profession.

Chapter 5 The Patent Monopoly: Factors Affecting the Attitude of Judges to the Monopoly Grant for Patents for Invention

As noted in chapter 4, one of the factors which may have influenced the judicial interpretation of patent specifications was the fact it awarded a monopoly. The attitude of judges to monopolies is examined in chapter 5. Their attitude to monopolies could have been formed by such matters as the history of abuse associated with the term 'monopoly'; the popular belief that all monopolies were void at common law; or that the monopoly was undesirable because of its economic impact as well as from a moral or religious perspective.

Once again, there was a diversity of approach within the judiciary. If a judge viewed the monopoly awarded by the patent grant in the same light as those monopolistic practices which had been condemned in a previous era, as a practice which took away a right from the public, this may have affected his reading of the patent specification. However, if the patent was viewed within a different context, that of public utility, the temporary monopoly awarded by the patent grant assumed a different guise. In this context, the monopoly for a new invention did not hinder the public. It did not take away a right that had existed before. If the invention were not of use to the public, it would simply fail, but if the invention was useful, then both the public and the inventor could reap the benefits. In that light, a temporary monopoly was an appropriate means to encourage useful inventions; the reward would be in proportion to the utility of the invention. Minor shortcomings in the patent specification need not undermine the patent.

It is possible that some judges did not regard patentees as highly as those who produced literary works. A scant regard for the creative input of an inventor may have affected how some judges saw the monopoly for an invention. It is also possible that vested interests may have had a role to play. Pressure by manufacturers to get rid of a troublesome monopoly or pressure brought to bear by the patentee and his financial backers may have been a factor in determining the validity of a patent.

CHAPTER 6 THE PATENT AS A FORM OF PERSONAL PROPERTY

Finally, chapter 6 examines how the judicial perception of the position of the patentee may have been affected by another divisive issue within the judiciary: the concept of property at common law. Although the patent specification could be read in terms of a contractual relationship, the patent was treated as a species of property. However, whether the patent for invention and copyright were species of property recognised at common law was a matter debated in several high profile copyright cases in the eighteenth century. If a property right at common law was defined as a right exercisable against third parties in relation to a thing, what was the 'thing' that was the subject of patent protection? The common law did recognise certain forms of incorporeal property, not all of which could be said to be related to a material 'thing'. Yet there were judges who were adamant that neither copyright nor a patent for an invention was a form of property recognised by the common law: copyright was a species of property created by statute (the Statute of Anne 1709) and the patent owed its existence to an act of the royal prerogative regulated by the Statute of Monopolies.

Whether a judge saw the patentee as having a privilege stemming from an act of the royal prerogative regulated by statute or as having a right to prevent another copying and selling an invention at common law could have affected the view a judge took of the position of the patentee. The common law was usually associated with concepts of natural justice and reason. A right at common law would, therefore, imply that the right was founded on natural justice and reason. However, a temporary 'privilege' awarded in the name of the crown, and regulated by statute, may have lacked the moral imperative of a natural right.

Chapter 6 also explores another aspect of the discussion of the patent as a form of property. A judge's understanding of the legal nature of property may have affected substantive patent law. If a judge considered that the common law required a proprietary right to be related to a physical thing, he may have transferred that concept to patent law. The patent – giving a temporary right to exclude others from exploiting the patentee's invention – was incorporeal property. If it was seen in the same way as an incorporeal hereditament, as "a right issuing out of a thing corporate (whether real or personal)" as "not the thing corporate itself ... but something collateral thereto",[11] this could have led the judge to look for "a thing corporate" to which the patent right was connected. This may have led him to accept a machine or substance, or possibly even an instrument, as the subject matter of a patent, but not a process. The chapter examines whether there is a correlation between the legal concept of property becoming broader and the *de facto* acceptance by the courts of protection by patent for a process, as separate from the product made. If so, this would

---

11   William Blackstone, *Commentaries on the Laws of England*, (12th ed.), London 1793, II, 20.

indicate that a growing underlying acceptance of the notion of 'intellectual property' may materially have affected the development of patent law during this period.

Chapter 7 From the Industrial Revolution to the Digital Revolution: The Software Challenge

The subject matter of patents had started to change in the eighteenth century: rather than being granted for the encouragement of whole new industries, they increasingly concerned new techniques. In the late twentieth-early twenty-first century, a very new form of technology began to be the subject of patent applications: digital technology. This digital technology now had to be fitted into a legal paradigm for patents that had largely been developed in response to the mechanisation technology of the Industrial Revolution.

By the mid-twentieth century, the old Statute of Monopolies had been replaced. The Patents Act 1949 would in turn be superseded by the Patents Act 1977, which is the statute English judges have to interpret today. The UK Patents Act 1977 was based on, and intended to give effect to, the European Patent Convention 1973 (EPC). The Act's European connection is significant because the English courts acknowledged that while they were not bound by the decisions of the Boards of Appeal of the European Patent Office, those decisions should be taken into account. Both the UK Patents Act and the EPC specifically excluded computer programs "as such" from patentability.

In this chapter, a brief examination is made of the attempts by the English courts to determine the patentability of computer programs. When was a computer program simply a computer program "as such", and therefore non-patentable, and when was a computer program more than a computer program "as such", and therefore patent eligible? Different approaches would develop. A diversity of approach within the English judiciary surfaced in several early decisions. A rift would also later open up between the older 'technical effect' approach developed by the Boards of Appeal of the European Patent Office and adopted by the English courts, and the 'any hardware will do' approach applied more recently by the judges in the Boards of Appeal.

It is argued in this study that as computer programs are essentially a method the program is the process by which a computer is instructed to perform the discussion on the patentability of computer programs should be seen within the historical context of the legal debates on process patents. When placed in this context, the legal issues on the patentability of computer programs become markedly familiar. In some ways these issues are not significantly different from the issues confronting the judges hearing patent disputes in the late eigteenth-early nineteenth century. In trying to understanding present day discussions, it is contended that this historical perspective is a valuable one.

1   THE PATENT COURTS AND COURT REPORTING

In general, the only examination of the validity of a patent before its enrolment was a determination by the law officers as to whether the patent would be legal under the Statute of Monopolies. However, the law officer's report seems to have been usually a matter of course and the system was probably administered in a most cursory way (see paragraph 4.3). The validity of a patent was only really tested if a dispute was brought before the courts.

During the period examined in this study, there was no specific common law court which heard patent disputes. All the common law courts had the capacity to hear patent cases. The court structure of the eighteenth-early nineteenth century was by no means a coherent one and there was often an overlapping of jurisdiction between the courts. A decision on a patent dispute by one senior court would not prevent essentially the same issue being brought to trial, by the same plaintiff, before a different senior court. The same case could also be heard by the same court on more than one occasion.

Cases were generally first heard at *nisi prius*: a trial before a single judge and a jury. A verdict reached at *nisi prius* had to be returned to the full court before the judgment could be filed. Motions by counsel for new trials or in arrest of judgment were routine. The case could be reconsidered by the full court if judgment had been reserved at *nisi prius* or an objection to the verdict had been filed. The verdict could be endorsed or the case could be heard again if a motion for a new trial was granted. Whereas a new trial was to bring the case before a jury to determine the facts of the case, matters of law arising from a proceeding were tried on a writ of error. Cases were brought on a writ of error before the Court of King's Bench from the courts of Common Pleas and Exchequer. The highest level of review was the House of Lords.

Depending on the remedy required, a patentee could find it necessary or expedient to bring an action before an equity court. The patentee could apply to the equity courts for such equitable remedies as an injunction, which would prevent the infringement of a patent until its validity had been tried in a court of common law, or an application for an account of any profits wrongfully obtained by a person who had infringed a patent. Actions brought before the common law courts were tried before a jury. The courts of equity did not make use of a jury, which meant that if issues of fact were raised, it would be necessary to have these issues transferred to a common law court.

1.1   The Court Structure

After the mid-eighteenth century, a shift in jurisdiction for patent cases took place. Although the common law courts had heard several significant patent cases in the sixteenth and early seventeenth century, until the mid-eighteenth century it was the Privy Council which was the main forum for disputes concerning the validity of patents. After the mid-eigtheenth century, the Privy Council relinquished its jurisdiction in patent validity cases to the common law courts.

1.1.1   Privy Council

It was the crown's prerogative to issue letters patent. The crown had the power to grant privileges for the sake of the public good, although prima facie they appeared to be clearly against the common right.[1] In the sixteenth century, under Elizabeth I, the granting of patents for new inventions introduced to the realm gathered momentum. As the patent was a royal privilege, Elizabeth I had been adamant that she had absolute jurisdiction in all disputes arising out of patent grants. The validity of the royal grant was not a matter for the common law courts. This was challenged in 1601 by parliament, but the bill was dropped when the Queen conceded that the validity of her patent grants should be left to the common law courts. The test case was *Darcy v. Allin 1602* and Hulme considers that "with this case commences the history of the English common law patent system".[2] *Darcy v. Allin* 1602 may have been seen as a victory for the common law courts, but it was not a resounding victory. The common law courts would hear only a few patent cases in the seventeenth century. Even after the passing of the Statute of Monopolies, which came into force in 1624, the Privy Council still had a dominant role in resolving patent validity cases. It would retain that role until well into the eighteenth century. This is rather surprising given that Section II of the Statute of Monopolies 1624 states:

> That all monopolies, and all such commissions, grants, licences, charters, letters patent, proclamations, inhibitions, restraints, warrants of assistance, and all other matters and things tending as aforesaid, and the force and validity of them and of every of them, ought to be and shall be forever hereafter examined, heard, tried and determined by and according to the *common laws of this realm, and not otherwise.*

---

1   Year Book, 40 Ed. III, (fol. 17, 18).
2   E. Hulme, "The History of the Patent System under the Prerogative and at Common Law", *Law Quarterly Review* (1896) 12, p. 151.

14

The words marked here in italics would seem to indicate that the common law courts would have the jurisdiction to hear patent validity cases. Yet, even Hulme, who is eager to date the history of the common law patent system back to the case of *Darcy v. Allin*, admits that the period from the Statute of Monopolies to the mid-eighteenth century is one "being almost barren of recorded common law decisions". What Hulme's research in the archives of the Privy Council did reveal, however, were records showing that the Privy Council was hearing patent validity cases long after the passing of the Statute of Monopolies.[3]

With its origins in the King's Council, the *curia regis*, the powers exercised by the Privy Council were the powers which the crown could exercise under the royal prerogative. The Privy Council had long administered a civil, as well as a criminal, jurisdiction. For example, the Privy Council would come to the aid of the Court of Admiralty in the hearing of merchants' cases, in particular those in which foreign merchants were concerned, as these were seen as connected to the promotion of trade. The use of arbitration in these civil cases was characteristic of the Council's proceedings, with these arbitration committees being composed of both laymen (often merchants) and common law lawyers. Under the Tudors and early Stuarts, the Council had been composed almost entirely of non-lawyers, but when legal advice was necessary, it would address the common law judges or the law officers of the crown.[4] A form of arbitration was offered to patentees by the Privy Council until the mid-eighteenth century.

As noted above, the competence of the Privy Council in patent cases arose because the grant of a patent was an act of the royal prerogative, as was its revocation. A patentee could petition the Privy Council to have an alleged infringer summoned before the Council on a charge of contempt of the royal prerogative. The Council would also hear complaints brought by tradesmen and manufacturers against patentees. The usual procedure in matters of patent validity was first to have a case referred to a committee of the Privy Council and then the committee would refer the case to the law officers.[5]

Davies' research shows that a revocation clause began to appear regularly in the patents of James I and, with the exception of a short period after the Restoration in which it was omitted from patents, this clause gradually became a fixed feature of all patents of invention. The clause usually stated that if on the examination of the patent before the Privy Council, or a specified number of its members, the grant was certified to be inconvenient or prejudicial to the realm, the patent would be made void. In the late seventeenth and eighteenth century, it generally mentioned the lack of novelty or that the patentee was not the first

---

3   E. Hulme, "Privy Council Law and Practice of Letters Patent for Invention from the Restoration to 1794", *Law Quarterly Review* (1917) 33, p. 63.

4   John P. Dawson, "The Privy Council and Private Law in the Tudor and Stuart Periods", *Michigan Law Review* 48, No. 4 (1950), pp. 406, 408, 426, 428.

5   MacLeod, *Inventing the Industrial Revolution: the English patent system, 1660-1800* (1988), pp. 58-59; Hulme, "Privy Council Law and Practice of Letters Patent for Invention from the Restoration to 1794" (1917), p. 191.

inventor as two grounds of revocation. From the registers it would seem that occasionally the Privy Council referred questions of novelty or priority of invention to the common law courts before using its powers under the clause to revoke a patent. Davies found evidence of revocations made under this clause by the Privy Council as late as 1779.[6] MacLeod notes that although the Privy Council could instruct the Attorney-General to prosecute the infringers of a patent that was unusual. More often the Council referred the parties to the civil jurisdiction of the common law courts; it was open to either party in a dispute to bring his case before a common law court. Given the paucity of recorded decisions in patent cases in the common law courts before the Privy Council ceded its jurisdiction, presumably it was more common for settlements to be reached out of court.[7]

The transition period, in which the common law courts rather than the Privy Council assumed importance in deciding the validity of patents, was the mid- eighteenth century and, according to Hulme, the trigger was Dr. James's case. In 1752, a petition was presented for the revocation of James's patent of 1747. The petition was dismissed by the Privy Council, upon which the petitioner, Walter Baker, requested that the clerk of the Privy Council be ordered to attend the trial against James for perjury that was to take place in the Court of King's Bench and to produce the original affidavit. According to Hulme, this led to a quarrel between the Privy Council and Lord Mansfield and, as a result of having considered its constitutional position, the Privy Council decided to cede its jurisdiction to the law courts.[8] Oldham, however, considers this theory as to why the transfer of jurisdiction took place to be 'somewhat speculative'. A less dramatic, but equally plausible explanation for the cessation of Privy Council jurisdiction in his opinion could simply have been that the increasing number and complexity of patent applications meant that the transfer was the practical option.[9] While it is quite possible that the Privy Council no longer wished to be put to the trouble of determining patent validity, given that it has been estimated that in the second half of the eighteenth century no more than twenty-two patent cases came before the senior common law courts (see paragraph 1.2), the patent case load of the Privy Council in the preceding period could not have been overwhelming.

The James case was not the very last case where an application was made to the Privy Council for the revocation of a patent. One application of interest is the petition signed by thirty-four instrument makers in June 1764. With the support of the Spectacle-makers' Company, Francis Watkins sought to upset Peter Dollond's patent for achromatic lenses. Having been ordered by the court to stop making achromatic lenses, the petitioners com-

---

6   D. Seaborne Davies, "The Early History of the Patent Specification", *Law Quarterly Review* (1934) 50, pp. 102-104.

7   MacLeod, *Inventing the Industrial Revolution: the English patent system, 1660-1800* (1988), p. 59.

8   Hulme, "Privy Council Law and Practice of Letters Patent for Invention from the Restoration to 1794" (1917), pp. 189, 194

9   James Oldham, *English Common Law in the age of Mansfield*, Chapel Hill and London 2004, p. 199, fn. 47.

plained to the Privy Council that they would be ruined if they were not allowed to make achromatic refracting telescopes. They argued against a patent that covered such a substantial part of a given trade. The Privy Council, however, declined to hear the petition and the defiant opticians were forced to face Peter Dollond in court; Dollond would win both in King's Bench in 1764 and in Common Pleas in 1766.[10] From Hulme's research, it would appear that the petition brought by Simpson and Balfour in 1794 to revoke the Cunningham's Scotch Patent was the last application to the Privy Council to revoke a patent. No further proceedings are recorded in the Privy Council Register for this case. Having searched the Registers from 1794 until 1810, Hulme could find no more applications.[11]

1.1.2   The Common Law Courts

The three superior courts at common law at this time were the Court of Common Pleas, the Court of King's Bench and the Court of Exchequer, which all sat at Westminster Hall. Common Pleas and King's Bench were common law courts; the Court of Exchequer had a mixed jurisdiction as both a common law and equity court.

The Court of Common Pleas was originally the court that heard actions in which the king had no interest, and the only court in which real actions could be brought. Hearing property and debt cases, it had jurisdiction over most civil cases. The jurisdiction of the Court of King's Bench extended to, on the Crown side, the competence to hear criminal cases and, on the plea side, actions of trespass, appeals of felony and hearing cases brought on a writ of error from the other courts of record, Common Pleas and Exchequer.

Within this framework, the Court of King's Bench was excluded from hearing common pleas. However, without the business of debt and real actions, there was little on the rolls. This deficiency was later addressed by the use of various procedural devices; legal fictions had enabled the Court of King's Bench to acquire jurisdiction over most common pleas during the course of the sixteenth century. The bill procedure of the King's Bench and the relative speed of its procedures made the court attractive to litigants. This would lead to competition between the two courts for business, particularly as judges and court officials were paid by the case. By the mid-eighteenth century, the victor was clearly the Court of King's Bench. It has been estimated that a steady increase in trial dockets in this court generated a massive load of business, averaging between 200-300 trials per term.[12] Baker strongly suspects that the general success of King's Bench, at the expense of Common Pleas, in the second half of the 18th century was due to the personality of Lord Mansfield,

---

10 Richard Sorrenson, "Dollond and Son's Pursuit of Achromaticity 1758-1789", *History of Science* (2001) xxxix, pp. 40-41, fn. 37 and 40.
11 Hulme, "Privy Council Law and Practice of Letters Patent for Invention from the Restoration to 1794" (1917), p. 193.
12 Oldham, *English Common Law in the age of Mansfield* (2004), p. 48.

his active and creative approach to commercial issues standing in stark contrast to "the 'sleepy hollow' of the Common Pleas".[13] This is disputed by Oldham. It was not the advent of Lord Mansfield that precipitated the decline of Common Pleas; the business of that court had been in decline for some time before Mansfield's arrival. Nor was the stagnation in business a matter of personalities, but more the consequence of certain traditional procedural requirements, such as the necessity to have the representation of a Sergeant-at-Law. Charles Pratt (later Lord Camden), who took over from Chief Justice Willes in 1761, was considered by contemporaries to be both eloquent and able. His successor, William De Grey, was also favourably depicted in the newspapers of the time.[14] With respect to patent cases, more patent cases were heard by King's Bench than by Common Pleas. In some cases, however, a dispute concerning the same patent was heard by both courts.

The cases generated by Arkwright's second patent are a good illustration of the multi-plicity of proceedings on essentially the same issue. Arkwright himself brought two cases for the infringement of his second patent. In *Arkwright v. Mordaunt* 1781, which was heard in the Court of King's Bench before Lord Mansfield, the court found against Arkwright. *Arkwright v. Nightingale* 1785 was heard by the Court of Common Pleas and this time, before Lord Loughborough, Arkwright was successful. Shortly after this victory, the patent came before the Court of King's Bench for a second time, with Buller, J. acting as the trial judge. This time the action had not been initiated by Arkwright, but by the Attorney-General in the name of the crown. It was commenced by a writ of *scire facias* to repeal the patent (see below). *R v.Arkwright* 1785 would result in the annulment of Arkwright's second patent. Arkwright later moved for a new trial, but Lord Mansfield made it very clear that the court could see no reason to grant Arkwright's request for a new trial, which would have set the whole process in motion again.[15]

Until 1841, the third central court, the Court of Exchequer, was both a court of law and a court of equity. It could hear all actions between subjects except for real actions. It also enforced the rights of the crown against subjects. However, its principal jurisdiction was as a court hearing revenue cases and controlling the Exchequer and the revenue officials. The equity jurisdiction of the court was extensive, but it would not interfere in a case which was before the Court of Chancery. Holdsworth notes that the time of the judges of this court was not fully occupied.[16] Before the nineteenth century, patent applications to the Court of Exchequer seem to have been rather infrequent.

---

13   J.H. Baker, *An Introduction to English Legal History*, London 2002, p. 50.
14   Oldham, *English Common Law in the age of Mansfield* (2004), p. 47-48.
15   Richard Arkwright, *The Trial of a Cause Instituted by Richard Pepper Arden, Esq*, London 1785, p. 191.
16   Holdsworth, *A History of English Law* (1964), vol. XIII, p. 556.

1.1.3   The Equity Courts

As noted above, the Court of Exchequer was for centuries both a court of law and a court of equity. The High Court of Chancery, however, functioned primarily as a court of equity. The jurisdiction of equity courts was quite distinct from that of the common law courts and this distinction can be seen with respect to patent disputes. It was not the task of the equity courts to determine the validity of patents. That lay within the competence of the common law courts. However, the equity courts offered remedies that were not available in the common law courts, and it was for this reason that a patentee might seek redress in the Court of Chancery (see paragraph 1.4). In order to understand the jurisdiction of equity courts in patent cases, it is necessary to look, if only very briefly, at the way in which these courts developed.

Whereas the common law formed the general law of the land, an equity jurisdiction had arisen in response to the formalisation of the writ system; it became impossible to bring an action in the common law courts if the claim did not fall within the scope of an existing writ. This had led to frustrated litigants petitioning the king's chancellor, who was an adviser to the king and a member of the King's Council. Prior to the Reformation, the chancellors had tended to be churchmen, schooled in canon law and civil law. When the Court of Chancery eventually separated from the King's Council, the Lord Chancellors who presided over the Court were prepared to use these sources to develop principles of equity.[17]

Initially proceedings were relatively flexible, as the chancellor based his decision on the facts of each individual case. The grounds for the ruling lay in the moral sphere, decisions being made according to 'conscience', not according to existing common law rules. Over time, there was a shift away from an appeal to the individual conscience of the chancellor to an appeal to 'equity', as the Court of Chancery developed its own principles. During the seventeenth century, the equitable jurisdiction became a more formalised one. Lord Nottingham, appointed chancellor in 1673, believed that equity should offer more certainty and not be dependent upon the personal determinations of any given chancellor. In the eighteenth century, although discretion remained an important factor in the courts of equity, the use of precedents increasingly formed the basis for deciding cases.

By the mid-18th century, there was little of that early flexibility to be detected in the procedures of the Court of Chancery. Indeed, the very word Chancery, notes Baker, "had become synonymous with expense, delay and despair".[18] A reluctance to grant equitable relief until all the facts had been presented and ordered, and excessive trial documentation, meant that Chancery proceedings were notoriously slow and costly.

---

17   Peter Stein, *Roman Law in European History*, Cambridge 1999, p. 88.
18   Baker, *An Introduction to English Legal History* (2002), p. 111.

1.2   PATENT ACTIONS IN THE COMMON LAW COURTS

The patent actions brought before the common law courts involved either an action to annul a patent or an action brought by the patentee to prevent the infringement of his patent. If a patent was to be declared void officially, it had to be annulled by the crown on a writ of *scire facias*. However, if a patentee brought a civil action for infringement, but failed in that action, in practice that failure would mean the end of his patent.

Until 1883, an action to repeal a patent was commenced by a writ of *scire facias*. The three grounds upon which a patent might be revoked by the writ were set out in Coke's *Fourth Institute*: where two patents had been granted for the same thing, the first patentee could have a *scire facias* to repeal the second; where a patent had been granted on a false suggestion or where the king had granted anything which by law he could not grant.[19] When a party wished to have a patent formally annulled, this required an objection to the patent to be lodged in the Petty Bag Office, which was part of the Chancery apparatus.

In England, letters patent were granted under the royal prerogative and sealed with the Great Seal. Consequently, an action to revoke a patent required the crown to decide whether to commence proceedings. The decision to proceed was taken via the crown's agent in patent matters, the Attorney-General. It was the Attorney-General who would sign the writ of *scire facias*, which would initiate the proceeding against the patentee.[20] Very often the initiative for annulment arose from manufacturers in the major industries. For example, in the case of *R v. Arkwright* the party pressing for the annulment was a consortium of cotton manufacturers. In *R v. Murray* 1803, the *scire facias* action against Murray was instigated by Boulton and Watt to repeal Murray's patent, granted in 1801, for an air pump for steam engines. Possibly influenced by the status of Boulton and Watt, and their remarkable success in legal actions, the day before the trial was due to be heard before Lord Ellenborough in King's Bench, the defendant withdrew his plea and his patent was cancelled.[21]

It is interesting to note Buller, J.'s comment in *R v. Arkwright* 1785 about the use of this writ: that although the writ had been used often in former times, the proceeding by *scire facias* to repeal a patent "is somewhat new in our days; none such has occurred within my memory".[22] However, in the Michaelmas term of that same year, Buller would preside over another *scire facias* patent case, *R v. Else* 1785, which was a trial of major interest to the country's lace manufacturers. More cases for annulment would follow, for example *R v. Boileau* 1799, *R v. Cutler* 1816, *R v. Metcalf* 1817, *R v. Hadden* 1826, *R v. Fussell* 1826,

---

19   Edward Coke, *Institutes of the Laws of England*, London 1797, Fourth Institute, p. 88
20   John Hewish, "From Cromford to Chancery Lane: New Light on the Arkwright Patent Trials", *Technology and Culture* (1987) 28, p. 85.
21   *R v. Murray* 1803, 1 HPC 522/3 RA 235-236.
22   Arkwright, *The Trial of a Cause instituted by Richard Arden, Esq* (1785), p. 172.

R v. Daniell 1827. The crown had a remarkable success rate: in all these cases, the verdict was for the crown and the patent was declared void.

The more frequent action was the one brought by the patentee for the infringement of his patent. From the mid-eighteenth century to the end of the 1830s, the number of enrolled patents had increased considerably. The number of patents effectively in force in 1750 has been estimated at 102. By 1840, that number had risen to 3,327.[23] It is not possible to know with any certainty how many patent disputes were brought to court during this period. Dutton, using B. Woodcroft's 'Patents for Invention: Reference Index', draws the conclusion that in the second half of the eighteenth century, no more than twenty-two cases came before the superior courts of Westminster. He makes the following estimation: Dollond's case is the first major case, followed by four in the 1770s, nine in the 1780s, and eight in the 1790s. The new century saw an increase, with eleven between 1800 and 1810, three between 1810 and 1815, eighteen cases between 1815 and 1820, and twenty-nine in the 1820s. In the early 1830s there were thirteen, but after 1835 there was a significant increase with thirty-four cases being heard between 1835 and 1840.[24]

Dutton is right to approach these figures with caution. Making an accurate estimate of the number of patent cases in this period is difficult. The reporting of cases was not consistent, particularly in the eighteenth century, and there are few reported cases before 1800. Dollond's case illustrates the point. Dollond's grant of patent was dated 1758, but the first lawsuits were brought by Peter Dollond, the son of the patentee. Sorrenson's research has revealed that Peter Dollond brought an action against Francis Watkin and his new partner Addison Smith in King's Bench in 1763 and another action in 1764. These were the first of twelve actions Dollond would bring against various opticians.[25] None of the cases appears in a series of reports. Davies, in his introduction to his compilation of patent cases published in 1816, considered that one reason why there were so few reports was that many, or perhaps most patent trials, had been heard at *nisi prius* (see below). The reports had been largely confined to those cases which had come before the court upon motions for a new trial, or cases reserved at *nisi prius* for the opinion of the court or for some other reason making it necessary to be heard by the full bench.[26]

Some cases, like Dollond's, are known primarily because they were cited in reported cases. For example, Godson refers in his patent treatise to the case of *Cartwright v. Amatt* 1800, heard before Lord Eldon when he was Chief Justice of the Court of Common Pleas, as being not reported but mentioned in arguments (in the reports of *Harmar v. Playne* by

---

23   B.R. Mitchell and P. Deane, *Abstract of British Historical Statistics*, 1962, pp. 268-269, in Appendix C, H.I. Dutton, *The patent system and inventive activity during the industrial revolution 1750-1852*, Manchester 1984.

24   Dutton, *The patent system and inventive activity during the industrial revolution 1750-1852* (1984), p. 71.

25   Sorrenson, "Dollond and Son's Pursuit of Achromaticity 1758-1759" (2001), p. 40.

26   John Davies, *A Collection of the Most Important Cases Respecting Patents of Invention*, London 1816, p. 14.

Vesey junior in Chancery in 1807 and East in King's Bench in1809).[27] Some cases only appear in the trial notebooks of the judges or in newspapers or pamphlets (see below). That the number of reported patent cases increased can, however, be safely said. This increase is immediately apparent from the division of the volumes in Hayward's collection of patent cases. Hayward's first volume of patent cases covers the period 1600 to 1828; the second volume is already restricted to the seven years between 1829 and 1836, and volume three to only the four years between 1837 and 1841.

1.3   Patent Judgments and Verdicts in the Common Law Courts

Cases could be heard either at *nisi prius* by a single judge and a jury or before the full court at one of the superior courts at Westminster, the latter being known as a trial at bar. The words *nisi prius* were in the opening clause of a writ commanding a sheriff of a county to summon a jury and bring the jury to the court at Westminster on a certain day, unless before then the king's judges had previously visited that county. The trial was to take place at Westminster only if it had not already taken place in the county, but in practice it was usually arranged that the king's justices would first have come to the counties. This solved the logistical problem of making sure that the jury, which had to be composed of men from the relevant locality, would be in court if the hearing was to take place outside their own county. These local trials were found to be convenient: instead of being tried at Westminster in the superior courts, *nisi prius* proceedings allowed cases to be heard in the counties. The chief justices of King's Bench and Common Pleas, and the chief baron of the Court of Exchequer could act as justices at *nisi prius* proceedings for the county of Middlesex. However, if a case was considered to be of great importance and complexity, a motion could be brought to have the case heard at bar at Westminster. This required the jury and witnesses to come for the trial of the case to Westminster.[28]

Under the *nisi prius* system, the assize judges on circuit would try questions of fact that were ready to be heard by a jury. The task of the trial judge ended when the jury verdict had been given. The verdict was returned to the full court, comprising three or four judges, so that they could give judgment in the case. Unless there had been any formal defect in the *nisi prius* proceeding, the judgment would be entered as a matter of course the following term. However, the court at Westminster would refrain from entering judgment if cause were shown. This required one of the parties to make an *ex parte* motion for a 'rule *nisi*'. This was an order for the opposing party to show cause against what was sought. If the

---

27 Richard Godson, *A Practical Treatise on the Law of Patents for Inventions and of Copyright*, London 1823, p. 157 referring to 11. East. 107 and 14. Ves 131.
28 Giles Jacob, *A New Law Dictionary*, London 1782: see 'Nisi prius'; Richard Burns, *A new Law Dictionary: intended for general use, as well as for Gentlemen of the Profession*, Vol. 2, London 1792, pp. 153-154.

opponent was successful the rule was discharged, otherwise it was made absolute. If the verdict had been for the plaintiff, the defendant could bring either a motion for arrest of judgment or a motion for a new trial. A motion for arrest of judgment was to show cause against the plaintiff's rule *nisi* for judgment and was confined to matters intrinsic to the record; an error had to be apparent from the face of the record. A motion for a new trial was to raise matters extrinsic to the record. A motion for a new trial gave the court in banc wider powers to consider issues arising from the trial. By the mid-eighteenth century, new trials were being granted not only after trials at *nisi prius*, but also after trials at bar (see below). Once the court in banc had actually given its judgment, the only remedy for a dissatisfied party was to ask for a writ of error.[29]

1.3.1   Nonsuit

Trials in the common law courts were before juries. The judge would sum up all the pertinent matters of fact, which were to be decided by the jury, and the jury would return its verdict (see below). In adjudicating on matters of fact, the jury's role could be quite considerable. However, in certain circumstances, the judge could dismiss a case before the jury considered its verdict. The decision was then a 'nonsuit'. A nonsuit judgment could be entered on several grounds. It could be appropriate because the plaintiff was guilty of delays or defaults. The defence counsel could ask for a nonsuit at the end of the plaintiff's case, which would be ordered if the judge considered that the plaintiff had failed to show sufficient evidence to justify putting the case before the jury. A plaintiff could also be nonsuited because of the discovery of some error or defect, even if the jury was already at the bar and ready to deliver its verdict.[30]

Patentees were regularly nonsuited. As noted above, before 1800 few patent cases were reported. However, Lord Mansfield's own trial notebooks show that a nonsuit judgment was the fate of quite a number of plaintiffs.[31] From an examination of the reported cases, it is evident that the grounds for nonsuits in patent cases varied but a deficiency in the patent specification was a common cause. This deficiency could taken various guises: the court considered that the plaintiff had taken out a patent for more than he had discovered,[32] particularly where the specification had not distinguished between the new improvement

---

29 Baker, *An Introduction to English Legal History* (2002), pp. 135-136, 138-139.
30 Burns, *A new Law Dictionary: intended for general use, as well as for Gentlemen of the Profession* (1792), p. 158-159.
31 For example *Horton v. Harvey* 1781, *Yerbury v. Wallace* 1768 and *Taylor v. Luckett* 1770. See James Oldham, *The Mansfield Manuscripts and the growth of English Law in the eighteenth century*, London 1992, p. 733.
32 For example *Campion v. Benyon* 1821, 129 ER 1187.

and the old invention,[33] or that the specification was misleading.[34] Other grounds included that the invention was considered not to be new,[35] or had no utility.[36] The new rules of pleading, which came into operation in the Easter Term of 1834, in combination with Lord Brougham's Act of 1835 which allowed amendments to the patent specification, meant that a nonsuit ruling would become less common.[37]

1.3.2   Motion for a New Trial and a Writ of Error

When a general verdict had been brought in by a jury, the disappointed party could move for a new trial before the verdict was confirmed by the court. This entailed having the case heard again before a different jury, if there was doubt concerning the validity of the jury's verdict. In *Bright v. Eynon* 1757, Mansfield considered that the courts had become more liberal in granting new trials and were prepared to look at the particular circumstances of the case. New trials were now being granted not only after a hearing at *nisi prius*, but also after trials at bar (by the full court). Mansfield was of the opinion that it was only proper to grant a new trial where "there was a reasonable doubt, or perhaps a certainty, that justice has not been done" and that it was expedient to have the case heard again in the same common law court.[38]

As Mansfield observed in *Bright v. Eynon*, granting a motion for a new trial was not necessarily an ill reflection on the original jury. Jurors may have heard too much about the case before its trial and become prejudiced without being aware of it or the hearing of the case may have been very long and complicated. As most general verdicts included legal consequences as well as matters of fact, Mansfield pointed out that in drawing these consequences the jury may have been mistaken and have drawn an inference contrary to the law.[39] Failures by the judge were a ground for a new trial: the jury could have mistaken the law or have been misdirected. In principle, a new trial was only granted where there were strong grounds to show that a new trial was warranted, and not because of "nice and formal objections".[40] There was another ground upon which this motion could be made. The defeated party could argue that he had been surprised by a piece of evidence, which he would have been able to answer had he been aware of it. It was indeed upon this latter

---

33   For example *Macfarlane v. Price* 1816, 171 ER 446.
34   For example *Savory v. Price* 1823, 1 CPC 432.
35   For example *Hill v. Thompson* 1818, 1 WPC 249.
36   For example *Manton v. Parker* 1814, 1 CPC 278.
37   Summed up in *Jupe v. Pratt* 1837, 1 WPC 145.
38   *Bright v. Eynon* 1757, 1 Burr 393-395.
39   *Ibid.*, 393.
40   Burns, *A new Law Dictionary: intended for general use, as well as for Gentlemen of the Profession* (1792), pp. 151-152.

ground that Arkwright had attempted, unsuccessfully, to move for a new trial upon his patent's annulment on *scire facias*.

Whereas a new trial was a means to correct errors in the determination of the jury verdict, a writ of error was to determine matters of law. The prior judgment of a superior court could then be reversed or affirmed. For example, having lost in the Court of Common Pleas, Hornblower and Maberly brought a writ of error against Boulton and Watt in1799. The case in error was heard by King's Bench. The principal ground for the writ of error was the legal point that Watt's invention was only for a principle, not for a manufacture. That a second argument was awarded to Hornblower was, according to Lord Kenyon "rather from a deference to the very respectable opinions given in the Court of Common Pleas on the former occasion than from any doubt we entertained on the subject". The judgment given in favour of Boulton and Watt in Common Pleas was affirmed.[41]

1.3.3   Juries in the Common Law Courts

As mentioned above, in the common law courts, patent cases were heard before juries. Juries in the eighteenth century did not represent a cross-section of the community. Those eligible to act as jurors were men who represented neither the highest levels nor the lowest levels of the social hierarchy. Exemptions from jury service were granted to those of high social standing, those of Barons and above, and to various others, including legal personnel. To be empanelled by a sheriff, a juror was expected to hold an interest in land. This was justified on the grounds that men of estate were less likely to succumb to bribes and bias than those of lesser social standing.[42] Nonetheless, the property qualification for jurors, at least until the Reform Act 1832, was less stringent than for most parliamentary electors.[43]

Upon a motion of the parties, a special jury could be ordered to try issues in the courts of King's Bench, Common Pleas and Exchequer. The special jury was introduced to deal with cases that were "of too great nicety for the discussion of ordinary freeholders".[44] The litigant applying for a special jury had to pay the fees unless the judge certified, in accordance with statutory requirements, that the cause required a special jury. Oldham's examination of Mansfield's trial notes reveals that about 600 cases were designated as having been tried by special juries in the period 1764 to 1786 alone. By the early nineteenth century, special juries were being used extensively.[45] Special juries in patent cases were common. A special jury seems to have been attractive to patentees: "We are plaintiffs and shall have

---

41   *Hornblower and Maberly v. Boulton and Watt* 1799, 8 T.R. 95-108.

42   Samson Eure, *Trials per pais: or, the law of England concerning juries by nisi prius, &c*, London: 1766, p. 109.

43   A.H. Manchester, *A Modern Legal History of England and Wales 1750-1950*, London 1980, p. 91.

44   Burns, *A new Law Dictionary: intended for general use, as well as for Gentlemen of the Profession* (1792), p. 46.

45   Oldham, *English Common Law in the age of Mansfield* (2004), p. 25.

a special jury", declared James Watt in a letter to Thomas Wilson, "Captain Morcom should not sell the bears skin till he has killed the beast, to be certain of setting our patent aside is rather too bold, we have good reason to hope the contrary".[46]

If a juror was to be a member of a special jury, however, he was expected not only to hold an interest in land, but also to be of a certain social standing. Prior to the nineteenth century there were no statutory qualifications for special jurors. Such conditions were first imposed in the County Juries Act 1825, by which special jurors were required to be merchants, bankers, or esquires (or persons of higher degree). The composition of that special jury could vary depending upon the nature of the case. The court could order a jury of merchants to try merchant affairs. Oldham has argued, however, that it is not correct to treat the terms 'merchant jury' and 'special jury' as synonymous. A committee was set up in 1817 by the Mayor and Aldermen of London to examine the lists of persons qualified to serve on juries for the city of London, including the composition of special juries. It reported that special juries in London did not consist exclusively of merchants. Oldham notes that while it is true that most of the special juries empanelled before Lord Mansfield in the trials held at the Guildhall in the City of London were composed of merchants, there were many cases utilizing special juries where the jurors were not merchants. There could be a special jury consisting of gentlemen.[47] It is of interest to note in this context that the special jury which was called together to hear the case of *R v. Arkwright* in 1785 was mixed: those empanelled to join the existing special jury members included a broker, a bell manufacturer, a 'chinaman' but also a gentleman.[48]

As regards the task of the jury, by the eighteenth century it was a well-established principle that it was not the task of the judge to pronounce upon a question of fact, nor that of the jurors to pronounce upon questions of law. Matters of fact were the province of "twelve indifferent men" and the task of the judge was "to declare as the law is upon the fact found ... For the law arises upon the fact".[49] Although juries did not decide upon matters of law, there was sometimes a thin line between what was fact and what was law. It was a problem recognised by Lord Mansfield; when asked his opinion on a pamphlet recommending the introduction of jury trial in Scotland in certain types of cases, Mansfield identified the main inconvenience as the difficulty of differentiating between law and fact.[50]

The questions of fact that could be put to a jury in a patent case were primarily whether the invention was new, whether it had been invented by the one claiming to be the inventor and whether the specification was sufficiently clear to enable a skilled artisan to make the invention based on the description given in the specification. Yet in determining the clarity

---

46 Cornish Record Offices, *Letter Watt to Wilson regarding cause in Common Pleas 30 June 1796*, AD 1583/9/35.

47 Oldham, *English Common Law in the age of Mansfield* (2004), pp. 22-24.

48 Arkwright, *The Trial of a Cause instituted by Richard Pepper Arden, Esq* (1785), p.11.

49 Eure, *Trials per Pais: Or, the Law of England Concerning Juries by Nisi Prius &c* (1766), p. 7.

50 Oldham, *English Common Law in the age of Mansfield* (2004), p. 16.

of a specification, or whether an invention was new, the line between fact and law could become blurred. In *Hill v. Thompson* 1817, the chancellor, Lord Eldon, apparently found it necessary to point out the distinction between fact and law, although the role of the jury was not pertinent to decisions he would make in a court of equity. In that case, one of the issues Lord Eldon dealt with was the role of the jury with respect to the patent specification. He explained that the specification must make a clear distinction between an existing machine and the new improvement to that machine, because if more than the improvement was claimed in the specification, the patent would fail in its entirety. While Lord Eldon accepted that the "utility of the discovery" and the "intelligibility of the description" and such like issues were matters of fact for the jury "whether or not the patent is defective in attempting to cover too much, is a question of law". In considering the facts of that case, which concerned iron smelting, Eldon stated that the question of law was whether the patentee claimed in his specification the benefit of the actual discovery of lime, as a preventive of 'cold short', or whether he claimed no more than the invention of that precise combination and processes which were described in the specification.[51] What a patentee claimed as his invention in the specification was a question of law to be determined by the judge, whether the specification was sufficient to enable a skilled artisan to make the invention was a question of fact, to be determined by the jury.

Lord Eldon's remark is of particular interest in relation to the case of *Bovill v. Moore*, where the patent at issue was one for a machine for the manufacture of bobbin lace. It was heard in Common Pleas in 1816. The main issue raised here was whether the invention was a new machine, built upon a new combination of parts from the beginning, or whether it was only an improvement on an existing machine. The case had been tried in the Hilary Term at Guildhall by Lord Chief Justice Gibbs. The jury had then been asked to answer the question whether the invention was new: "do you find that the combination of parts up to the crossing of the threads is not new?" which was answered in the affirmative by the jury. A juryman added the observation: "The threads taking a new direction, and certainly the most valuable part to the plaintiff, is a new invention; but we are of the opinion it is nothing more than an improvement." Determining whether an invention was new was a matter of fact for the jury. However, the jury was also asked whether more than an improvement was being claimed. Gibbs, C.J. had put the question to the jury in the following terms: "whether you think he has in his specification described an invention, as I have stated to you, to a greater extent than the proof goes to establish."[52] Did this question go to determining whether the patent was defective in attempting to cover too much, which was, according to Lord Eldon a matter of law for the judge? The line between determining

---

51 *Hill v. Thompson* 1817, 1 WPC 237-238.
52 *Bovill v. Moore* 1816, 1 CPC 348.

what was fact and what was law seems to have been blurred. Had this prompted Lord Eldon's remark in *Hill v. Thompson*?

It would seem that the line between fact, the province of the jury, and law, the province of the judge, remained problematic. In a footnote to the *Hill v. Thompson* case, Webster added the following: that in the case of *Neilson v. Harford* 1841 it had been argued that in Lord Eldon's opinion "the expression 'intelligibility of the description', as a question for the jury, was co-extensive and synonymous with the expression 'meaning of the specification'".[53] That may have been counsel's interpretation, one that was presumably favourable to his client, but a reading of *Hill v. Thompson* does not justify ascribing this opinion to Lord Eldon. Eldon does indeed say that the 'intelligibility of the description' is a matter of fact for the jury. However, Eldon pointed out that determining what a patentee claimed in his specification was a question of law. This would seem to indicate that the meaning of the specification was a matter of law and distinct from whether the specification was sufficient, which was a matter of fact. Certainly the court in the *Neilson v. Harford* case did not consider intelligibility and meaning to be synonymous. As Webster notes: "But the Court of Exchequer held that these were essentially distinct; that the meaning of the specification was for the court, and that the court were to tell the jury what the specification had said, the interpretation of terms of art being left to the determination of the jury, according to the evidence; that the jury were to determine whether that which the specification says, is a sufficient description."[54]

It is interesting to conjecture how far observations made by juries on such matters as what was a new invention and whether the specification was sufficient were instrumental in shaping concepts in patent law. Lord Mansfield seems to have respected his juries. In his examination of Mansfield's notebooks, Oldham notes that in only a very small percentage of the thousands of cases recorded did Mansfield disagree with the verdict reached by the jury.[55] In the eighteenth century, the participation of jurors was more direct and active than it is today. Noteworthy in this context is the observation made by a juror to Lord Mansfield in *Morris v. Bramson* 1776. The patentee of a stocking frame had brought an action for the infringement of a patent of 1764 for a machine for a set of needles to be applied to a stocking frame for making oylet holes. The issue here was whether an addition to an old stocking frame was the proper subject of a patent. Lord Mansfield received a letter from a juror saying that if the objection to this patent was on the ground that it was only for an addition to an old machine, that objection would revoke almost every patent. Citing this case in *Boulton and Watt v. Bull*, Buller, J. stated that Lord Mansfield considered

---

53 *Hill v. Thompson* 1817, 1 WPC 237, fn (h).
54 *Ibid.*, 237.
55 Oldham, *English Common Law in the age of Mansfield* (2004), p. 17.

this to be "a very sensible letter" and since that time a patent for an addition would be seen as good, as long as it was only for the addition.[56] (See paragraph 3.3.2.3).

As the case of *Morris v. Bramson* shows, relevant observations by jurors could be endorsed by the judges themselves. In *R v. Arkwright* 1785, for which there is a detailed, verbatim report, one juror made a comment during the examination of a witness which was immediately taken up by Buller, J. himself:

> "Q: Is there any other method by which you think the same purpose would be answered, by making use of the same length of spindle which you see there?
> A: It is suggested, the idea of an horizontal motion of this part of the machine, at the same time as it is making this rotatory motion.
> A juror: There is not a word of that in the specification.
> Mr. Justice Buller: No, not a word in it, all this is the conclusion of a very ingenious, sensible man."[57]

Jurors were at liberty to ask questions of witnesses during the course of a trial. In *R v. Arkwright*, several of the jurors' questions were concerned with the actual working of Arkwright's machinery, a model of which had been brought into the court for the purpose of demonstration. Although in his opening address to the jury, Bearcroft, counsel for the crown, had pointed out that "the subject matter which you are to look at, being a piece of machinery, consisting of many parts, some of them minute, the whole of it considerably complicated, with which persons in common life have no acquaintance or familiarity", some jurors asked very pertinent questions. For example, a witness was asked by counsel whether the wheels and rollers used to elongate the thread for spinning worked upon the same principle as those for roving:

> "A: I think rollers moving over one another, and elongating any thing, whether thread or cotton, are in principle the same.
>
> A Juror: Is not the diameter of the axis of the roller you are now speaking of, intended to determine the size of the thread?"[58]

A jury was at liberty to reach a verdict before all the witnesses had been heard; it could inform the judge of its verdict at any point in the proceeding. If the jury had found, for example, that the testimony given by the plaintiff's witnesses was so compelling that it was

---

56   *Boulton and Watt v. Bull* 1795, 2 H. Black 489.
57   Arkwright, *The Trial of a Cause instituted by Richard Pepper Arden, Esq* (1785), p. 136.
58   *Ibid.*, p. 12, 141.

considered unnecessary to allow the defendant's witnesses to testify, the jurors could elect to inform the judge of their verdict. This was not usual but it was commonplace for a jury to reach a verdict without retiring, or if it did retire to have only the briefest of deliberations.[59] This speedy decision-making was indicated in the reports by a statement to that effect. For example, in *R v. Arkwright*, the reporter notes, "The jury, without a minute's hesitation, brought in their verdict"[60] and *Hare v. Harford* 1803, a brewing case, in which a quick verdict was reached "without any hesitation" despite the contrary opinions of the scientists called as witnesses for the opposing sides.[61]

Oldham points out that in reaching a verdict, the eighteenth century jury was considered to have a moral obligation to follow the direction of the judge and his construction of the applicable laws, although there was no legal obligation imposed upon the jury to do so. He notes that trial judges frequently directed juries to find for one party or the other, and juries ordinarily complied.[62] While an examination of patent cases in this period confirms his conclusion, that juries generally reached a verdict as directed, that was not always the case. Of interest in this context is the case of *Bramah v. Hardcastle* 1789. Lord Kenyon had, at the conclusion of his summing up, told the jury that the patent was void, the invention not being new, and hence they should find for the defendant. The jury, however, found for the plaintiff, the patentee. The verdict stood.[63]

1.4 Patent Actions and Judgments in the Courts of Equity

The courts of equity offered patentees several remedies that were not available in the common law courts. These remedies were discovery, injunction and account. An application could be made to a court of equity for discovery. An order for discovery gave the patentee the opportunity to examine the work of the alleged infringer in order to ascertain whether that manufacture did indeed constitute an infringement of the patent. It was not uncommon practice for a patentee to apply for an order of inspection if the alleged infringer refused to allow a voluntary examination. This required a case of 'reasonable suspicion' to be made out in court.[64] It was considered prudent to apply to the court of equity to appoint persons to inspect manufactures.[65] The importance of this remedy is illustrated in a letter sent from James Watt to Thomas Wilson in 1791 regarding the dubious originality of Hornblower's engine:

---

59 Oldham, *English Common Law in the age of Mansfield* (2004), p. 59.
60 Arkwright, *The Trial of a Cause instituted by Richard Pepper Arden, Esq* (1785), p. 187.
61 *Hare v. Harford* 1803, 1 CPC 186.
62 Oldham, *English Common Law in the age of Mansfield* (2004), p. 68.
63 *Bramah v. Hardcastle* 1789, 1 CPC 171-172.
64 *Morris v. Bramson* 1776, 1 CPC 34 Carpmael fn.
65 Godson, *A Practical Treatise on the Law of Patents for Inventions and of Copyright* (1823), p. 182.

"If they mean to keep the construction of the Engine secret on the hopes to prevent our being able to prove the infringement they deceive themselves for if we do not obtain proof in an easier manner we shall make application to the L[or]d Chancellor to enforce a discovery of their manner of working which we are informed by Counsel will be the easier obtained, on account of their pretending to work under a patent, and consequently ought to have no secrets, and the patent itself will prove great part of what we desire. It seems to us to be in vain to apply to Mr Hornblower, but as you are to be at Bristol, it will be right to apply to Mr Winwood informing him that we conceive the Engine to be an encroachment upon us, and that we are determined to try the matter with them, and that in order to save expense to both parties we wish to know, whether they will permit persons appointed by us to inspect and examine the construction and working of the Engine; or whether we must take the legal steps to procure such examination. In my opinion it will be their interest to face the matter at once as attempts at concealment can only involve them as well as us in expense, and cost what it will we shall certainly endeavour to right ourselves, as long as our money lasts which expensive as Law is, will we expect work out the term of our exclusive privilege."[66]

Proceedings had to be brought in equity for an injunction and an account. The patentee would file a bill requesting an injunction to prevent the defendant's continued use of the patentee's invention and for an account of any profits made by the defendant from that use. The action of account could in practice operate as a form of equitable damages. An order to keep an account could be made so that the patentee could be compensated if vindicated.

Ordering an account could also act as a counterweight to an injunction, as a means of protecting the defendant. If an injunction would cause great hardship to the defendant, and it was not certain that the validity of the patent would be upheld at trial, it was at the discretion of the court not to order an injunction but instead order the defendants to keep an account of any profits made using the disputed invention.[67] One example is *Liardet v. Johnson* 1777, where the patent at issue was for the composition of cement. Although Chancellor Bathurst granted Liardet an injunction to prevent Johnson using that composition until the issue had been resolved in the common law court, the injunction was expressly ordered not to restrict Johnson from finishing the houses mentioned in the affidavit, which he had already begun to cover with cement. Johnson did, however, have to

---

66   Cornish Record Office, Boulton and Watt Letters, AD 1583/5/9.
67   *Hill v. Thompson* 1817, 1 WPC 238.

submit an account with respect to those houses in case the common law court would direct an account at the hearing.[68]

However, it was common for an injunction to be granted until the legal question of the validity of the patent could be tried. Where a patentee had enjoyed a reasonably long and undisputed possession of the patent, the Court of Chancery considered that there was less risk involved in granting the injunction until the legal question could be tried than in dissolving it, for the patent could prove to have been valid.[69] It was even intimated in *Hill v. Thompson* 1817, by the chancellor, Lord Eldon, that an injunction could be granted unconditionally. The court would grant an injunction to a person who had exclusive enjoyment of a patent on the basis that the court would give credit to his apparent right and immediately grant an injunction to prevent any invasion of that right. The injunction would continue until that apparent right was undermined. This pronouncement was later taken as an authority to show that the court could grant an injunction absolutely, without imposing any conditions on the patentee. The burden of invalidating the patent was then on the alleged infringer either by bringing an action in his own name or by instituting a *scire facias* action. However, it was not usual to grant this type of injunction, as the patentee was generally compelled to bring an action to defend his patent in the common law court.[70] The Court of Chancery could dissolve an injunction if it had reasonable grounds for doubt.

In *Beeston v. Ford* 1829, Lord Chancellor Lyndhurst summed up the general rules: where a patentee has for a number of years enjoyed the exclusive possession of a patent, the court would not allow that possession to be disturbed and would grant an injunction until trial at law, whatever doubt there may be as to the validity of the patent. However, if such possession could not be proved, the court would not grant its protection, but would send the parties to a court of law to decide the question.[71] Godson, writing his treatise on patents in 1823, considered that it was advantageous for a patentee to proceed in equity for an infringement before recourse to the common law courts. This was because the remedy in equity was for instant relief; the court of equity could restrain an alleged infringer from any further use of the patent right immediately. The defendant would then have no right to continue using the invention until the validity of the patent had been determined by a court of common law.[72]

---

68 *Liardet v. Johnson*, 62 ER 1001.
69 *Harmar v. Playne* 1807, 1 CPC 257.
70 *Hill v. Thompson* 1817, 1 WPC 236 and fn (g).
71 *Beeston v. Ford* 1829, 1 CPC 491.
72 Godson, *A Practical Treatise on the Law of Patents for Inventions and of Copyright* (1823), pp. 183-189.

1.5   PARLIAMENT

In the eighteenth century, if a patentee wished to extend his patent beyond the time limit laid down by the Statute of Monopolies, he needed to approach parliament to obtain a private Act of Parliament. The private bill procedure applied to all bills for the particular interest or benefit of any person. It is clear from *The Method of Proceedings, in Order to Obtain a Private Act of Parliament* by W. Owen, published in 1767, that the procedure was both time consuming and costly, with fees having to be paid to various individuals at various stages. From *The Method of Proceeding* the following main stages can be outlined: first a petition to the Lords had to be drawn up, which was then presented to the House and read and referred to two judges; then a bill was drawn up and left with the judges, witnesses were arranged and examined; a copy of the bill was then signed by the judges and the judges' report was drawn up; then a brief of the bill had to be presented to the Lord Chancellor who informed the House of its contents; the bill was read a first time and a second time several days later; the bill was then committed to a committee and then read a third time; it was then carried down to the House of Commons where it was also read twice; it was then voted upon and, when passed, returned to the House of Lords to await royal assent.[73]

Owen's instructions on private Act procedure are concerned with unopposed private bills beginning in the Lords, the Commons proceedings being treated as a formality. With the establishment of the office of Lord Chairman, it would seem that by the early 1830s all necessary amendments to unopposed bills starting in the Commons would be made in committee of that House, so that the committee procedure in the Lords was a formality. Similarly, for an estate bill begun in the Lords, the evidence taken in committee in the Lords was considered sufficient for the Commons.[74] Although the end product of the private bill procedure was a piece of legislation, nonetheless there were judicial aspects to the proceedings. Holdsworth notes three stages in which the judicial aspect of private bill legislation was prominent: proceedings on the petition of the bill, on the second reading and the committee stage. In particular, proceedings before committee were of an essentially judicial nature. The main distinction between the role of a court and the committee was that the judicial inquiry in committee was preliminary not to a judgment but to a legislative act.[75]

However, these committees were not totally impartial. In 1621, it had been argued that members of the House ought not to draw private bills, for a member would later be a judge and ought to be indifferent. The rule was not observed. Any patentee who needed a private

---

73   W. Owen, *The Method of Proceeding in Order to Obtain a Private Act of Parliament*, London 1767, pp. 5-24.
74   Shelia Lamberts, *Bills and Acts: Legislative Procedure in Eighteenth-Century England*, Cambridge 1971, p. 95.
75   Holdsworth, *A History of English Law* (1964), vol XI, pp. 325-332.

bill had to find a sponsor in the House. Lambert notes in her study that all bills were ostensibly promoted and introduced by members, and it was essential for any outside group to obtain the interest of some members, at least to the extent of going through the formal procedures in the House, if a bill were to succeed. Many members themselves had private interests coinciding with those of the outside groups; many had causes they sought to promote. It would not be until 1830 that a resolution of the House of Commons finally prohibited members from having any interest in parliamentary agency.[76]

In the eighteenth century, the House of Commons was still an assembly of landed proprietors, but the number of those involved in business was on the increase. It has been estimated that by the early eighteenth century a significant proportion of the House of Commons (20.7%) was already involved in some form of business, ranging from venture capitalists and great industrialists to provincial manufacturers. Even those whose interests remained on the estate could still be involved in some form of business, for example canal building and the exploitation of natural resources such as timber, coal and tin.[77] It was usually the Member of Parliament who had been recruited to help the bill pass through parliament who would be appointed as chairman of the committee.[78]

The methods used by Matthew Boulton and James Watt upon their application to extend James Watt's patent for an improved steam engine are illustrative of parliamentary lobbying in the eighteenth century. Watt's bill was opposed, the chief opposition being formed by the mining interest, which hoped to get free use of the engine as soon as possible. Robinson outlines the strategy Boulton and Watt used to marshal their forces in parliament to secure the passage of the bill. Friends who could bring influence to bear were approached. Local ties were used; Boulton had considerable influence with the leading families in the Midland counties. Indeed, the lobby for the patent extension reflected the powerful social connections developed by Boulton and his friends. Nor was Boulton unaware of the economic interests of Members of Parliament. However, it was a combined operation: Watt himself was apparently able to call upon the support of fifteen out of the forty-five Scottish M.Ps.[79] Their efforts were rewarded: the Fire Engine Act was passed in 1775 extending Watt's first patent to 1800. To be granted an extended period of twenty-five years would prove quite exceptional; after the 1835 Act, patent extensions were allowed for a further seven years, but shorter periods were also not uncommon (see below).

In order to extend a patent by Act of Parliament certain criteria had to be met. On the one hand, the invention had to be of substantial benefit to the public and on the other

---

76 Lambert, *Bills and Acts: Legislative Procedure in Eighteenth-Century England* (1971), pp. 63-64.
77 Eveline Cruickshanks, Stuart Handley and D.W. Hayton, *The History of Parliament: The House of Commons 1690-1715*, Cambridge 2002, Vol. I, pp. 289, 300-301.
78 Holdsworth, *A History of English Law* (1964), vol. XI, p. 341.
79 Eric Robinson, "Matthew Boulton and the Art of Parliamentary Lobbying", *The Historical Journal* (1964) Vol. 7, No. 2, pp. 216-224.

hand there had to be clear evidence that the patentee had not had sufficient opportunity to exploit his invention. Patentees drafted their petitions with these two criteria in mind. A good example is the petition of Joseph Bramah, who wished to extend his patent for a new sort of lock. His fourteen-year term being almost up, he argued:

> "your petitioner hath not hitherto had it in his power to reimburse himself any part of the great expense he hath incurred, nor hath he any prospect of being enabled so to do, or to carry his said invention to the height of perfection and cheapness he is persuaded it is capable of, unless the term of the said letters patent is prolonged, the effect of which prolongation your petitioner humbly presumes will be ultimately beneficial to the public."[80]

However, after an Act, introduced by Lord Brougham, to 'Amend the Law Touching Letters Patent for Invention' in 1835, petitions for the extension of a patent were heard only by the Judicial Committee of the Privy Council. Before 1835, about twenty-five applications to extend patents had been considered by various select committees. Between 1835 and 1852, in the period in which renewal applications were examined by the Judicial Committee of the Privy Council, seventy-seven cases were considered.[81] With the transfer of patent extension hearings to the Judicial Committee of the Privy Council, Lord Brougham stressed that a strong case would have to be made out to justify an extension, as "these applications are any thing rather than matters of course. This is an extraordinary jurisdiction which has been conferred on the judicial committee by the legislature, and it is to be exercised only on the most special grounds alleged and proved in reference to each case". He made clear that the criteria would be unaffected: the applicant would have to prove that the usual term was insufficient, given the nature of the invention, to allow the patentee to reap the proper reward for his invention, and that the invention was of merit and of use to the public.[82]

Dutton argues that the reluctance of parliament and the Judicial Committee of the Privy Council to extend patents unless a very clear case was made, together with the cost, explains why only a hundred or so inventors bothered to apply.[83] Nonetheless, it would seem that where a clear case was made, there was an apparent willingness to assist the patentee. With respect to extensions by a private Act, as noted above, James Watt's patent was prolonged by parliament for the extraordinarily long period of twenty-five years. Liardet obtained an Act in 1776 to extend his patent for cement for a period of eighteen

---

80   Joseph Bramah, *The petition and case of Joseph Bramah, of Piccadilly, engineer, inventor of the patent locks for the security of life and property*, London 1798: The Petition A.
81   Dutton, *The patent system and inventive activity during the industrial revolution 1750-1852* (1984), p. 155.
82   Jones's Patent, 1 WPC 579.
83   Dutton, *The patent system and inventive activity during the industrial revolution 1750-1852* (1984), p. 155.

years, on condition that a specification of preparing and applying it should be enrolled within four months of the Act.[84] Another example is provided by the extension of James Turner's patent of 1792 for the invention of a yellow colouring. That Turner had been forced to instigate various actions in law and equity to defend his patent was taken into account, and that the damages awarded had been only nominal. It was considered that Turner had not been properly compensated for his invention nor given the opportunity to bring his invention to perfection. The Act granted Turner an extension of eleven years.[85] After 1835, the Judicial Committee of the Privy Council was also prepared to be sympathetic to patentees' claims for an extension. For example, under Lord Lyndhurst a series of patent extensions were granted. In 1837 alone, these patent extensions included Swaine's patent for a method of producing and preserving artificial mineral waters which was prolonged for seven years, Wright's patent for combinations and improvements in machinery for making pins for five years, and Bodmer's patent for improvements in machinery for preparing, roving and spinning cotton and wool for seven years.[86]

1.6 LAW REPORTS

It was Burrow's reports of King's Bench cases that would usher in the new era of law reporting: his reports set high standards both with respect to accuracy and attention to detail. His efforts did not go unnoticed by the judiciary: in keeping with the general respect with which these reports were treated is the remark made by Aston, J. that a case had been "treated in a most able and masterly manner in the reports of Sir James Burrow".[87] The mid-eighteenth century was to mark a watershed in the way in which cases were reported. Henry Cowper and Sylvester Douglas would follow in the footsteps of James Burrow. They were professional reporters, writing their reports with a view to publication.

In his Preface to volume 1 of *Reports of Cases argued and determined in the Court of King's Bench* of 1790, Sylvester Douglas noted that "the evidence of a very great part of the law of England almost entirely depends" upon the "fidelity and accuracy" of the law reports. "Yet it has somehow or other happened that little or no care has been taken, nor any provisions made, to render the evidence of judicial proceedings certain and authentic."[88]

The law reporting prior to this period was both haphazard and often of poor quality. There had once been a special office of reporter, but that office had fallen into disuse by the beginning of the reign of Henry VIII and was only temporarily revived under Bacon's

---

84 *Liardet v. Johnson* 1780, 62 ER 1001.
85 Turner's patent, 1 WPC 84-85.
86 Respectively 1 WPC 560-1, 1 WPC 561, 12 ER 1089.
87 *Doe v. Horde* 1777, 2 Cowper 698.
88 Sylvester Douglas, *Reports of Cases argued and determined in the Court of King's Bench*, London 1790, pp. vi-vii.

chancellorship in the reign of James I. With the demise of the Year Books, the last being compiled in 1535, the early reports began to appear. Of the earlier reports, three series of reports may be distinguished as the most significant: reports of cases compiled by Edmund Plowden from the 1550s to 1570s; by Edward Coke, the first eleven reports appearing between 1600 to 1615 and the last two after his death; and, to a lesser extent, those of Edward Bulstrode, his collection being put together between 1656 and 1659. Edward Coke's reports were long so highly respected that they were cited simply as 'The Reports'. Coke's style of reporting was, however, rather different from the modern approach. Coke would add in his own comment and not distinguish, as Plowden had, his own views from those he was reporting. Baker ascribes this way of reporting not to dishonesty, but as reflecting the medieval view that the correctness of the doctrine reported was more important than the historical precision of the report, with reports being seen more as instructional law books built around actual cases than as accurate representations of those cases.[89] It is not inconceivable, however, that Coke's ego was also instrumental in determining his style of reporting.

The printing of law reports took place in the middle of the seventeenth century. Historians generally view the reports of the period 1650 to 1750 as being "mostly of an inferior nature".[90] What was reported was rather ad hoc: reports were often made by individual practitioners for their own use and the cases they reported were simply the cases in which they had been personally involved. However, publishers were aware that there was a market for law reports and collections of cases were made for publication. Some of these collections were of dubious quality. Sometimes reports were published under the names of distinguished lawyers or judges, but an actual connection with these eminent persons is questionable.[91] Accuracy and detail suffered as law reports in this period were often edited for publication years after the cases had been heard. So poor was the quality of some reports that judges were openly critical. In *Slater v. May* 1704, Chief Justice Holt had been moved to remark "upon the observation upon 4. Mod. see the inconveniencies of these scambling reports, they will make us appear to posterity for a parcel of blockheads".[92] Lord Mansfield was also prepared to voice his dissatisfaction. He was aware of "the danger of inaccurate reports".[93] For example, Lord Mansfield informed the defendant's counsel in one case that he should not have quoted from Moseley's Reports.[94] His criticism was not reserved only for the works of little known reporters: even Blackstone's reports could be found wanting: "We must not always rely on the words of reports though under great names: Mr. Justice

---

89 Baker, *An Introduction to English Legal History* (2002), p. 183.
90 *Ibid.*
91 Manchester, *A Modern Legal History of England and Wales 1750-1950* (1980), pp. 23-24; Theodore F.T. Plucknett, *A Concise History of the Common Law*, London 1956, p. 280 and Baker (2002), p. 182.
92 *Slater v. May* 1704, 2 Ld Raym 1072.
93 *Ackworth v. Kempe* 1778, 1 Doug. 42.
94 *Quantock v. England* 1770, 5 Burr 2629.

Blackstone's reports are not very accurate."[95] This seems a little harsh as in the previous year Mansfield had referred to a "very correct" report of a case from Blackstone's own notes.[96]

James Burrow began to publish his law reports of the cases heard in the Court of King's Bench in 1756. His motivation for doing so was the constant pestering he had endured by those who wished to use his notes. In the Preface to his first volume, Burrow points out that he did not take his notes in short hand and was careful to reproduce the sense of what was said rather than the actual words. He took care that "the case and judgment, and the outlines of the ground or reason of decision, are right".[97] In Burrow's reports a clear distinction is drawn between the material facts of the case, the arguments set out by counsel and the grounds for the judges' decisions. References to authorities and other cases were placed in the margin along with the key points. Sometimes Burrow entered an observation, for example in *Rose v. Green* 1758 mention is made in the text of counsel's speech of the case of *Duncombe v. Walter*. Counsel states that this case is badly reported in several reports, but he also refers to the report of Thomas Raymond and is prepared to cite from Skinner's reports. In a note in the margin, Burrow has added "None of these reports of this case are well drawn up, except Sir Thomas Raymond's: and that is only an argument, with an adjournatur".[98]

In the latter days of his reporting career, Burrow added a personal note at the end of volume 4 of his reports. He explained that what he had chosen to report was based upon certain criteria: there had to be a determination or illustration of some point of law involved in the case; cases that could be decided easily were of no interest to him, nor cases that were so particular that they were unlikely to become useful as precedents. With great modesty, he suggested that he might not have done justice to the matter, or perhaps the language, either of the court or the bar. However, upon one ground he was satisfied: "I flatter myself that I have with tolerable accuracy stated the cases and also the points upon which the judgment turned."[99] It was accuracy that Burrow was striving for in his reporting.

Whereas Baker argues that Lord Mansfield's abilities attracted reporters of high quality, in particular Burrow, and later Henry Cowper and Sylvester Douglas,[100] Lieberman wonders if it is not the case that Lord Mansfield is considered to be a man of such ability exactly because of the high quality of the King's Bench reporters. Although Lord Mansfield is generally praised by contemporaries and subsequent historians for ushering in a period of legal creativity and innovation, Lieberman sounds a word of warning. He notes that a

---

95   *Devon v. Watts* 1779, 1 Doug. 92.
96   *Ackworth v. Kempe* 1778, 1 Doug. 42.
97   Preface 1 Burr iii, ix and x.
98   *Rose v. Green* 1758, 1 Burr 438.
99   4 Burr 2583.
100 Baker, *An Introduction to English Legal History* (2002), p. 184.

number of modern scholars have argued for a more modest appraisal of Lord Mansfield's judicial leadership: that Lord Mansfield was not as innovative as often depicted, but rather his contribution should be seen in terms of legal consolidation and refinement.[101] It is within this context that Lieberman's following remark should be read:

> "Mansfield, as his contemporaries fully recognized, was singularly blessed in the private reporters he attracted, and it is easy to mistake the novelty and distinctiveness of his judicial leadership simply on account of the unmatched quality of the law reports covering his tenure at King's Bench."[102]

It is hard to understand why Lieberman needs to interpret this relationship of judge/reporter within the framework of an apparent contest of abilities: whether the real talent was Lord Mansfield's or his reporter's. The functions of judge and reporter are quite distinct. While Burrow admits he often used his own words to report cases, it is a huge leap to presume the "distinctiveness" of Lord Mansfield's leadership was dependent upon Burrow's penmanship and that of his successors. Burrow's pride as a reporter is manifest in his insistence upon accuracy. That makes it improbable that Burrow's reports, no matter how lucid, were more than a diligent account of what had actually taken place. His successors would strive for that same level of accuracy. The quality of the grounds for the decision-making was Lord Mansfield's own.

Burrow's successor in King's Bench was Henry Cowper. Cowper acknowledged that there was much discussion in the profession at that time concerning the proper method of reporting and that each individual reporter had to make his own choice. His style was to state the pleadings concisely and to give the arguments delivered by counsel for both sides as comprehensively as the subject matter dictated. As to the judgment of the court, he had endeavoured to be "faithful, accurate, and full, as the assistance of short hand, and the most earnest attention could enable me to be".[103]

By the time Douglas took over as the reporter of King's Bench cases, the best method of reporting had still not been settled. Douglas outlined two main methods in his Preface: those who report at great length with respect to facts and counsel's arguments, giving almost verbatim renditions of the advocates' speeches, even when these advocates were representing the same party; and those who only gave a brief summary of the case together with the point decided, thereby omitting all the arguments by counsel and most of the reasoning of the judges. He considered there to be advantages and disadvantages to both approaches, and had himself attempted to steer a middle course between these two extremes.

---

101 David Lieberman, *The province of legislation determined*, Cambridge 1989, pp. 99-100.
102 *Ibid.*, p. 89.
103 Preface, 1 Cowper iii-iv.

Douglas set out the nature of this middle course he had chosen to adopt in thirteen points in the Preface. The gist of that approach comprises: to state what was material in the pleadings or evidence; to summarize the main points of counsel's arguments; to state the judgments of the court using his own notes and the notes of others; to place in the margins notes to illustrate or confirm doctrines laid down in the text and an abstract of the principle points of the case; to consult the original authors of cases cited.[104] There was one principle in particular that bound Douglas clearly to Burrow and Cowper:

> "There is no species of publication which demands a more scrupulous accuracy than those histories of judicial proceedings and decisions to which the name of *Reports* has been long appropriated".[105]

Despite continuing differences of style between individual reporters and the way in which reports were drafted in different courts, the main principles, in particular the requirement of accuracy, laid down by Burrow, Cowper and Douglas, were assimilated and law reporting became increasingly standardized. The next step was to ensure that case reports were published shortly after the decision had been reached. That was achieved under the court reporters Durnford and East, whose reports cover King's Bench cases between 1785 and 1800. Their example was followed by the other court reporters: Henry Blackstone in Common Pleas in 1788, Vesey in the Court of Chancery in 1789, Anstruther in the Court of Exchequer in 1792 and in 1812 by Dow in the House of Lords. With this regular series of reports, a short period of 'authorised reports' emerged. These were reports prepared by reporters who were known to and approved of by the judges. Only their reports could be cited in court. The monopoly was short-lived. The expense of the authorised reports prompted competition. An early rival was the series Law Journal Reports, founded in 1822. The privilege of exclusive citation was taken away by Denman C.J., in King's Bench in 1832 and the other courts followed his lead.[106]

There had, however, by this time long been another source of law reports: the newspapers of the day. Oldham points out that the London newspapers during the second half of the eighteenth century contained a surprising amount of information about court proceedings. The nature of the case was set out and the arguments of the parties were summarized. Comments made by the judge to the jury were frequently reported. Reports usually included a brief editorial statement about the importance of the case to the public. These reports often appeared verbatim, or almost so, in several newspapers. Having compared these newspaper reports with published reports (if there was a published report) and various

---

104 1 Douglas Preface xi-xvi.
105 *Ibid.*, Preface v.
106 Holdsworth, *A History of English Law* (1964), vol. XII, pp. 112-117, vol. XIII, pp. 425-427 and W.T.S. Daniel, *The History and Origin of the Law Reports*, London 1884, pp. 265-266.

manuscript sources, Oldham came to the conclusion that the newspaper reports were for the most part reliable representations of basic factual information.[107] In 1776, James Burrow had voiced a different opinion, stating that it would be a great pity to leave the reporting of the decisions of the court to "the ignorant, erroneous and false reports of newspapers, monthly historians, and collectors for book-sellers", although there was possibly an even worse fate, and that was to leave reporting to "the posthumous publication of defective and imperfect notes of gentlemen who cursorily took them, merely for their own use and as helps to their own memories, without any thoughts of making them public".[108]

While it is beyond the scope of this study to conduct a general analysis of the reliability of newspaper law reports, a sample patent case was examined in order to draw a comparison between the reporting of the patent case in the newspaper and a very detailed report of that case. The patent case selected was *R v. Arkwright* because of the verbatim report of *R v. Arkwright* that is available, published as *The trial of a cause instituted by Richard Pepper Arden, Esq*. The report of 12 November 1785 in *The Times* is not concerned with the main trial but with the motion brought by Serjeant Adair on 10 November for a new trial on behalf of his client, Arkwright. This motion is also covered in the detailed report. The law report in *The Times* first sets out the background to the motion. It explains that the action to repeal Arkwright's patent was on the ground of the lack of a sufficient specification and that the invention was not original. The reader is told that there had been two previous trials, the circumstances of each case had been "exactly similar" but the verdicts had been different. In the proceedings on *scire facias* a general verdict had been given for the King. Arkwright's counsel is named as Adair and a summary of his reasons is given as to why the court should grant a rule for a new trial. The summary is a fair representation of Adair's principal arguments as presented in the detailed published report.

The Times report then devotes a paragraph to what was said by Justice Buller, who had been the presiding trial judge, and the final paragraph sets out the decision of Lord Mansfield. *The Times* reporter had adeptly focused upon the most newsworthy point made by Buller at this motion hearing: that after having listened to the previous trial evidence for five or six hours, he had perceived that the defendant had "not a leg to stand on". Perhaps a little journalist licence had been used here, as the detailed report speaks of four or five hours of trial proceedings rather than five or six, but the statement as to "not a leg to stand upon" is the same. With respect to the reporting of Lord Mansfield's statement, the words are very similar to those in the detailed report. *The Times* report has all the main points: that there was "no colour for the rule"; that the ground urged for a new trial was that more evidence could be produced; that there were two questions to be tried, the specification

---

107 James Oldham, "Law Reporting in the London Newspapers, 1756-1786", *American Journal of Legal History* 31 (1987), pp. 177-179.
108 4 Burr 2584.

and the originality of the invention; that these questions were stated on the record. Rather surprisingly, the reporter does not quote Mansfield as having said "there is not a child but must know they were to try the questions there stated", as appears in the verbatim report, but opts for a more neutral "so that everybody must know what was to be tried".[109]

This is, of course, an examination of only one newspaper report, but it would seem to confirm Oldham's conclusion. *The Times* report of this motion hearing would appear to be a fair representation and a good summary of the arguments, when compared with the more detailed published case report. However, Oldham admits that, given the large number of newspapers published during the period he examined (1756-1786), it was not possible to study them all. And while Burrow's distain for newspaper reports might have been coloured by his own professional pride, presumably he had some grounds for voicing his distrust.

In some instances, however, the only reports of cases that are available are newspaper reports or pamphlets. This is the fate *of Liardet v. Johnson* 1778. Although considered by Hulme to be a very significant case in the development of patent law (see chapter 4), the only law report of *Liardet v. Johnson* in a law report series is concerned with the hearing in the Court of Chancery on 5 July 1780. That law report was added as a note to the case of *Thomas v. Jones* 1842. According to the note, the report of the Liardet case in Chancery was found in the 20th volume of Serjeant Hill's manuscript and was reported by Douglas. It would have been cited if arguments had been addressed to the court on whether the court would grant a perpetual injunction after a verdict of law, whether the verdict was in an action brought by the plaintiff in equity, and not in an issue or action directed by the court.[110] From this Chancery report, it appears that the case of *Liardet v. Johnson* had been heard twice at common law. It was first heard at Westminster before Lord Mansfield and a special jury. A motion for a new trial had been granted and the second trial had been heard during the Trinity term, again before Lord Mansfield. Although the defendant had produced a considerable amount of new evidence at the second hearing, the special jury in the second trial again found for the plaintiff. No motion for a new trial was submitted after the second verdict. However, as the cause was at issue in the equity court, it was then heard before Eyre, B.[111] These two trials at common law were not reported in any law report series. The first trial was, however, reported in various papers: *The Morning Post* of 23 February 1778, *The Public Advertiser* of the same day and the *St. James's Chronicle* 21-24 February 1778. Information about the second trial is mainly to be gleaned from pamphlets published by the parties after the hearing.[112]

---

109 *The Times*, 12 November 1785; p. 3; Issue 276; col. A and Arkwright (1785), pp. 187-191.
110 *Liardet v. Johnson* 1780, 62 ER 1000.
111 *Ibid.*, 1002.
112 John Adams and Gwen Averley, "The Patent Specification: The Role of Liardet v Johnson", *Journal of Legal History*, (1986) Vol. 7, p. 165.

The Morning Post article consists of a couple of paragraphs. Setting out that the case was tried in King's Bench before Lord Mansfield and a special jury, it explains to its readers that the action was for the infringement of a patent and an Act of Parliament granted to Liardet. The defendant Johnson had taken out a patent for a very similar composition of stucco, but his defence was not based upon his own patent but upon whether Liardet could show that his composition was a new and useful invention and whether the specification was sufficient. It refers to the witnesses who were called as being "some of the most eminent and experienced architects, plasterers, and builders". These witnesses gave evidence to show the novelty and utility of the plaintiff's invention and that the verdict of the jury was in favour of the plaintiffs, which fully established the validity of the patent.[113]

The newspaper report deals only with the main lines of the case and gives no detail about the concept of 'novelty'. The reader is only told that the witnesses knew of no stucco that would be resistant to the British climate until that of Liardet came into use. Further information is largely to be found in the pamphlets produced by the opposing parties. These pamphlets Hulme described as "paper warfare", although this paper warfare was useful in that it has preserved not only the substance of the speeches by counsel, but also a verbatim report of Lord Mansfield's address to the jury.[114] The pamphlets published by the parties are the main source for the second trial. It is in the Adams' family reply to Johnson's pamphlet in which Mansfield's summing up to the jury is recorded.[115]

As mentioned above, the reporting of patent cases was not consistent, particularly in the eighteenth century. The case of *Liardet v. Johnson* illustrates how the absence of a report in a law report series can hinder the analysis of the development of patent law in this period. It may be difficult to determine whether a particular case represented an authority and constituted a precedent. Hulme argues that the case of *Liardet v. Johnson* signifies a turning point in the interpretation of the patent specification.[116] This is disputed by Adams and Averley. They point out that later authorities mistakenly identify *Liardet v. Johnson* as the case of the trusses, and Buller's 'Nisi Prius' would seem to record the outcome of the case incorrectly. It is this mistaken outcome that finds its way into Carpmael's and Webster's compilations of patent cases. Similar confusion arises in the treatises; for example, Godson too confuses the Liardet case with the case on trusses. That the case is not well recorded, is one of the reasons Adams and Averley bring forward to argue that the case is not of central importance and that it is certainly not a landmark in the develop-

---

113 *Morning Post*, 23 February 1778, No. 1667, p. 2, col. 4, cited in E. Hulme, "On the History of Patent Law in the Seventeenth and Eighteenth Centuries", *Law Quarterly Review* (1902) 18, pp. 283-284.
114 *Ibid.*, p. 284.
115 Adams and Averley, "The Patent Specification: The Role of Liardet v Johnson" (1986), p. 165.
116 Hulme, "On the Consideration of the Patent Grant Past and Present" (1897), p. 317.

ment of patent law.[117] The issue of the role of *Liardet v. Johnson* in the development of patent law is dealt with in chapter 4.

1.7 Summary

After the mid eighteenth century, the common law courts became the principal forum for the hearing of patent disputes. Patent cases were not confined to any one of the common law courts in particular. There were two main forms of patent action. The more common action was a civil action for the infringement of a patent, brought by the patentee against an alleged infringer. The other form of action was initiated by a writ of *scire facias*, where an objection to the patent had been lodged and the crown, via the Attorney-General, had decided to proceed. This writ was issued by the Attorney-General, on behalf of the crown and was brought against a patentee in order to annul the patent.

In actions for infringement, the same case could be heard on several occasions; at *nisi prius* before a single judge and jury and again if a rule for a new trial was granted; it could be heard in the superior courts of Westminster before the full court to confirm or discharge a rule *nisi*. Points of law could be referred to the Court of King's Bench on a writ of error. Patentees could apply to the equity courts for the equitable remedies of discovery, injunction and account. In the eighteenth century, if a patentee wished to extend his patent beyond the statutory period of fourteen years he needed to apply for a private Act of Parliament. After Lord Brougham's Act of 1835, applications for patent extensions were heard by the Judicial Committee of the Privy Council.

In the common law courts, patentees were regularly nonsuited and hence their actions for infringement would fail. Where the hearing ran its full course, the evidence was presented to a jury for its verdict upon matters of fact. It was common practice to assemble a special jury to hear patent cases. The line between what was fact, which was the province of the jury, and what was law, which was the province of the judge, was not always entirely clear in patent cases at this time. If a verdict was brought in against the patentee in a civil action for infringement, in effect the patent lost its validity, even though it was the *scire facias* proceeding by the crown which was the formal means of revoking a patent.

In the latter part of the eighteenth century, not all patent cases were reported. The existence of non-reported cases can sometimes be ascertained from judges' trial notebooks, newspaper reports and contemporary pamphlets. The accuracy and reliability of law reports improved dramatically with James Burrow's reports of King's Bench decisions under Lord Mansfield. The high standards of reporting he set were maintained by the following generations of court reporters.

---

117 Adams and Averley, "The Patent Specification: The Role of Liardet v Johnson" (1986), pp. 162, 165-166.

2   Division Within the Judiciary: Were Some Judges 'Hostile' to Patentees?

A common complaint made by patentees and their supporters during this period is that the judiciary did not look upon patents favourably. For example, James Watt in a letter to Robinson, regarding a patent for a lamp, warned: "if he \Mr. K/ were to have a patent for his particular method of supplying the lamp his enemies would unite again[s]t him as they have done against Argand and he would find his purse too shallow for Westminster hall from which Good Lord deliver us."[1] The annulment of Arkwright's second patent of 1775 caused some concern among patentees, particularly those whose patents affected important sectors of industry like cotton and mining. Watt himself had appeared as an expert witness for Arkwright, and his testimony on Arkwright's behalf can be read as an attempt to support the position of a patentee who, like himself, was constantly having to face the infringement of his patent. After the annulment, Watt appears to have collaborated with Arkwright in writing a paper suggesting reforms to the patent system (he would later produce more detailed suggestions for patent law reform).[2] From the examples cited by Dutton, the distrust of some patentees for the court system seems to have persisted well into the nineteenth century. Writing in the early 1830s, Charles Babbage considered that the system "stab the inventor through the folds of an Act of Parliament and rifle him in the presence of the Lord Chief Justice of England" and John Farley was of the opinion that "Appeal to the law has proved itself to be a system of delusion".[3]

That patentees would use emotive language is understandable. They had interests to defend, and often financiers to satisfy. The decision to bring an action for the infringement of a patent, or where the patentee had to defend his patent against annulment, meant expense and, given the court procedures of the day, inevitable delays. Even a successful plaintiff could feel bitter that he had been forced to undergo the lengthy process of defending his patent in court. A recurrent theme in the letters from James Watt senior to his friends and colleagues is his distress and, at times quite literal, fatigue caused by these legal proceedings. In a letter to his old friend, Joseph Black, in 1795 he states: "I should have wrote to you sooner, but have been engaged in the disagreeable business of our lawsuit and out of health and spirits." In another letter dated the following year, in which he asks

---

1   Eric Robinson and Douglas McKie (eds.), *Partners in Science: James Watt & Joseph Black*, London 1970, Letter 104, p. 150.
2   A.N. Davenport, *James Watt and the Patent System*, The British Library 1989, p. 22.
3   *Quarterly Review* XLIII, 1830, p. 333 and *Westminster Review* XXII, 1835, p. 471. Cited in Dutton, *The patent system and inventive activity during the industrial revolution 1750-1852* (1984), p. 70.

Robinson to appear as a witness in the case against Maberley, he confesses that the matter "has for years been a torment to me" and "At present had not Mr. Boulton and myself the assistance of our sons we must give it up, though the stake is very great".[4]

What is surprising, however, is that such emotional and ill-defined language as "hostile" and "prejudiced" to describe the attitude of judges to patentees in this period has found its way into the accounts of historians. In his standard work on the history of English law, William Holdsworth turns his attention to commerce and industry in the eighteenth century. He remarks that the commercial advantages of encouraging inventors by the grant of patent rights were recognised by the courts. In a footnote, he refers to the judgment of Eyre, C.J in *Boulton and Watt v. Bull* 1795 that improvements of this kind should be encouraged as reflecting "the general view", although he notes Lord Kenyon's famous statement in *Hornblower v. Boulton and Watt* 1799, in which Kenyon confessed that he was not one of those who greatly favoured patents. Holdsworth considered that this 'general view', typified by Eyre's opinion in *Boulton and Watt v. Bull*, showed that the courts "had by that time quite got over their prejudice against patents, which had been due to the early association of patent rights with pernicious monopolies".[5]

Dutton blames a great deal of the uncertainty afflicting patent law during this period on the "excessively hostile attitude of some judges" and fixes the cessation of general hostilities at a later period than Holdsworth, asserting that a change in the attitude of judges did take place but the more favourable approach was adopted in the 1830s. A period of "early prejudice against patents" was now to give way. There would be, as one observer put it, a "continually relaxing aversion on the part of the Courts of Law". Although it was a slow process, Dutton considers that much of the change took place between 1830 and 1840.[6] Dutton's assessment of the judiciary's attitude is endorsed by MacLeod, although she considers that prior to the mid-eighteenth century, there is no evidence that judges held any "anti-patent prejudices". However, "Mounting competition among patentees and manufacturers turned patent litigation into a bear pit in the closing decades of the eighteenth century, and the odds were stacked against patentees". Indeed, it seems to her paradoxical that the number of patents rose in the late eighteenth century given the "reported hostility of judges and juries to patents, combined with the new judicial emphasis on the specification and readiness to set it aside on a technicality".[7] While avoiding such terms as 'hostile' or 'prejudice', Hulme notes: "an attitude of rigorous rather than benevolent interpretation was commonly assumed in the Court of Common Law."[8] The general picture that emerges

---

4   Robinson & McKie, *Partners in Science: James Watt & Joseph Black* (1970), Letters 153 and 162, pp. 212-213, 231.

5   Holdsworth, *A History of English Law* (1964), vol. XI, pp. 430-431 and fn. 1, p. 431.

6   Dutton, *The patent system and inventive activity during the industrial revolution 1750-1852* (1984), pp. 76-77, 78, 81.

7   MacLeod, *Inventing the Industrial Revolution: the English patent system, 1660-1800* (1988), pp. 58, 74, 145.

8   Hulme, "On the Consideration of the Patent Grant Past and Present" (1897), p. 318.

from these accounts is one in which patentees were treated unfavourably, even sometimes with hostility, by a significant section of the judiciary.

To allege that judges were "hostile" or "prejudiced" is to imply some measure of bad faith on the part of judges who did not find in favour of patentees. These terms are normative, pejorative labels. The concepts they describe are subjective. As such, it is questionable how useful they can be as guides in an academic analysis. That the use of such terms as "hostile" and "prejudiced" is both imprecise and misleading is perhaps the reason why Dutton and MacLeod see 'hostility' to patents in a period in which Holdsworth considers the general view of judges to have become quite favourable to patents. What criteria have to be fulfilled before a judge can be described as "prejudiced" against patentees or "hostile"? Much has been made of Lord Kenyon's statement in *Hornblower and Maberly v. Boulton and Watt* 1799 cited above that he was not one who greatly favoured patents.[9] However, these commentators invariably fail to mention that in that same case Lord Kenyon then went on to state that he was against a too literal interpretation of the words of the patent for "there is no magic in words" and actually found in favour of the patentees, Boulton and Watt.[10] Is a judge like Lord Kenyon 'prejudiced' because he had specifically said that he is not one "who greatly favour patents" even if he is still prepared to find for a patentee? Is a judge like Lord Ellenborough who did announce that patents were "a species of property highly important, as it respects the interests of the individual, and with him also the interests of the public"[11] still not 'hostile' given his propensity to set aside patents for grammatical irregularities?

A more constructive and fruitful approach to understanding the attitude of judges to patents, in the latter part of the eighteenth century and the early nineteenth century, arises if an examination is made of the divergence in the interpretation criteria used by judges in reaching their decisions. These criteria were affected by whether a judge adopted a formalist or teleological approach to interpretation. This divergence was present but less conspicuous where a traditional area of law was concerned. As Simpson points out, there may be wide differences in the way in which propositions of law are formulated (even when agreeing, judges may be saying different things), yet there is at the same time a very considerable measure of agreement as to the practical application of the law in actual cases.[12] Judges may have been critical of the criteria used by other judges, but if the decision reached was consistent with received ideas within the existing legal order, the criticism was muted. Criticism would not be muted if a judge attempted a too radical modification of the existing legal paradigm (see below).

---

9   *Hornblower and Maberly v. Boulton and Watt* 1799, 8 T.R. 98.
10 *Ibid.*, pp. 98-99.
11 *Huddart v. Grimshaw* 1803, 1 CPC 225.
12 A.W.B. Simpson, *Legal theory and legal history: essays on the common law*, London 1987, p. 372.

In the mid-eighteenth century, patent law was new to the common law courts. There was no well-established legal matrix in place, as was the case with such legal domains as the law of real property and wills. Consequently, members of the legal community could not fall back on years of accepted practice. In these circumstances, the divergence in interpretation would come more explicitly to the fore. Without recourse to a settled body of received wisdom, judges' decisions would be more individualistic. Decisions would be more dependent upon the preference of a particular judge for a certain mode of interpretation, filtered through the judge's own frame of reference. Judicial decisions were, therefore, often experienced by patentees as inconsistent with each other or as out of step with the world as they saw it.

2.1   The Role of the Judge: Modern Insights

To accuse a judge of hostility or prejudice implies that some judges were using their position to shape a system of patent law that was loaded against patentees. This raises a major issue: do judges create law? Only if a creative function exists, whether in a primary or derivative form, is it relevant to examine the *attitude* of judges to patents in this period. Whether judges have a creative function is a question that has been addressed by many academics over the years and the debate continues. The positivist theory sees the law as essentially a rule based, closed system with a restrictive interpretational role for the judge. Critical legal movements, however, have rejected the marginal role assigned to judicial creativity in the formalist approach. Non-legal as well as legal factors could influence the judicial decision-making process. While these counter-movements have acknowledged that in practice the judge has a creative function, the extent of that creativity has been disputed. Some scholars maintain that judges simply create law as they see fit, others have argued that judicial creativity is not arbitrary, but only secondary and limited by the general legal order. It is beyond the scope of this study to deal with the issue in any depth, and the short discussion that follows below simply attempts to highlight some of the main arguments.

2.1.1   The Formalism Approach

The legal positivist theory of law sees the law as a system of rules. If the law is a system of rules, the task of the judge is restricted. The judge's function is to apply these given rules to the facts of individual cases. This apparently simple premise is, however, fraught with difficulties. What facts are the relevant facts to which the rules must be applied? How, and by whom, should these rules be interpreted?

The need for the interpretation of rules can never be entirely excluded. However, the line between the interpretation and the creation of rules is not always obvious. Justinian recognised the risk of judicial rule creation and tried to prevent it by prohibiting judges from interpreting his *Corpus iuris civilis*. Judges were required to submit cases that needed interpretation to the *augusta auctoritas*, to which was reserved the competence to interpret laws (Codex I, 17, 2, 21). Napoleon is said to have been horrified when he heard of the first commentary on his *Code Civil*, declaring: "Mon code est perdu!" These two examples led Vogenauer to comment: "In the thirteen centuries separating the two emperors from each other, there were plenty of attempts completely or at least partially to stifle the interpretative activities of judges and legal scholars."[13]

The standpoint of several prominent legal scholars in the nineteenth century would set the tone in Europe: there must be a sharp distinction between the competence of the judge and that of the lawgiver. Dumont's work *De la Codification*, which appeared in 1803 and leaned upon Jeremy Bentham's views on codification, was adamant that judicial decision-making must be a more or less automatic application of the legal code. Von Savigny's analysis of legal interpretation similarly stressed this distinction. The judicial interpretation of a new law or even of a custom was only permissible if it were "reine Auslegung" and not "Fortbildung des Rechts".[14] Judicial interpretation must contribute to the application of a law but should not form new law, even if this new law stemmed from the existing law.

The fear that judicial interpretation would become the law itself was not confined to civil law jurisdictions. In England, Francis Bacon reminded his fellow common law judges in *The Essays*, published in 1625, that the function of the judge must be "*jus dicere* and not *jus dare*; to interpret law, and not to make law, or give law".[15] In a well-known sermon, the English bishop Hoadley pointed out in 1717: "whoever has an absolute authority to interpret any written, or spoken laws, it is he who is truly the lawgiver, to all intents and purposes: and not the person who first wrote, or spoke them."[16] Jeremy Bentham considered the blurring of the distinction between *jus dicere* and *jus dare* to be a major ground for criticising the English legal system in the eighteenth century. Bentham has been hailed as an early prime exponent, or even the founding father, of legal positivism.[17] Bentham's analysis of judicial decision-making in the eighteenth century led him to conclude that judges did have a creative function. However, it was a function that he believed they should not have, as a creative capacity on their part adulterated legislative law and undermined legal certainty. His ideal was the destruction of customary law and its replacement by a code that would be so complete and clear that it would cover every case. It would not need

---

13 Stefan Vogenauer, "Statutory Interpretation", in Jan Smits (ed.), *Elgar Encyclopedia of Comparative Law*, Cheltenham 2006, p. 681.
14 J.H.A. Lokin, *Tekst en Uitleg*, Groningen 1994, pp. 1-3.
15 Francis Bacon, *Essays moral, economical and political*, London 1798, p. 248.
16 Vogenauer, "Statutory Interpretation" (2006), p. 681.
17 H.L.A. Hart, *Essays on Bentham: Studies in Jurisprudence and Political Theory*, Oxford 1982, pp. 17-18.

an interpreter. Interpretation was an arbitrary system, "An indistinct danger [that] hovers over every head", and the use of such a method meant there could be no security.[18]

Modern positivists have been more prepared than Bentham to accept a role for judicial interpretation, even if only a modest role. While Hart analyses law in terms of a system of rules, he distinguishes between primary and secondary rules. These secondary rules are necessary in order to specify the ways in which the primary rules may be ascertained, introduced, eliminated or varied. The 'open texture' of law leads Hart to recognise an element of judicial discretion in the system. However, he maintains that the application of law is normally settled by rules and only in a few atypical cases is the matter open to judicial discretion. That Hart would seek to marginalize judicial discretion is understandable, as it would otherwise subvert his rule-based model.[19] Hart's theory has been criticised by Dworkin. Dworkin contends that law consists not only of rules, but also of policies and principles, in particular the latter, which are evoked in hard cases to which the rules alone afford no clear outcome.[20] Posner contends that it is Hart's failure to reconcile the practice of judges to his theory of positivism which opened him up to Dworkin's criticism.[21] However, this would appear to be a general shortcoming in the positivist, rule-based model of law: it ignores the *practice* of judicial decision-making by focusing on a rule based theoretical construct of judicial decision-making.

2.1.2   The Creative Approach

In an empirical study of judicial decision-making which appeared in 2008, Hartendorp concluded that the rational positivist model was a failure. His conclusion is interesting because the study concerned judges making decisions in civil actions not in a common law system, but in a codified system of law (in the Netherlands). The rational, positivist model was rejected by Hartendorp because it failed to take into account other essential aspects of judicial decision-making. The observations made by the judges in this study made it clear that, in practice, decision-making was formed not just by applying a theoretical knowledge of the law, by applying rules, but also by taking other non-legal factors into account derived from 'non-rational' forms of knowledge. Logic played a more restricted role than that of 'practical wisdom'.[22]

---

18   Jeremy Bentham, *The Theory of Legislation, translated from the French of Etienne Dumont by Richard Hildreth*, first published in French in 1802/Oceana Publications: 1975, I. xvii, pp. 94-95.
19   Hilaire McCoubrey and Nigel D. White, *Textbook on Jurisprudence*, London 1996, pp. 38, 46-47.
20   *Ibid.*, 35.
21   Richard A. Posner, *Law and Legal Theory in England and America*, Oxford 1996, p. 15.
22   R.C. Hartendorp, *Praktisch gesproken: Alledaagse Civiel Rechtspleging als praktische Oordeelsvorming*, Rotterdam 2008, pp. 35-36, 167, 211.

The rejection of the formalist approach has a much longer history. An early sceptic of formalism was the American judge, Oliver Wendell Holmes. From his experience in the common law courts, he argued that judicial decision-making was not simply a logical exercise in which an established rule of law was applied to the facts of a particular case:

> "... the life of the law has not been logic, it has been experience. The felt necessities of the time, the prevalent moral and political theories, intuitions of public policy, avowed or unconscious, even the prejudices which judges share with their fellow men, have a good deal more to do than the syllogism in determining the rules by which men should be governed."[23]

The idea that the law could be dealt with as if it contained only the axioms and corollaries of a book of mathematics was dismissed. He rejected the "official theory" that each new decision follows syllogistically from existing precedents. Unlike Bentham, Holmes did see the origin of the common law in customs. Over the centuries these customs had disappeared, but the rule had remained and been given a new form, as "new reasons more fitted for the time have been found for them". The ones who had fitted these new reasons to the old rule were the judges. "The very considerations which judges most rarely mention, and always with an apology, are the secret root from which the law draws all the juices of life. I mean, of course, considerations of what is expedient for the community concerned."[24]

Holmes always maintained that one of the most important of the non-legal factors affecting judicial decision-making was public policy. Others would voice similar views. For example, Herman Oliphant in his book *A Return to Stare Decisis*, which appeared in 1928, questioned the usefulness of the ratio decidendi as a device for the legal reasoning of the judges, considering that the choice was more often based not on legal logic, but on reasons of policy or morality.[25] Paul Vinogradoff acknowledged that judges could not disregard the changes of views taking place in society at large in the settlement of disputes. The change of views taking place in society would affect the movement of judicial case law.[26] The premise that judicial decision-making takes into account non-legal factors would form the basis for rule scepticism and a rejection of formalism.

Would it therefore be more correct to maintain that in practice judges create the very law they apply? In the common law system, the ratio decidendi forms the precedent of a case. This precedent must be followed in subsequent cases where the material facts of the earlier case can be deemed to be similar to the material facts in the present case before the judge. Whether a precedent will be followed therefore depends upon whether a judge

---

23   Oliver Wendell Holmes, *The Common Law*, Chicago 1881/2000, p. 1.
24   *Ibid.*, pp. 35-36.
25   McCoubrey & White, *Textbook on Jurisprudence* (1996), pp. 212-213.
26   Paul Vinogradoff, *Common Sense in Law*, New Jersey, 2006/1914, pp. 195-196.

considers the material facts in the present case to be similar or not. The judge will not have to follow precedent if he can distinguish the material facts in the present case from those in the former case. This process of determining similarity makes it possible for a judge to modify the previous rule by ignoring some fact that earlier judges regarded as important, in other words the judge determines that the fact is not a material fact, or by emphasising a fact which previous judges considered unimportant. As the material facts of two different cases can never be identical, the determination of similarity will also depend upon the judge's application of analogy. Commenting upon judicial decision-making in the common law system, Peter Stein maintains:

> "judges do in fact create new law when they make a decision which constitutes a precedent, yet formally the fiction is preserved that the judges are merely declaring what has always been the common law and (when they overrule an earlier decision) correcting their predecessors' misapprehensions."[27]

Does a judicial decision depend purely upon the personal views of the judge concerned? Bentham certainly believed so: "The judge, now conforming to the law, and now explaining it away, can always decide a case to suit his own designs."[28]

For Bentham, the need to avoid the personal discretion of a judge in the decision-making process was one of the main factors for implementing a codified system of law. However, there are those who would maintain that the function of a judge in a codified system is no less creative than that ascribed by Bentham to the judicial decision-making process in a common law system. Lokin argues that attempts to reduce the role of the judge to being only the mouthpiece of a code have always been doomed to failure. One example he provides is that of the French law on the judicial organisation promulgated in 1790. This law contained a 'référé législatif'. Judges were not to make regulations, but refer questions to the legislative body if it were necessary: "soit d'interpréter une loi soit d'en faire une nouvelle." The consequence was predictable; the judges refused to reach decisions and referred every case to the legislature. Robespierre's wish to eliminate the word 'jurisprudence' from the French vocabulary had succeeded, but not quite in the way he had intended. A certain level of judicial interpretation had to be allowed. Cambacérès would argue in the National Convention in 1793 that to expect a code to have predicted every case was simply fanciful.[29] Lokin is convinced that the judge's role must be a creative one: every text needs interpretation, not just the unclear ones but also the clear ones. It is a misunderstanding to limit the creative role of the judge to that of finding the law, as does

---

27 Peter Stein, *Regulae iuris: from juristic rules to legal maxims*, Edinburgh 1966, pp. 16-17.
28 Bentham, *The Theory of Legislation, translated from the French of Etienne Dumont by Richard Hildreth* (1975), I. xvii, p. 94.
29 Lokin, *Tekst en Uitleg* (1994), p. 9.

Scholten (see below). While acknowledging that Scholten has swept away many misconceptions concerning the role of the judge, Lokin considers that Scholten's analysis is not radical enough; apparently Scholten was not prepared to follow his analysis through to its logical conclusion. That conclusion must be that the text of a law is an empty shell. It is only through judicial interpretation that the literal text of a law may remain the same over a long period of time, for the interpretation of that literal text will have taken on different meanings over that time. This is because the law is not found; it is the judge who gives the law its content.[30]

2.1.3   The Bounded Creativity Approach

If judges do have a creative role, are judges' decisions arbitrary: do the existing legal parameters simply function as camouflage for judicial law making, as Bentham argued? Or do judges only create law within the bounded confines set by existing legal parameters? C.K. Allen is a spokesman for the latter approach. He acknowledges that judges in "a derivative or secondary sense" make law, but only in this sense. Theirs is not an original act of creation. Every act of interpretation shapes something new, in a secondary sense. A judge cannot, however much he may wish to do so, sweep away what he believes to be the prevailing rule of law and substitute something else in it place. "In this sense it is no 'childish fiction' to say that he does not and cannot 'make' law."[31]

Allen's approach is similar, in this respect, to that of the Dutch civil law scholar, Paul Scholten. Scholten's work is highly respected within the Netherlands, but is little known in common law jurisdictions. Scholten argued that the function of the judge is essentially a creative one, but it is restricted by the given legal order. Just like Holmes, who was describing a common law system, he rejected any model of judicial decision-making which was based on judges mechanically applying existing rules to the facts of a case. Rather than simply applying existing rules to determined facts, the rule has to be found either by interpretation or by analogy or refinement.[32]

Scholten saw the law as embedded within society. Every law is based upon an appreciation of social interests, and is aimed at exerting an influence on what happens in that social reality. As society is constantly changing, so legal regulations may come to cover areas for which they were not intended. The meaning of a legal rule has to be determined within the totality of the legal context; in relation to meaning and the common use of language, and in relation to the social relationships that it regulates. A legal measure is

---

30 *Ibid.*, pp. 26-30.
31 C.K. Allen, *Law in the Making*, (7th ed.) Oxford 1978, pp. 308-309.
32 Paul Scholten, *Asser's Handleiding tot de Beoefening van het Nederlands Burgerlijk Recht: Algemeen Deel*, Zwolle 1974, p. 6.

part of a chain of serial regulation; other measures will have preceded it. The new legal measure replaces these but at the same time is related to them. There is continuity in the law, but it changes every day by its application.[33]

For Scholten, a judicial decision cannot be seen as a deduction made from a closed system. Law is an open system, for the law is never complete, not only because it is the imperfect product of human beings, but also because it is constantly being added to. There is more to being a judge than simply applying existing rules to established facts. The process of subsumption itself, whereby the minor premise, the particular facts of a case, is brought under the major premise, is a creative act. Why is this fact relevant and that fact not relevant? The judge is looking for those facts which are of importance to the decision and he cannot interpret which facts are of importance without having a rule as the starting point. Facts can only be seen from the perspective of the rule, the decision.[34] It is interesting to note in this respect that Scholten's analysis of the way in which a judge interprets facts echoes Popper's ideas on the relationship between observation and theory: "I believe that theory at least some rudimentary theory or expectation always comes first; that it always precedes observation."[35]

Before the facts can be fitted into the framework of a rule, Scholten argues that the rule has to be found. It is not ready waiting for the judge: there are rules, but the judge has to decide which rule is the right rule for this particular case.[36] Every decision is, therefore, at the same time an application of the rules and a creation: the one who decides on which rule is applicable is also determining the application. The judicial decision adds something new to the system.[37] If the very selection of the applicable rule is a creative act, this undermines the formalist argument that the judge applies rules to facts in a neutral or mechanistic way. It also undermines the modern positivists' contention that only in a few atypical cases is judicial discretion relevant. It means that every decision made by a judge, whether the outcome of a relatively simple or a relatively complex case, relies upon the exercise of a creative function.

Scholten set out a radical new approach to understanding the role of judicial decision-making. It was radical because he saw the judicial decision-making process not only as an intellectual exercise, but also as an intuitive one.[38] Finding the law is never a matter of applying the text of a law to a case in a mechanistic manner, but rather a creative process demanding the construction of a just solution. The law cannot be understood without

---

33 *Ibid.*, pp. 34-35.
34 *Ibid.*, pp. 75-76, 121.
35 Karl R. Popper, *Objective Knowledge: A Evolutionary Approach*, Oxford 1974, p. 258.
36 Scholten, *Asser's Handleiding tot de Beoefening van het Nederlands Burgerlijk Recht: Algemeen Deel* (1974), pp. 120-121.
37 *Ibid.*, pp. 76-77.
38 Scholten, *Asser's Handleiding tot de Beoefening van het Nederlands Burgerlijk Recht: Algemeen Deel* (1974), pp. 130-132.

reference to legal principles, which provide the moral element of the law. The decision will therefore have a moral component: for a decision is always also a matter of conscience. However, the decision is not arbitrary. One reason that it is not arbitrary is exactly because a decision is a matter of conscience: a judge must be able to declare: "I can do no other."[39] Nor can a judicial decision be arbitrary because it must fit within the legal order in which it is made and it is this requirement which restricts the apparent freedom of the judge. The necessity to provide grounds for a decision is the guarantee that this apparent freedom is not abused.[40]

Just as Scholten rejected the formalist premise of a distinction between morality and law, for a decision is always a matter of conscience, he also rejected the view that codification made interpretation unnecessary. That was an illusion. Interpretation would be necessary to redress apparent gaps or lack of clarity. The question was what form should this interpretation take? Should it be grammatical, historical or teleological (serving social goals)? As to an historical interpretation, why would it be permissible to explain one legal provision by using another legal provision made at a different time? And how would a grammatical interpretation be possible if an explanation according to the words would be different from one according to the system? As every law is based on an appreciation of social interests, Scholten argued that the meaning of a law can, therefore, only be understood in the context of human relations and that requires a place to be made for sociological or teleological interpretation.[41]

Scholten's analysis of judicial decision-making has much to offer for an understanding of judicial decision-making in general, regardless of distinctions between common law and civil law systems. While seeing judicial decision-making as a creative act, nonetheless Scholten considers this creative act to be limited in that it must fit within certain parameters. These parameters are the authority that has been vested in the judicial function by any particular community and that there is a logical connection between the judge's reasoning and the facts. Whether the grounds for applying a rule in a particular way are considered to fit will depend upon whether they appears consistent with the legal order as a whole.[42]

2.2   The Role of the Judge: Eighteenth Century Legal Treatises

If influential legal treatises, by writers such as Hale and Blackstone, are consulted the impression they give is that judges in the eighteenth century were to conceive of their role in formalist terms. The task of the judge was simply to apply existing rules of law to the

---

39 *Ibid.*, pp. 130, 133.
40 *Ibid.*, p. 131.
41 *Ibid.*, pp. 2-4, 34-35.
42 *Ibid.*, pp. 130-131.

facts of individual cases. They did not create law: *jus dicere* not *jus dare* was indeed the maxim. This reluctance to acknowledge a creative function for a judge, even at a secondary level, would pose problems for these writers. Apparent inconsistencies required explanation. All too often these explanations were not intellectually satisfactory and would provide an easy target for the sharp wit of a critic like Bentham.

Matthew Hale's *The History of the Common Law*, written in 1665 but not published until 1713, would become an important and respected book in the eighteenth century. Hale, who had himself acted as a judge (in Common Pleas, as Lord Chief Baron of the Exchequer and finally as the Lord Chief Justice of the King's Bench), observed that judicial decision-making functions in a different way from parliamentary law making. Although judicial decisions bind the parties in a case, as a law between the parties in the case in question, they do not make a law properly so called, as that function is reserved to the king and parliament. However, judicial decisions do have "a great weight and authority in expounding, declaring and publishing the law" and "though such decisions are less than a law, yet they are a greater evidence thereof than the opinion of any private persons".[43]

In this reading, judicial decisions are evidence of a law, but they are not in themselves law. However, Hale was aware of a problem: if judges do not create law, if that is the task of the king and parliament, how could the common law have developed? In tracing the historical development of the common law from early times through to his own day, Hale accepted that law changes: the common law, at the time of Henry II, when Glanville wrote, was different in some particulars from that in the time of Henry III, when Bracton wrote, although it was not possible to pinpoint the exact time when that change began. That the law undergoes a process of change is only to be expected, for "there must of necessity be a provision of new, and other laws successively answering to the multitude of successive exigencies and emergencies, that in a long tract of time will offer themselves". One way for Hale to deal with this problem was to see an invisible hand of parliament in the development of the common law: "doubtless many of those things that now obtain as common law had their original by parliamentary acts of constitutions though those acts are now either not extant or made before Time of Memory".[44] Yet Hale goes on to acknowledge that the common law consists of more than parliamentary acts lost in time: "So that use and custom, and judicial decisions and resolutions, and acts of parliament, though not now extant, might introduce some new laws, and alter some old, which we now take to be the very common law itself."[45] Hale's summary of the components of the common law indicates that he saw not only statutes but also custom and judicial decisions as having

---

43 Matthew Hale, *The History of the Common Law of England*, Chicago 1971, p. 45.
44 *Ibid.*, pp. 4, 39.
45 *Ibid.*, p. 40.

contributed to the process of legal change and the formation of what had become accepted as the common law.

The theory that the common law had developed from extinct statutes was still current in the eighteenth century. It was a theory which served to diminish the role of judges: judges had not developed the common law in their courts, but had simply applied the law laid down in vanished statutes. This reading of the history of the common law was referred to in an editorial footnote by Edward Christian in Blackstone's *Commentaries*. Christian quotes Wilmot, L.C.J., who was of the opinion that "the common law is nothing else but statutes worn out by time. All our law began by the consent of the legislature, and whether it is now law by usage or writing is the same thing". He then also cites Hale in this footnote: "That many of those things that we now take for common law were undoubtedly acts of parliament, though now not to be found of record." Christian himself acknowledges that the greatest part of the common law probably owed its origin to extinct statutes, but also considered that much of the common law had been introduced by usage.[46]

The citations in the footnote stand in stark contrast to the text of the *Commentaries* itself. Blackstone identifies the "first ground and chief corner stone of the laws of England" to be "general immemorial custom, or common law, from time to time declared in the decisions of the courts of justice".[47] It is revealing that when Blackstone does allude to an early statute, the statute of treasons in the reign of Edward III (25 Edw. III. c. 2), he considered its effect was simply to declare and enumerate those offences which were already treason at common law. Blackstone did acknowledge that statutes might be necessary to deal with the imperfections of human laws, and the mistakes and unadvised determinations of unlearned (or even learned) judges.[48] However, Blackstone put his faith in the common law rather than in statute law:

> "For to say the truth, almost all the perplexed questions, almost all the niceties, intricacies and delays (which have sometime disgraced the English, as well as other, courts of justice) owe their original not to the common law itself, but to innovations that have been made in it by acts of parliament."[49]

Given this opinion on statute law, it would only be logical that Blackstone would relegate statute law to a minor role in the development of the common law.

If the common law was immemorial custom declared by the courts, was there a creative role for the judge? Blackstone addresses the role of the judge in his Introduction to the *Commentaries*. Following in Hale's footsteps, Blackstone sees the task of the judge to

---

46   Blackstone, *Commentaries on the Laws of England* (1793) Editorial note (7), vol.1, Introd. p. 74.
47   *Ibid.*, Introd., p. 72.
48   *Ibid.*, Introd., p. 86.
49   *Ibid.*, Introd., p. 9.

expound and declare, but not to make law. Judges act as the "depositary of the laws"; it is within the judiciary that knowledge of the common law is to be found and it is this body that determines the validity of customs and maxims. However, a judge is:

> "sworn to determine, not according to his own private judgment, but according to the known laws and customs of the land; not delegated to pronounce a new law, but to maintain and expound the old one." "For it is an established rule to abide by former precedents, where the same points come again in litigation; as well to keep the scale of justice even and steady, and not liable to waver with every new judge's opinion."[50]

Blackstone does, however, point to an exception to this rule. A judge may deviate from precedent where the former judgment is "contrary to reason or to divine law". For a former decision which is "manifestly absurd or unjust" is not bad law, it is actually not law at all. It has been erroneously determined, which means even in such cases "judges do not pretend to make a new law, but to vindicate the old one from misrepresentation". He concludes:

> "The doctrine of the law then is this: that precedents and rules must be followed, unless flatly absurd or unjust."[51]

In order to maintain his argument that judges do not create law, Blackstone has to present unjust or absurd decisions as never having been law. In this respect Edward Christian's comments are again of interest. His two footnotes make it clear that he did not accept Blackstone's opinion on this matter. In footnote (3) he points out that notwithstanding whether such decisions are manifestly absurd and unjust "they must be religiously adhered to by the judges in all courts, who are not to assume the characters of legislators. It is their province *jus dicere*, and not *jus dare*". He backs up his argument first by citing Edward Coke (noting Coke's "enthusiastic fondness for the common law") and then by citing a more recent source, Francis Hargrave. Hargrave stated that although arguments based on inconvenience deserve attention "if the rule of law is clear and explicit, it is in vain to insist upon inconveniencies; nor can it be true that nothing, which is inconvenient, is lawful, for that supposes in those who make laws a perfection, which the most exalted human wisdom is incapable of attaining, and would be an invincible argument against ever changing the law". In footnote (4) Christian concludes: "Precedents and rules must be followed even when they are flatly absurd and unjust, if they are agreeable to ancient principles." Citing an example of such an absurd law, he continues: "it is the clear law of England, and can

---

50 *Ibid.*, Introd., pp. 68-69.
51 *Ibid.*, Introd., pp. 69-70.

only be abrogated by the united authority of the king, lords, and commons, in parliament assembled."[52]

It has been argued that when Blackstone attributes this discretion to ignore absurd or unjust decisions to judges, the rationale behind this opinion may have had a more practical than theoretical justification. As noted in the previous chapter, the reporting of cases before the mid-eighteenth century was haphazard and frequently inaccurate. Holt, in *Slater v. May* 1704, had famously decried the idiocy of some of the reporting and there were various reporters whose works were considered to be particularly unreliable. The exception for "flatly absurd or unjust" may well have meant little more than allowing judges not to be bound by dubious and unsoundly reported precedents.[53] It is possible that the unreliability of earlier reporting may have influenced Blackstone's opinion. Nonetheless, by granting this discretion to judges, Blackstone appears to be allowing for what he has previously excluded, that the judge's "own private judgment" had a role to play. An opportunity for creative interpretation does apparently exist, at least in the negative. The decision as to whether a precedent is "flatly absurd or unjust" is the province of the individual judge; it depends upon his view of that previous decision. It would therefore appear that Blackstone is caught between his formalistic description of the role of the judge and an acknowledgment of the sphere in which an individual judge's experience and worldview operates.

The reference to ignoring "flatly absurd or unjust precedents" is not the only evidence to indicate that Blackstone was aware that the judge appeared, at times, to have a competence that was beyond that of the *bouche de la loi*. It is apparent in his analysis of statutory interpretation. Although the wording of a statute was of importance, Blackstone states that there are other factors to be taken into account than the letter of the law:

> "The fairest and most rational method to interpret the will of the legislator, is by exploring his intentions at the time when the law was made, by signs, the most natural and probable. And these signs are either the words, the context, the subject-matter, the effects and consequences, *or the spirit and reason of the laws.*"

He adds:

> "From this method of interpreting laws, by the reason of them, arises what we call equity".[54]

---

52   *Ibid.*, fn (3) and (4)), pp. 69-70.
53   Allen, *Law in the Making* (1978), pp. 228-229.
54   Blackstone, *Commentaries on the Laws of England* (1793), Introd., pp. 59, 61 [my italics].

As will be seen in the following chapter, which examines the statutory interpretation of the Statute of Monopolies, Blackstone was not a lone voice pleading for the equitable construction of statutes. He was enunciating a form of statutory interpretation with a tradition that went back several centuries. Vogenauer's examination of cases indicates that the equitable interpretation of statutes persisted from the Year Book period to 1830.[55] Blackstone was simply voicing the attitude to statutory interpretation that was current at the time he wrote his *Commentaries*. Christian himself, who in his footnotes did not always fully endorse Blackstone's opinions, stood firmly behind this means of construing statutes. Penal statutes should be construed according to the "strict letter in favour of the subject", if there were any ambiguity, and "remedial statutes must be construed according to the spirit; for in giving relief against fraud, or in the furtherance and extension of natural right and justice, the judge may safely go beyond even that which existed in the minds of those who framed the law".[56]

Blackstone refers to the definition of equity by Grotius: "the correction of that wherein the law by reason of its universality is deficient."[57] However, Blackstone was keenly aware that by recognising the concept of equity to be a general factor in influencing the interpretation of statutes by common law judges, a very sensitive issue had been brought to the fore. The whole question of equity was particularly sensitive in the English system because of the institutional arrangement: equity was a separate system with its own courts, its own principles and its own remedies quite distinct from the common law and its courts. In the eighteenth century the question of judicial creativity almost invariably involved the discussion of the classical doctrine of equity in law.[58] The institutionalised distinction between equity and the common law in the English system bedevilled the discussion of equity. As Lieberman points out, the need felt by any legal system to balance the claims of equity against the stability of legal rules was transformed in England into a constitutional issue regarding the extent to which Chancery might interfere with and overrule the common law.[59]

In his *Commentaries*, Blackstone made it clear that although equity had a role to play, that role was limited. Equity and law had their own spheres. Blackstone warned that:

> "the liberty of considering all cases in an equitable light must not be indulged too far; lest thereby we destroy all law, and leave the decision of every question entirely in the breast of the judge. And law, without equity, though hard and

---

55 Stefan Vogenauer, *Die Auslegung von Gesetzen in England un auf dem Kontintent*, Tübingen 2001, Part II, pp. 669-779.
56 Blackstone, *Commentaries on the Laws of England* (1793), Introd., p. 88 note (19).
57 *Ibid.*, Introd. p. 61.
58 David Lieberman, *The province of legislation determined*, Cambridge 1989, p. 74.
59 *Ibid.*, p. 78.

disagreeable, is much more desirable for the public good, than equity without law: which would make every judge a legislator, and introduce most infinite confusion; as there would then be almost as many different rules of action laid down in our courts, as there are differences of capacity and sentiment in the human mind."[60]

This idiosyncratic relationship of equity and law in the English system undoubtedly made some members of the bar and the judiciary wary of a creative role for the judge.

Blackstone stressed that reason was fundamental in order to discover the laws of nature and, through them, the laws of England. Although Blackstone urged the reader that "law is to be considered not only matter of practice, but also as a rational science",[61] it was not Blackstone's intention that any individual should consider, by using this process of reasoning, that his own critical faculties were superior to the wisdom that had been accumulated over the centuries. He believed that throughout all legal history there ran a mysterious purpose which was of its own force improving institutions: "the fundamental maxims and rules of the law ... have been and are everyday improving and are fraught with the accumulated wisdom of ages." This force was more powerful than anything man could achieve. It was this belief which is behind the often quoted analogy made by Blackstone: "Our system of remedial law resembles an old Gothic castle, erected in the days of chivalry, but fitted up for a modern inhabitant."[62] Even if the decisions of the courts were only evidence of the law rather than the law itself, precedents were of importance not only to maintain legal certainty but as a vehicle for this 'wisdom of ages'.

The comment that "law is to be considered not only as matter of practice, but also as a rational science" is, however, a particularly revealing one. Boorstin remarks that although Blackstone treated the law as a closed, logical system, he sometimes confused it with appealing to experience. On the one hand, a rule of law was stated in such a manner as to make it appear that the law was merely recognizing a physical fact, rather than creating a rule by its own fiat. On the other hand it was explained as part of everyday experience. The use of the two methods of rationalising the law sometimes led Blackstone into a difficulty greater than mere ambiguity.[63] Blackstone's reference to the right of judges to ignore absurd precedents and "the liberty of considering all cases in an equitable light", even if this should not be indulged too far, indicate an implicit awareness that the judge's task involved more than simply applying existing rules to the facts of a case. Langbein has recently argued that Blackstone very well knew how much room for discretion judges had.

---

60   Blackstone, *Commentaries on the Laws of England* (1793), Introd., p. 62.
61   *Ibid.*, II, p. 2.
62   *Ibid.*, II, p. 2, IV, p. 442, III, p. 268.
63   Daniel J. Boorstin, *The Mysterious Science of the Law, An Essay on Blackstone's Commentaries*, Chicago 1996, pp. 127-133.

This may be the reason why Blackstone did not make the sound argument that the collegiality of the superior courts (which decided by majority vote) would serve as a corrective to any arbitrariness on the part of a single judge.[64] It is difficult to gauge the extent to which Blackstone may have been aware of the inconsistencies of his arguments, but in his unwilling to recognise judicial creativity, even when apparent, he was not alone. A perfect illustration of this purposeful blindness is available in the *Commentaries* itself, in the footnotes of Edward Christian.

In a footnote in the Introduction to the *Commentaries*, Christian wants to show that although Acts of Parliament now lost in time may once have formed the greatest part of the common law, custom *"even of modern date"* has contributed to the common law. He uses the example of the law of the road, that horses and carriages should pass each other on the whip hand: "This law has not been enacted by statute, and it is so modern, that perhaps this is the first time that it has been noticed in a book of law. But general convenience discovered the necessity of it, and our judges have so far confirmed it, as to declare frequently at *nisi prius*, that he who disregards this salutary rule is answerable in damages for all the consequences."[65] This rule is acknowledged by Christian as a rule not enacted by parliament. It is also acknowledged that it is not a custom from time immemorial that has shaped the common law; indeed it is "so modern" it has probably not been presented in a law book before. The obvious conclusion, therefore, is that judges have simply made this law during their hearings at *nisi prius*. It is a conclusion that Christian apparently cannot draw.

The importance of Blackstone's preference for a formalistic interpretation of the role of the judge in his *Commentaries* cannot be overemphasised: his *Commentaries* was seen by many as a source of authority. Eight editions of the *Commentaries* appeared during Blackstone's lifetime. After Blackstone's death, fifteen editions were produced by various editors between 1783 and 1849. Holdsworth describes Blackstone's book as one that was at once seen as a classic by his contemporaries and by later lawyers. It was praised by Lord Mansfield as the perfect students' book soon after it appeared; and it was cited with approval by him in 1768.[66]

While undoubtedly influential, Blackstone's *Commentaries* was not, however, without its critics, some more explicit in their criticism than others. The restrictive, formalist description of the judge's role presented in Hale and Blackstone was utterly rejected by Jeremy Bentham. In his *A Comment on the Commentaries*, written between 1774-1776, Bentham set out to expose the inconsistencies and inadequacies of Blackstone's treatise on the common law of England and one important element in that debunking was the role

---

64   John H. Langbein, "Blackstone on Judging", in Wilfred Prest (ed.), *Blackstone and his Commentaries: Biography, Law, History*, Oxford and Portland 2009, pp. 67-68.
65   Blackstone, *Commentaries on the Laws of England* (1793), fn (7), Introd., p. 74 [my italics].
66   Holdsworth, *A History of English Law* (1964) vol. XII, pp. 715-716.

of the judge. In Bentham's opinion there was no doubt that the English judiciary in the eighteenth century exercised a creative function. The judiciary did not simply interpret existing rules of law: the judges were the creators of the very rules they were applying. Law making and adjudication were not the separate systems they should be, but in practice one and the same.

Bentham did not endorse the idea that the laws of England were ultimately derived from the laws of nature: "of the Law of Nature, as I have often said, I know nothing, since it is a non-entity."[67] Nor did he accept the argument that the origins of the common law were to be found in immemorial custom. It was absurd to argue, as did Blackstone, that judges did not make law but simply implemented the law that already existed in the form of ancient conventions: "what is called the Unwritten Law is made not by the people but by judges: the substance of it by judges solely: the expression of it, either by judges, or by lawyers who hope to be so." The cases were not examples of the rules, but the sources of the rules themselves. "As a system of general rules, the common law is a thing merely imaginary."[68] This conclusion prompted him to argue against the common law, with its 'mythical' roots in custom, and for written law in a codified form: custom "has no more force than what the act of a judge can give it" but "an act of parliament is superior to any act of a judge".[69]

In his *A Comment on the Commentaries*, Bentham paid particular attention to Blackstone's argument that judges were not bound by absurd or unjust decisions. Picking up on the inconsistency, he derides Blackstone's reasoning that these decisions were not bad law but actually not law at all. This was a method, says Bentham with rather typical cynicism, which "I must own I should not have thought of putting into practice". By declaring that these laws were not bad laws, but no laws, Blackstone had reasoned "according to an old established recipe which he learnt from the brethren of the trade" which would allow a judge to give a contrary opinion if he so wished.[70] For what did "contrary to reason" mean other than "contrary to what I like". "This then is the rule which our Author [Blackstone] has found to give a judge to whom a preceding determination is proposed. 'Follow it', says he, 'unless it is most evidently contrary to what you like'."[71]

Bentham similarly attacked Blackstone's rules for the interpretation of statutes. For Bentham, the interpretation of a law by judges too often meant getting rid of the clear intention of the legislator and substituting it for a presumption by the judge of his own idea of what was the intention of the legislator: "Where the law is fixed, though it be difficult,

---

67 Jeremy Bentham, *A Comment on the Commentaries and A fragment on Government*, J.H. Burns and H.L.A. Hart (eds.), London 1977, I.8, p. 61.
68 *Ibid.*, Comment II.7 p. 223 and II.1 p. 119.
69 *Ibid.*, II.9 p. 238.
70 *Ibid.*, I.6 p. 54.
71 *Ibid.*, II.5 p. 198.

obscure, incoherent, - the citizen always has a chance to know it. … But let a judge dare to arrogate to himself the power of interpreting the laws, that is to say, of substituting his will for that of the legislator, and everything becomes arbitrary; no one can foresee the course which caprice will take."[72] Blackstone's rules of construction were in essence nothing more than a means for judges to change legislation which they disliked. Citing the example of the statute which made void all leases by ecclesiastical bodies for longer terms than three lives or twenty-one years, Bentham remarks that the judicial construction by which leases exceeding that period, if made by a bishop or dean, would not be void was simply the alteration of the statute. "The judges did not like the remedy provided by the legislature: they therefore put another they like better in its room: substituting their own fluctuating and unconjecturable notions of expediency in the room of the simple expression of the legislator's will." For there was nothing to construe, the words could not have been plainer.[73]

Bentham's criticism of the English legal system was radical. In assessing the effect of his criticism on the legal community, it must be borne in mind that Bentham was an outsider. He had withdrawn from the professional community of lawyers, for he had not flourished as a legal practitioner, and referred to himself as a 'non-lawyer' in several of his works.[74] Nor had his vitriolic attacks on judicial law-making endeared him to that community. Furthermore, Bentham had his own agenda. What was needed, in his opinion, was a thorough overhaul of the legal system. There must be an end to the muddle that was the common law and an end to what he considered to be judicial legislation. For as Postema notes, Bentham's attack was not restricted to Blackstone, but was directed against the whole system of thought, the dominant way of conceiving of law.[75] Bentham, unlike Blackstone, openly recognised a creative role for the judge in the common law. Indeed, it was one of the main reasons why the common law had to be swept away in favour of codification. His rejection of the creative function was far more absolute than Blackstone's, for while Blackstone denied that judges made law, he did ascribe to their function a wider scope for interpretation than Bentham would have found permissible.

2.3 The Role of the Judge: The Eighteenth-Early Nineteenth Century Bench

The influence of the legal profession as a professional community upon judicial decision-making should not be underestimated. It has been argued that judicial decision-making

---

72 Bentham, *The Theory of Legislation, translated from the French of Etienne Dumont by Richard Hildreth* (1975), I. xvii p. 94.
73 Bentham, *A Comment on the Commentaries and A fragment on Government* (1977), II.2 pp. 139-140.
74 H.F. Jolowicz, "Was Bentham a lawyer?", in George W Keeton and Georg Schwarzenberger (eds.), *Jeremy Bentham and the law: a symposium*, London 1948, p. 5.
75 Gerald J. Postema, *Bentham and the Common Law Tradition*, Oxford 1986, p. 312.

must be seen within a social context.[76] A judge is aware of the opinions and expectations of others, including those of fellow judges and courtroom advocates. This form of 'social control' appears, for example, to have affected Lord Mansfield post *Perrin v. Blake* 1769 in his approach to real property cases. On the other hand, that same case can be used as an example to illustrate Scholten's belief that judicial decision-making is, and indeed must be, a matter of conscience: that a judge cannot in all conscience reach a different decision, even if this requires him to render a dissenting opinion (see below).

In Kuhn's analysis of scientific professional communities (which is also applicable to other forms of professional communities), what professional communities share are paradigms: models from which spring particular coherent traditions. It is this sharing of paradigms which mainly prepares the student for membership into the professional community within which he will later practice. The professional community joins men who learned the bases of their field from the same concrete models. These members have undergone a similar education and professional initiations; in the process they have absorbed the same technical literature and drawn many of the same lessons from it. Exposure to the same paradigm ensures that their subsequent practice will seldom evoke overt disagreement over fundamentals: "Men whose research is based on shared paradigms are committed to the same rules and standards."[77] This is why the emergence of new theories is usually preceded by a period of professional insecurity. Numerous attempts are made to modify the old theory in order to eliminate any apparent conflict. Where anomalies cannot be assimilated, a paradigm shift will eventually take place. The transfer of allegiance from paradigm to paradigm is a conversion experience that cannot be forced. This may take time for, as Max Planck remarked: "a new scientific truth does not triumph by convincing its opponents and making them see the light, but rather because its opponents eventually die, and a new generation grows up that is familiar with it."[78]

There are parallels to be drawn with the legal community. Plucknett described the legal profession of the eighteenth century as being "small and very powerful".[79] In the eighteenth century, there were few senior judges – "twelve men in scarlet"- and relatively few counsel. Simpson characterises the legal profession at this time as a small, tightly organized group. The law was its possession. Simpson argues that a customary system of law can function only if mechanisms exist for the transmission of traditional ideas and orthodoxy. The members of the group have to operate within the boundaries of received ideas and practice. There would be strong pressure against innovation and anything more than the most modest originality of thought would be treated as heresy. Through such institutional

---

76   Hartendorp, *Praktisch gesproken: Alledaagse Civiel Rechtspleging als praktische Oordeelsvorming* (2008), p. 143.
77   Thomas S. Kuhn, *The Structures of Scientific Revolutions*, Chicago 1996, pp. 10-11 and 177.
78   *Ibid.*, pp. 67-68, 78, 151.
79   Plucknett, *A Concise History of the Common Law* (1956), p. 200.

arrangements as apprenticeship, residence in the Inns of Court, organised dispute and argument, and judges sitting in banc, members of the profession knew each other personally. In this tightly cohesive group, there was a wide measure of consensus upon basic ideas and values, as well as upon what views could be considered as tenable. This is revealed in the relative paucity of dissenting opinions: only twenty during the thirty years Lord Mansfield presided over King's Bench and all the decision were unanimous in the period 1756-1765.[80] Duman describes the bar as exhibiting a "corporate unity" virtually unaffected by the passage of time: a description of the profession in the late Middle Ages could as easily have been used for the eighteenth or nineteenth century. "The entire professional milieu of the barrister and judge created a unique occupational outlook."[81]

As will be shown below, the legal community of the eighteenth century was less cohesive than Simpson or Duman portrays it. Lemmings has pointed to the decline of the Inns of Court in the eighteenth century. Their decline was significant because the Inns had long been the primary forum for the development and maintenance of communal life. The mid-eighteenth century Inns, suffering as they were from low levels of residence and participation from students, barristers and benchers, seem to have contributed little to developing a sense of profession identity. The decline of their collective rituals, which had developed with the educational regimes in place by the fifteenth century, illustrate the poverty of their corporate life.[82]

The legal community was also a less homogenous community than Kuhn's depiction of a scientific community. Judges came from different social backgrounds: varying from impoverished aristocracy to the lower ranks of society. Particularly relevant, given Kuhn's emphasis on similar education, is the different educational backgrounds of the judges sitting on the bench in the eighteenth century. Furthermore, within the judiciary there were significant differences of opinion regarding the function of the judge and the scope for judicial discretion: there were those who were staunch supporters of the formalist approach, whereas others were clearly prepared to interpret laws within a social context. This meant that although judges were using the same terminology, their reasoning was not necessarily the same. Division was always just under the surface.

Simpson is right to acknowledge the importance of shared "traditional ideas and orthodoxy". There was an emphasis on continuity within the legal community and any changes to the law had to be presented in terms of interpretation. There were indeed certain parameters which could not be ignored: what Scholten described as an intuitive feeling for operating within the legal order of the given community. Radical departures from accepted orthodoxy could not be countenanced. Where older, traditional areas of law were

---

80   Simpson, *Legal theory and legal history: essays on the common law* (1987), pp. 377, 380-381.
81   Daniel Duman, *The Judicial Bench in England 1727-1875*, London Royal Historical Society 1982, p. 11.
82   David Lemmings, *Professors of the Law: Barristers and English Legal Culture in the Eighteenth Century*, Oxford 2000, p. 295.

concerned, there was a more general, 'intuitive', understanding as to how far those boundaries could be pushed and divisions within the judiciary were therefore often not so conspicuous. However, this cohesion should not be exaggerated. There was division within the judiciary. At times, these inherent divisions within the judiciary would come prominently to the fore, either because of occasional deviance by a judge from a traditional paradigm or because the area of law at issue was still in development.

2.3.1   Internal Divisions: Divergent Backgrounds within the Community

In his Introduction to his *Commentaries*, Blackstone laments the deterioration in the social standing of the legal profession. Whereas in the time of Fortescue, there were two thousand students at the Inns of Court who were *filii nobilium* or gentleman born, by the time of Coke, the number had dropped to no more than a thousand students whose background made the Inns "neither commodious nor proper for the resort of gentlemen of any rank or figure".[83] Blackstone was using these figures to make a point. Although, in Boorstin's words, the *Commentaries* was "written specifically for the squirearchy, merchants and law students of eighteenth century England",[84] it was important to Blackstone that an academic study of the common law would appeal to the higher ranks of society. Arguably, this was not Blackstone simply exhibiting an inherent faith in the wisdom of the higher classes (an attitude that would be lampooned by Bentham).[85] Blackstone observes in his Introduction that: "most gentlemen of considerable property, at some period or other in their lives, are ambitious of representing their country in parliament."[86] Ignorance of the science of the law not only adversely affected the work of legal practitioners, but also that of members of parliament responsible for the drafting of legislation. By giving legal instruction to those who formed, or would form England's parliament, Blackstone hoped that England's common law would not be undermined by unwise legislation. As mentioned above, Blackstone blamed "innovations that have been made in it by acts of parliament" for any shortcomings in English law.[87]

An examination of the social backgrounds of the chief justices in the latter part of the eighteenth century-early nineteenth century does show some diversity, even though towards the end of the eighteenth century, the ranks of the judiciary would become increasingly dominated by men from the urban middle classes.[88] As Blackstone indicated, the highest

---

83   Blackstone, *Commentaries on the Laws of England* (1793), Introd., pp. 24-25.
84   Boorstin, *The Mysterious Science of the Law: an Essay on Blackstone's Commentaries* (1996), pp. 4-5.
85   Bentham, *A Comment on the Commentaries and A fragment on Government* (1977), III. 8, p. 466, III. 11 and 12 p. 467.
86   Blackstone, *Commentaries on the Laws of England* (1793), Introd. 8.
87   *Ibid.*, Introd. 9.
88   Duman, *The Judicial Bench in England 1727-1875* (1982), p. 177.

ranks of society were underrepresented. There were few members of the aristocracy to be counted amongst the judiciary, although one of its members would be hugely influential. Lord Mansfield, born William Murray, did come from a noble family; he was one of the younger sons of the impoverished fifth Viscount of Stormont. There were some members of the judiciary who came from very humble backgrounds. For example, Charles Abbott, who later became Lord Tenterden, had a father who owned a barbershop in Canterbury. Lord Eldon, who as Lord Chancellor presided over the Court of Chancery for many years, was born John Scott, the son of a coal fitter. Others belonged to the gentry, for example, Lord Ellenborough, born Edward Law, was the son of an English prelate who came from substantial yeomen stock. Not all of the judges were English: Lord Mansfield was born in Scotland, as was Alexander Wedderburn, who later became Lord Loughborough. Having studied law at the University of Edinburgh, Loughborough practiced as an advocate in Edinburgh before becoming a member of the English bar. Indeed, for a short period, both the Chief Justice of the Court of Common Pleas (Lord Loughborough) and the Chief Justice of the Court of King's Bench (Lord Mansfield) were Scotsmen. John Copley, later Lord Lyndhurst, who presided as Lord Chancellor over the Court of Chancery and Chief Baron of the Court of Exchequer for periods during the 1820s and 30s, was born in the United States.[89]

The judges had different educational backgrounds prior to their call to the bar. Most of the senior judges were university educated. Lord Mansfield, for example, was an Oxford scholar. The letters written to the Duke of Portland (where he suggests a course of study, including such writers as Cicero, Grotius and Pufendorf), may indicate the nature of Mansfield's own studies at Oxford.[90] Lord Ellenborough, a Cambridge man, was a classical scholar but also "well initiated in mathematical science". Lord Tenterden, educated at Oxford, was an accomplished classics scholar but, unlike Ellenborough, "remained a stranger to the exact sciences".[91] By contrast, Lord Kenyon had no university education. Without a university degree, it had been necessary, according to the regulations in place at the time, for Kenyon to be a law student at the Inns for five years before he could be called to the bar.[92]

Some judges were well grounded in systems other than the English common law. Mansfield was a man of considerable learning. He was familiar not only with English common law and the principles of equity, but also with several other legal systems. His early biographer, John Holliday, stresses Mansfield's "perfect knowledge of the Roman

---

89 John Campbell, *The Lives of the Chief Justices of England*, London 1874, vol. IV p. 149, 310, Holdsworth, *A History of English Law* (1964), vols. XIII p. 595, XVI p. 5.

90 C.H.S. Fifoot, *Lord Mansfield*, Oxford 1977, p. 29.

91 Campbell, *The Lives of the Chief Justices of England* (1874), vol. IV p. 148 and p. 319.

92 *Ibid.*, IV, p. 46.

law".[93] Mansfield was also expert in Scottish law. Although Mansfield had left Scotland at a young age, he had studied Scottish law and appeared in many Scottish appeals to the House of Lords. Indeed his earliest practice had been in these appeals. Holdsworth argues that it was because of Mansfield's knowledge of other bodies of law outside the common law that he was able to come to a conclusion as to what constituted right and reasonable principles, and his guiding sources were the principles of equity and Scots law. The attraction of Scottish law was that some of its rules were more reasonable than English law and the Scottish lawyer was not looking for the appropriate writ, but for the appropriate legal principle which allowed a system to be built up using logical and deductive methods rather than the empirical inductive English method of decided cases.[94]

According to Campbell, although Mansfield did indeed pay much attention to Scottish law and expressed satisfaction with the methodical arrangement and precise definitions of Mackenzie and Stair: "his true delight was to dip into French juridical writers, to see how Roman law and feudal law had been blended, and to pore over the commercial code recently promulgated there." This 'Ordonnance de la Marine', was a code "which he hoped one day to introduce here by well-considered judicial decisions – a bright vision that was afterwards realized".[95] Lord Kenyon was cited by Campbell by way of contrast. Campbell, admittedly not a great admirer of Kenyon, points to Kenyon's "scanty education". He was apparently unable to read a single page of the Pandects, and was wholly unacquainted with the Roman civil law.[96] It is possible, however, that Kenyon's unpopularity with many barristers and attorneys (his partiality or distain for certain counsel was notorious), may have encouraged anecdotes about his ignorance of Latin.[97]

Mansfield's interest in comparative law would lay him open to attack. He would be derided by Lord Redesdale for his interest in law north of the border and by Junius, the pseudonym of an unidentified but relentless critic, for his interest in continental law, in particular Roman law. Junius: "you have made it your study to introduce into the court where you preside measures of jurisprudence unknown to Englishmen. The Roman code, the law of nations and the opinion of foreign civilians are your perpetual theme."[98] Lord Camden, in a thinly veiled attack on Lord Mansfield, stated: "I am not wise enough to determine which of the two laws is most perfect, the Roman or the English. This I know… that although almost every country in Europe hath received that body of laws, yet they have been with a more stubborn constancy at all times disclaimed and rejected by England. For which reason, (and not through any disrespect to the argument [Mansfield's] I have

---

93   John Holliday, *The Life of William late Earl of Mansfield*, London 1797, p. 120.
94   Holdsworth, *A History of English Law* (1964), vol. XII, p. 556.
95   Campbell, *The Lives of the Chief Justices of England* (1874), vol. III, p. 188.
96   *Ibid.*, vol. IV, pp. 40, 77-78.
97   Douglas Hay, "Kenyon, Lloyd", in *Oxford Dictionary of National Biography*, at <www.oxforddnb.com>, 15431, p. 6.
98   Fifoot, *Lord Mansfield* (1977), p. 188.

been endeavouring to answer) I choose to lay aside all that learning as not being relevant in Westminster-hall."[99]

If knowledge of other systems of law may have affected the attitude of some judges and have caused some diversity of values, there was also a lack of uniformity with regard to their education in the common law itself. The common law could only be learned in practice at the Inns of Court and not at a theoretical level before Blackstone accepted the chair founded by Viner. Learning the common law took the form of an apprenticeship and the educational component was what the student "could pick up from chance instruction or such studies as fell his way".[100] By the eighteenth century, formal legal education at the Inns was virtually non-existent.

Blackstone was disparaging of this system of education. The law student was subjected to a "a tedious lonely process to extract the theory of law from a mass of undigested learning; or else by an assiduous attendance on the courts to pick up theory and practice together, sufficient to qualify him for the ordinary run of business". This emphasis on practice rather than theory left the law student commencing his study "at the wrong end":

> "Making therefore due allowance for one or two shining exceptions, experience may teach us to foretell that a lawyer thus educated to the bar, in subservience to attorneys and solicitors, will find he has begun at the wrong end. If practice be the whole he is taught, practice must also be the whole he will ever know: if he be uninstructed in the elements and first principles upon which the rule of practice is founded, the least variation from established precedents will totally distract and bewilder him: *ita lex scripta est* is the utmost his knowledge will arrive at; he must never aspire to form, and seldom expect to comprehend, any arguments drawn *a priori*, from the spirit of the laws and the natural foundation of justice."[101]

What Blackstone sketches is a form of training that would promote a 'black-letter' approach to the law. (It would appear that, once again, Blackstone is caught between his outwardly formalist approach to the role of the judge and his recognition of the need for intelligent interpretation.) In his recent study of the English legal culture in the eighteenth century, Lemmings concluded that even if barristers had been conscientious students, the nature

---

99 James Oldham, *English Common Law in the age of Mansfield*, Chapel Hill and London 2004, p. 360. Lord Camden was giving judgment in *Doe v. Kersey* 1765; the case was reported in pamphlet form.
100 A.H. Manchester, *A Modern Legal History of Engand and Wales 1750-1950*, London 1980, p. 55.
101 Blackstone, *Commentaries on the Laws of England* (1793), Introd. pp. 30, 32.

of their legal education at the Inns was not conducive to "producing lawyers who were sensitive to the social purposes of the law".[102]

There are also examples of personal rivalry and dislike, which must have, to some extent, undermined the cohesiveness of the judicial community. A well-known example is the relationship between Mansfield and Kenyon. Mansfield did not want Kenyon to succeed him in King's Bench. In the hope of seeing Buller, his favourite, in that position, Mansfield remained in office longer than he himself desired. Buller had a close association with Mansfield, to the extent that some of the judgments delivered by Mansfield were actually written by Buller. This does not mean that Buller and Mansfield never disagreed, but they were apparently able to persuade the other without rancour.[103] In the latter days of Mansfield's chief justiceship, it was often Buller who acted as the trial judge (and indeed it was Buller who would hear several important patent cases). Mansfield's resistance to Kenyon as a candidate for King's Bench was an insult Kenyon would not forget. His chagrin would occasionally surface: for example, Kenyon had openly sneered at some of the decisions of King's Bench which in his eyes were fusing law and equity.[104]

Kenyon was not Mansfield's only detractor. There were other judges who were quick to disparage Lord Mansfield for his approach to precedent and equity, such as the Lords Eldon, Redesdale and Camden (see below). Fifoot notes a certain discomfort between Mansfield and Blackstone, as Blackstone "shrank under the immediate eye of his patron", leading Bentham to comment on the "heart-burning between the noble and learned lord and the author of the *Commentaries*".[105] One more example of personal antagonism is provided by the relationship between Abbott (Lord Tenterden) and Justice Best. Apparently, Charles Abbott could scarcely conceal his dislike of Best, J. (who later transferred to Common Pleas).[106] Likes and dislikes may also have affected relationships between judges and counsel. According to Campbell, Lord Kenyon had a "strong dislike" for Edward Law (later Lord Ellenborough) and was pleased with any opportunity to put him down. With approval, Campbell notes that under Ellenborough "a more liberal and scientific mode was restored of treating commercial questions, the civil law and foreign jurists were quoted with effect, and the authority of Lord Mansfield was again in the ascendant".[107] Presumably, it was this frame of mind that Kenyon had found so offensive. On the other hand, Campbell

---

102 Lemmings, *Professors of the Law: Barristers and English Legal Culture in the Eighteenth Century* (2000), p. 144.
103 James Oldham, "Eighteenth-Century Judges' Notes: how they explain, correct and enhance the Reports", *American Journal of Legal History* 31 (1987), pp. 36-38.
104 Campbell, *The Lives of the Chief Justices of England* (1874), vol. IV p. 82.
105 Fifoot, *Lord Mansfield* (1977), p. 47.
106 Campbell, *The Lives of the Chief Justices of England* (1874), vol. IV p. 358.
107 *Ibid.*, vol. IV, pp. 190-191, 217.

accuses Abbott of have unduly favoured one counsel in particular, James Scarlett (the future Lord Abinger).[108]

While the study of the law and the exercise of the profession did bind these men together and induce certain shared values and beliefs, the homogeneity of the judiciary should not be exaggerated. Different social backgrounds, educational backgrounds, personalities and experiences would affect the way in which these judges would construe their role and consequently the way in which the law would be interpreted. In this respect, it is interesting to note Popper's deduction that we filter our observations through our own worldview: we observe only what our problems, our interests, our expectations, and action programmes, make relevant.[109]

2.3.2   Internal Divisions: The Style of Interpretation

Judges had very different ideas about their interpretative function. As Allen points out: "some judges will always play safe and some will be astute to mitigate the *rigor juris* in accordance with common sense, justice and social requirements."[110] Lieberman points to a schism between Blackstonean conservatism and the Mansfield reformist zeal.[111] While it is understandable that this 'schism' is described in terms of conservatism and reformism, these are the symptoms rather than the cause. The underlying cause was whether a formalistic approach or a purposive, teleological approach was adopted.

The function of precedent – whether precedents illustrated principles or whether they were the substance of the common law – set Lord Mansfield apart from some other members of the bench. The extent to which Lord Mansfield respected precedent is a subject of scholarly debate. Oldham argues that the system of common law was sufficiently resilient to allow Mansfield considerable manoeuvring room, but nonetheless Mansfield did acknowledge the importance of precedent (often urging barristers to search thoroughly for authorities or doing so himself), and if the cases on point were unequivocally against his inclination, he would yield.[112] Lieberman too argues that Mansfield, despite contemporary complaints to the contrary, never entirely ignored precedents even though Mansfield saw the essence of England's law to be principle not precedent.[113] Fifoot does not consider that Mansfield set out to flout precedent: he did not seek to subvert the decisions of his predecessors. However, Fifoot immediately adds a proviso: Mansfield did challenge

---

108 *Ibid.*, p. 359.
109 Karl R. Popper and John C. Eccles, *The Self and its Brain*, London and New York 1977, p. 134.
110 Allen, *Law in the Making* (1978), p. 345.
111 Lieberman, *The province of legislation determined* (1989), p. 142.
112 Oldham, *English Common Law in the age of Mansfield* (2004), p. 30.
113 Lieberman, *The province of legislation determined* (1989), p. 126.

authority, not by defiance, but by ingenuity, resorting to such tactics as attacking the competence of the early law reporters.[114]

Certainly Lord Mansfield had a more radical approach to precedent than Blackstone: it was not the details of the case, but the principle revealed in the case that was significant. These principles could be principles of morality or policy. In *Jones v. Randall* 1774, the matter at issue was a wager. Mansfield argued that the wager would not stand if it were against principles: either against the principles of morality, as the law of England prohibits everything which is *contra bonos mores*, or against the principles of "found policy". These general principles must govern a decision, for the law does not consist in particular cases:

> "The law of England would be a strange science indeed, if it were decided upon precedents only. Precedents only serve to illustrate principles and to give them a fixed authority. But the law of England, which is exclusive of positive law enacted by statute, depends upon principles; and these principles run through all the cases, according as the particular circumstances of each have been found to fall within the one or other of them."[115]

In a number of his decisions, Mansfield pointed to the danger of focusing on the particulars of an individual case. In *Fisher v. Prince* 1762 he stated: "The reason and spirit of cases make law, not the letter of particular precedents", and in *Hankey v. Jones* 1778: "There is no greater fault in citing cases than that of drawing general conclusions from particular premises."[116]

The attitude to the function of precedent impacted upon another controversial issue: the relationship between the common law and equity. If precedent was revealed principle rather than forming the substance of the law, where was the line between equity and law? According to Heward, Lord Mansfield himself was not prepared to exclude equitable principles from the common law court, as these principles were so fundamental he considered that they had a role to play in all courts.[117] There are certainly enough cases to show that Mansfield did believe that equity, in the sense of natural justice, should prevail. In *Alderson v. Temple* 1768 he stated:

> "The most desirable object in all judicial determinations, especially in mercantile ones, (which ought to be determined upon natural justice, and not upon the niceties of law) is, to do substantial Justice."[118]

---

114 Fifoot, *Lord Mansfield* (1977), p. 214.
115 *Jones v. Randall* 1774, 1 Cowper 39.
116 *Hankey v. Jones* 1778, 2 Cowper 751, *Fisher v. Prince* 1762, 3 Burr 1364.
117 Edmund Heward, *Lord Mansfield*, Chichester and London 1979, pp. 170-171.
118 *Alderson v. Temple* 1768, 4 Burr 2239.

Mansfield did not see the common law and equity as two totally distinct jurisdictions in this respect, for the rules of the common law themselves were "drawn from the fountain of justice".[119] This appeal to natural justice is a theme running through many of his cases. In *Towers v. Barrett* 1786, an action for money had and received, Mansfield referred to that action as one "founded on principles of eternal justice".[120] In *Moses v. Macferlan* 1760, Mansfield dealt with the objection that no assumpsit lies, except upon an express or implied contract, as follows: "If the defendant be under an obligation, from ties of natural justice, to refund; the law implies a debt and gives this action, founded in the equity of the plaintiff's case, as it were upon a contract (*quasi ex contractu*) as the Roman law expresses it."[121]

These principles could serve social goals. As Mansfield's early biographer John Holliday noted: "His ideas went to the growing melioration of the law, by making its liberality keep pace with the demands of justice, and the actual concerns of the world."[122] In various cases, Mansfield would allude to the need to see the law within a social context. With respect to the general rule that a married woman could not hold property, either real or personal, Mansfield remarked in *Corbett v. Poelnitz* 1785:

"This is the general rule. But then it has been properly said that, as the times alter, new customs and new manners arise: these occasion exceptions; and justice and convenience require different applications of those exceptions within the principle of the general rule."[123]

In *Johnson v. Spiller* 1784, Mansfield stated: "But *quicquid agant homines* is the business of the Courts, as the usages of society alter, the law must adapt itself to the various situations of mankind."[124]

Lord Mansfield's appeal to principle rather than precedent, and his tendency to apply principles which some believed belonged exclusively to the competence of the equity courts, would alienate those judges who supported a 'black-letter' approach to the law. Criticism of Mansfield would by no means be limited to the venom of the anonymous Junius. Campbell notes how Lord Eldon, Lord Kenyon, and Lord Redesdale were accustomed to "shake their heads at Murray", because "he ventured to view questions of law scientifically, and, where he was not restricted by precedents, to deal out justice in a manner that would not have suggested itself to a mere formalist".[125] Of Kenyon's influence over King's Bench, Campbell remarked:

---

119 *Omychund v. Barker* 1744, 1 Atkyns 33.
120 *Towers v. Barrett* 1786, 1 T.R. 134.
121 *Moses v. Macferlan* 1760, 2 Burr 1008.
122 Holliday, *The Life of William late Earl of Mansfield* (1797), p. 121.
123 *Corbett v. Poelnitz* 1785 1 T.R. 8.
124 *Johnson v. Spiller* (1784) 3 Doug 373.
125 Campbell, *The Lives of the Chief Justices of England* (1874), vol. III, p. 313.

"And from the stout resistance which then continued to be offered in Westminster Hall to all attempts to relieve the administration of justice from wretched technicalities, Lord Chief Justice Kenyon was long hailed as the Restorer of the rigid doctrines to be deduced from the Year Books."[126]

Whereas Mansfield and a few of his colleagues believed that some sort of fusion between the principles of law and equity should take place, most lawyers still thought that the courts of law and equity should remain separate and each of them should work on their own separate lines.[127] Any interpretation of the common law that was perceived as based upon the application of principles which belonged to the equity courts, would therefore be subject to the intense disapproval of a significant section of the legal profession. For example, the Lords Camden, Kenyon, Thurlow and Eldon all openly disapproved of a fusion of law and equity.

Taking into account "the actual concerns of the world" was considered by formalist judges to be outside the ambit of the profession. When Kenyon stated in *Ellah v. Leigh* 1794: "I confess I do not think that the courts ought to change the law so as to adapt it to the fashions of the times: if an alteration in the law be necessary, recourse must be had to the Legislature for it", this was most probably a reaction to Mansfield's opinion in *Johnson v. Spiller* 1784.[128] In *Compton v. Collinson* 1790, Mansfield's decisions in cases involving married women's property were clearly considered quite radical by some members of the legal profession. In the Compton case, the counsel for the defence remarked: "As to the modern cases of *Ringstead v. Lady Lanesborough*, *Barwell v. Brooks*, and *Corbet v. Poelnitz*, many able lawyers have been surprised at the extent of the doctrines laid down in them."[129]

One of Mansfield's most outspoken critics was the former Chief Justice of Common Pleas and Chancellor, Lord Camden. In Lord Camden's opinion, the business of the common law judge was "to tell the suitor how the law stands, not how it ought to be", and how the law stands could be found by "attending to the old black letter of our law" and judges should never pretend to decide upon a claim of property "without founding their judgment upon some solid written authority, preserved in their books or in judicial records".[130] Camden would not countenance those who, in Edmund Burke's words before the House of Lords, argued that the "antique rigour" of the law should give way to "the accommodation of human concerns" or "keep pace with the demands of Justice".[131]

---

126 *Ibid.*, vol. IV, p. 39.
127 Holdsworth, *A History of English Law* (1964), vol. XII, p. 557.
128 *Ellah v. Leigh* (1794) 5 T.R. 682.
129 *Compton v. Collinson* 1790, 1 H. Black 339.
130 *Donaldson v. Beckett* 1774, William Cobbet, *Parliamentary History of England*, vol. 17, London 1813, col. 998-999.
131 Lieberman, *The province of legislation determined* (1989), p. 98.

How innovative Mansfield's leadership of King's Bench was has been the subject of dispute. Fifoot was of the opinion that Mansfield came "neither to destroy nor to innovate but to fulfil".[132] He notes that the legal reaction to the new society was hesitant and the innate conservatism of the legal profession was reinforced by the poverty of the reports and the personality of the judges. While Blackstone's mind was still dominated by the legacies of feudalism, Lord Mansfield wished to free the law from technical preoccupation and from long since antiquated dogmas.[133] Lieberman argues that, given the strong pressure for continuity within the common law system, it is unlikely that Mansfield could have accomplished so much had he been operating in as much of a legal vacuum as his admirers supposed.[134] Lieberman has queried the extent to which Mansfield may be seen as the herald of a new legal age. He agrees with Simpson, whose examination of contract law in this period led him to declare: "Mansfield was no innovator in legal matters" and that "his ideas commonly involved no more than a bold and striking affirmation of views expressed by others". Furthermore, much of the law on negotiable papers was actually systematised by one of Mansfield's predecessors, Sir John Holt.[135]

Whether or not Mansfield was building upon a foundation laid by others, what is evident, however, is that Mansfield's approach to the law differed significantly from that of some other members of the bench. Mansfield adopted a purposive, teleological approach to the law: the law functioned within a social context and had to be responsive to that context. It was not a closed system. It was an approach that stood in stark contrast to the black-letter approach of judges like Kenyon and Eldon. Noting that Kenyon had first attracted attention because he could reproduce relevant black-letter precedents on demand, and Eldon had established his reputation by arguing the technicalities of conveyancing, Lemmings considers it not surprising that when men like Kenyon and Eldon reached the top of their profession they would act instinctively according to the microscopic world they knew: "they implemented, maintained, and justified its irrational rules, and worked to insulate it against the threat of outside influence."[136] Lemmings somewhat overstates his case. As will be seen in paragraph 5.1.3, Kenyon did place the laws on forestalling, regrating and engrossing foodstuffs in a social context, even if his objection to market reasoning was out-dated by 1800, and Lord Eldon was one of the few judges who suggested that a patent could be taken out 'even for a new method' (see the case of Hill v. Thompson 1817, in paragraph 3.3.2.2). However, the reputation these judges had as black-letter judges

---

132 Fifoot, *Lord Mansfield* (1977), p. 84.
133 *Ibid.*, pp. 14, 26, 216.
134 Lieberman, *The province of legislation determined* (1989), p. 100.
135 *Ibid.*, pp. 99-100.
136 Lemmings, *Professors of the Law: Barristers and English Legal Culture in the Eighteenth Century* (2000), p. 315.

among their contemporaries is one indicator that their dominant style of interpretation was formalistic.

2.3.3   Perrin v. Blake *1769-1772: The Internal Divisions Unmasked*

The case history of *Perrin v. Blake* is a perfect illustration of these divisions and tensions within the judiciary. Where a more familiar area of law was concerned, judges may have applied somewhat different reasoning, but there was a greater tendency for the outcome to be within the parameters prescribed by traditional orthodoxy. Those parameters could be stretched a little, but they could not be entirely flouted. Too obvious radical departures could not be countenanced, as was made evident by the disapprobation heaped upon Mansfield by many members of the legal community for his decision in *Perrin v. Blake* 1769. *Perrin v. Blake* shows the conflict between formalism and the teleological approach. A number of underlying issues rose to the surface: how creative was the role of the judge; what was the relationship between common law and equity and should social developments colour the interpretation of the law?

The case of *Perrin v. Blake* concerned a plantation in Jamaica, which had been bequeathed in a will. William Williams had made provisions in his will in case his wife should have an additional child. If that child were female, she would receive a sum of money; if male he would share the estate, both real and personal, equally with the existing son, John Williams. He stated in his will that "it is my intent and meaning that none of my children shall sell and dispose of my estate for a longer time than his life", and with that intent, the residue of the estate went to John William and any male infant from his wife for life and in remainder to Isaac Gale and his heirs during the natural lives of his sons, the remainder to the heirs of the said sons; the remainder to his daughters for their natural lives, the remainder held by Isaac Gale and his heirs during the natural lives of his daughters; the remainder to the heirs of the said daughters. As no infant was born, John Williams remained the only son. There were also three daughters, one of whom was Hannah Blake, the respondent in this action. The issue was whether John Williams took any estate, and if so, what kind of estate. Upon the recommendation of the Privy Council, the case was brought to the King's Bench. If the King's Bench was of the opinion that John Williams was seised in fee, or in tail, of the whole or any part of the premises, then the previous judgment would be reversed; if the court would certify that John Williams was not seised of any estate of inheritance in the premises, then the appeal would be dismissed.

The case depended entirely upon the construction of the will. Counsel for Hannah Blake argued that what was of importance was the intention of the testator, which was very clearly to give only an estate for life to his son. However, there was a problem which the defence had to deal with: the operation of the legal expression "heirs of the body". It was necessary for the defence to distinguish this case from the case of *Coulson v. Coulson*, where the intention of the testator had not been sufficient to overcome the legal function of the term "heirs of the body". Counsel argued that in the present case, the introductory clause indicating the testator's intention was sufficient, despite the testator's use of "inaccurate or unapt words".[137]

For the plaintiff it was argued that the expression should only be construed in accordance with its strict legal meaning "otherwise you let in a flood of inconveniency, by rendering the rules of construction entirely dependent on the caprice of individuals". Shelley's case had stated: "That in any instrument, if a freehold be limited to the ancestor for life, and the inheritance to his heirs, either mediately or immediately, the first taker takes the whole estate: if it be limited to the heirs of his body, he takes a fee tail; if to his heirs, a fee simple." This rule, laid down by Lord Coke, had been revived in *Coulson v. Coulson* and had since been made the standard for conveyancers. Its authority had been used to settle many estates.[138]

In response, Lord Mansfield pointed out before the case was stood over for judgment that there had been many cases and a great diversity of opinion on this issue. He then added: "It should be considered, that the different temper of the times may have occasioned considerable difference; and the want of due attention to this has occasioned the courts to run into many absurd distinctions, which had now better be forgotten."[139] Mansfield was always prepared to see the law within a social context.

Certain remarks made by the judges of King's Bench in delivering their judgments in 1770 are very revealing. In his judgment, Willes, J. began by apologising if he differed from his brothers. He states: "It is the duty of a judge to decide upon the most rational scheme that occurs to him; and he had better adhere to that opinion which he has formed, than give way to the undue influence of others, however erroneous his own opinion may in fact be." (This seems to underscore the "Here I stand: I can do no other" approach, which is an important element of Scholten's theory on conscience: see above). Willes' teleological approach is apparent as he states: "that I shall ever discountenance, as much as I can, anything which savours of ancient strictness and policy, and where I can possibly depart with justice from an old maxim the policy of which has now ceased, I certainly will." The rule in Shelley's case was a product of feudal policy, and the reasons for it were now antiquated. His guides in this case were to be "reason and humanity". Words have "no charm or magic, but their effect is constituted by the sense they bear". For as Lord Cowper had observed in an earlier case: "if the law could invariably adhere in all cases to the technical expressions, without any deviation, in the most natural and proper case, the common law

---

137 Francis Hargrave, *Collectana Juridica*, London 1791, vol. I, pp. 286-287.
138 *Ibid.*, pp. 287-288.
139 *Ibid.*, p. 295.

would become a mere matter of memory instead of being a system of judgment and reason."[140]

In a similar vein Aston, J. remarked: "I admit the rule in Shelley's case to be law; but I deny the consequence, that it is an invariable rule to be applied on every devise. This is an old rule of feudal policy, the reason of which is long since antiquated, and therefore it must not be extended one jot." He noted that it had been laid down in several cases that courts of law must decide upon intent, as well as courts of equity. He concluded that "If we now comply with the testator's intention, we shall act agreeable to reason, law and convenience. The system of law and equity will be uniform, and the parties saved much expense and trouble."[141]

Lord Mansfield voiced his agreement with Aston and Willes and similarly placed the old rule within its historical, social context: it had arisen at a time when an estate for life could have no other purpose than to cheat the lord of his feudal services, and hence the law had sensibly ordered that in such cases it should be an estate tail. However, although the rule was clear law, it was not a general proposition. The legal import of words must govern where the intent is doubtful, but in this case there was no doubt as to the intent. "If the words be not ambiguous, or if the declaration be plain, that the legal sense of the words must yield." *Coulson v. Coulson* was not as settled law as had been argued. Nonetheless, Mansfield clearly anticipated resistance from the legal community for his stance. In telling words he stated:

> "and I do not doubt but there are, and have been always, lawyers of a different bent of genius, and different course of education, who have chosen to adhere to the strict letter of law; and they will make a difference between trusts and legal estates, to the harassing of a suitor; ... And if courts of law will adhere to the mere letter of law, the great men who preside in chancery will ever devise new ways to creep out of the lines of law, and temper with equity."[142]

That Mansfield expected some resistance is not surprising: although the court had found for the defendant, a member of his bench, Yates, J., had delivered a dissenting opinion. Yates declared that, just as Willes, he had to stand by the opinion he had formed. That opinion was that rules of law were more important than a testator's intention: "we had better adhere to the law, and let a thousand testators' wills be overthrown." What Yates expresses is a formalistic, black-letter approach to the law:

---

140 *Ibid.*, pp. 297-301.
141 *Ibid.*, pp. 305-308.
142 *Ibid.*, pp. 319-322.

"These technical expressions are the measures of property in legal devises; and the law having fixed a determinate meaning, the law will not permit their sense to be perverted, but *direct the judges ever to adhere to them without the smallest departure.*"[143]

Yates was prepared to admit that the original reason for the rule in Shelley's case had long since ceased, that its origins were indeed to be found in feudal policy. However, unlike the other members of the bench, he did not consider that to be a reason to discount it: it had long been the law of the land, and should thus remain so as long as parliament did not intervene. Furthermore, Yates considered that the rule in itself was "reasonable and just". In the cases which Yates brings to the fore to substantiate his opinion, the emphasis of his argument is on the technical meaning of legal terms. For example, he quotes Lord Maccles-field in the case of *Backhouse v. Wells* who had said: "if the word had been *heirs* instead of *issue*, the judgment of the court must have been different." For "As to testators, individuals must not control the general law which is established by legislative authority and long experience: if we forsake this, we open a door to uncertainty; and when we set up the tes-tator's intention in contradiction to the legal sense of his words, we confound landed property".[144]

Given the decision of the King's Bench, a writ of error was brought to the Exchequer Chamber in 1772. The King's Bench decision would be reversed and Blackstone was one of the judges who considered the judgment of King's Bench to have been erroneous. Blackstone distinguished different categories of rules of law. There were those that were "irrevocably established", fundamental rules which, having stood the test of ages, could not be exceeded or transgressed by the intention of a testator, no matter how clear and manifest that intention might be. There were other rules of a more arbitrary and artificial kind, less "sacred" because they were not founded upon great principles of legislation or policy. Some of these rules were only rules of interpretation or evidence to ascertain the intention of parties. These more flexible rules allowed for exceptions; fundamental rules did not.[145]

Once again, Blackstone's opinion reveals a certain tension between his formalistic ideals and his acknowledgment of judicial discretion. Yet Blackstone was quick to point out the limits to any judicial discretion: it had no role to play with respect to fundamental rules of property founded on great principles of public convenience or necessity. It was irrelevant if these principles had arisen from feudal policy; hardly any rule of the law of real property had not a "feudal tincture". Whatever their origins, such rules had now been

---

143 *Ibid.*, pp. 309, 310, 311-312 [my italics].
144 *Ibid.*, pp. 312-313, 317.
145 Francis Hargrave, *A Collection of Tracts relative to the Laws of England*, Dublin 1787, vol. I, pp. 493-494.

adopted into the common law of England "incorporated into its body and interwoven with its policy, that no court of justice in this kingdom has either the *power* or (I trust) the *inclination* to disturb". The law of real property had been formed into a fine system, full of "unseen connections and nice dependencies", so that if one link in the chain were broken, the whole would be endangered. And once again Blackstone was at pains to point out that even apparently antiquated rules were wise rules: for the rule in Shelley's case was not merely a narrow feudal principle, but in fact for "the liberal and conscientious purpose of facilitating the alienation of the land". Furthermore, even if *Coulson v. Coulson* had been decided on dubious grounds, one would have to "tremble at the consequences of shaking its authority" now it had been established for thirty years and half the titles of the kingdom were built upon its doctrine.[146]

Lieberman sees *Perrin v. Blake* as offering valuable insight into "the nature and limits of judicial law reform during the period".[147] What the case reveals is an important factor in the conflict between conservatism and reformism: a conflict between the formalistic style of judicial interpretation and the teleological. As an arch proponent of the teleological approach, Mansfield had been prepared to see even the sacred English law of real property within a social context. He had done it before, and had encountered opposition before. Mansfield's decision in *Wyndham v. Chetwynd* 1757, to give effect to a testator's wishes, would later bring him into conflict with Lord Camden, while Camden was Chief Justice of the Court of Common Pleas. Lord Camden's attack on Mansfield's opinion in Wyndham came in 1765 in *Doe v. Kersey*. Camden:

> "it is not my business to decide cases by my own rules of justice, but to declare the law as I find it laid down." For "the discretion of a judge is the law of tyrants; it is always unknown; it is different in different men; it is casual, and depends upon constitution, temper and passion."[148]

Perrin v. Blake marked a turning point for Mansfield. The weight of the opposition he now encountered from the legal community subdued him. Oldham notes that the fight went out of Mansfield on property questions. A conservatism, unlike his approach to other areas of the law, crept into property questions generally after his reversal in *Perrin v. Blake*. Mansfield apparently decided that property was one area where it was more important to enforce rules for the sake of certainty than for the sake of common sense. As he stated in

---

146 *Ibid.*, pp. 498, 502 and 508.
147 Lieberman, *The province of legislation determined* (1989), p. 142.
148 Oldham, *English Common Law in the age of Mansfield* (2004), p. 359-360. *Doe v. Kersey* was reported in pamphlet form.

Atkyns v. Davis 1783 "I don't care (indeed I am afraid judicially) to make such an extensive innovation in property, contrary to the sense of mankind for 200 years".[149]

2.4   Analysing the Attitude of Judges in Patent Disputes

At the beginning of this chapter, three models of judicial decision-making were presented: the formalist approach, the creative approach and the bounded creativity approach. A good model requires observing facts in the real world and testing out various hypotheses which could explain these facts. A model must be falsifiable. This process of conjecture and refutation, as Popper observed, is the way to increase knowledge.[150] If the assertions a model makes do not correspond with observations in the real world, the model has to be rejected. Therefore, if it is apparent that judges do more than apply legal rules to the facts of a case in a mechanistic fashion, the purely rule-based model must be set aside. If it appears that judges cannot create law arbitrarily, that model must be rejected.

In analysing the opinions of judges in patent cases, it will be argued in the following chapters that the judge had a creative role, even those judges who adopted a formalist approach. The decision-making process, as Scholten pointed out, is in itself an inherently creative one. In hearing a patent case, the judge had to determine which facts were the relevant facts. That determination itself was a creative act. The judge had to decide whether the facts of the present case were analogous to the facts of a previous precedent. For example, was not disclosing that only one sort of salt had marine acid, without which the colour yellow could not be made, the same situation as not making it clear that bituminous schistus in the state found and known in England could be used in the process (issues respectively in *Turner v. Winter* 1787 and *Derosne v. Fairie* 1835)? As well as deciding upon which facts were the material facts, the judge had to apply the principles of law to those facts. Yet during the period examined here, not all judges interpreted the Statute of Monopolies and the patent specification in the same way. Applied as a model of reality to explain judicial decision-making in patent cases, it would appear that a purely rule-based model of law fails.

Were all of these judges in practice simply creating patent law consistent with their own legal notions and their own frames of reference? Even a formalist approach has a creative aspect, as a rule is selected based upon an individual judge's determination of which facts are the relevant facts. A teleological approach, whereby a given law is interpreted in terms of the purpose of that law within the context of the society of the day, points to another creative possibility within a decision-making process. Yet even if a creative function for judges is acknowledged, and the influence of non-legal factors, this does not necessary

---

149 *Ibid.*, pp. 360, 363.
150 Popper, *Objective Knowledge: an Evolutionary Approach* (1974), p. 260.

imply that the judicial decision-making in these cases is purely arbitrary. A judge has to give grounds for his decision, showing a logical connection between the facts and the rule which he has selected for application to those facts. If a judge's discretion is not arbitrary, a decision which appears to be based upon the wrongful application of a rule to the particular facts of the case would presumably appear to be inconsistent with the prevailing legal order and would not be approved by the legal community as a whole. Scholten argued that a decision must fit within existing legal parameters, constituting a totality of meaning, language and social relationships. An intuitive understanding of these parameters would mean that most decisions would fit within that prevailing legal order.

Where the prevailing law rests upon strongly established and generally accepted authorities, a judge who misapplies or flouts those accepted authorities will generally fall foul of the professional community. A too creative manipulation of authority in an attempt to mask a change in direction opens up the judge to criticism from his peers. A good illustration of the limits to judicial discretion is provided by the case of *Perrin v. Blake*. The treatment meted out to Lord Mansfield was in the form of open, and very vocal, criticism of the decision reached in that case by King's Bench. Many lawyers, and in particular conveyancers, considered that the King's Bench decision had been reached by rejecting the application of a settled rule of law, which was applicable to the facts of the case: the rule laid down in Shelley's Case. It was one of the few decisions made by Lord Mansfield that would be reversed. In cases dealing with land and wills, affecting the sacred core of English property law, Mansfield would find himself more hemmed in by the legal community than in matters dealing with merchant law. Mansfield decided commercial matters under a separate system of legal rules: the law merchant. This allowed him to draw upon foreign legal authorities, equitable principles associated with the law of nations and certain legal analogies and categories derived from the common law itself.[151] The law of real property would not give Mansfield the same scope for flexibility and precedent building. The law of real property already had substantially set parameters, set not just by a considerable body of accepted legal precedents, but also by a set of common non-legal assumptions held by the legal profession with respect to the role of property in society (see chapter 6).

Perrin v. Blake would seem to indicate that a model of judicial reasoning in which a judge is free to create any law of his own choosing or that a case decision is entirely dependent upon the particularities of an individual judge should also be rejected. Fundamental criticism of a decision, such as that suffered by Mansfield because of *Perrin v. Blake*, would make a judge very aware of the disapproval of the professional community. In later cases on the same point, Mansfield's King's Bench would not again depart from or reexamine the technical rule laid down in Shelley's Case. It was this rule which was confirmed to be the rule applicable to *Perrin v. Blake* when the case was reheard by the Court of

---

151 Lieberman, *The province of legislation determined* (1989), pp. 104-106.

Exchequer.[152] Patent law was new to the common law courts in the mid-eighteenth century and had not built up a substantial body of precedents. It did not have a traditional foundation, as was the case with older areas of law. There was, therefore, more room for judicial individualism. Yet even here within a relatively short time, an explicit, radical departure from what the majority considered to be the current state of the law would cause a stir. As will be seen in the following chapter, Eyre's opinion that a method fell under the statutory term 'manufacture' remained a matter for discussion for some years.

The internal divisions always present within the judiciary, but in general less conspicuous in the decision-making in more established areas of law, would surface openly in the development of patent law. Whereas some judges considered that their role was to abide by the strict letter of what they deemed to be the existing patent law, others preferred to interpret that law according to what they considered to be the spirit of the law. The factors taken into consideration in interpreting patent law would vary depending upon the nature of the approach adopted by the judge. In a predominantly formalistic approach, the emphasis would be on such matters as grammar, word formulation or the historical context of a statute. In a teleological approach, the emphasis would be more on the "spirit" of the law, interpreting the law within a contemporary social context. Dutton appears to equate 'hostility' on the part of some judges with judges interpreting the law "in the strictest possible sense, allowing no error, however immaterial".[153] What Dutton is describing is a formalistic approach. Even if a mechanistic, restrictive interpretation of a patent is evident, this does not necessarily imply that the judge adopting that interpretation was hostile to or prejudiced against patentees in particular. Those judges who adopted a "play safe", or formalistic, approach towards interpreting patent law may well have had a tendency to interpret other areas of law in the same way. For example, Yates' formalistic style of interpretation above in *Perrin v. Blake* would be reflected in his approach to copyright and patents in *Millar v. Taylor* 1769 (see chapter 6). Patent law would be subjected to a period of uncertainty, caused by the push and pull of conflicting judicial approaches to interpretation, until the parameters became more settled.

2.5 Summary

It has been argued by various scholars that some judges were 'hostile' or 'prejudiced' against patents. The attitude of judges to patents is only pertinent if judges have a creative function, either original or derivative. For this purpose, a brief outline is given of the different models of judicial decision-making: the positivist approach, the creative approach and the bounded creativity approach.

---

152 *Ibid.*, p. 140.
153 Dutton, *The patent system and inventive activity during the industrial revolution 1750-1852* (1984), p. 77.

From the prominent legal treatises of the eighteenth century, it would seem that the role of the judge was conceived of in a restrictive, formalist manner. These treatises exhibit a certain tension between the theory of a rule-based approach to judicial decision-making and the actual practice of the courts. It is also apparent that there were divisions within the bench at this time regarding the role of the judge. Although the legal community of the eighteenth-early nineteenth century was small and shared certain values and orthodoxy, its cohesive nature should not be overestimated. Judges came from different social and educational backgrounds, and the interpretation of the law would be filtered through their own frames of reference.

What is very evident is the split within the judiciary as to styles of interpretation. On the one hand there were judges who endorsed a formalistic style, such as Lord Kenyon and Lord Camden. On the other hand there were those who preferred a teleological approach, such as Lord Mansfield and most of the members of the King's Bench while he presided. This internal division within the judiciary is illustrated by the case of *Perrin v. Blake*, heard in the period 1769-1772. *Perrin v. Blake* also serves to illustrate the failure of both a rule bound model to describe judicial decision-making or the boundless, creative approach. Whereas judges do have a creative role, it is not boundless but must fit within the parameters of the legal order.

It is argued here that it is more fruitful to analyse judicial decision-making in patent cases in terms of these differing styles of judicial interpretation a formalist or teleological approach rather than in terms of hostility or prejudice. This difference in styles of interpretation was always present within the judiciary but in more established areas of law it was less conspicuous. Even if judicial reasoning would differ in these cases, there was a high probability that the decision would fall within the accepted parameters. Disapproval would be the lot of a judge who attempted a too radical departure from accepted orthodoxy. Patent law was a new area of law, without a traditional foundation. The different styles of interpretation would be more clearly exposed.

3   Patent Law: The Interpretation of the Statute of Monopolies 1624 from the 1750s to the 1830s

During this period, there were two major elements of patent law that were subject to judicial interpretation. One was the Statute of Monopolies 1624, in particular Section VI, which outlined under which circumstances an exception to the general prohibition on monopolies could be made for an invention. The other element was the patent specification. The specification will be examined in the following chapter.

From the 1750s to the 1830s, there was very little patent 'law' in the sense of the word indicated by Hale, as being made by the king and parliament. Brougham's Patent Law Amendment Act in 1835 was the first piece of legislation on patents since the Statute of Monopolies 1624. The 1835 Act instigated a change of forum for hearing applications for patent extensions; the Privy Council, rather than parliament, was given the power to grant an extension for any period not exceeding seven years. Patentees were also given the right to amend mistakes either in the title or in the specification of their inventions. In 1839 there would be another Act to amend the 1835 Act (and one in 1844), but there would be no comprehensive legislative intervention in patent law until the Patent Act 1852. The Statute of Monopolies therefore remained the primary legislative source throughout this period. In itself, the Statute of Monopolies only provided a very basic framework. Only one section, Section VI, dealt with the criteria for patents for inventions. For the Statute to become a useful legal tool, it needed judicial interpretation, which in turn would produce a body of case law and a set of precedents. By the mid-eighteenth century, there had been too few patent disputes in the period since the Statute for a substantial body of case law to have been built up. The common law courts had heard several patent cases in the seventeenth century, but thereafter their role seems to have been minimal. In the seventeenth century and until the mid-eighteenth century, patent validity cases had also fallen under the jurisdiction of the Privy Council. When the common law courts became the primary forum, after a procedural dispute with the Privy Council, Hulme notes, "the common law judges were left to pick up the threads of the principles of law without the aid of recent and reliable precedents".[1]

Throughout the period examined in this study, the common law courts were interpreting the validity of patents within the context of the terms of the Statute of Monopolies. If the

---

1   Hulme, *On the Consideration of the Patent Grant Past and Present* (1897), p. 318.

Statute was to be a practical legal instrument, clarity was needed as to what the law would protect and what it would not. During this period, the economy of Britain was changing, as manufacturing industries increased not only in importance but also in sophistication. A technical invention could be valuable because it produced a new or improved substance, or new machinery. However, even an innovation that produced no new or improved end product but consisted only in a process by which known artefacts were used to produce a known product but more cheaply and more efficiently was also valuable. If the courts were only prepared to protect a physical thing as a 'manufacture', the patentee of a process separate from the vendible substance would not enjoy legal protection.

How the terms of the Statute would be understood by the courts would depend upon which style of judicial interpretation was being applied. Those judges who favoured a teleological approach, would be more likely to be pragmatic, adjusting the meaning of the Statute to serve the interests of the society of the day. Other judges, who had more formalist ideas concerning the role of the judge, would seek to interpret the Statute either by understanding its wording within the historical context of the Statute or by applying what they considered to be a more literal understanding of the terminology of the Statute.

3.1   The Importance of the Statute of Monopolies

The view that the Statute formed the foundation of British patent law has been challenged by a number of historians. One ground for this challenge has been that the Statute was simply declaratory of the existing common law. It is interesting to note that the first legal treatise on patents, John Collier's *An essay on the law of patents for new invention* which appeared in 1803, did indeed consider the Statute to be merely of a declaratory nature. Collier: "The statute of the 21st of James cannot be correctly said to impose any new restraints, but to prevent license being substituted for law, by avoiding the doubts and difficulties attending the legitimate exercise of the prerogative. Hence in *perpetuum rei testimonium*, the parliament deemed it proper to interpose, and to declare what is, and what shall be, the law of the land."[2] Hulme, writing at the end of the nineteenth century, interprets several of the Statute's sections as consistent with the pre-1623 common law (see below). Boehm points out that the Statute relied heavily in language and in content on King James' *Book of Bounty*. The only new features the Statute presented were the limitation of patents to a maximum of fourteen years and the provision that they should be tried at common law.[3]

The importance of both the Statute of Monopolies, and the case law it generated, has been more recently disputed by Sherman and Bently. The ground for this dismissal is not

---

2   John Dyer Collier, *An Essay on Patents for new Inventions*, London 1803, pp. 119-120.
3   Klaus Boehm, *The British System I*, Cambridge 1967, p. 16.

whether or not the Statute was simply a restatement of the common law, but that this particular piece of legislation in itself was only of minor significance. According to Sherman and Bently, the prominence that has been given to the Statute of Monopolies, as having laid the foundations of patent law, is the product of a nineteenth century rewriting of history: "The Statute of Monopolies played, at best, a minimal role in pre-modern patent law." While not suggesting that the Statute of Monopolies had no role to play in the history of intellectual property, nonetheless they argue that the foundation of patent law is not to be found in this Statute but in the Royal Charters and Royal Letters Patent of the Crown. This can be seen for example in the way patents were presented in the Report of the 1829 Select Committee on Patents. As well as being treated in a similar way as other Acts (or patents), the Statute "was derided by the fact that in those rare instances where it was specifically mentioned, it was said to be 'chiefly declaratory of what had been held to be law by judges'". The authors call upon us to "resist the temptation to rewrite history in our own images" and admit that the Statute of Monopolies was only of minimal significance.[4]

That Sherman and Bently minimise the impact of the Statute of Monopolies on the development of patent law is consistent with their estimation of the role of the courts in this process. More significant than case law interpreting the Statute, in their opinion, was the process of drafting patent bills and legislation, even if these were not always successful. Such attempts had the effect of concretising ideas, of forcing commentators to determine in more detail the nature of the law. "Although these processes were presented as if they were reducing the pre-existing law to a codified form, given that patent law did not exist in any recognisable form at the time it is more accurate to say that they were creating rather than finding the law." Cited, as an example, is the bill drafted by Godson in 1831, one of the features of which was to clarify the meaning of the word 'manufacture'.[5]

The clauses in the letters patent were certainly instrumental in helping to shape patent law. For example, as noted below in paragraph 3.3, the condition in the Statute of Monopolies that a patent grant should not be "generally inconvenient" had appeared as a clause in royal grants of patent long before the Statute of Monopolies came into force. The Statute in itself provided little in the way of detail upon which a comprehensive body of patent law could be built. However, the Statute and the case law that it generated cannot be dismissed as an irrelevancy. The Statute of Monopolies was the measure by which all the patent cases were judged by the courts. A good illustration is provided by the case of *Hornblower v. Boulton and Watt* 1799. In his judgment, Grose, J. actually quotes most of Section VI of the Statute before summing up that the questions concerning the disputed

---

4   Brad Sherman and Lionel Bently, *The Making of Modern Intellectual Property Law: The British Experience 1760-1911*, Cambridge 1999, pp. 208-209.
5   *Ibid.*, pp. 105-106.

patent were whether it was a patent for the sole working or making of any manner of new manufacture, whether the patentee was the first inventor, and whether it was contrary to law, mischievous to the state or to trade or generally inconvenient.[6] As will be seen below, the interpretation of the terminology of Section VI is what formed the case law throughout this period.

The Statute and the accompanying case law are not ignored in the 1829 Report. The appendix to the 1829 Report consists of a summary of the major patent cases detailing the grounds for the decisions, which was provided by John Farey, who was a witness before the committee. The Statute is also discussed by another witness, who was a member of the bar: Benjamin Rotch. Rotch was a barrister known for his scientific knowledge, himself a patentee, who had appeared as counsel in several patent cases. Rotch is critical of the Statute of Monopolies and argues that the main source of the problems confronting patent law was indeed the Statute of Monopolies itself. He comments:

> "the words of the statute, which are extremely well calculated for those times, do not happen now at all to hit the necessities of the present period. The consequence is, that the judges are constantly straining the meaning of this Act to make it meet the necessity of the times. Thus it depends on the extent of laxity that a judge will venture to give as to what the law at this particular day in any particular court happens to be on patents."

The remedy Rotch suggests:

> "to put all this straight, is to adopt the common sense decisions of the judges, and to form a statute which shall embrace those objects which, although without the pale of the Act, are every day the object of patent grants, and sanctioned and supported as such in courts of law by the judges."[7]

Rotch's reference to "the common sense decisions of the judges" is an acknowledgment of the role of the judges. The courts had been faced with the practical application of patent law to actual cases. They had been confronted with industrial practices that were evolving in terms of specialisation and proficiency. A coherent, regulatory framework that would take into account the infinite permutations and variations of manufacturing ingenuity did not exist by the 1830s. Arguably, it never could exist. Yet the Statute and the case law it had generated undoubtedly formed a starting point for judicial decision-makers, treatise writers and for reformers.

---

6   *Hornblower v. Boulton and Watt* 1799, 8 T. R. 100.
7   *Select Committee Report 1829*, pp. 107-108.

It is interesting to note that when the first treatise on patents was written in 1803, Collier referred to the statute of James as follows: "From this period the doctrine of our law of patents may be properly said to commence, for by its salutary operation the pernicious system was wholly destroyed."[8] Collier devoted several chapters to an examination of the Statute and how it had been construed by the courts. Apparently, Collier did consider the Statute and its case law to be significant. His work appeared at the very beginning of the nineteenth century, thus presumably it cannot be described as a nineteenth century rewriting of the historical significance of the Statute. In the preface to his essay on patents for invention, Collier describes his work as "an attempt to collect scattered fragments so that the whole that relates to commercial patents is in an obvious form".[9] Whether Collier succeeded is a matter of opinion. Nonetheless, to state, as do Sherman and Bently, that "patent law did not exist in any recognisable form" before legislative attempts were made in this field goes too far. That approach underestimates the significance of the case law which had been built up already.

By the time Godson drafted his bill in 1831, there was already a body of case law in place. It was sufficiently recognisable to have made it possible for this same Godson to write *A Practical Treatise on the Law of Patents for Invention and of Copyright* in 1823, and it is worth noting here the word "Practical" in the title of that treatise. Furthermore, in Book II, where Godson deals with patents for invention, he states "the law of patents of inventions as it now stands rests for support on the statute of 21 James".[10] The approach adopted by Godson in the first part of Book II is to explain patent law in terms of the judicial interpretation of the Statute of Monopolies (before addressing the law relating to the specification). The Statute clearly influenced the basis for Godson's own legislative attempts. What Godson was trying to clarify in his 1831 bill was a term from the Statute of Monopolies: "manufacture". The case law generated by the Statute was important because it brought practical issues to the fore, which had to be dealt with as they arose. That the meaning ascribed to the terms of the Statute by the judges may not always have kept up with social and technological developments, does not imply that patent law did not exist in any recognisable form by the early nineteenth century. It would indeed be a curious phenomenon if attempts at legislative reform would have been totally uninfluenced and distinct from the main forum for the development of patent law in this period: the courts.

Much of the story of the development of patent law in the latter part of the eighteenth century and early nineteenth century must be told in terms of the attempt by judges to convert Section VI of that Statute into a practical instrument. Judges were trying to imbue the terminology of the Statute with meaning. Without clarity of meaning there were no

---

8   Collier, *An Essay on Patents for new Inventions* (1803), p. 19.
9   *Ibid.*, p. vii.
10   Godson, *A Practical Treatise on the Law of Patents for Inventions and of Copyright*, (1823), p. 44.

proper criteria by which the validity of a patent could be judged. Finding that clarity of meaning was not a straightforward process. If the Statute, as drafted in 1623, was to a large extent a restatement of the common law at that time, that restatement was a very concise one. The Statute itself provided no more than the barest of outlines of a law for patents for invention. It had to be coloured in by judicial interpretation. In that respect the Statute was "what has been held to be law by judges". It is argued here that the Statute of Monopolies was of fundamental importance, irrespective of whether it was or was not simply declaratory of the common law at the time it was passed. It is important not because of its legislative impact in 1624 but because it would form the basis for the development of the law in the courts in the eighteenth and early nineteenth century. Given that there was no comprehensive legislative intervention until 1852, this period of judicial determination is of crucial importance and its contribution to major concepts in patent law should not be underestimated.

3.2   The Criteria for Statutory Interpretation

What criteria did judges use in the eighteenth and early nineteenth century to interpret the Statute of Monopolies? In trying to understand the 'intention of the legislature', the wording and syntax of the text of statutes have long played a dominant role as an interpretative tool in the English courts. This emphasis on a text-orientated interpretation has often been brought to the fore by commentators as differentiating the approach of the common law courts from that of their continental neighbours. Whereas English courts adhere to a strict interpretation, based on the literal meaning of words or the grammatical construction of a sentence, the judges in civil law systems interpret in accordance with the purpose or design of the statute. Lord Denning, one of the most influential judges in the second half of the twentieth century, made the following comparison:

> "We have for years tended to stick too closely to the letter – to the literal interpretation of the words", whereas under the 'European method' … the judges do not go by the literal meaning of the words or by the grammatical structure of the sentence. They go by the design or purpose which lies behind it. When they come upon a situation which is to their minds within the spirit – but not the letter – of the legislation, they solve the question by looking at the design and purpose of the legislature – at the effect it was sought to achieve. They then interpret the legislation so as to produce the desired effect. This means that they fill in gaps, quite unashamedly, without hesitation. They ask simply: what is the sensible way of dealing with this situation so as to give effect to the presumed purpose of the legislation … To our eyes – short-sighted by

tradition – it is legislation, pure and simple. But to their eyes, it is fulfilling the
true role of the courts. They are giving effect to what the legislature intended,
or may be presumed to have intended."[11]

Lord Denning here refers to a tradition of the literal interpretation of statutes. What
Vogenauer has argued, however, is that the dominance of the literal rule of statutory
interpretation had not always been the English tradition. The English courts, just like their
continental neighbours, have gone through periods of change with respect to statutory
interpretation. Two modes of statutory interpretation can be distinguished in English
courts: one mode in which the judge kept precisely to the wording of the statute, and the
other by which the judge could deviate from the text in the name of equity. Even where
the wording was clear, this latter mode saw judges deviate from the wording in order to
bring the law in line with equity, justice and reason. The early restrictive approach leaning
heavily on wording and grammar gave way to a more liberal approach to statutory interpretation in the period from the Year Books to about 1830. It was only after 1830 that strict
literalism became the dominant interpretative method in the English courts.[12]

Vogenauer cites a number of legal works and cases to support his argument that the
equitable approach to statutory interpretation triumphed over one primarily dominated
by wording and grammar in this period before the 1830s. A more liberal method of interpretation emerges from the work *Discourse upon the Exposition and Understanding of
Statutes* that appeared in 1571. This work, probably written by Thomas Egerton, who
would become Lord Ellesmere at the beginning of the seventeenth century, states that: "for
sometimes it [statute[shall be construed strictly- that is according to the words and no
further. Sometimes the words by equity are stretched to like cases. Sometimes they are
expounded against the words."[13] This equitable construction of statutes was described in
the reports of the barrister Edmund Plowden. In *Eyston v. Studd* (1574) he comments as
follows: "it is not the words of the law, but the internal sense of it that makes the law, and
our law (like all others) consists of two parts, viz. of body and soul, the letter of the law is
the body of the law, and the sense and reason of the law is the soul of the law." For the
judge "ought not to rest upon the letter only….. but he ought to rely upon the sense, which
is temperated and guided by equity".[14] That Plowden espoused the equitable construction
of statutes is highly significant: Plowden's law reports were still compulsory literature in
the Inns of Court in the eighteenth century.[15]

---

11 *James Buchanan and Co. Ltd v. Babco Forwarding and Shipping* (UK) Ltd (1977) Q.B. 213-214.
12 Vogenauer, *Die Auslegung von Gesetzen in England und auf dem Kontinent*, (2001), Part II, pp. 669-670,
    685,778-780. Egerton Discourse, *Eyston v. Studd* and Heydon's case are cited by Vogenauer.
13 *Ibid.*, pp. 683-684, Egerton, Discourse s. 123.
14 *Ibid.*, p. 687, *Eyston v. Studd* (1574) 2 Plowd 465, 467.
15 *Ibid.*, p. 687.

In Heydon's Case 1584, it was stated that four things should be considered in the interpretation of all statutes: what was the common law before the Act was made, what was the mischief and defect for which the common law did not provide, what remedy had the parliament resolved upon to cure the defect, and what was the true reason for the remedy. This 'mischief rule' meant that judges must construe the statute taking these four points into account in order to determine the true intent of the makers of the Act. Although Heydon's case gave instructions for the use of several interpretation criteria, that in combination would serve to find the hypothetical will of the legislator, Vogenauer maintains that most of the time the courts only mentioned a single point from Heydon's case, not all four considerations.[16]

Blackstone provided a list of interpretative criteria in his *Commentaries*. Blackstone saw wording as the place to begin but, as noted in the previous chapter, there were other factors to be taken into account. These included what the intentions of the legislature had been at the time when the law was made, the effects and consequences, and the spirit and reason of the laws. He introduced the mischief rule in its complete formulation.[17] Blackstone's treatment of statute law would long be viewed as a source of legal authority. The need to interpret statutes according to the spirit of the law was stressed by Blackstone in the Introduction to his *Commentaries* and he returned to it again in Book III:

> "It is said, that a court of equity determines according to the spirit of the rule, and not according to the strictness of the letter. But so also does a court of law. Both, for instance, are equally bound, and equally profess, to interpret statutes according to the true intent of the legislature. In general laws all cases cannot be foreseen; or if foreseen, cannot be expressed: some will arise that will fall within the meaning, though not within the words, of the legislator; and others, which may fall within the letter, may be contrary to his meaning, though not expressly excepted. These cases, thus out of the letter, are often said to be within the equity, of an act of parliament; and so cases within the letter are frequently out of the equity. Here by equity we mean nothing but the sound interpretation of the law; though the words of the law itself may be too general, too special, or otherwise inaccurate or defective. These then are the case which, as Grotius says, *lex non exacte definit, sed arbitrio boni viri permittit*; in order to find out the true sense and meaning of the lawgiver."[18]

---

16 *Ibid.*, pp. 677-681, Heydon's Case 1584, 3 Co Rep 7b per Roger Manwood.
17 *Ibid.*, pp. 670, 681.
18 Blackstone, *Commentaries on the Laws of England* (1793), III. p. 430.

That Blackstone refers to Grotius here is consistent with his whole approach to statutory interpretation, leaning as it does upon the civilian tradition. Vogenauer points out that in his *Commentaries* Blackstone applied maxims which went back to the Digest. He borrowed from Cicero. The links with Pufendorf in the *Commentaries* are clear; the similarities in language between Blackstone's text on statutory interpretation and that of Pufendorf in the English translation of *De jure naturae et gentium* are unmistakable. Although Blackstone cites civilian scholars, even more often Blackstone uses continental literature implicitly.[19]

The equitable construction of statutes was a method of interpretation that was still being applied in the mid-eighteenth century and would persist into the early nineteenth century. Vogenauer cites various examples. In *Halsey v. Hales* 1796 Lord Kenyon stated: "We are called upon in this case to decide according to the strict letter of the Act of Parliament: but that is not the true line of construction, for Lord Coke says *qui haeret in litera haeret in cortice*.[20] We must therefore consider what is the fair meaning of the Act." In *R v. Inhabitants of Everdon* 1807, Lord Ellenborough stated: "it would indeed be a grievous construction if we were bound to adopt the literal sense of the words of the statute... This is the plain sense and spirit of the Act, though somewhat straining upon the words of it: but no other construction can be put on them consistently with the general object of the Act." In the same case, Grose, J. stated: "The letter of the statute is sufficiently plain according to the common understanding of the words; but that would mitigate so strongly against the spirit and object of it, that we cannot be governed by the letter without entirely defeating the very wholesome law."[21]

However, Vogenauer considers that by the second part of the eighteenth century, the use of the equitable construction was already in decline. He notes that the courts would give clear wording the preference, if this would not lead to absurd consequences. Parker, C.B. stated in *Mitchell v. Torup* 1766: "In expounding acts of parliament, where words are express, plain and clear, the words ought to be understood according to their genuine and natural signification and import, unless by such exposition a contradiction or inconsistency would arise in the act by reason of some subsequent section, from whence it might be inferred the intent of parliament was otherwise."[22] Several other cases are cited to show a shift against equitable construction, including Lord Mansfield in *Atcheson v. Everitt* 1775 and Justice Buller in *Jones v. Smart* 1785.[23]

In *Atcheson v. Everitt* it was alleged by the defendant that a new trial should be granted for an action of debt upon the statute against bribery. The grounds for granting a new trial

---

19   Vogenauer, *Die Auslegung von Gesetzen in England und auf dem Kontinent* (2001), Part II, pp. 772-773.
20   Cited by Vogenauer, *Die Auslegung von Gesetzen in England und auf dem Kontinent* (2001), Part II, p. 701, fn. 191.
21   *Ibid.*, pp. 720-721, fn 303.
22   *Ibid.*, p. 692, fn. 138.
23   *Ibid.*, p. 703, fn. 205, 206.

was that evidence had been given by a Quaker and that evidence could not stand. Quakers did not give an oath but an affirmation, and testimony on an affirmation in a criminal cause was excluded by statute. Although Mansfield admitted that he did not know why this exception had been made "but it is made, and must be followed". He then added: "The effect, however, is, that it is an exception not to be extended by equity. In remedial cases, the construction of statutes is extended to other cases within the reason or rule of them. But where it is a hard positive law, and the reason is not very plainly to be seen, it ought not to be extended by construction."[24]

This indeed sounds like a shift away from an equitable construction. However, appearances are somewhat deceptive. The statute clearly states criminal cases must be examined on oath. This is acknowledged by Mansfield. But the question that Mansfield then poses is what is a 'criminal cause'? How should these words in the statute be interpreted? Citing Blackstone's work, he points out: "Penal actions were never yet put under the head of criminal law, or crimes. The construction of the statute must be extended by equity to make this a criminal cause. It is as much a civil action, as an action for money had and received. The legislature, when they excepted to the evidence of Quakers in criminal causes, must be understood to mean causes technically criminal; and a different construction would not only be injurious to Quakers, but prejudicial to the rest of the King's subjects who may want their testimony."[25] While apparently not extending the construction of the statute by equity, indeed arguing that it must be extended by equity to make this penal action a criminal case, Mansfield achieves the liberality of interpretation he had pleaded for in *Omichund v. Barker* 1744. It seems like a classic example of what Fifoot alleged: that Mansfield's challenge to authority was not met by defiance, but by ingenuity.[26] Nonetheless, a resort to an ingenious approach could indicate that a shift away from the equitable construction of statutes was taking place at this time and that Mansfield was aware of it.

Ten years later in the case of *Jones v. Smart*, this shift seems even more apparent. In that case, Buller, J. stated: : "... we are bound to take the act of parliament, as they have made it: a *casus omissus* can in no way be supplied by a court of law, for that would be to make laws." Several other judgments in that same case reflected Buller's approach. Lord Mansfield stated: "To be sure, absurd consequences may seem to follow from giving a privilege to the son, which the father has not: but the question is, has the statute done it or not?" His approach is echoed by Ashhurst, J.: "I cannot think that it was their intention purposely to exclude the father, but in fact they have done it" and any change would be for the legislature "if they think proper".[27] Even Lord Kenyon seems to favour a more

---

24 *Atcheson v. Everitt* 1775, 1 Cowper 391.
25 *Ibid.*, 391.
26 Fifoot, *Lord Mansfield* (1977), p. 214.
27 *Jones v. Smart* 1785, 1 T.R. 48, 51-52.

restrictive approach in *Hutson v. Hutson* 1796: "I think it would have been more wise in deciding cases on the rule of Geo. 2. to have adhered to the letter of it than to have gone into the circumstances of each particular case, especially as that rule was made to explain a former rule in the reign of Charles the Second; since an explanatory rule, like an explanatory statute, should never be extended by construction."[28]

Vogenauer highlights another aspect of this movement towards a more literal form of statutory interpretation which was taking place in the latter part of the eighteenth century. At one time, it had been quite common for judges to refer to parliamentary debates as an aid to interpretation. For centuries, judges used their own knowledge of what had passed in the House or asked others for information, such as those who had participated in legislative proceedings and based their understanding of the statute on this information. A case from 1366, illustrates the point: "we will advise with our companions who were at the making of the statutes".[29] Yet in the eighteenth century, this too was in decline. The turning point is considered to be *Millar v. Taylor* 1769, with Willes, J. formulating what would later be referred to as the exclusionary rule:

> "The sense and meaning of an Act of Parliament must be collected from what it says when passed into a law; and not from the history of changes it underwent in the House where it took its rise."[30]

King's Bench would restrict the use of these records. As Vogenauer noted, Blackstone did not even include records of parliamentary debates in his list of interpretation criteria.[31]

Nonetheless, the rejection of the use of records of parliamentary debates as an aid to statutory interpretation was not consistent. In cases after *Millar v. Taylor* 1769, some judges still referred to parliamentary debates. For example, in *Atcheson v. Everitt* 1775, Lord Manfield: "With regard to the exception against the testimony of Quakers in criminal prosecutions, it was occasioned by a strong prejudice in the minds of the great men who passed the stat. 7 and 8 Wm. 3. c 34. I have looked into the debates of those days, and find that every step and section of the act was fought hard in the House of Commons, and carried by small majorities."[32] And in *R v. Webster* 1789, Lord Kenyon remarked: "And I have also had an opportunity of knowing, since that determination, that our opinion coincides with that of the gentlemen who drew the act."[33]

---

28 *Hutson v. Hutson* 1796, 7 T.R. 8-9.
29 Vogenauer, *Die Auslegung von Gesetzen in England und auf dem Kontinent* (2001), Part II, p. 671.
30 *Millar v. Taylor* 1769, 4 Burr 2332.
31 Vogenauer, *Die Auslegung von Gesetzen in England und auf dem Kontinent* (2001), p. 671.
32 *Atcheson v. Everitt* 1775, 1 Cowper 390.
33 *R v. Webster* 1789, 3 T.R. 75.

What Vogenauer describes is general tendencies. As mentioned above, Vogenauer cites *Jones v. Smart* as an example of the tendency towards a more restricted approach to statutory interpretation. However of interest in this case is the dissenting opinion of Willes, J. Willes gives several grounds for his opinion, including a grammatical one. Nonetheless, the thrust of his opposition is that the game laws are already sufficiently oppressive and should not be extended by implication: "And wherever a law is productive of tyranny, I shall ever give my consent to narrow the construction." Willes states that what he most relies upon are the "unaccountable absurdities which must flow from a different interpretation".[34] At the opposite end of the spectrum was Charles Abbott, the later Lord Tenterden. As Vogenauer points out, Abbott had never favoured the equitable construction. Even during the period in which the equitable construction of statutes had been common, Abbott had always personally been against it. As Chief Justice of King's Bench, in *R v. Inhabitants of Turvey* 1819 he stated: "I have often lamented, that in so many instances, the courts have departed from the plain and literal construction of the statutes relating to the settlement of the poor…. I shall feel myself bound to construe these acts of parliament according to the plain and popular meaning of their words." For Abbott, the wording of statutes was an absolute priority in interpretation. Nonetheless, Abbott himself was not always consistent. As late as 1824, he said in a judgment: "The object of these provision is, that the creditors of the insolvent should have notice… and I think the words of the sixth section ought to receive a liberal construction. If we were to construe them literally, it would follow as a consequence that… Now that would impose great difficulties upon insolvents, and would be attended with great inconvenience."[35] What these inconsistencies in statutory interpretation could indicate is a transitional phase. At the end of the eighteenth century, statutory interpretation by judges was moving away from the once dominant equitable construction to the more literal construction.

Did this shift affect the interpretation of the Statute of Monopolies in the latter part of the eighteenth century and early nineteenth century? Given that patent disputes had only, in effect, become part of the caseload of the common law courts from the mid-eighteenth century, the Statute, despite its age, had not yet been subject to extensive interpretation by the judges of the common law courts. If the judicial attitude to the Statute of Monopolies is examined over this period, it cannot be said that the 1830s marked a more literal approach to the Statute. From the time the common law courts took over from the Privy Council in the mid-eighteenth century, there had been judges who had sought to interpret the Statute either in a historical context or in a manner which appeared to them as literal. This affected their determination of the term 'manufacture', as being a material thing, a thing made by

---

34 *Jones v. Smart* 1785, 1 T.R. 49-50.
35 Vogenauer, *Die Auslegung von Gesetzen in England und auf dem Kontinent* (2001), pp. 701, 739-740, *Forman v. Drew* 1825 4 B and C 18.

the hands of man. It was in the 1830s that a wider interpretation of the term 'manufacture' became apparent and it was at the beginning of the 1840s that the term was openly accepted as including a process separate from a substance. The 'spirit' of the Statute rather than its literal meaning seems to have come to the fore in the 1830s.

It would appear that during the period under consideration here, it was not a shift from equitable to literal statutory interpretation that was of importance in determining the meaning of the terminology of Section VI, but whether the judge in question was one who in general favoured a formalist approach to the interpretation of laws or not. Even if that judge announced that he was not restricting himself to the literal text of a statute, his preference for formalism would appear in other ways. A good example of a judge who favoured the equitable interpretation of statutes but remained a formalist in his approach is Lord Kenyon.

At first sight, given Kenyon's reputation as a formalist, it may seem rather surprising that Kenyon would reject an interpretation of a statute based on "the strict letter of the Act of Parliament", as noted above in the case of *Halsey v. Hales*. On closer analysis, Kenyon's concept of equitable statutory interpretation was restrictive, despite his acceptance that the literal text should not always be the determining factor. This was because his form of 'equitable construction' was not dynamic but static. He did not seek to place a statute within a present or future social context in order to interpret it, but within the context at the time the statute was made. That would determine what the legislature had meant, not any personal presumptions about the 'spirit' of the law and the demands of the present. In the *Halsey v. Hales* case, Kenyon examined the object of the legislature at the time the law at issue was made in order to determine whether that case fell within the meaning of the exception to the Act: "I think the object of the legislature was to prevent persons, who had no marketable estates, making improvident bargains in granting annuities: but they thought that a person who could bring a real security to market was not subject to such impositions, and therefore they provided by the last section that the act should not extend to any annuity secured by lands of equal or greater annual value whereof the grantor was seised in fee-simple or fee-tail."[36] This static component in equitable construction, the need to look back in time to determine the meaning rather than to interpret according to a more modern concept of the spirit of that particular law, was explicitly acknowledged by Blackstone. As Blackstone had said in his *Commentaries*: "The fairest and most rational method to interpret the will of the legislator, is by exploring his intentions *at the time when the law was made*, by signs, the most natural and probable."[37] Upon this reading, the meaning of the Statute of Monopolies would depend upon the context in 1623. Clearly,

---

36   *Halsey v. Hales* (1797) 7 T.R. 196.
37   Blackstone, *Commentaries on the Laws of England* (1793), Introd. p. 59 [my italics].

not abiding by "the strict letter of the Act of Parliament" was not necessarily synonymous with a progressive interpretation of a statute, one tuned to the needs of the present.

As noted in chapter 2, Lokin argues that the text of a law is an empty shell. It is only through judicial interpretation that the literal text of a law may remain the same over a long period of time, for the interpretation of that literal text will have taken on different meanings over time. That description would certainly seem applicable to the wording of Section VI of the Statute of Monopolies. As will be seen below, whereas the wording of Section VI remained the same, not all the concepts behind that wording remained the same throughout the period examined. These shifts in meaning were not dictated by an accompanying shift in statutory construction, from equitable to literal. The term 'new manufacture' would be interpreted far more liberally in the 1830s, the period in which Vogenauer considers statutory interpretation switched from equitable to literal, than in the preceding century. The shifts were rather the product of the dynamics of the pull and push of judicial teleological and formalist approaches.

3.3 The Judicial Interpretation of Section VI of the Statute of Monopolies 1624

The Statute of Monopolies declared that all monopolies were against the laws of the realm and would be void. Nonetheless, the Statute made several exceptions to the prohibition on monopolies. One exception was laid down in Section VI:

> "That any declaration before mentioned shall not extend to any letters patents and grants of privilege for the term of fourteen years or under, hereafter to be made, of the sole working or making of any manner of new manufactures within this realm, to the true and first inventor and inventors of such manufactures, which others at the time of making such letters patents and grants shall not use, so as also they be not contrary to the law, nor mischievous to the state, by raising prices of commodities at home, or hurt of trade, or generally inconvenient."

In applying this section to patent disputes, it was necessary for the judges to interpret the meaning of several phrases. The phrase 'any manner of new manufactures' raised the problem of what was to be understood as new and as a manufacture. The term 'true and first inventor' would depend upon the meaning ascribed to the word 'inventor'. Which manufactures would not be 'generally inconvenient' would fluctuate according to the economic theory being applied. Indeed, economic considerations seem to have been integral to the judicial interpretation of patent law, affecting not only how a judge would read the proviso on 'hurt of trade', but also colouring what he deemed to be a new manufacture, who was an inventor and what was generally inconvenient. How flexible a judge was in his interpretation depended upon whether he adopted a formalistic or a teleological approach to judicial decision-making.

3.3.1   The 'True and First Inventor'

In the Tudor period, several categories of persons were the recipients of the grant of a patent. These included a person who had created an invention himself and the first importer of an invention into England. This importation of an invention could take the form either of importing from a foreign country a device that had already been made there or by bringing to England foreign workmen with the required knowledge and expertise to make the product domestically. Patentees could be creative inventors or importers. Two of the sixteenth century patents listed by Hulme illustrate this dual approach. George Cobham was granted a patent for a dredging machine in 1562, the patent stating that the patentee represents that 'by diligent travel' he had discovered a machine to scour the entrances to harbours and the patent was for the importation of a number of these machines. On the other hand, a patent of 1563 to Burchsard Cranick was for an engine "lately invented, learned and found out by Cranick, and to be unlike anything devised or used within the realm".[38] Even where the patent concerned an invention based on individual empirical research, rather than an importation of an existing invention, the patentee was not necessarily the inventor himself. The practice of assigning patents appears to have been of long standing. For example, the patent granted to Cornelius de Vos in 1564 to make alum and copperas was shortly after assigned to Lord Mountjoy.[39]

In determining what the word 'inventor' meant when the phrase "true and first inventor" was drafted in the Statute of Monopolies, Hulme considers that the Statute did not introduce a new definition.[40] The pre-1623 reading of the word 'inventor' encompassed one who either invented or introduced the invention into the realm. Hulme concluded that: "Invention, i.e. the exercise of the inventive faculty, was not an essential qualification – institution of the manufacture, from whatever source derived, was the valid consideration of the patent grant under the statute."[41] The position of the importer was not an anomaly because the exercise of the inventive faculty was not required under the common law. That requirement would come later: "The development of the language has since narrowed the connotation of the term 'inventor' to exclude the individual.... who has brought in a new

---

38   Hulme, "The History of the Patent System under the Prerogative and at Common Law" (1896), pp. 145-146.
39   *Ibid.*, pp. 146-147.
40   E. Hulme, "The History of the Patent System under the Prerogative and at Common Law: A Sequel", *Law Quarterly Review* 16 (1900), p. 55.
41   Hulme, "On the History of Patent Law in the Seventeenth and Eighteenth Centuries" (1902), p. 281.

manufacture."[42] As noted above, Boehm too sees the Statute, for the most part, as simply a declaration of the common law. He notes that Coke states specifically that Section VI added nothing to the existing patent law, leaving patents "no better than they would have been if this Act had never been made" except to exempt them from the general prohibition on monopolies.[43]

Hulme's line of argument has been followed by a number of other historians. According to Davies, the introduction of a trade as an 'invention' was not an abuse of the patent system, but in keeping with the aims of the Tudor and Stuart statesmen to encourage trade and commerce.[44] This is the line adopted by Van Zijl Smit. He argues that the words and phrases in the Statute of Monopolies should be understood in terms of "a mercantilist framework of calculated state interventionism". The focus was on the introduction of whole new industries, not new knowledge about units of technology. This is apparent in the meaning of the words 'true and first inventor'.[45] Similarly, Dent considers that the patent grants under Elizabeth and James reflected policies aimed at employment, trade and regulation. Patents may be seen as specific practices that furthered, quite deliberately, these policy goals of the elite.[46]

That the introduction of a new trade fell under the term 'invention' has led some historians to argue that the requirement of invention, in the sense of a creative act, came later than the Statute of Monopolies. For example, Fox argued that the requirement of inventive ingenuity was "simply a refinement added to patent law by the courts" as patent litigation developed.[47] This reading of the history of the word 'inventor' in the Statute has been disputed by Prager. While Prager accepts that the English legal practice of the fifteenth, sixteenth and seventeenth centuries used the words 'inventor' and 'importer' interchangeably in many instances, he argues this does not justify the theory that invention was hardly an issue. On the contrary, inventive merit was clearly established under Elizabeth I and was merely disregarded by corrupt courtiers and officers. He cites several sixteenth century cases, such as Matthey's patent for certain types of knife handles and Hastings' patent for a certain kind of cloth, as examples of cases where the patent was held to be void for lack

---

42   Hulme, "The History of the Patent System under the Prerogative and at Common Law: A Sequel" (1900), p. 55.

43   Boehm, *The British Patent System I* (1967), pp. 16-17.

44   Seaborne Davies, "The Early History of the Patent Specifaction" (1934), p. 96.

45   Dirk van Zijl Smit, *The Social Creation of a Legal Reality: A Study of the Emergence and Acceptance of the British Patent System as a Legal Instrument for the Control of New Technology*, Edinburgh 1981, pp. 72-74.

46   Chris Dent, "Patent Policy in Early Modern England: Jobs, Trade and Regulation", *Legal History* vol. 10 (2006), pp. 73, 94.

47   Harold G. Fox, *Monopolies and Parents: a Study of the History and Future of the Patent Monopoly*, Toronto 1947, p. 227.

of inventive merit. Furthermore, he argues that Bircot's case uses the word 'invent' in the modern sense of the word: "it is much easier to add than to invent".[48]

While Getz rejects the idea that invention in the modern sense of the word was either a ground or a condition of the grant in this earlier period, he does argue that the distinction between inventors and importers was being more sharply drawn by the middle of the eighteenth century, as there was a greater understanding of the differing social functions performed by each than there had been in Tudor and Stuart times. This change in attitude was not attributable to any one cause, but a complex of factors. These included the increasing power of industrialists and a shift in emphasis from trade to manufacture.[49] Sherman and Bentley argue that although the language of creativity was not used with any degree of consistency until the early part of the nineteenth century, creativity was a concern extending to all forms of intellectual property during the eighteenth century. Looking at the embryonic patent law "we see that in a series of decisions and commentaries which began to appear at the end of the eighteenth century the law gradually developed a picture of what it meant to invent or create a machine or a chemical process". They add in a footnote that the "belief that patents could only be granted to creators of inventions was also eventually used to argue, successfully, against the granting of patents for the mere publication, introduction or importation of an invention".[50]

The law would long understand the term 'inventor' to encompass one who had not necessarily used his creative faculties. The importer as 'inventor' would still be good law in the early nineteenth century. While there are numerous instances of judges voicing admiration for a patentee's ingenuity, throughout the period examined in this study there are strong indications, as will be seen below, that although creativity was a factor it was still not the determining factor. More significant than individual creativity was the introduction of the use of the invention to England.

3.3.1.1   The 'True and First Inventor' in Legal Treatises
There are no specific treatises on patent law during the eighteenth century, which means for this period it is necessary to look at what is said on this subject in more general legal treatises. Of interest in this context, is a general treatise on statute law written early in the eighteenth century. The book *Readings upon the Statute Law*, was written in the 1720s, by an author identified only by his profession (as a 'Gentleman of the Middle Temple'). Having set out the provisions of the Statute of Monopolies, the writer identifies seven

---

48   Frank D. Prager, "Standards of Patentable Invention from 1474 to 1952", *University of Chicago Law Review* 20 (1952), pp. 70-72.

49   L. Getz, "History of the Patentee's Obligation in Great Britain", *Journal of the Patent Office Society* 46 (1964), pp. 75, 77-78.

50   Sherman and Bently, *The Making of Modern Intellectual Property Law: The British Experience 1760-1911* (1999), p. 44 and fn 4.

properties or qualifications set out in Section VI that an invention must have in order not to be caught by the general prohibition on monopolies. He then concludes "yet this Act, if they have all these properties, sets them in no better case than they were before this Act". These words echo Coke's words, maintaining that the Statute did not alter the previous common law approach to patents for inventions. The 'Gentleman of the Middle Temple' then notes that an invention will be considered new even if "the thing was practised beyond sea before, for the Statute speaks of new manufactures within this realm; so that if it be new here, it is within the Statute, for the Act intended to encourage new devices useful to the kingdom, and whether learned by travel or by study, *it is the same thing*".[51]

Describing creative invention and imported invention as "the same thing" is common-place in legal texts far into the eighteenth century and the early nineteenth century. Blackstone offers little insight into the interpretation of "true and first inventor", as his treatment of patents in his *Commentaries on the Laws of England* is confined to a few sentences, which for the most part simply repeat Section VI of the Statute. His editor, Edward Christian, added in a footnote that the patent is granted on condition that "the invention is new, or new in this country".[52] Wooddeson, like Blackstone before him, pro-duced a treatise based on his Oxford lectures. Like his predecessor, patent law occupies very little space in that treatise: less than two pages. He states that "if the invention be new in England, a patent may be granted, though the thing was practiced beyond sea before: for the statute speaks of new manufactures within this realm; and it was intended to encourage new devices of public utility; and whether they are learned by travel or by study makes no difference".[53]

This dual approach does not seem to have changed by the time Collier wrote the first treatise on patent law in 1803. Collier notes that the use and publication of an invention in a foreign country, however ancient, does not prevent it from being considered a new invention for the purpose of patent law if it is new to England. He cites the case of *Edgberry v. Stephens* as authority and that Eyre referred to that case in the Boulton and Watt trial; the first introducer of a manufacture practiced beyond the seas would be deemed to be the first inventor. This was to encourage new devices whether acquired by travel or study. He adds: "This construction is now universally admitted in our courts." It is possible that Collier himself had certain reservations concerning this approach but: "whether this con-struction be logically correct is not material." The introduction of these discoveries was of great importance for the improvement of the trade of the realm.[54]

---

51 Gentleman of the Middle Temple, *Readings upon the Statute Law*, vol. IV (1723-1725), pp. 241, 243 (my italics).

52 Blackstone, *Commentaries on the Laws of England* (1793), II, 407, fn 8.

53 Richard Wooddeson, *A systematical View of the Laws of England; as treated of in a Course of Vinerian Lectures, read at Oxford, during a Series of Years, commencing in Michaelmas Term, 1777*, vol. 2, London 1792-1793, pp. 395-396.

54 Collier, *An Essay on Patents for new Inventions* (1803), pp. 100-101.

The inventor as either creator or importer was still considered to be good law when Godson wrote his treatise on the law of patents for inventions in 1823. In the section 'Of the inventor', Godson provides three categories of 'inventor': "a discoverer of a new thing, a publisher of an invention or an introducer of a foreign invention." A discoverer is defined as he who first finds out a thing of which a limited monopoly may be granted. If the principle of the invention be taken from a scientific work, the patentee is not an inventor in the eyes of the law: "In vain will it be urged that the patentee has embodied the principle, that the method of reducing it to practice is his own discovery, and that great genius has been exerted to form the subject." With respect to a publisher, if two persons separately discover the same thing, the one who obtains a patent for it before the other has made the matter public is the first and true inventor. The authority is cited as Dollond's patent (see below). Godson notes that this doctrine was confirmed in the case of *Forsyth v. Reviere*. The third category of inventor was the introducer. If the object of the patent were new in England, he would be deemed the inventor. Godson specifically points out that the importer as inventor was still within the ambit of the law, citing *Wood v. Zimmer* as an authority.[55]

3.3.1.2   The 'True and First Inventor' in Case Law

A number of patent disputes heard by the common law courts concerned the matter of who was the true and first inventor. As noted in chapter 1, there are few reported patent cases in the eighteenth century. Determining the court's attitude to the term 'inventor' in this period, therefore, must be gleaned from what evidence has remained. One of the earliest cases which deals with the matter is the case of *Dollond v. Champney* 1766. MacLeod states: "The first major patent case at common law since the early seventeenth century was Dollond's in 1766, in which the judiciary began to address the thorny problem of the proper consideration for a patent."[56] Research carried out by Richard Sorrenson would indicate that in fact the 1766 case was not the first case in the series. Peter Dollond brought several actions for the infringement of a patent granted to his father in 1758 for making achromatic lenses. Records indicate that Dollond had already brought an action before King's Bench in 1763 and 1764 and had gone to Chancery to enforce the earlier judgment in his favour.[57] Although the *Dollond v. Champney* case was not reported, it was probably the 1766 case against James Champney, heard before Lord Camden in Common Pleas, that was the one cited in the reported case of *Boulton and Watt v. Bull* 1795.

In *Boulton and Watt v. Bull*, Buller, J. observes that the objection to Dollond's patent at the time appears to have been that he was not the first inventor. It had been argued that a certain Dr. Hall had made the same discovery before him, but this Dr. Hall had "confined

---

55   Godson, *A Practical Treatise on the Law of Patents for Inventions and of Copyright* (1823), pp. 52-56.
56   MacLeod, *Inventing the Industrial Revolution: the English patent system, 1660-1800* (1988), p. 61.
57   Sorrenson, "Dollond & Son's Pursuit of Achromaticity 1758-1789" (2001), p. 40, fn 40 on p. 53.

it to his closet". It was held in Dollond's case that as Dr. Hall had not made his discovery public, Dollond was to be considered the first inventor.[58] It would appear, at least from this reading of Dollond's case, that the term 'first inventor' was taken to mean the one who first made an invention public, whether or not he was the original creator. For the purposes of the Statute of Monopolies, the first person to disclose the invention to the public, even if he was not chronologically the first inventor was the "true and first inventor". Creativity was secondary to disclosure. The impetus to trade was apparently still the governing factor in the 1760s.

In the case of *Roebuck v. Stirling*, heard in House of Lords in 1774, the patent was for making sulphuric acid. The respondents argued that the substitution of lead vessels for glass vessels in this process was not a new discovery, because at the time the patent was granted this method was known. The appellants argued that "the rule adopted in England is, that the person who first used the invention within the realm, whether he is the original inventor or brings the invention from foreign parts, is entitled to a patent".[59] Although the appeal was dismissed, it was not on this ground.

Although the argument for the inventor as importer is set out in several cases in the eighteenth century, there do not seem to have been many cases, or at least reported cases, where one of the parties to the dispute was an importer rather than a creative inventor (or an assignee of a creative inventor). That makes one of the cases found in Lord Mansfield's trial notebook of particular interest. In *Ensell v. Quintin* the dispute did concern a case where the 'inventor' was the importer. The case of *Ensell v. Quintin* 1778 hinged upon whether the plaintiff was "the first inventor in his majesty's kingdom of the art of making and manufacturing plates or sheets of glass ... in the manner practised in Germany and other parts abroad". Various witnesses were called, including Blydel for the plaintiff who declares that the use is German and "I never heard of it made in England till Plaintiff". Unfortunately, Mansfield's notes do not reveal how the case was resolved nor is this supplied by any surviving court records.[60]

A confirmation of the importer as inventor appears in *Boulton and Watt v. Bull* 1795 in Eyre's opinion. In his judgment, Eyre, C.J. comments upon the case of *Edgeberry v. Stephens* 1691:

"That case establishes, that the first introducer of an invention practised beyond sea, shall be deemed the first inventor: and it is there said, the act intended to

58 *Boulton and Watt v. Bull* 1795, 2 H. Black 470.
59 *Roebuck v. Stirling* 1774, 1 WPC 46.
60 Oldham, *The Mansfield Manuscripts and the growth of English law in the eighteenth century*, (1992), pp. 757-758.

encourage new devices, useful to the kingdom; and whether acquired by travel or study, it is the same thing."[61]

This was apparently not simply considered to be good law at the end of the eighteenth century, but into the nineteenth century. The reward of a patent went to one who was not necessarily the original inventor but to the one who had brought the benefit of the invention to society. In *Forsyth v. Riviere* 1819, it was made clear that what was important in the eyes of the law was not who was the original inventor, but who first published or introduced the invention to the country. In the words of Abbott, C.J.:

> "if several simultaneously discover the same thing, the party who first commu-
> nicates it to the public, under a patent, is entitled to the benefit of it; the law
> not requiring that the patentee should be literally the first inventor, or finder-
> out of something new, but that it was sufficient if the patentee be the first
> publisher or introducer of the invention."[62]

The same point was made by Abbott (as Lord Tenterden) ten years later in *Lewis v. Marling* 1829. Lord Tenterden stated: "It is no doubt incumbent on the plaintiffs to show that their machine is new, but it is not necessary that they should have invented it from their own heads; it is sufficient that it should be new as to the general use and public exercise in this kingdom."[63]

If a patentee was claiming to be a creative inventor, did he also have to have made the machine in question himself? Of interest here is the case of *R v. Arkwright* 1785. In this case, the prosecution set out to demonstrate that Arkwright's second patent for roving and carding was essentially the same as the first, expired, patent for spinning. There are comments made by Bearcroft for the prosecution and Adair for the defence with respect to the meaning of the term inventor. Bearcroft stressed that Arkwright *himself* must be the inventor: "it must be a new invention by the patentee himself: Mr. Arkwright, therefore, if this is a new invention, must have been the inventor of it himself." He added that Arkwright's skill was simply in recognising a good invention and that he himself was never a "practical mechanic".[64] In response, Adair argued that the inventor does not also have to be the maker. Adair: "a smith or a carpenter, or a workman of any other description, does the manual part", but Arkwright was nonetheless the inventor, and it was Arkwright who was in charge of the numerous workmen employed in making the machines.[65] Buller did

61 *Boulton and Watt v. Bull* 1795, 2 H. Black 491.
62 *Forsyth v. Riviere* 1819, 1 CPC 404.
63 *Lewis v. Marling* 1829, 1 WPC 492.
64 Arkwright, *The Trial of a Cause instituted by Richard Pepper Arden, Esq* (1785), pp. 21, 167.
65 *Ibid.*, p. 113.

not correct Adair's assertion: that another was responsible for the physical making of the invention did not mean that the one who had thought through the invention was not the inventor.

The judicial recognition of this distinction is an interesting one, given the discussions on the legal definition of property which arose in court during copyright cases. As will be seen in chapter 6, stress was generally put upon the physical form of the subject matter of the patent, rather than upon an inventive idea. Yet in *R v. Arkwright*, apparently the 'inventor' was the person with the idea and he did not have to be able to put that idea into a physical form himself. Later cases confirmed the importance of the inventor as being the one with the idea. Godson, in the supplement to his treatise of 1832, concluded that it was a rule of law: if a servant makes a new discovery by himself, the invention is his property; but if a master plans and a servant only executes with alterations of his own, the master is the true inventor of the machine.[66] The case of *Crossley v. Beverley* in 1829 indicates a further shift towards the legal protection of the idea, as long as that idea did at some point take on a physical form. In this case, the patentee of a gas apparatus had made certain improvements to the machine between the time he took out the patent and the time he enrolled his specification. The specification described those improvements and the patentee claimed the machine so improved as his invention. Brougham, representing the alleged infringer, contended that a person could not take out a patent for the idea of a machine which had not been constructed, and that it was not sufficient if the idea had been put into practice between the taking out of the patent and the enrolment of the specification. That argument was rejected by Abbott, Lord Tenterden: there was no authority for the argument that an improvement could not be made between the time of taking out the patent and disclosing the invention. The patent was not invalidated.[67]

It would appear that the importation of a new device into England, which would be of commercial benefit to the realm, was long considered by the law as equally worthy of the protection of a patent as was the actual creation of a new device. Invention, in the modern sense of that word, was apparently not the highest good during this period; the commercial impetus given to the country's trade was the highest good. Whether the invention had been discovered by travel or by study, it was "the same thing": one was not more significant than the other. The importer as inventor long remained good law. As noted above in the case of *Lewis v. Marling*, as late as 1829 Lord Tenterden had repeated that it was not necessary for an 'inventor' to have invented it from his own head; it was sufficient if it were new as to the general use and public exercise in England. More than a decade later, this had apparently not changed. As Pollock, appearing as counsel for the plaintiff in *Crane v. Price* 1842, noted: "What merit in respect of the invention is due to the introducer of a

---

66   Richard Godson, *Supplement to a Practical Treatise on the Law of Patents for Invention*, London 1832, p. 4.
67   *Crossley v. Beverly* 1829, 109 ER 24-25.

manufacture from abroad? But the rights of such patentees are recognised by law. It is for the benefit to the country and the public that the patentee is rewarded."[68]

3.3.2   'New manufactures'

In referring to 'new manufactures', the Statute of Monopolies raised two interpretational issues: what could be described as 'new' and what was to be understood by the term 'manufacture'. Dutton contends that it was the absence of a clear and unambiguous definition of what kind of invention could be the subject of a patent that was one of the major causes of the confused state of the law: "In a period when the quantity and quality of inventive activity were changing rapidly, the meaning of 'new manufacture' as applied by the courts was often variable and obscure, and sometimes manifestly out of touch with the needs of a changing industrial economy."[69] Dutton is correct to point out that there was no clear and unambiguous definition. It was caused by different styles of judicial interpretation.

After the mid-eighteenth century, it became the task of the judges of the common law courts to interpret the Statute of Monopolies. As noted above, there was little case law and hence a paucity of settled principles. Without well-determined boundaries, an individual judge's preference for an interpretational style became more apparent. The distinction between a formalist approach and a teleological approach became particularly evident in the legal construction of what was to be understood by the term 'manufacture' in the Statute. This point was made by Benjamin Rotch in his testimony before the 1829 Select Committee on Patents for Invention. Using the example of bleaching cotton, he pointed out that mixing acid and water together may be an improvement of great value to the manufacturer, "in the present time when everything depends on the excellence, the rapidity or cheapness with which you do a thing". He notes:

> "In fact, three patents out of four are taken out for new processes, by which well known ends are obtained; that cannot be considered as a new manufacture; a new process by which you obtain an old manufacture is not a new one; it is a mere mode of putting together known elements to effect a known end. But some judges, my Lord Tenterden for one, are so open to the necessity of granting patents for these things, because they are so vastly important, that they will say 'that is the meaning of the word manufacture'. Another who is a

---

68   *Crane v. Price* 1842, 1 WPC 402.
69   Dutton, *The patent system and inventive activity during the industrial revolution 1750-1852* (1984), p. 72.

statute lawyer, would say 'nonsense; manufacture means no such thing, this is only a process.'[70]

As will be seen below, some judges maintained that the subject of a patent must be a physical, vendible object in order to be classed as a 'manufacture' under the Statute. The reasoning behind this decision was either because the judge considered this was the intention of parliament at the time the Statute of Monopolies was passed, or because he was of the opinion that the word 'manufacture' should be used within the legal context in its literal, etymological form. For these judges, a principle or a method was clearly excluded from the category of 'manufacture' and was not patentable.

Other judges were not so dogmatic. Some judges considered that the term 'manufacture' should be interpreted in terms of benefit and utility, according to their own conceptions of public policy, rather than by a literal or historical approach. Those judges who wished to include methods and processes as manufactures, hence protecting the numerous, and often valuable, chemical processes, often either indulged in linguistic acrobatics to class them as 'manufactures' within the context of the Statute of 1624 or simply ignored the problem by not raising the matter (the latter being the simplest approach if even the defendant's own counsel did not raise it as an objection).

3.3.2.1   'Manufacture' Defined in Legal Treatises

The word 'manufacture' seems to have been used, in general, in several slightly different ways throughout the eighteenth century. The word was still used in the eighteenth century to describe a whole industry, for example, 'the woollen manufacture' or 'the linen manufacture'. This use is interesting in the light of the argument that, at the time the Statute of Monopolies was passed, the focus was on the importation of whole new industries (see below). Manufacture is also found used in the sense of a trade. One example of this use is in Giles Jacob's *The Law Dictionary*, which appeared in 1797. In setting out the meaning of an Elizabethan statute on apprenticeship, Jacob explains that as the statute only refers to a trade at the time the statute was made "it seems to follow, that a *new manufacture, which to all purposes may be called a trade, is yet not a trade within this statute*".[71] The word manufacture is also used in the sense of a 'commodity', as something that can be bought and sold. One example of this use can be found in Nathan Bailey's very popular etymological English dictionary (by the end of the eighteenth century, twenty-eight editions had appeared). Bailey defined the noun 'manufacture' to be "any sort of commodity made by the work of the hands", its etymology being *manus* and *factura*.[72] As will be seen below,

---

70 *Select Committee Report 1829*, pp. 107-108.
71 Giles Jacob, *The Law Dictionary: Explaining the Rise, Progress and Present State of the English Law*, vol. 1, London 1797, Apprentice III [my italics].
72 N. Bailey, *An Universal Etymological English Dictionary*, Edinburgh 1800.

this is essentially the definition of manufacture given by Lord Kenyon in *Hornblower v. Boulton and Watt* 1799.

It is interesting to note, however, that the patent grants made under Elizabeth and James I were not always for a thing that could be described as "something made by the hands of man". As noted above, the word manufacture could be found used in the sense of a whole industry or trade. One example of such use would be the 1598 patent for the sole importation of playing cards.[73] If the Statute were only declaratory of the usage before its passage, given that the Statute refers to "the true and first inventor and inventors of *such manufactures*", then the manufacture here would have referred to the sole importation of a trade, not the thing that had been made. Nor did this change after the Statute of Monopolies. Davies has discovered patents that were granted in the eighteenth century for such subjects as fishing for whales and a patent for the insurance of horses. These illustrate, in his opinion, "the latitude taken in the interpretation of the term 'manufacture' even late in the eighteenth century".[74] It should be noted, however, that the eighteenth century patents to which Davies refers may not have been tried in court; they had passed through the law officers and had hence been enrolled.

The general legal treatises in the eighteenth century provide little detail concerning the meaning of the word 'manufacture'. Christian does not examine what is meant by the term 'manufacture' in his editions of Blackstone's *Commentaries*. Neither does Wooddeson address the matter of patents in sufficient detail to define the term 'manufacture', although he does deal (if very briefly) with what may be considered to be 'new' (see below). The issue of what is understood by 'manufacture' is addressed in more detail in Collier and Godsons' treatises on patents, which appeared early in the nineteenth century. Collier asserts: "A patent cannot be granted for a method or principle, its object must be some substantial thing produced." Collier goes on to note: "It is now completely decided in Westminster Hall, that if a patentee denominate his discovery a method, when in fact the thing invented is something substantial, the verbal inaccuracy shall not vitiate the grant."[75] In the appendix, where he presents a list of patents between 1 January and 31 March 1803, he adds:

> "The mere inspection of the following list will show how necessary it is that patentees should be informed of the rules laid down in the law of patents. It will be seen how great a portion of the grants appear by their titles to be extended not to any piece of mechanism, utensil or manufacture, but to a process, method or principle for which no patent can be valid. It is, however, some

---

73   Hulme, "The History of the Patent System under the Prerogative and at Common Law: A Sequel" (1900), p. 51.

74   Seaborne Davies, "The Early History of the Patent Specification" (1934), pp. 96-97.

75   Collier, *An Essay on Patents for new Inventions* (1803), pp. 75, 130.

consolation to reflect, that what is stated as such is often the application of a method, process or principle in some substantial form, for which a patent can be maintained. It is now understood, that where this construction can be given, it will be applied *in the most beneficial sense for the patentee*; and that no advantage will be taken of minute verbal criticism, to render the royal grant nugatory, and to disappoint the inventor of this equitable reward."[76]

Although Lord Chief Justice Eyre had seemed to "insinuate that a patent for a method might be good", in *Boulton and Watt v. Bull*, Collier was of the opinion that it had since been "completely decided that such a patent would be void".[77]

Writing twenty years later, in 1823, Godson considered the term 'manufacture' in the Statute to have "not yet been accurately defined; for the objects, which may possibly come within the spirit and meaning of that Act, are almost infinite". He then attempts to sum up what falls within the meaning of new manufacture. It may be a substance or thing made; a machine, or instrument; an improvement, or addition; a combination or arrangement of things already known; a principle, method or process carried into practice by tangible means; a chemical discovery; a foreign invention. It is interesting to note that Godson was of the opinion that the first of these, 'substance', "appears peculiarly to have been contemplated by the legislature as the most proper object for a patent" and in this context he mentions Kenyon's definition: a manufacture is something made by the hands of man.[78]

Godson is less emphatic than Collier with respect to the status of a method: "that a mere method of making a thing, or a process, or a manner of operating, cannot be the subject of a patent, is not quite so clear. Much discussion has taken place on this rule." Godson, like Collier, is convinced that the simple use of the term 'method' will not invalidate a patent. "And therefore, it is now clearly established, that if the patentee claim a method, and yet in the specification describe some tangible matter, the grant is valid. In other words, though the patent is for something called a method, yet the real subject of the grant is either a substance, machine, improvement or combination." Nonetheless, he is doubtful that a method without this corporeal dimension is sufficient for a patent: "It is conceived that such a device, method, or process, cannot be a manufacture within the meaning of the statute of James, because it is destitute of one of the qualities absolutely necessary to be found in a new manufacture, or subject proper for a patent – materiality. The description given by that very learned judge, Eyre, C.J. is not of any thing that can be made. There is nothing corporeal, – nothing tangible – nothing that can be bought or sold; no instrument by which the supposed benefit is produced, and which might, as an article of trade, be

---

76 *Ibid.*, Appendix p. 50 (my italics).
77 *Ibid*, fn 131.
78 Godson, *A Practical Treatise on the Law of Patents for Inventions and of Copyright* (1823), pp. 57-58.

purchased and used by another person."[79] With respect to a principle as a manufacture, even though Eyre thought there could be patent for an embodied principle: "It is the better opinion that a patent for the application of a principle must be as bad as one for the principle itself." As it would seem impossible to specify a principle or describe its application to all cases, this would be a strong reason why it cannot be the subject of a patent.[80]

However, Godson is aware of a problem; the status of what he refers to as 'chemical discoveries'. He notes how many of these discoveries there have been and how important they are to the community. He points out that it is the opinion of many persons, that if methods or processes in general cannot be the subject of patents, yet a chemical process ought to be considered a new manufacture within the meaning of the statute. Godson's reading of the law at that time was that a chemical discovery would only fall under the description of manufacture "when it gives the community some substance, or compound article, new and unused, vendible and beneficial".[81]

Godson is not dogmatic on this point, however, because he considers that there are authorities to show that "a mere process of a chemical discovery is a new manufacture". In this context, he cites Justice Dallas in *Hill v. Thompson* 1818: "a patent for combinations and proportions, producing an effect altogether new, by a mode and process or series of processes, unknown before, or to adopt the language made use of at the bar, it is a patent for a combination of processes altogether new, leading to one end." "From whence it might be inferred that a chemical process may be the subject of a patent."[82] That is a possible inference, but it was not necessarily the reading Dallas intended. Dallas appears to have been quoting what had been argued in the case: "*But it is said*, it is a patent for combinations and proportions...and this being the nature of the alleged discovery, any use made of any of the ingredients singly, or used in partial combination, omitting some and making use of all or some, in proportions essentially different, and yet producing a result equally, if not more beneficial, will constitute no infringement of the patent." Dallas did not specifically deal with the status of chemical discoveries, but he did find against the patentee on the grounds that no infringement had been proved and that the invention was not new.[83]

What Godson makes clear in his 1832 supplement is his belief that the issue of method, principle or process needs to be resolved by legislation: "Some careful enactment is much wanted which should clearly define this rule of law." He then sums up:

"Great care will be required in framing a new act to give a proper definition to the subject of a patent, particularly as to first principles and chemical discoveries.

---

79 *Ibid.*, pp. 82-84, 88.
80 *Ibid.*, pp. 80-81.
81 *Ibid.*, p. 96.
82 *Ibid.*, p. 97.
83 *Hill v. Thompson* 1818, 1 CPC 383-4, 392 [my italics].

There should be a body of law made expressly for the discoveries in chemistry, because the rules which apply to the inventor of a machine do not adapt themselves to the discoverer of a chemical truth.

How far the first discoverer of a principle should be protected in a monopoly of the principle, and not be confined to the means by which he brings it into use, is a question of great difficulty; but it seems to be very dangerous to give a monopoly of the principle."[84]

3.3.2.2   'Manufacture' Defined in Cases

Turning to the case law itself, the case of *Boulton and Watt v. Bull* 1795 is worth examining in some detail. It provides an insight into how the panel of judges who heard this case interpreted the term 'manufacture' and their understanding of previous cases. In *Boulton and Watt v. Bull*, one of the major issues was to determine whether the patent specification described a 'manufacture' as laid down in the Statute. In his specification, Watt had described his invention as a "*method* of lessening the consumption of steam and consequently fuel in fire engines". However, was that a 'manufacture'? The plaintiff's counsel stated that the term manufacture meant "any thing made or produced by art" and it was irrelevant if the invention had been described as a method in the patent and then as an engine in the Act to prolong the patent. The plaintiff's counsel observed that "almost all the patents upon record, that have been granted to those, who have made discoveries or improvements in the mechanic arts, being for the method of doing the thing, and not the thing done". When asked by Heath, J. "Is there any instance of a patent for a mere method?" he pointed out that Dollond's patent was for "an invention of *a new method* of making the object glasses of refracting telescopes". Similarly Hartley's patent was for his *method* of securing buildings from fire. He concluded his opening statement by noting: "So likewise are the numerous patents, that have been granted for the different improvements which have been made of late years in chemistry and medicine." Henry Blackstone, the reporter of this case, added in a footnote that a great variety of patents of this kind were then cited all to the same point.[85]

The defendants argued that there was no new mechanical invention by Watt, but simply a principle and what had been described was the method to apply that principle. The principles were old; they had been applied in Newcomen's steam engine, for it had long been known that steam had an expansive power and was condensed by cold. What was new was the application of those principles. That was not the subject of a patent.[86]

---

84 Godson, *Supplement to A Practical Treatise on the Law of Patents for Invention* (1832), pp. 16, 24.
85 *Boulton and Watt v. Bull* 1795, 2 H. Black 468, fn (a).
86 *Ibid.*, 470-471.

In *Boulton and Watt v. Bull*, Rooke, J. considered that method meant a mode or manner of effecting, so that a new method implied a new mode of construction. He explained that: "patents for a method or art of doing particular things have been so numerous, according to the lists left with us, that method may be considered as a common expression in instruments of this kind. It would therefore be extremely injurious to the interests of patentees, to allow this verbal objection to prevail." He then turned his attention to the meaning of the word 'principle', noting that it may mean either the elementary truths of a science or consequential axioms based on those truths. In this case, Watt had not discovered a new natural principle; his invention was a new mechanical employment of principles already known. Hence the mechanical improvement and not the form of the machine was the object of the patent: "whether the patentee call it a principle, invention, or method, or by whatever other appellation, we are not bound to consider his terms, but the real nature of his improvement, and the description he has given of it, and we may; I think, protect him without violating any rule of law."[87]

Heath, J. considered that the term 'manufacture' covered two classes: the first class machinery and the second substances formed by chemical and other processes. However, the end result must be something vendible, otherwise it could not be a manufacture. Heath: "I approve of the term *manufacture* in the statute, because it gives us to understand the reason of the proviso, that it was introduced for the benefit of trade." The interpretative approach Heath applies here is an historical one; the purpose of the Act at the time the statute was passed is the reasoning that should be applied to determine the meaning of 'manufacture'. For Heath, the aim of the Statute was clearly a commercial one: to improve trade. Therefore, there had to be a vendible machine or substance as the subject of a patent, something that could be bought and sold. Nonetheless, he acknowledged that a patent for a method would not necessarily be void. According to Heath, many patents that used the term *method* were not actually for a method but had been described "using an inaccuracy of expression". On closer analysis, the patent was for a vendible substance. That was the case with respect to Dollond's patent: "A patent for an improvement of a refracting telescope, and a patent for an improved refracting telescope, are in substance the same." A patent must be for a vendible matter, and not for the principle. "The grant of a method is not good, because uncertain, the specification of a method or the application of principle is equally so, for the reasons I have alleged."[88]

Buller, J. was emphatic that principle alone could not be the foundation of a patent. In his judgment, he defines a principle as "the first ground and rule for arts and sciences, or in other words the elements and rudiments of them". Therefore: "The very statement of what a principle is, proves it not to be the ground for a patent. A patent must be for some

---

87   *Ibid.*, 478-479.
88   *Ibid.*, 481-483.

new production from those elements and not for the elements themselves." He then examined whether a principle "reduced into practice" was a suitable subject for a patent. He was of the opinion that a principle reduced into practice could only "mean a practice founded on principle, and that practice is the thing done or made, or in other words the manufacture which is invented". The true foundation of all patents must be the manufacture itself. The same line of reasoning is applied to a method as a subject of a patent: "I think it is impossible to support a patent for a method only, without having carried it into effect and produced some new substance." "When the thing is done or produced, then it becomes the manufacture which is the proper subject of a patent."[89]

Like Heath, Buller considered that mechanical and chemical discoveries could be described as manufactures as long as the patent was for a new article; it did not matter that the items of which they were composed were known before as long as the patent was for the specific compound article produced, not for all the ingredients. As an example of a mechanical invention he cites the fire engine. The first inventor of the fire engine could not have a patent for the method and principle of using iron; the patent must be for the fire engine. Similarly, if the invention is a medicine to prevent fever, the patent could not be for the method and principle of using antimony; it would have to be for the specific compound powder.[90]

Eyre's judgment in this case is always singled out because his line of argument deviated from those of the other three. He advanced a seemingly radical idea of what may be protected by a patent: a method devoid of a physical component. The reasoning behind this premise is teleological: patents for methods were regularly granted and legal protection should not be withheld, particularly not where that invention was of benefit to the public. His reading of the Statute of Monopolies is equitable: a method falls within the meaning of 'manufacture', if not within the word. Eyre is concerned with the spirit of the Statute, how it should be applied to the present, not with what may have been intended at the time the Statute was passed.

In his judgment, Eyre openly acknowledged the paucity of material on patent rights, remarking: "I think we are here upon ground which is yet untrodden." He observed that the words 'any manner of new manufacture' fell very short of the words 'any thing' in the first section:

> "but most certainly the exposition of the statute, as far as usage will expound it, has gone very much beyond the letter. In the case in Salkeld, the words 'new

---

89 *Ibid.*, 485-487.
90 *Ibid.*, 487.

devices' are substituted and used as synonymous with the words 'new manufactures'".[91]

Eyre examined the argument that had been put forward that the term 'manufacture' was open to "extensive signification": 'manufacture' applied not only to things made but also to the practice of making. The category of things made included new compositions of things "such as manufactures in the most ordinary sense of the word" and secondly all mechanical inventions "for a new piece of mechanism is certainly a thing made". With respect to the category 'practice of making' may be classed "all new artificial manners of operating with the hand, or with instruments in common use, new processes in any art, producing effects useful to the public". If this effect is a new substance or composition of things, then the patent should be for this new substance or composition, without regard to the mechanism or process.[92] That made Dollond's case exceptional, as it was for "a method of producing a new object glass, instead of being for the object glass produced". Eyre's approach to Dollond's case, therefore, was not that the reference to 'method' was a verbal inaccuracy, but that, in this particular case, the term 'method' was used as an unnecessary alternative as there was a physical product.

However, "When the effect produced is no substance or composition of things, the patent can only be for the mechanism". The authority given by Eyre for this proposition was Hartley's case. Hartley's invention was to secure buildings from fire. Eyre argued that there was no substance or composition of things as the subject of the patent. It would be hard to maintain that it had been for the plates of iron, as those things were in common use. In Hartley's patent "the invention consisted in the method of disposing those plates, so as to produce their effect, and that effect being a useful and meritorious one, the patent seems to have been very properly granted to him, for his method of securing buildings from fire". The only possible reading of this case was, in Eyre's opinion, that it was a patent for a method, not for a substance and not for an effect, because the effect was "merely negative, though it was meritorious".[93]

Eyre pointed out that Hartley's patent was not the only one he had seen for a method, adding: "we may not shake the foundation upon which these patents stand. Probably I do not overrate it, when I state that two thirds, I believe I might say three fourths of all patents granted since the statute passed, are for *methods* of *operating* and of manufacturing, producing no new substances and employing no new machinery."[94] Eyre was aware of patents for new methods, where "the sole merit and the only effect produced was the saving of time and expense, which lowered the price of the article and therefore introduced it into

91   *Ibid.*, 491-492.
92   *Ibid.*, 492-493.
93   *Ibid.*, 494.
94   *Ibid.*, 494-495.

more general use". "Now I think these methods may be said to be new manufactures, in one of the common acceptations of the word, as we speak of manufactory of glass or any other thing of that kind."[95]

Eyre contended that a method like Hartley's, or a method that was only a cheaper and better way of producing a known substance, rather than producing a new substance, could in itself be the proper subject of a patent. Eyre explains his approach to the status of method as follows:

> "The advantages to the public from improvements of this kind, are beyond all calculation important to a commercial country, and the ingenuity of artists who turn their thoughts to such improvements, is in itself deserving of encouragement; and in my apprehension it is strictly agreeable to the spirit and meaning of the Statute Jac. 1. that it should be encouraged: and yet the validity of these patents, in point of law, must rest upon the same foundation as that of Mr. Hartley's."[96]

Eyre is adamant here that the benefit to society, rather than what he termed a "narrow construction of the word manufacture in this statute", is what is relevant. Watt's engine was a necessity for the working of the mines and, as such, was a necessity for many of the principal manufactures of the country. Coal in large quantities could be difficult to procure and expensive, so that any method which reduced the consumption of coal "will be of great benefit to the public". How could there not be a patent for a method when "intimately connected as it is, with the trade and manufactures of the country?" Eyre's reasoning is strongly teleological, and when Eyre refers to "the spirit and meaning" of the Statute of Monopolies, this is what he considers to be that spirit.[97]

Eyre's interpretation of 'manufacture' is significantly different from that of the other judges. His contention that a patent could be for a method was in direct contradiction to Buller's opinion. As noted above, Buller did not consider that a method, as separate from the new substance it had produced, could be patentable. Rooke and Heath did not seek to invalidate a patent simply because the term 'method' had been used: they were not prepared to adopt a strictly literal interpretation of this word at the cost of the patentee. However, the term 'method' must be reasoned away as a semantic misconception, a mistaken use of language on the part of the patentee. This in itself is striking given the rather one-sided presentation that appears in many accounts of the judicial interpretation of patents during this period: that the slightest inaccuracy would be sufficient to declare a patent void.

---

95 *Ibid.*, 494.
96 *Ibid.*, 494.
97 *Ibid.*, 494-495.

However, these two judges were of the opinion that if the patent truly was for a method, then the patent would be void. A method is not a manufacture. This is where they part company with Eyre. Collier, and later Godson, in their treatises, would also reject Eyre's approach. Godson pays particular attention to Eyre's judgment. He casts doubt upon the legality of Hartley's patent and remarks that it is worth noting that Eyre was the only judge who spoke in favour of its legality. While a patent for a method may be supported, the subject of it must be some material substance.[98]

There is, however, agreement between the judges in *Boulton and Watt v. Bull* with respect to a mere principle. A mere principle cannot be the source of a patent. Yet, Eyre states in his judgment:

> "Undoubtedly there can be no patent for a mere principle, but for a principle so far embodied and connected with corporeal substances, as to be in a *condition to act*; and to *produce effects* in any art, trade, mystery or manual occupation, I think there may be a patent."[99]

Again, this was directly contrary to Buller's opinion. Just as Buller considered there could be no patent for a method only, without it having produced some new substance, he argued there could be no patent for the practical application of a principle. The principle must have been 'reduced into practice'. As noted above, by 'reduced into practice' he understood 'the practice' to be "the thing done or made, or in other words the manufacture which is invented". It was Buller's opinion that was later endorsed by Godson in his treatise: "It is the better opinion that a patent for the application of a principle must be as bad as one for the principle itself."[100]

Hornblower v. Boulton and Watt 1799 once again concerned Watt's invention. The case was brought on a writ of error to the King's Bench from the Court of Common Pleas (see for procedure, paragraph 1.3.2). The point for consideration was whether the patent was for a manufacture or only for mere principles, for which no patent could be granted. In his judgment, Lord Kenyon stated that he was against a too literal interpretation of certain words for, as Lord Hardwick had said on a previous occasion "there is no magic in words". By comparing the patent and manufacture, it appeared to him that what was being claimed as a monopoly was "an engine or machine, composed of material parts, which are to produce the effect described". It fell, therefore, within the meaning of the term 'manufacture'. His understanding of the term 'manufacture' was, as noted, "something made by the hands of man".[101] With this definition of 'manufacture', Kenyon seems to

---

98 Godson, *A Practical Treatise on the Law of Patents for Inventions and of Copyright* (1823), pp. 83, 88.
99 *Boulton and Watt v. Bull* 1795, 2 H. Black 495.
100 Godson, *A Practical Treatise on the Law of Patents for Inventions and of Copyright* (1823), p. 80.
101 *Hornblower v. Boulton and Watt* 1799, 8 T.R. 98-99.

have opted for a very literal meaning of the word 'manufacture': the *manus* and *factura* definition, in other words there must be a thing that had been made by human hands.

Kenyon's judgment in the Hornblower case as reported in the *Term Reports in the Court of King's Bench* by Charles Durnford and Edward Hyde East is short. In that report, Kenyon points out that Watt's patent had been examined earlier in the Court of Common Pleas and that it was out of deference to the opinions given on that former occasion, rather than from any doubt on the subject, that the case was being heard again. However, interesting additional information on Kenyon's judgment is provided by a report of the case which appeared in *The Times* of 26 January 1799.

In *The Times* report, an outline is first given of the arguments advanced by Le Blanc for the plaintiff in error (Hornblower) and Rous for the defendants (Boulton and Watt). Le Blanc argued that the patent had not been given for the engine or any piece of mechanics, but it was only for the principle of doing a certain thing, not for the thing itself. Rous contended that the whole strength of the adversary's case consisted on a play on words, and if the Court were to adopt that reasoning, no patent that had ever been granted could possibly stand. His argument then became rather graphic. Speaking of Watt's invention: "By it a single bushel of coals would raise one foot high thirty millions of pounds weight. It possessed a force more than double the power of gunpowder. Could this operation be performed by a mere abstract idea – by a thing not tangible? If his learned friends were rashly to approach it as they had ignorantly spoken of it, they would be crushed like flies, and no trace of their existence would be left. Could anything incorporeal or which was not tangible, produce such effects?"[102]

It was a speech which seems to have appealed to Lord Kenyon, as in his summing up as reported in *The Times* he had a rather graphic example of his own to quote. Kenyon said that he had never understood the works of some of the modern philosophers who denied the existence of matter. He then referred to the treatise of a Dr. Beattie in which Beattie, in answer to these modern philosophers, had suggested carrying these philosophers to the cliffs of Dover and throwing them over. The doctor thought that by the time they had arrived at the end of their journey, they would very probably be convinced there was such a thing as matter. The reporter noted: "His Lordship said, he understood that reasoning extremely well." If Watt's patent had been a patent for a philosophical principle only, Kenyon thought it could not have been supported, but he had no doubt that this was a manufacture. What is also of interest is that, according to *The Times* reporter, Kenyon did not just say that a manufacture was "something to be made by the hand of man". This part was reported as follows: "His Lordship said that he had not a particle of doubt that this was a patent for a manufacture, for something to be made by the hand of man, made of

---

102 *The Times*, 26 January 1799; p. 3 Issue 4393; col C.

such materials, and to produce such an effect."[103] That a manufacture may produce an effect adds a more sophisticated dimension to the plain, literal definition of manufacture as 'something made by the hands of man'. Nonetheless, it is very clear that for Kenyon a 'manufacture' was a physical thing.

The report by Durnford and East devotes more space to the opinion of Grose, J. than to that of the Lord Chief Justice himself. Grose attempted to deal with a number of concepts in his opinion. Whether the Statute of Monopolies would permit a patent for a 'mere principle' to be classed as a new manufacture, was an issue which he thought he need not consider: "if I can show that this is a patent for a new manufacture, whether a patent for a mere principle be good or not will be immaterial." Despite this, he does, however, comment upon the point: "I am not prepared to say that a patent for a mere principle was intended to be comprehended within those words."[104] He also has an opinion about the patentability of a method. After describing Watt's method for lessening the consumption of steam and fuel, he says: "This method, however, if not effected or accompanied by a manufacture I should hardly consider as within the statute of James." In Watt's case, "I see that by pursuing the method pointed out a manufacture is produced." "Then the intention of the legislature is fulfilled."[105]

Lawrence, J., in reviewing the concepts of 'method' and 'principle' in his opinion in the Hornblower case, considered that the interpretation of these terms need not be unnecessarily narrow. He states: "Method, properly speaking, is only placing several things and performing several operations in the most convenient order: but it may signify a contrivance, or device; so may an engine, and therefore I think it may answer the word 'method'. So 'principle' may mean a mere elementary truth, but it may also mean constituent parts."[106] Such an analysis widens the definition of method and principle to include within the usage of those terms something tangible.

Examining the judgments in the major patent cases during the eighteenth century, the inescapable conclusion is that no definitive interpretation of manufacture had been formed. The majority of the judges trying these cases considered that the term 'manufacture' in the Statute required a physical, vendible product. This did not mean, however, that a patent describing itself as for a method would automatically be held void. As there were no settled legal definitions for method and principle, it had been left to individual judges to determine the usage of these terms. For one judge the word 'method' was simply a means of doing something, for another the term would be understood to include the device so produced or the instruments necessary to carry out the method. All the judges rejected the patentability of a bare principle, but when was a principle a bare principle? Was it a bare

---

103 *Ibid.*
104 *Hornblower v. Boulton and Watt* 1799, 8 T. R. 101.
105 *Ibid.*, 102-103, 105.
106 *Ibid.*, 106.

principle if it had been put to a practical application, or was it not possible to claim the application of the principle but only the tangible thing to which the principle had been applied? None of the judgments in the two major cases dealing with Watt's patent, however, indicates the terminology was being construed narrowly in a way unfavourable to the patentee; what they do indicate is uncertainty. The majority opinion at this time seems to have been that a patent describing itself as for a method would not fail only on this account, but some tangible element had to be the subject matter of the patent. Nor would a patent fail in which the working of a principle was essential, as long as the patent was not for the mere principle or for the application of a principle separate from the thing produced.

The definition of 'manufacture' was a problem that did not seem to have gone away in the nineteenth century. Godson's contention in 1823 that it was not clear "that a mere method of making a thing, or a process, or a manner of operating, cannot be the subject of a patent" is understandable. It was not clear. Eyre's reference to a 'method detached from all physical existence whatever' as the subject of a patent had sown the seeds of legal complication. Could the term 'manufacture' cover a means of doing something? If it could, then new issues arose. Different types of method were being discerned by the judiciary. There were those methods that made the vendible end substance a better product, and those methods that simply produced the same product but in a cheaper and more efficient way. There were methods that used well-known materials but in a hitherto unknown combination in order to achieve a new effect. There were methods in which absolutely nothing was new, but the process was now applied to a substance where nobody had ever thought of applying that process to that substance before. A certain amount of judicial sidestepping appears from the cases. If the patent included a material component, instruments that had been built to put the method into effect, then these instruments could be seen as the manufacture. If the specification was defective, the issue of method did not have to be addressed.

R v. Wheeler 1819 was a *scire facias* action to repeal a patent: the patent was described to be for "a new or improved method of drying and preparing malt". Abbott was not prepared to assert categorically that a method could be the object of a patent. He begins his judgment by defining the word manufacture:

> "the word 'manufactures' has been generally understood to denote either a thing made, which is useful for its own sake, and vendible as such, as a medicine, a stove, a telescope, and many others, or to mean an engine or instrument, or some part of an engine or instrument, to be employed, either in the making of some previously known article, or in some other useful purpose, as a stocking-frame, or a steam engine for raising water from mines."

However, Abbott adds:

> "Or it *may perhaps* extend also to a new process to be carried on by known
> implements, or elements, acting upon known substances, and ultimately pro-
> ducing some other known substance, but producing it in a cheaper or more
> expeditious manner, or of a better and more useful kind."

Abbott then further qualified his statement by adding:

> "Something of a corporeal and substantial nature, something that can be made
> by man from the matters subjected to his art and skill, or at the least some new
> mode of employing practically his art and skill is requisite to satisfy this word
> [manufacture]." [107]

Abbott readily accepted that a patentee could represent himself to be the inventor of a new
method for achieving an object if that object was to be achieved by the use of the patentee's
new engine or instrument. Reflecting on Watt's patent, Abbott considered that Watt's
patent for a new method of lessening the consumption of steam and fuel in engines did
have this element, as Watt's specification described certain parts to be used in the construction of these engines. The problem with Wheeler's patent was that there did not appear
to be any new instruments: "The patentee does not profess to be the inventor of any engine,
instrument, or organ: he says, that a coffee roaster, or a kiln, or any thing by which the
grains may be kept in motion during their exposure to the requisite degree of heat, may
be used."[108] Abbott brings to the fore, and questions, the status of a method several times:

> "*Or supposing* a new process to be the lawful subject of a patent, he may
> represent himself to be the inventor of a new process, in which case it should
> seem, that the word 'method' may be properly used as synonymous with pro-
> cess."[109]

> "Neither has he described any certain or precise process, *which admitting that
> there may be a patent for a process only*, ought unquestionably to be done." [110]

Unfortunately, Abbott did not find it necessary to determine whether a patent for a new
method of drying and preparing malt for the colouring of beer, might be "good as a patent

---

107 *R v. Wheeler* 1819, 106 ER 394-395 (my italics).
108 *Ibid.*, 396.
109 *Ibid.* 395.
110 *Ibid.*, 396 (my italics).

for the manufacture…if followed by a sufficient specification, which it probably might be", because in Wheeler's case the specification was defective.[111] Dutton compares the cases of *Hill v. Thompson* 1817 and *R v. Wheeler* 1819 to demonstrate the judicial confusion at this time. The 1819 case was a step backwards compared with the 1817 case. "In the 1817 case Hill *v.* Thompson, Eldon, L.C, suggested that a patent could be taken out 'even for a new method'. But within two years Abbott, J., could go only so far as to say that the 'word manufacture, *may perhaps* extend to a new process to be carried on by known implements'".[112]

In the early nineteenth century, the matter of whether a method could be the subject of a patent had still not been definitively determined. Abbott's words in *R v. Wheeler* reveal judicial acceptance of a method but his certainty pertains only to a method where the process had included the invention of "an engine, instrument, or organ" through which the process would be carried out. Unlike Eyre, Abbott seems to have been reluctant to make an explicit statement, declaring that the meaning of the term 'manufacture' extended to methods, because many patents were indeed granted for methods. As noted above, Eyre had openly stated that he saw no reason to "shake the foundation upon which these patents stand", particularly given their benefit to trade and manufacture. Abbott's reluctance to take a stand with respect to the status of method in *R v. Wheeler* may have been affected by the fact he had only become Lord Chief Justice in the previous year. Possibly Campbell was right to detect "a want of boldness" in Abbott.[113] Reflecting on the Wheeler case in his testimony before the Select Committee in 1829, Rotch had commented: "The King and Wheeler, attempts to determine what a new manufacture is; the words of his Lordship show how completely he is puzzled to make it mean what patents ought to be granted for at the present day, to meet the times." Rotch concludes: "That little word 'perhaps', sets us all at sea, and nobody can say positively what title to a patent the courts will support or will not."[114]

Whether inventions comprising a new process that acted on old materials could be construed as a manufacture under the terms of the Statute was addressed specifically in *Cornish v. Keene* 1837. In *Cornish v. Keene* the patent was for "an improvement or improvements in the making or manufacturing of elastic goods or fabrics applicable to various useful purposes". The defence had been granted a rule for a new trial having argued that a mere combination of objects known before could not be the subject of a patent. Tindal, C.J., however, had no doubt that the patent was for a manufacture as "it is a vendible article produced by the art and hand of man; and of all the instances that would occur to the mind when inquiring into the meaning of the terms employed in the statute, perhaps

---

111 *Ibid.*, 395-396.

112 Dutton, *The patent system and inventive activity during the industrial revolution 1750-1852* (1984), p. 74.

113 Campbell, *The Lives of the Chief Justices of England* (1874), vol. IV, p. 340.

114 *Select Committee Report 1829*, p. 108.

the very readiest, would be that of some fabric or texture of cloth". Even though the materials were old, the combination was new and the fabric so produced was altogether new. "It is a manufacture at once ingenious and simple."[115] Tindal seems not to have suffered from the doubts which had plagued Abbott in *R v. Wheeler.*

Dutton sees a shift taking place in the 1830s: "By the 1830s, the matter had become clearer. In 1834 James Russel managed to support his patent for a method (process), as did Derosne in the following year for his method of filtering the 'syrup of sugar'. But according to William Hindmarch, the leading patent lawyer of the time, it was not until the 1842 case of *Crane v. Price* that patentees could be said to have been fairly sure of what the courts meant, namely that methods and processes were suitable subjects for a patent."[116] The significance of *Crane v. Price* as a turning point is endorsed by Sherman and Bentley, noting that this case "settled the question as to whether a method or process as distinct from the thing produced could be the valid subject matter of a patent".[117] Although *Crane v. Price* was decided slightly later than the period examined in this study, it cannot be ignored as it brought to the fore arguments that had been advanced during this period.

In *Crane v. Price*, the plaintiff's invention was the application of anthracite or stone coal, combined with hot air blast in the smelting or manufacture of iron from iron stone, mine or ore. The patentee had specifically stated that he did not claim the use of a hot air blast nor the application of anthracite; what he claimed as his invention was the combination of using the hot air blast with the application of anthracite. The combination of the two had not been used before in the manufacture of iron, but the question was whether the combination could be the subject of a patent. Was the plaintiff's invention a manufacture within the intent and meaning of the Statute of Monopolies? The case was heard on several occasions before Tindal, C.J.

Pollock acted as counsel for the patentee in *Crane v. Price*. His submissions are particularly interesting, as the main line of his argument would be adopted by Tindal in his judgment. Pollock pointed out: "From the decided cases upon this subject it is not very easy to discover any general rule or principle by which the courts have been guided."[118] In Pollock's submissions on what constitutes a manufacture, the emphasis is not on the word 'manufacture' but on the word 'invention': "But it is said that the invention is not a manufacture for which a patent can be granted... Nothing is more fallacious than this mode of speaking of an invention; that it is only so and so." Pollock alludes to the number of cases in which the application of a well-known article, in a manner well-known before, in the

115 *Cornish v. Keene* 1837, 132 ER 536-537.
116 Dutton, *The patent system and inventive activity during the industrial revolution 1750-1852* (1984), pp. 74-75.
117 Sherman and Bentley, *The Making of Modern Intellectual Property Law: The British Experience 1760-1911* (1999), p. 108.
118 *Crane v. Price* 1842, 134 ER 246.

manufacture of an article well-known before, had been held to be the subject matter of a patent, and as examples he cites Derosne's patent and Hall's patent.[119]

What is then the 'manufacture'? Pollock: "Suppose the invention a mere process, then any change in the order of the process, or generally in the modus operandi constitutes a new manufacture."[120] Clearly this concept of 'manufacture' is a radical departure from the idea of a manufacture as a physical, vendible object. Examining previous decisions, Pollock concludes: "The uniform tenor of the decisions shows any modification in the manner of making an article of commerce, whereby the price is diminished, or the quality and general utility of the article produced are increased, to be a new manufacture, even though all the substances were known and used."[121]

In delivering the judgment of the court, Tindal stated: "We are of opinion, that if the result produced by such a combination is either a new article, or a better article, or a cheaper article, to the public, than that produced before by the old method, such combination is an invention or a manufacture intended by the statute, and may well become the subject of a patent."[122] He then added that such an assumed state of facts:

> "falls clearly within the principle exemplified by Abbott C.J. [in *The King v. Wheeler*] where he is determining what is and what is not the subject of a patent, namely, it may, perhaps, extend to a new process to be carried on by known implements or elements, acting upon known substances, and ultimately producing some other known substance, but producing it in a cheaper or more expeditious manner, or of a better and more useful kind. And it falls also within the doctrine laid down by Lord Eldon [in *Hill v. Thompson*], that there may be a valid patent for a new combination of materials previously in use for the same purpose, or even for a new method of applying such materials. But the specification must clearly express, that it is in respect of such new combination or application."[123]

Tindal states here that the assumed facts "falls *clearly* within the principle exemplified by Abbott", thereby apparently ignoring the implication of Abbott's use of the word 'perhaps'. Yet, as noted above, the word 'perhaps' was a word that Rotch had found very significant in his testimony before the Select Committee in 1829.

Tindal recognised, like Eyre previously, that patents for methods were regularly granted: "There are numerous instances of patents which have been granted where the invention

---

119 *Crane v. Price* 1842, 1 WPC 400.
120 *Ibid.*, 401.
121 *Ibid.*, 403.
122 *Ibid.*, 409.
123 *Ibid.*, 409.

consisted in no more than the use of things already known, the acting with them in a manner already known, the producing effects already known, but producing those effects so as to be more economically or beneficially enjoyed by the public." As examples of such patents he cited Hall's patent, for applying the flame of gas to singe off excess fibres of lace; Derosne's patent for filtering syrup of sugar through a filter to act with charcoal, where charcoal had been used for filtration purposes before except for the syrup of sugar; Hill's patent where the invention consisted only in the use and application of cinders thrown off by the iron smelting process, which had previously been treated as rubbish but could be used to produce good metal; Daniell's patent for improvements in dressing woollen cloth, where the invention was simply immersing a roll of cloth, manufactured in the usual way, in hot water.[124]

Tindal's acceptance of pure method also seems to be little more than an admission that in practice patents for processes had already been acknowledged by the courts and the issue had therefore been settled *de facto*. Indeed, in *Crane v. Price*, Tindal states that the "only questions" to be considered was whether a better and cheaper article had been produced and whether the combination described in the specification was new in England. In Crane's case, Tindal did not doubt that Crane's patent was for a cheaper and more efficient method; the yield of the furnace was higher and the expense of making iron was less. However, there was also a better end product; the nature, properties and quality of the iron were superior. Tindal's pragmatic approach seems to conform to the uniform tenor to which Pollock had referred. The rationale behind the concept of manufacture had shifted from being restricted to a physical, vendible product to considerations of "benefit and utility", to borrow Pollock's words.[125] It was the triumph of the teleological approach.

With respect to abstract principles, by the 1830s the dominant approach was that a principle could not be the subject of a patent unless it had been 'reduced into practice'. The barring of a bare principle from patentability does not seem to have been controversial. Most of the witnesses heard by the 1829 Select Committee endorsed the exclusion of principles from patent protection. Dutton notes: "Although there existed a strong presumption that principles could not be patented, it was not until the 1830s and 1840s that a principle 'reduced into practice' was generally accepted as a proper subject for a patent."[126] However, where the line was to be drawn between what was a bare principle and what was the application of that principle 'reduced into practice' was not always immediately apparent.

In the case of *Minter v. Wells* 1834, the issue was whether the patent was simply for the principle or a principle reduced into practice. The case concerned a patent for a chair

---

124 *Ibid.*, 409-410.
125 *Ibid.*, 402.
126 Dutton, *The patent system and inventive activity during the industrial revolution 1750-1852* (1984), p. 73.

with self-adjusting leverage. The case report shows a discussion between Godson for the defendants and the judges in the Court of Exchequer as to whether Minter's patent was a patent only for the principle of leverage:

> "Lyndhurst LCB (to Godson): You are using the word "principle" in a loose sense.
>
> Mr. Godson: The word principle certainly has never been very accurately defined, as applied to inventions; but it has never been doubted, that if you take one of the first principles in any science – for instance, the lever in mechanics – you cannot secure it by patent.
>
> LCB: This is a mechanical contrivance.
>
> Godson: Yes, my Lord; it is nothing more than one of the first principles.
>
> Parke B: But that not being applied in combination before, can that not be patented?
>
> Godson: No, my Lord; I apprehend not. If he claim the combination, and then sums up the invention for the principle, and not for that combination....
>
> Parke: It is only for the application of the self-adjusting leverage to a chair. Cannot he patent that?
>
> Godson: If that were so, then the words in which he makes his claim are bad.
>
> Parke: But his patent is the application of a self-adjusting leverage to a chair, which is admitted to be a new combination. Cannot that be the subject of a patent? It is the combination of the two things which he claims as the subject of his patent.
>
> Godson: If your Lordship thinks that that construction can be put upon it, that is another question.
>
> Parke: He claims the combination of the two, no matter in what shape or way you combine them.
>
> Godson: What is the combination?
>
> LCB: Why, the application of the self-adjusting leverage producing the effect, constitutes the machine; and he claims that machine, and the right to make that machine.
>
> Godson: If your Lordship translate this to mean machine, of course I have no further argument to use.
>
> LCB: It is evidently a machine consisting of a self-adjusting leverage producing that particular effect on the chair."[127]

---

127 *Minter v. Wells* 1834, 1 CPC 644.

It was decided that the plaintiff was not claiming a principle. He was claiming the application of self-leverage as manifest in a machine used for a chair and hence it was a 'clothed' principle.

This issue came up once again in the Court of Exchequer before Lord Abinger in the case of *Jupe v. Pratt*, heard in the period 1836-7. The disputed patent in this case had been awarded for a system to expand a table. Pollock, who appeared as counsel in this case, summed up as follows:

> "But although the law says, undoubtedly and correctly enough, that you cannot take out a patent for a principle, that is, for a barren principle, when you have clothed it with a form and given it body and substance, in which the principle may live and produce the benefit which you claim to result from it, why then in many cases (and it is a consolation to every just and honest feeling one has on the subject of invention), although you cannot have a patent for a principle in substance, you can have a patent for the spirit of your invention."[128]

Alderson, B. commented: "you cannot take out a patent for a principle; you may take out a patent for a principle coupled with the mode of carrying the principle into effect, provided you have not only discovered the principle, but invented some mode of carrying it into effect."[129]

Nor was it possible to claim a patent based on a 'double use': the discovery of a new application. Buller had mentioned this point in *Boulton v. Bull* 1795: "whether if a man by science were to devise the means of making a double use of a thing known before, he could have a patent for that, it was rightly and candidly admitted that he could not." Buller gave the example of Dr. James's fever powder. Dr. James could not have sustained a patent for the method and principle of using antimony. If an ingenious doctor would find out that the powder was also a specific cure for consumption, could he have a patent for the sole use of James's powder for consumption? Buller: "I think it must be conceded that such a patent would be void; and yet the use of the medicine would be new, and the effect of it as materially different from what is now known, as life is from death."[130]

Lord Abinger's address to the jury in *Losh v. Hague* 1838 makes this point clear: "The law on the subject is this: that you cannot have a patent for applying a well-known thing which might be applied to 50,000 different purposes, for applying it to an operation which is exactly analogous to what was done before. Suppose a man invents a pair of scissors to cut cloth with, if the scissors were never invented before, he could take out a patent for it.

---

128 *Jupe v. Pratt* 1837, 1 WPC 145.
129 *Ibid.*, 146.
130 *Boulton and Watt v. Bull* 1795, 2 H. Black 486-487.

If another man found he could cut silk with them, why should he take out a patent for that?"[131]

In his footnote to *Losh v. Hague*, Webster sums up as follows: "applications of this nature cannot be said to be 'any manner of new manufacture'; they may be called inventions, in one sense of the term, inasmuch as something may be said to have been found out, some discovery may be said to have been made; but they are not such as can be the subject matter of letters patent." "Cases of this kind are well described by the term 'double use'... there cannot be a patent for a double or new use of a known thing, because such use cannot be said to lead to any manner of new manufacture." Webster is asserting here a distinction between discovery and invention. A discovery is not in itself patentable. Webster does draw attention in his footnote to a large class of cases in which a new use of a known thing was the substance or essence of the invention. However, he considered that in all these cases a new manufacture was the result and therefore the invention could be protected by patent.[132]

What these discussions show is a lack of certainty in the courts regarding exactly what it was the law was protecting as a 'manufacture'. Did the subject matter of a patent have to be something physical? With respect to the patentability of a principle, the answer would appear to be 'yes'. An abstract principle could not be the subject of a patent. It only became patentable if it had been reduced into practice. On the other hand, by the 1830s a number of patents for a way of doing something, the method as distinct from the product, had been given protection by the courts. This protection also extended to cases where no new artefact or substance was being used in the method: the method consisted solely of a new combination of known things to produce a known article only better or more efficiently.

It is argued in chapter 6 that one of the factors affecting the development of a legal definition of manufacture may have been a judge's understanding of patents as a form of property. Formalist judges conceived of property at common law in terms of rights relating to a physical thing. This would imply that a manufacture, being the subject matter of a patent, must have a corporeal dimension. This traditional notion of what was property at common law may have initially stood in the way of a method being a manufacture.

3.3.2.3   'New'

The other element the Statute required, with respect to a manufacture, was that the manufacture be 'new'. There are two aspects to this question: whether an improvement or addition to an existing invention could be classed as a new manufacture and whether novelty was a prerequisite.

---

131 *Losh v. Hague* 1828, 1 WPC 208.
132 *Ibid.*, fn (f).

Tudor case law was distinctly against counting an improvement as a new manufacture. In 1571, Richard Matthew had obtained a patent for knife handles (also referred to as Matthey's patent). However the patent was disputed by the Cutlers' Company, one of its arguments being that it should not be restrained from using a slight improvement on an old industry. The complaint was upheld and the patent was declared void.[133] The seminal case was that of Bircot's patent, which involved a patent for a new method of smelting. It was held in Bircot's case that a mere improvement could not sustain a patent. The case had been reported with approval by Edward Coke in his 'Institutes', published shortly after 1600.[134]

In legal treatises in the earlier part of the eighteenth century, the rule in Bircot's case is presented as good law. The rule is repeated in the 1720s by the Gentleman of the Middle Temple in his *Readings upon Statute Law*: "such a privilege as is consonant in law, must be substantially and essentially newly invented; but if the substance was in *esse* before, and a new addition thereunto, though that addition make the former more profitable, yet it is not a new manufacture in law; and so was it resolved in the Exchequer Chamber, Pasch. 15 Eliz. in Bircot's case, for a privilege concerning the preparing and melting of lead ore; for there it is said, that that was to put but a new button to an old coat: and it is much easier to add than to invent."[135] Richard Wooddeson showed himself to be out of step in his *A Systematical View of the Laws of England*. Although the book appeared in 1792-1793, after the case of *Morris v. Bramson* in 1776, it still states: "But the invention must be substantially new, not an addition or improvement, rendering more profitable or convenient any design before in use."[136] One explanation may be that, as his lectures commenced in 1777, Wooddeson delivered his lecture before being aware of the effect of *Morris v. Bramson*. Unlike Blackstone's *Commentaries*, this work does not appear to have gone through various editions which were updated by editors.

By the time Collier and Godson were writing their treatises on patent law, the old law had clearly been rejected. Collier highlights the importance of Bolton and Watt's patent in this development. Noting that no fewer than thirteen patents had been assigned to improvements of the steam engine, "most of which would probably have been suppressed if the legal discussion on the patent of Boulton and Watt for an improvement on the same invention, had not completely decided the question on the competency and validity of patents for improvements, when those improvements are deemed material and useful".[137]

---

133 Hulme, "The History of the Patent System under the Prerogative and at Common Law: A Sequel" (1900), p. 150.
134 Coke, *Third Institute*, p. 184.
135 Gentleman of the Middle Temple, *Readings upon the Statute Law*, p. 241.
136 Wooddeson, *A systematical View of the Laws of England; as treated of in a Course of Vinerian Lectures, read at Oxford, during a Series of Years, commencing in Michaelmas Term* (1792-1793), p. 396.
137 Collier, *An Essay on Patents for new Inventions* (1803), Appendix p. 50.

Godson explains in his treatise that the doctrine in Bircot's case was overruled by Lord Mansfield in *Morris v. Bramson*, but that the patent must be confined to the addition or improvement. If the grant can be read as extending to the whole, it will be invalid, for the property in the addition or improvement can give no right to the thing that has been improved.[138] Godson sees this rule in terms of public policy: "it is not difficult to conceive that a person might endeavour to monopolize a known article of trade, by a patent for some immaterial alteration or addition to it, on the speculation the public would give him credit for the patent article being superior to the old one." Of interest here is that Godson adds that to prevent such deceit, the new manufacture or subject must be material and useful. "It must of itself be a thing of some consequence in commerce."[139] He then attempts to summarize what falls under the heading of a patentable improvement: in general the substitution of one material for another in making a manufacture is insufficient to support a patent; any particular machine, engine or instrument used in the production of a substance is a new manufacture, but it must possess the same properties as a substance; an addition must be useful; it must be a substantial improvement; it may be a combination or arrangement of things already known if a new effect is produced, which either produces a new article, or makes an old one in a better manner or at a cheaper rate; it could be substances mingled together, or different machines formed into one, or an arrangement of many old combinations, so as to produce an effect which was never before attained although in all instances of this kind of manufacture the ostensible object of the patent must be the new combined matter, and not any part of the old article, materials, ingredients, or machine.[140]

If the case law is examined, *Morris v. Bramson* 1776 appears to have been the turning point, although as a precedent the case is a little curious. At issue here was the infringement of a patent of 1764 for a machine for a set of needles to be applied to a stocking frame for making oylet holes. An action concerning this invention had already been tried previously in *Morris v. Else* 1766, where the verdict had been in favour of the patentee. The invention had been shown to be an improvement on a previous invention. *Morris v. Bramson* forms a curious precedent because there is no official recording of Mansfield's judgment in this case. It would appear that the precedent is based on Mansfield's reaction to a letter from a juror. In citing this case in *Boulton and Watt v. Bull* 1795, Buller, J. reported Mansfield as having said:

"I received a very sensible letter from one of the gentlemen who was upon the jury, on the subject whether on principles of public policy there could be a

---

138 Godson, *A Practical Treatise on the Law of Patents for Inventions and of Copyright* (1823), pp. 71-72.
139 *Ibid.,* p. 67.
140 *Ibid.,* pp. 68-77

patent for an addition only. I paid great attention to it, and mentioned it to all
the judges. If the general point of law, viz that there can be no patent for an
addition, be with the defendant, that is open upon the record and he may move
in arrest of judgment. But that objection would go to repeal almost every patent
that was ever granted."

Buller went on to add:

"Though his lordship did not mention what were the opinions of the judges,
or give any opinion himself, yet we may safely collect that he thought, on great
consideration, the patent was good and the defendant's counsel, although they
had made the objection at the trial, did not afterwards persist in it. Since that
time it has been the generally received opinion in Westminster Hall that a
patent for an addition is good. But then it must be for the addition only, and
not for the old machine too."[141]

In *Boulton and Watt v. Bull*, Buller clearly distanced himself from the approach in Bircot's
case. Taking up the example of a new button on an old coat given in Bircot's case, he states
he does not see the objection; it does not matter if the coat is old if the button were new.
What he then indicates is the danger of relying on antiquated case law:

"But in truth arts and sciences at that period were at so low an ebb, in comparison with that point to which they have been since advanced, and the effect
and utility of improvements so little known, that I do not think that case ought
to preclude the question."[142]

In other words, a black letter approach to the precedent would be an endorsement of an
antiquated law for which there was no justification. It is a line of argument against following
the strict letter of the law that appeared in the opinions of the King's Bench judges in the
case of *Perrin v. Blake* (see chapter 2). With the notable exception of Yates, J., the King's
Bench judges in that case openly rejected the continuation of antiquated rules which no
longer appeared to serve a purpose. Only Yates contended that even if the original reason
for a rule no longer applied, it should still be upheld if parliament had not intervened to
alter the law. On this basis, presumably Yates would have been against the overruling of
Bircot's case if he had still been in King's Bench when *Morris v. Bramson* was heard (Yates

---

141 *Boulton and Watt v. Bull* 1795, 2 H. Black 489.
142 *Ibid.*, 488.

had gone to Common Pleas a few years earlier, possibly because of his dissenting opinions in several significant cases).

Buller openly approved of an improvement or an addition as being the proper subject of a patent. However, this improvement or addition had to have a physical form. Buller had made it very clear that the term 'manufacture' required a substance; his understanding of this statutory term is therefore a literal reading of the word 'manufacture' as a thing made by the hands of man. The example he gives from Bircot's case is indeed such a physical thing: a new button on the old coat. Following this line of reasoning, an improvement to a method would presumably not have been endorsed by Buller because a patent for a method was, in his eyes, void. Yet Buller's approach regarding improvements is essentially pragmatic. He considered that the acceptance of an improvement as a subject of a patent had become the trend, not only by the courts but also by the parties themselves: "In later times, whenever the point has arisen, the inclination of the court has been in favour of the patent for the improvement, and the parties have acquiesced, where the objection might have been brought directly before the court."[143] Buller was prepared to recognise what was in effect already commercial practice. This is perhaps not surprising given that Buller had for years been Lord Mansfield's right-hand man and the man whom Mansfield wished to succeed him. Buller was endorsing what appeared to him to be a sensible state of affairs, one apparently already accepted within the manufacturing industry. His attitude to patents for improvements is in line, therefore, with Mansfield's teleological approach to commercial law. Mansfield had relied on merchant support to develop the commercial law: he had paid attention to the opinions of these merchants and had cultivated the cooperation of the merchant community in London.[144]

An earlier case in which an improvement had been discussed was *R v. Arkwright* 1785, a case in which Buller himself had acted as the presiding judge. Mr. Bearcroft, counsel for the Crown in that case, had explained in some detail to the jury the law relating to improvements. It would seem from his explanation, one that was not queried by Buller, that the only point of issue was not whether improvements could be the subject of a patent but whether the patentee had clearly distinguished between the new invention, being the improvement for which he had a claim, and the old invention, being an invention which he could not claim. A patent which did not make this precise distinction between the improvement and the existing invention would fail. Bearcroft cited the case of *Williams v. Brodie* as an example. In that case it had been acknowledged that William's improvement of inserting a pipe for conveying air into the old stove was "excessively ingenious and perfectly equal to maintain a patent", but because Williams had not distinguished between

---

143 *Ibid.*, 488-489.
144 Lieberman, *The province of legislation determined* (1989), pp. 112-113.

his new addition and the old stove in his patent claim, the judge found against Williams.[145] That the crown could grant a patent for an improvement was also explicitly acknowledged a few years later in *Bramah v. Hardcastle* 1789.[146] In 1795, when *Boulton and Watt v. Bull* was tried, whether an improvement or an addition could be the subject of a patent does not seem to have been at issue. What was at issue was whether there had been a clear distinction made by the patentees between the improvement and the old invention. In the case of Watt's patent, Buller considered that Boulton and Watt were claiming more than just the improvement, and for this reason he decided against them.[147]

In *Boulton and Watt v. Bull*, Eyre, C.J. had also distanced himself from Coke's approach to patents for additions. With respect to Bircot's case: "the principle on which that case was determined has been, as my brother Buller observes, not adhered to."[148] Grose, J. in *Hornblover v. Boulton and Watt* 1799 was even more outspoken in his rejection of the old law concerning additions and improvements. When examining whether a patent could be granted for an addition, Grose stated: "If indeed a patent could not be granted for an addition it would be depriving the public of one of the best benefits of the statute of James. Lord Coke's opinion therefore seems to have been formed without due consideration, and modern experience shows that it is not well founded."[149]

By the end of the eighteenth century, it had become settled law that an improvement could be the subject of a patent. Van Zijl Smit contends that the change of attitude by the courts to improvements reflected a shift in the perceived function of the patent system: from the encouragement of whole new industries to the encouragement of new techniques.[150] Bircot's case had been explicit in its rejection of patents for improvements, but it had been equally explicitly overruled by the latter part of the eighteenth century. This more liberal approach by the courts took place well before the 1830s, the period Dutton sees as heralding a more favourable judicial disposition to patentees. The judicial acceptance that in principle a patent could be granted for improvements would suggest that the teleological style of interpretation had predominated over a black letter approach in this particular respect.

The acceptance of improvements or additions as the subject of a patent was a significant step, but it in turn ushered in a new phase of uncertainty. The legal uncertainty was no longer as to whether an improvement or addition was the valid subject matter of a patent. The uncertainty was in determining whether the patentee was right to claim that the invention was not an improvement but an entirely new invention itself, or whether the

---

145 Arkwright, *The Trial of a Cause instituted by Richard Pepper Arden, Esq* (1785), p. 162.
146 *Bramah v. Hardcastle* 1789, 1 CPC 170.
147 *Boulton and Watt v. Bull* 1795, 2 H. Black 488, 490.
148 *Ibid.*, 491.
149 *Hornblower v. Boulton and Watt* 1799, 8 T.R. 104.
150 Van Zijl Smit, *The Social Creation of a Legal Reality: A Study of the Emergence and Acceptance of the British Patent System as a Legal Instrument for the Control of New Technology* (1981), p. 90.

patentee had made a clear distinction in the patent claim between the improvement he had invented and the old, existing invention. Part of this uncertainty can be ascribed to the need for judges to understand the scientific techniques set out in the specification (see chapter 4).

The treatment of improvements and additions illustrates the push and pull effect of judicial decisions on the development of patent law during this period. Allowing improvements sprang from a teleological approach. It was an acknowledgment of the importance of advances in techniques for the industry of the day; it was a rejection of antiquated law which had been geared up to the working of whole industries rather than specific techniques. Yet whether a patentee would lose the patent protection for the improvement could be determined on how literally a judge was prepared to read the wording of a specification, together with the patent title and recitals. If the judge did come to the decision that the patentee was claiming more than just the improvement or addition, the whole patent was declared invalid. If the patent was bad as to a part, it was deemed bad as to the whole. This was apparently standard law by 1818. In delivering the judgment of the Court of Common Pleas in *Hill v. Thompson* 1818, Dallas, J. stated: "if any part of the alleged discovery, being a material part, fail (the discovery in its entirety forming one entire consideration), the patent is altogether void; and to this point, which is so clear, it is unnecessary to cite cases."[151] In *Hill v. Thompson* although the court accepted that obtaining iron from the cinder and slag that had before been thrown away was new, the patentee also appeared to have claimed the application of lime to iron made from cinders, an application which the evidence indicated had been known before. As one claim was deemed invalid, the patent was wholly void.

This rule was applied, but "not without great reluctance" by Abbott, C.J. in *Brunton v. Hawkes* 1821. In that case, Abbott considered himself to be bound by the precedent laid down in *Hill v. Thompson*: "It appears to me, that the case of *Hill v. Thompson*, which underwent great consideration in Common Pleas, is decisive upon that question.... the Court of Common Pleas held, that admitting there was novelty in the one, yet as there was no novelty in the other, the patent was wholly void."[152] In *Brunton v. Hawkes*, Abbott acknowledged that the plaintiff's mode of making cables and anchors was of benefit to the public, and for that reason he said: "I should wish that he who introduced it might be entitled to sustain the patent." Abbott was clearly unhappy to find himself in the position of having to declare the whole patent void: "I feel myself compelled to say, that I think so much of the plaintiff's invention as respects the anchor is not new; and that the whole patent is, therefore, void."[153]

---

151 *Hill v. Thompson* 1818, 1 WPC 249.
152 *Brunton v. Hawkes* 1820, 106 ER 1037-1038.
153 *Ibid.*, 1037.

A few years later, in *Lewis v. Marling* 1829, it seems that Abbott jumped at the opportunity to ameliorate the harshness of this rule. In the Lewis case, the plaintiff had made a machine for shearing which included a brush and this was part of the machine at the time of the patent. However, before the machine was made for sale, the patentees discovered that the brush was superfluous. The defendants argued that as part of the invention had failed, the brush being of no use, then the patent was void entirely, as stated in *Hill v. Thompson*. Abbott agreed that if the patentee described something in his patent as being an essential part, which turned out not to be essential or even useful, the patent would be void, as this would be misleading the public. That was not the case if the part concerned, which had turned out not to be useful, had not been described in the specification to be essential. He commented: "Several of the cases already decided have borne hardly on patentees, but no case has hitherto gone the length of deciding that such a claim renders a patent void, nor am I disposed to make such a precedent."[154] What Abbott's words reveal in *Brunton v. Hawkes* and *Lewis v. Marling* is his judicial discomfort with the strictures imposed by the concept of a patent as being for an entire, indivisible consideration. In 1835, a piece of legislation was passed which helped patentees in this respect. Under the Act introduced by Lord Brougham it became possible for patentees to amend their specifications and to disclaim any part of the title of the invention or the specification. It was a move explicitly applauded by Baron Parke in *Morgan v. Seaward* 1837: "It is a satisfaction to know that this objection will not necessarily, in the present state of the law, destroy the patent, as the objection is one which will probably be removed by the Attorney-General under the 5 and 6 Will. 4, c. 83."[155]

The second aspect of 'new' manufacture was whether the word 'new' in the Statute required novelty, new in the sense of never having existed before. Hulme argues that to understand 'new' in the sense of 'novel' would be mistaken. The term 'new manufacture' in the Statute is not a demand for novelty, as want of novelty could not be raised as a separate issue apart from prior user. The definition of new in the statute is precise: "which others at the time of making such letters patent and grants shall not use." It is explained by the clause in the letters patent which avoids the grant on proof that the said invention 'is not a new manufacture as to the public use and exercise thereof'. But that does not mean there must be novelty.[156] Hulme: "For all practical purposes therefore it was sufficient for the patentee to prove that the industry had not been carried on within the kingdom within a reasonable limit of time to render his grant unassailable on the score of novelty."[157] A good illustration of the point Hulme was making is the case of *Calthorp's Administrators v. Wayman* 1676, which concerned an engine to saw marble. The court held that it was

---

154 *Lewis v. Marling* 1829, 109 ER 361-362.
155 *Morgan v. Seaward* 1837, 150 ER 881.
156 Hulme, "On the History of Patent Law in the Seventeenth and Eighteenth Centuries" (1902), p. 281.
157 Hulme, "The History of the Patent System under the Prerogative and at Common Law" (1896), p. 153.

not material that the sawing engine had been used beyond the sea (there was evidence it had already been in use for fifty years in Holland) "if it were not here known nor used before".[158]

This understanding of the word 'new' does not appear to have changed significantly throughout this period. The key requirement was whether the invention had been used within the country before the patent was issued, not whether it was an entirely new invention. The first to bring the invention into public use in the realm would have his patent upheld, even if he was not chronologically the first inventor and even if that first inventor was a fellow countryman. This was the rule laid down in Dollond's case, which had deemed Dollond to be the first inventor rather than Dr. Hall. It was reiterated by Bayley in *Lewis v. Marling* 1829, on a motion for a new trial of that case: "it is no objection that someone else has made a similar discovery by his mind, unless it has become public. So if I introduce a discovery, bona fide made, I may have a patent for it."[159] In *Morgan v. Seaward* 1837, Sir F. Pollock, appearing for the plaintiff, maintained that the requisite of novelty in an invention was restricted:

> "Then, all which the statute requires in this respect is, that the grant shall be 'to the first and true inventors of such manufactures which others at the time of the making of the grant did not use.' And all that the letters patent themselves require, is, that the invention shall be new as to the public use and exercise thereof in England or the colonies." [160]

In delivering the judgment of the court in *Morgan v. Seaward*, Parke, B. affirmed Pollock's synopsis of the law. The judge explained that 'new' was to be understood "in the legal sense of that word". That legal sense was "if the invention be not a new invention as to the public use and exercise thereof in England, the patent should be void".[161]

What, however, would constitute 'public use and exercise'? Lord Mansfield had considered the matter of novelty in *Liardet v. Johnson* 1778. The case was heard twice by Lord Mansfield. According to contemporary accounts (neither of the two trials of this case was reported in a series of reports), Mansfield looked at two aspects: the law of prior user and the law of prior publication. The earlier case of *Calthorp's Administrators v. Wayman* 1676, as noted above, had indeed mentioned two criteria: that the invention should not be 'known' or 'used' in England before. It would appear, therefore, that actual use was not the only determining factor. In the Liardet case, a number of dictionaries, which had been published

158 *Calthorp's Administrators v. Wayman* 1676, 84 ER 966-967.
159 *Lewis v. Marling* 1829, 1 WPC 496.
160 *Morgan v. Seaward* 1837, 150 ER 877.
161 *Ibid.*, 879.

prior to the patent, were brought in evidence by the defendant in an attempt to show that the composition of the stucco used by Liardet was known before.

With respect to prior use, Mansfield summed up as follows:

> "It is not a man's having made an attempt; it is not a man's having suggested an idea; it is not a man's having it in a closet; it is not a man's hitting upon it by accident and not pursuing it farther, knowing he has hit upon a good composition, but it must be something in the trade that is followed and pursued. It is not an invention that a man may have made use of in an instance or two, and dropped it, and never claimed it after, that will prevent another inventor (without any privity of knowledge of those materials) if he really hits upon those materials and makes a composition of service to artists."[162]

Elements set out in this opinion would be taken up in later cases. As Mansfield had indicated, earlier attempts at the invention, if they remained at the level of experiments, would not invalidate a later patent for prior use. In *Jones v. Pearce* 1832, Patterson, J. told the jury that if they thought Mr. Strutt's carriage wheel, based on the suspension principle, was only an experiment, and the plaintiff had come afterwards and remedied the defects with his own invention, there was no reason to say that Jones' patent was not good.[163] In *Macintosh v. Everington* 1836, it was pointed out by the Attorney-General, John Campbell who was acting on behalf of the plaintiff, that: "Many of the most important inventions by which the manufactures of this country have been so greatly improved have been but one step beyond what has been done for ages, and many have been but one stage beyond fruitless experiments which have been made and abandoned."[164] The jury was satisfied that Macintosh's process to make waterproof fabrics had not been known in the country before and found for the plaintiff.

In *Morgan v. Seaward* 1837, the meaning of the term 'public use' was discussed at some length. In this case, the construction of the paddle wheels had only been disclosed to connected persons intending to take a share of the patent. Parke, B.: "A disclosure of the nature of the invention to such a person, under such circumstances, must surely be deemed private and confidential." It would not be possible "To hold this to be what is usually called a publication of the invention in England." The case would be quite different if the patentee had constructed machines for sale, and sold them to any one of the public who would buy the invention, before his patent because then the invention would not be new at the date of the patent. "This was laid down in the case of *Wood v. Zimmer*, and appears to be

---

162 Hulme, "On the History of Patent Law in the Seventeenth and Eighteenth Centuries" (1902), p. 286.
163 *Jones v. Pearce* 1832, 1 WPC 124.
164 *Macintosh v. Everington* 1836, 2 CPC 190.

founded on reason: for if the inventor could sell his invention, keeping the secret to himself, and, when it was likely to be discovered by another, take out a patent, he might have, practically, a monopoly for a much longer period than fourteen years."[165] Prior publication required that there must have been some use or exercise of it in England in a sense that could be called "public".

Remarking upon this issue, Alderson, B. said: "It is certainly a most important question, what are the limits of what a man may do without its being a publication, and a question on which much remains to be discovered: the law is in a very confused state." Alderson referred to two cases: those of Dr. Brewster and of Dollond. If the whole issue revolved around public *use* of the invention, Alderson asked, why had Dr. Brewster lost the benefit of his invention of the kaleidoscope when it had only been previously published in a book? It had not been used, although it had been made known to all the world. In the Dollond case, Dollond was deemed to be the first inventor as he had been the first one to bring the object glasses into public use. Alderson: "If Dr. Hall had published his discoveries in a book, I apprehend that would have put an end to Dollond's patent, although Dr. Hall had never made an object glass in his life."[166] Alderson's observation was a reminder that, despite the apparent focus on public use in determining whether an invention was a new manufacture, public use was not the only criterion; the invention must also not have been known in England.

When would the law consider that an invention had been made known? Alderson indicated that the simple fact of publishing a description of the invention would be sufficient, without that invention having ever been used. Alderson concluded that the courts had failed to bring clarity to the question of 'public use': "Much obscurity has been introduced into this question by the use of loose expressions and dicta."[167] It would seem that by the late 1830s, the issue of what exactly constituted prior use, or prior publication, was still to be resolved.

3.3.3   *'Contrary to the Law, nor Mischievous to the State, by Raising Prices of Commodities at Home, or Hurt of Trade, or Generally Inconvenient'*

The Statute of Monopolies granted the patentee of a new manufacture a monopoly for fourteen years. However, the awarding of trading monopolies was still a contentious issue in the eighteenth century. Under the Tudors and Stuarts, the word 'monopoly' had become associated with corrupt and unjust practices; the earlier abuse of monopolies had linked the word to a form of protection which appeared to benefit a few individuals at the expense

---

165 *Morgan v. Seaward* 1837, 150 ER 880.
166 *Ibid.*, 878.
167 *Ibid.*

of the country at large. The wider issue of monopolies, and how a lingering negative connotation may have affected the attitude of some judges with respect to monopolies for
patents for invention, is examined in chapter 5.

The Statute of Monopolies set down the conditions under which a patent grant could
be revoked. As well as specifying the particular abuses of 'raising prices of commodities
at home, or hurt of trade' as grounds for revocation, the Statute included the more wide-
sweeping criterion of 'or generally inconvenient' as a ground for declaring the monopoly
grant void. A clause stating that a patent could be revoked for 'inconveniency' appeared
in the terms of a patent grant of 1575. The clause gradually came into regular use in the
crown's letters patent. It conferred the power on the crown or the Privy Council to revoke
a grant of patent on proof that it was 'inconvenient'; it was a power that the Privy Council
did not hesitate to use.[168] The Statute of Monopolies simply adopted this language in its
proviso concerning patents for inventions.

The term 'generally inconvenient' must have posed problems for those judges in the
eighteenth and early nineteenth century who supported a formalist approach to adjudication. Such a wide term as 'inconvenient' made a literal interpretation problematic. Indeed,
this was recognised by Buller in *R v. Arkwright*: "if it is open to inconvenience, it is open
to every reason you can suggest" (see below). Furthermore, an analysis of the case law after
the Statute of Monopolies indicates that what was, or was not, deemed inconvenient shifted.
By the latter part of the eighteenth century the interpretation of the term "generally
inconvenient" was clearly not tied to what the legislature might have considered to fall
under the heading of 'inconvenient' in 1623.

In the eighteenth and early nineteenth century, the formal judicial vindication for a
patent being set aside as "generally inconvenient" was that it was not considered to be in
the best interests of the public. The judges' opinions were explicit that the monopoly
awarded by a patent was in return for a benefit to the country. A few examples of such
statements in the eighteenth and early nineteenth century will suffice: Buller, J. in *Turner
v. Winter* 1787: "The consideration, which the patentee gives for his monopoly, is *the
benefit which the public are to derive* from his invention after his patent is expired.";[169] Lord
Ellenborough in *Huddart v. Grimshaw* 1803: "this is a species of property highly important,
as it respects the interests of the individual, and with him also *the interests of the public*.";[170]
Abbott, C.J. in *R v. Wheeler* 1819: the inventor "represents to the crown, that he has invented
this or that thing, and that he is the first and sole inventor thereof, etc; and the crown
yielding to his representation, and willing to give encouragement to all arts and inventions

---

168 Seaborne Davies, "The Early History of the Patent Specification" (1934), pp. 102-103.
169 *Turner v. Winter* 1787, 1 T.R. 604.
170 *Huddart v. Grimshaw* 1803, 1 WPC 86.

that may be *for the public good*, grants to the patentee the sole liberty and privilege of using his said invention, for a certain term, under the conditions before noticed".[171]

If the benefit to the realm, the public good, was being put forward by the courts as the consideration for the patent grant, it is hard to see how judges could ignore considerations of public policy in their determinations. In the pre-modern English patent system, the patent system was one of registration rather than of examination. The validity of a patent only became an issue if there was a dispute between interested parties. The courts then in effect determined whether the patent was void, either by deciding in favour of the infringer in a private action or for the crown in a *scire facias* proceeding to repeal the patent grant. As the public good had been declared to be a factor in determining the validity of a patent, it had to be taken into account.

Lord Loughborough famously announced that public policy should not play a role in a private law action between individuals. In *Arkwright v. Nightingale* 1785, he stated:

> "but nothing could be more essentially mischievous than that questions of property between A and B should ever be permitted to be decided upon considerations of public convenience or expediency. The only question that can be agitated here is, which of the two parties in law or justice ought to recover?"[172]

However, even if a patent had survived a private action, a patent could still be revoked on a writ of *scire facias*. The public interest was then acknowledged as a factor. When the matter of Arkwright's second patent was heard again later that same year, this time as a *scire facias* proceeding to repeal the patent, Buller acknowledged the importance of the public interest:

> "The decision of this cause, it is admitted, is of very great importance to the public upon the one hand, and to the individual who has the patent upon the other. The value is likewise stated to be very extensive; and besides, there have been two different decisions upon the question. It was for these reasons I chose to give the cause a much fuller and more patient hearing, than I should have thought either necessary or proper, if it had been merely an action for damages between two individuals."[173]

The proviso of the Statute of Monopolies itself made public policy an issue that had to be taken into consideration by the courts: public policy could not be separated from a condition

---

171 *R v. Wheeler* 1819, 106 ER 394.
172 *Arkwright v. Nightingale* 1785, 1 WPC 61.
173 Arkwright, *The Trial of a Cause instituted by Richard Pepper Arden, Esq* (1785), p. 172.

requiring that the patents granted should not be detrimental to the State, by raising prices of commodities at home, or be harmful to trade, or 'generally inconvenient'. What changed was the interpretation of 'generally inconvenient' by the courts: what the courts had deemed to be 'inconvenient' in Coke's day was no longer deemed to be inconvenient by the early nineteenth century. This is seen, for instance, in the change of attitude by the courts towards labour-saving machinery.

3.3.3.1   Mechanisation

The two criteria, that a patent should not harm trade or be generally inconvenient, seem to have been read in the seventeenth century as a statutory enactment of existing common law. Hulme notes that in the sixteenth century, the sole test of the monopoly contrary to the law, as defined by Coke, was that the grant should not seek to restrain the public of any freedom or liberty that they had had before, or hinder them in their lawful trade.[174] If the public was not thus to be restrained, in effect what was required was the introduction of a new trade or industry. A monopoly could be granted for a "new trade into the realm" that was "for the good of the realm". These conditions for a monopoly grant appeared in counsel's submission in the case of *Darcy v. Allin* 1602.[175] Monopolies that would restrain a man from carrying out his lawful trade, which in turn could mean that man's unemployment, had not been condoned by the common law courts. It was a line of reasoning that had appeared in several cases at the beginning of the seventeenth century, such as *Claygate v. Batchelor* 1610.[176] It was the thrust of the Clothmakers of Ipswich case 1614, as reported by Coke: no man could be prohibited from working in any lawful trade.

Coke was adamant that taking away a man's trade was tantamount to taking away a man's life. It was odious. It followed, therefore, that any invention that would "turn so many labouring men to idleness" was 'inconvenient'. To illustrate the point, he described a new invention that would thicken bonnets and caps in one day in the time it would normally take fourscore men. The court had ordered that the caps should be thickened by manual labour and not by the new method.[177] Greater efficiency in an old industry was apparently not a major consideration, and most certainly not where that efficiency would conflict with one of the other significant aims of the patent system under Elizabeth and James I: to increase employment. Hulme sees the case of Lee's application for the stocking frame, which is said to have been rejected on the ground that the machine would supersede manual labour, as evidence that before 1623 the inventor's rights were at first regarded as

---

174 Hulme, "The History of the Patent System under the Prerogative and at Common Law" (1896), p. 153.
175 *Darcy v. Allin* 1602, Noy 182 (74 ER 1139).
176 Dent, "Patent Policy in Early Modern England: Jobs, Trade and Regulation" (2006), pp. 82-83.
177 Coke, *Third Institute*, pp. 181, 183-184.

of doubtful validity if it seemed that the invention would prejudicially affect an existing industry.[178] Laying off men was seen as prejudicial.

The social desirability of mechanisation was still a moot point in the latter part of the eighteenth century. After having attempted to hold up mechanisation by smashing the machinery in 1767 and 1779, cotton spinners and others had petitioned parliament in 1780 against "an evil of great magnitude ... the introduction of patent machines and engines of various descriptions". The cotton spinners did not deny that the machines were more efficient, but argued that their use would cause unemployment and that the lower quality of machine produced goods would have a negative effect upon British trade.[179] The legal categorization of labour-saving devices as 'generally inconvenient' survived into the eighteenth century. In his *Readings upon the Statute Law*, which appeared in the 1720s, the Gentleman of the Middle Temple repeated Coke's example of the bonnets and caps as good law.[180] However, by the time Wooddeson delivered his Vinerian lectures at Oxford in the 1770s, it would seem that the courts had adopted a different attitude:

> "it has been maintained, on the principle of its not being generally inconvenient, that the inventor of an engine to do as much work in a day as might employ many labouring hands, is not entitled to accept a patent by this statute. Because to deprive industrious manufacturers of their ordinary means of subsistence was considered as a general inconvenience. This notion however seems now exploded, because the cheapness of useful commodities on the one hand countervails the supposed inconvenience on the other."[181]

The issue of labour-saving devices as "generally inconvenient" was brought to the fore by Bearcroft, as counsel for the crown in *R v. Arkwright* 1785. He presented it as being the most serious of all the objections to Arkwright's patent because it was "prejudicial and inconvenient to the public in general", affecting not just the parties themselves. His reasoning was that the grant of the patent would lead to the loss of the manufacture in the country because it would cause unemployment in England. He estimated that if Arkwright's patent was deemed good "you will rob upwards of 30,000 people of their manual labour in this business, and of the means of their supporting themselves by their industry". Being deprived of the "industrious exercise of this business in this country", the labourers would be driven away and would take their skills with them to a foreign country.[182]

---

178 Hulme, "The History of the Patent System under the Prerogative and at Common Law" (1896), p. 152.
179 Van Zijl Smit, *The Social Creation of a Legal Reality: A Study of the Emergence and Acceptance of the British Patent System as a Legal Instrument for the Control of New Technology* (1981), p. 94.
180 Gentlemen of the Middle Temple, *Readings upon the Statute Law* (1723-1725), p. 241.
181 Wooddeson, *A systematical View of the Laws of England* (1792-1793), p. 396.
182 Arkwright, *The Trial of a Cause instituted by Richard Pepper Arden, Esq* (1785), pp. 21-22.

The issue of inconvenience, however, was not tried in *R v. Arkwright*, as it was ruled out by Buller, J. The reason for the submission being struck out was a procedural one: no facts had been brought to the fore by the prosecution prior to the hearing in order to prove general inconvenience. Buller held firm against the contention, put forward by the team of prosecution counsel representing the crown, that it was self-evident that the unemployment caused by such labour-saving machinery was 'generally inconvenient'. Mr. Lee argued for the crown that stating the facts was not necessary as: "I conceive it may be fairly assumed, there is no one thing of equal importance, in any country, to the employing of the inhabitants that compose it." An invention that did not require human hands, that would thus deprive men, women and children of sustenance, "I should conceive such a thing, upon proof, would be directly a public inconvenience, and destructive of the happiness of mankind. And yet it would not be necessary to show that was the nature of it, but only to state that". Mr. Erskine objected that no more was required than to repeat the words of the Statute of Monopolies itself. The crown did not have the power to grant a patent that was prejudicial and inconvenient to the king's subjects in general: "Here then the statute says, no patent shall be enforced which is inconvenient to the subjects; and we aver, that is the case." Their arguments were dismissed by Buller on the following ground:

"Where the act of parliament states particular facts, and makes certain acts a crime, there it is sufficient to state it in the words of the act; but here no act at all is stated, no notice is given upon what ground you mean to go; if it is open to inconvenience, it is open to every reason you can suggest; and the party is not prepared to bring an answer to it, he has no opportunity of answering…Therefore they should state those facts that they think prove the general inconvenience, and it will be for the jury to decide upon the truth or falsehood of those facts; it once established by the jury such facts existed, then it would be a question of law, whether this was an inconvenience." [183]

Saving labour was apparently not accepted by Buller as synonymous with 'inconvenience', and hence requiring no further facts to be put into evidence. That labour-saving machinery could in fact lead to greater employment had been alleged in a former case brought by Arkwright to defend his patent. In 1782, Arkwright had brought an action against Mordaunt. A pamphlet had been produced setting out Arkwright's reasons for applying to parliament for an extension of his patent at the time of that former trial. This pamphlet was cited in *R v. Arkwright* at the end of the prosecution case, primarily as evidence that Arkwright had purposely not made his specification clear (for further detail see chapter 4). However, several other interesting points arose from this pamphlet. Arkwright had

---

183 *Ibid.*, pp. 31-33.

acknowledged that the introduction of his machinery had reduced labour, but "though the price of labour, by the introduction of these inventions, has greatly decreased, yet the business has increased in a most extraordinary degree" and that employment, rather than unemployment, had been the result: "he has established a business that already employs upwards of five thousand persons, and a capital, on the whole, of not less than £200,000 a business of the utmost importance and benefit to this kingdom."[184] The point was taken up by the defence counsel, Adair, even though inconvenience was not an issue to be tried. Presumably, he considered that the matter might have had an impact on the jury even though inconvenience could not be submitted as a ground for revocation by the prosecution. Adair pointed out that:

> "the cotton manufactory was, in fact, increased to a great degree since Mr. Arkwright discovered these new inventions in this manufacture. Another thing, which I should have mentioned first, is, to appeal to your knowledge, whether the number of hands employed have not increased; whether the quality of the manufacture is not become manifestly better in every particular; and whether the price of it, notwithstanding the existence of Mr. Arkwright's patent, is not lessened: if all those effects had been produced to you, it would be in vain, if my learned friend was permitted to go on upon such general allegation as that, it would be in vain to prove to you, the continuance of that patent is ruinous to the public, the commencement of which was of such advantage to the man-ufactories; but that the continuance of a patent which is a partial monopoly to a particular purpose, may produce some inconveniencies to those engaged in the same branch of manufacture, is a proposition impossible to be denied; but that is an inconvenience which the law has recognized, and which they must submit to, if the party is entitled to the protection of the law."[185]

By the end of the eighteenth century, a swing was taking place. From 1660 to 1750, the promise to create employment had remained a common consideration by applicants for patents. MacLeod notes that the balance between creating employment and saving labour, in the patentees' consideration, began to shift perceptibly in the mid-eighteenth century. She suggests that the more relaxed attitude to labour-saving machinery discernable in the latter part of the eighteenth century was probably because the population pressure had eased and markets had widened. In the 1790s, forty-seven patentees actually cited their inventions as labour-saving (although that still represented only 7% of all patents). The new interest in labour-saving inventions was probably connected to labour shortages, as

---

184 *Ibid.*, pp. 100, 102.
185 *Ibid.*, pp. 105-106.

the rapidly expanding cotton, iron and coal industries in the 1790s intensified the demand for labour.[186]

By the latter part of the eighteenth century, more efficient machinery and methods in existing industries were not, therefore, considered by the courts to be necessarily pernicious to public welfare. If more could be produced at a lower price, not only could members of the public buy commodities more cheaply, but also larger scale production at a competitive price was good for trade, which in turn was good for employment. In the two major cases concerning Watt's patent for his fuel saving steam engine, no objection had been made by the defendants that the engine was mischievous to the state, hurtful to trade or generally inconvenient. Having observed this had not been contended, Grose, J., in the Hornblower case 1799, commented: "On the contrary every man's experience, as far as report goes, tells him that the invention has infinite merit, is for very many purposes highly beneficial to the public, and is in great request."[187]

As noted above, in his opinion in *Boulton and Watt v. Bull* 1795, Eyre had openly supported patents for new methods, where the only effect produced was the saving of time and expense. One of the reasons for his support was because these methods "lowered the price of the article and therefore introduced it into more general use" and "The advantages to the public from improvements of this kind, are beyond all calculation important to a commercial country". When Watt's patent was tried before King's Bench in 1799 in the action brought by Hornblower in error from Common Pleas, Lord Kenyon did, however, voice his reservations about patents. That reservation was framed in terms of public policy: the effect that a patent, as a monopoly, had upon working people. Having confessed that he was "not one of those who greatly favour patents", he acknowledged that in many instances the public received benefit from them but "striking the balance upon this subject, I think great oppression is practised on inferior mechanics by those who are more opulent".[188] His concern echoes that of a previous age: monopolies should not hinder a man from carrying out his lawful trade (see chapter 5).

However a shift in the attitude of the courts with respect to labour-saving machinery was discernable. It was confirmed by Collier, writing at the very beginning of the nineteenth century. He states that the construction of what was deemed to be mischievous to trade had altered in the courts: "it has been discovered that the preservation and improvement of the trade of this country has, in an eminent degree, depended upon the application of machinery to save human labour, and the principal objects to which patents have been directed, are for this express purpose."[189] In the early nineteenth century, increased efficiency in manufacturing processes had become a criterion in assessing the validity of a patent. It

---

186 MacLeod, *Inventing the Industrial Revolution: the patent system, 1660-1800* (1988), pp. 160-162, 168.
187 *Hornblower v. Boulton and Watt* 1799, 8 T.R. 100-101.
188 *Ibid.*, 98.
189 Collier, *An Essay on Patents for new Inventions* (1803), pp. 38-39.

was a factor that was affecting the legal definition of the term 'manufacture' in the Statute. As noted above in *Hill v. Thompson* 1817 and *R v. Wheeler* 1819, the importance of new processes that produced a known substance in a cheaper or more efficient way, or produced a better product, was acknowledged by the judges in these cases. When *Crane v. Price* was heard in 1842, efficiency was a major criterion in favour of the validity of a patent. The issue in that case was simply whether the invention, which was the subject of the patent grant, meant the product could "be more economically or beneficially enjoyed by the public".[190] Increased efficiency had become a significant factor in assessing the benefit to the realm from a patent grant. A patent promoting greater efficiency either through better methods or through labour-saving mechanisation (even in an existing industry) would no longer be deemed "generally inconvenient". Once again a line of judicial reasoning which took into account the perceived needs of the day had moulded the law.

3.3.3.2   Utility

The Statute of Monopolies itself does not refer to any requirement of utility. The argument that a patent should be for a useful invention was essentially based on Coke's commentary upon the Statute. Lord Coke stated that, at common law, in order to support a monopoly there must be '*urgens necessitas et evidens utilitas*'.[191] Lack of utility, as a potential ground to have a patent set aside, was argued in terms of it being 'inconvenient' and 'mischievous'. There should not be a patent for something that was not useful. The early case of *Edgeberry v. Stephens* 1691 had said that "the act intended to encourage new devices *useful* to the kingdom". Specific reference to the requirement of usefulness was made by judges throughout the eighteenth and early nineteenth century, among others, by Eyre in *Boulton v. Bull*, Buller in *R v. Arkwright*, Ellenborough in *Huddart v. Grimshaw*, Eldon and Dallas in *Hill v. Thompson*.[192]

It is interesting to note that the defence counsel in *R v. Arkwright* 1785, sergeant Adair, had in passing dismissed the criterion of usefulness as a legal requirement. His comments would seem to imply that the question of usefulness could be left to the market, rather than the law. In words reminiscent of Adam Smith's (see chapter 5) Adair said: "the reward is proportioned exactly to the ingenuity: if his invention is worth nothing, he will derive no profit to his family; if ingenious and valuable to the public, he will derive an adequate profit during the time, and the public would receive the benefit in reversion."[193] The courts, however, did take usefulness into account in determining the validity of a patent throughout the period under consideration.

---

190 *Crane v. Price* 1842, 134 ER 248.
191 Coke, *Third Institute*, p. 184.
192 Summed up in *Morgan v. Seaward* 1837, 150 ER 876.
193 Arkwright, *The Trial of a Cause instituted by Richard Pepper Arden, Esq* (1785), p. 106.

In the case of *Manton v. Parker* 1814, the conclusion that the invention was pointless was instrumental in declaring that the patent was void. It concerned the infringement of a patent for a 'new invented hammer for the locks of fowling pieces'. The invention was to let air out of the gun barrel while ramming down the wad. The plaintiff was nonsuited, Thompson, C.B. declaring: "It seems to me…. that the utility of this invention and the purpose of this patent wholly fail."[194] In the following year, *Manton v. Manton* was heard in the Court of Common Pleas. Gibbs, C.J. observed that it was necessary to show that an invention "is not only new but that it is useful to the public".[195] He reiterated this point in *Bovill v. Moore* 1816: "In point of law it is necessary that the plaintiff should prove that this is a new and useful invention."[196] In *Hill v. Thompson* 1817, Lord Eldon stated that the invention must be novel and useful, and that the utility of the discovery was a matter for the jury to decide.[197] Apparently, usefulness was generally accepted in the courts as a proper legal criterion, even if there was no specific reference to utility in the Statute of Monopolies. That makes the statement by Parke, J. in *Lewis v. Marling* 1829 of particular interest.

In *Lewis v. Marling*, the invention included a brush which, at a later stage of development, became superfluous. It had been argued by the defendant that as part of the invention was not useful, the whole patent failed. That argument was dismissed by Tenterden because the part of the machine that had turned out not to be useful was not essential, and the plaintiff had not claimed that part of the machine to be essential in the patent description. In *Lewis v. Marling*, Parke, J. stated that the proper criterion for determining the validity of the patent was not usefulness but whether the invention was new: "there is no case deciding, that a patent is on that ground void, although cases have gone the length of deciding, that if a patent be granted for three things, and one of them is not new, it fails in toto." Reviewing the Statute of Monopolies, he comments: "The condition, therefore, is, that the thing shall be new, not that it shall be useful; and although the question of its utility has been sometimes left to a jury, I think the condition imposed by the statute has been complied with, when it has been proved to be new."[198]

Lewis v. Marling was heard in King's Bench. However, when the issue of usefulness was brought up for discussion in *Morgan v. Seaward* in the Court of Exchequer in 1837, Parke (now a Baron of the Exchequer Court) seems to have at least partly retracted this statement. It should be pointed out that *Morgan v. Seaward* was not decided upon the matter of utility. As noted above, Morgan's patent had been for two inventions, one connected to the steam engine and the other to paddle wheels. The patent suggested that these

194 *Manton v. Parker* 1814, 1 CPC 278.
195 *Manton v. Manton* 1815, 1 CPC 287.
196 *Bovill v. Moore* 1816, 1 CPC 338.
197 *Hill v. Thompson* 1817, 1 WPC 237.
198 *Lewis v. Marling* 1829, 109 ER 361-362.

two inventions were improvements. Evidence indicated that one of them was not an improvement; the steam engine was deemed useless. Following the precedent laid down by *Hill v. Thompson*, even though the invention with respect to the paddle wheels would have sustained a patent, as part of the patent was bad, that meant the whole patent was void.

Given, therefore, that the issue in *Morgan v. Seaward* was whether one of the inventions covered by the patent was an improvement, Parke, B. considered that it was not necessary to deal with the question of whether the utility of each part of an invention was essential to the patent, if that utility was not suggested as a ground for the patent grant. In other words, it was not necessary to consider the effect of finding part of the invention not useful. Nonetheless, in his judgment in this case, Parke did comment upon the concept of usefulness. He states:

> "A grant of a monopoly for an invention which is altogether useless, may well be considered as 'mischievous to the state, to the hurt of trade or generally inconvenient', within the meaning of the statute of Jac. 1, which requires, as a condition of the grant, that it should not be so, for no addition or improvement of such an invention could be made by anyone during the continuance of the monopoly, without obliging the person making use of it to purchase the useless invention; and on a review of the cases, it may be doubted whether the question of utility is any thing more than a compendious mode, introduced in comparatively modern times, of deciding the question, whether the patent be void under the statute of monopolies."

Parke then added:

> "And we do not mean to intimate any doubt as to the validity of a patent for an entire machine or subject which is, taken altogether, useful, though a part or parts may be useless, always supposing that such patent contains no false suggestion."[199]

This latter statement is consistent with the finding for the patentee in *Lewis v. Marling*: only part of the invention was deemed useless, and no suggestion had been given in the description of the patent that the redundant part was essential. In *Manton v. Parker*, the lack of utility had defeated the patent but in that case the whole purpose for which the patent had been taken out was shown to be useless, not just an inessential part.

---

199 *Morgan v. Seaward* 1837, 1 WPC 197.

However, it would appear that a shift had taken place in Parke's opinion since *Lewis v. Marling*. In *Morgan v. Seaward*, Parke seems to accept that usefulness was a criterion under the Statute of Monopolies itself in order to determine whether a patent was mischievous to the state, hurtful to trade or inconvenient. In *Lewis v. Marling*, he had pointed out that the Statute imposed no such condition of utility, and what was relevant was whether the invention was new, not whether it was useful.

Pollock, counsel for the plaintiff in *Morgan v. Seaward*, was quick to point out Parke's former statement in *Lewis v. Marling*, that the condition under the Statute of Monopolies was whether the thing was new, not whether it was useful. He argued that there was a good reason why the Statute did not in fact impose any condition as to utility: "Whether a thing be new or not is a pure question of fact; but whether it be useful or not, with reference to previously existing things of the same kind, is a question of opinion, and a question admitting of all possible shades and degrees of difference."[200] Pollock certainly had a point. The utility of an invention was not necessarily clear-cut. As will be seen in the following chapter, even scientists called as expert witnesses did not always agree upon the utility of an invention or parts of an invention. Much would depend upon a judge's own personal assessment as to whether an invention was useful or not, or whether a part of an invention was useful, and if that part were not useful, whether it had been described in the specification as an essential part. Despite these difficulties, the general tendency of the courts throughout this period seems to have been to take utility into account and a finding of lack of utility was a ground for judges to set aside a patent as mischievous to the state or inconvenient.

3.4   SUMMARY

When judges analysed the terminology of the Statute of Monopolies, their approach would be affected by their personal style of interpretation. Those with a teleological style would tend to adopt a more pragmatic attitude towards the interpretation of the terms in the Statute. If the purpose of the Statute was to promote trade and commerce, as long as an invention was useful, it was beneficial to the public and good for commerce, why should the inventor not enjoy legal protection? Other judges did not endorse this approach. They looked to interpret the Statute of Monopolies within its historical context and preferred a more literal interpretation of the Statute's wording.

With the exception of the term "true and first inventor", which throughout this period referred either to a creative inventor or the importer of an invention, the concepts underlying the phrases in the Statute did not remain static and their meaning would shift. There was a certain "pull and push" effect: a 'push' in the development of the meaning of a term

---

200 *Morgan v. Seaward* 1837, 150 ER 878.

often followed by a 'pull' to place restrictive boundaries around that development. The 'push' would often come from judges whose interpretation of the law was teleological, as these judges sought to bring the law in line with what they considered to be the demands of a more modern society. The 'pull' would come from judges who preferred a formalist approach to the law and would be an attempt to pull the interpretation back to one closer to a more literal interpretation of the Statute or existing case law.

This process can be seen with respect to whether a method was a 'new manufacture' according to the Statute of Monopolies. A teleological interpretation of the term 'new manufacture' could enable a judge to accept a pure method as an appropriate subject of patent protection, as a 'manufacture'. However, some judges considered that the term 'new manufacture' should be understood in its historical context; what would parliament have considered to be a manufacture in 1624 at the time the Statute of Monopolies came into force. Those judges who preferred a more formalist interpretation of the law would seek to 'pull' the legal definition of 'manufacture' back to a more literal understanding of the Statute. These judges were reticent to divest the term 'manufacture' of some corporeal element: if a manufacture was to be understood as a thing made by the hands of man, then some form of 'thing' was required as the subject matter of the patent. As techniques increasing became the subject matter of inventions, and hence of patents, there was a growing tendency on the part of the judiciary to accept the validity of patents that had been granted for methods. Differences in interpretation led to a period of legal uncertainty as to the status of method. This uncertainty was sometimes openly acknowledged by judges, or avoided by reaching a decision on a different basis. *Crane v. Price* in 1842 is generally acknowledged as the case which finally decided that a method separate from the product made could be the subject of a patent.

The tension between pragmatism and a black-letter approach can be illustrated by looking at the 'new' aspect of the term 'new manufacture'. A similar pattern can be seen with respect to the legal status of improvements. The case of *Morris v. Bramson* 1776, heard by Lord Mansfield, in effect ended the prohibition on improvements and additions as the subjects of patents. Mansfield was apparently concerned with the spirit, the purpose of the Statute, and would not be deterred by antiquated case law which had barred improvements from being patentable. He was not the only judge who considered Bircot's case (1572) to be outdated or find Coke's opinion on the matter to be misguided and backward. *Morris v. Bramson* in practice initiated a new phase in patent law; it widened the ambit of patent law to protect a class of techniques, improvements and additions that would not previously have enjoyed legal protection. Yet once this major pragmatic step had been taken to allow an improvement to be the subject of a patent, legal provisos were quickly found to hedge in this new development. The push forward in the form of the acceptance of the patentability of improvements was followed by a formalistic response to the description of the improvement. Although an inventor could patent an improvement, the wording describing that improvement had to be precise to distinguish the improvement from the original invention. Using a formalistic approach, a judge could cite any imprecision in that delineation as a ground to invalidate the patent in its entirety.

The interpretation of "generally inconvenient", as a ground to revoke a patent, was one that was hard to separate from considerations of public policy. The understanding of this term by the judiciary did undoubtedly shift as the English economy gradually moved towards greater industrialisation. Patents which had as their subject matter methods or machinery that would increase efficiency were increasingly commonplace in the latter part of the eighteenth/early nineteenth century. Labour-saving machinery, in Coke's time rejected by the courts as a proper subject of a patent for reasons of public welfare, was no longer a ground for the courts to invalidate a patent. An important criterion was whether the invention was efficient and, taken as a whole, useful.

What emerges from this judicial struggle to give meaning to the Statute of Monopolies is not a story of unremitting 'hostility' by the courts towards patentees in the pre-1830s period. Words were not always interpreted strictly against the patentee: even by the end of the eighteenth century, the courts would not invalidate a patent simply because the term 'method' had been used. The 1830s did not mark an abrupt shift in attitude. The purposeful, teleological, approach had always coexisted with the formalist, literal approach: the judges who 'pushed' rather than 'pulled' had always been there and in certain respects their interpretation would have become clearly dominant by the 1830s.

4 Patent Law: The Interpretation of the Patent Specification from the 1750s to the 1830s

The second element of patent law dealt with by the courts during this period was the patent specification. Unless the petition applying for the patent grant was contested, the law officers required no further disclosure of the invention than what had been vouchsafed in the application by the petitioner. It was only after the grant of patent had been made that the patentee was obliged to enrol a specification, within a certain period of time, describing his invention. What was described in the specification had to correspond with the title and recitals of the patent grant. The adequacy of the specification only became an issue if the patent was disputed and its sufficiency was then determined by the court. During the period under consideration in this study, a shift took place in the way in which the courts would interpret the specification.

4.1 The Introduction of the Patent Specification

It is generally accepted that the patent specification first appeared as a regular feature of patent practice in the early part of the eighteenth century. Prior to the early eighteenth century, the crown did not require a specification, or indeed any other form of written disclosure, to support its letters patent. This did not mean, however, that no obligations were imposed upon the patentee in return for the privilege of the monopoly grant.

An important goal of Tudor and Stuart policy was to bring in new trades and manufactures to the realm. What the crown demanded in return for the privilege of a patent grant was the patentee's promise to introduce and put the manufacture into working. This was the consideration for the grant of a monopoly in the early patent system and it required personal effort and supervision on the part of the patentee. Statements made by those petitioning for a patent grant indicate that candidate patentees expected that working the manufacture would be a condition of the grant. The applicant promised to introduce and bring into practice an industry which would prove beneficial to the country. Further evidence for this form of consideration is provided by the clauses inserted by the crown in the letters patent. A common clause was to give the patentee a time limit within which the invention had to be up and running. The same effect could be achieved by the so-called apprenticeship clause, which stipulated that the patentee must teach his 'art and science' to Englishmen. These time and apprenticeship clauses in the letters patent later became obsolete, probably because preference was given to a clause revoking a grant for 'inconveniency', a term which would cover the failure to introduce the industry within a reasonable time. The conclusion is that it was not the disclosure of the invention that was important in this earlier period, but the undertaking to work the grant which constituted the essential consideration.[1] This requirement of personal effort and supervision is reflected in the Statute of Monopolies. According to Coke's commentary on the Statute, in his *Third Institute*, the period of fourteen years was chosen for the duration of the monopoly because it was thought that it would enable the patentees to train two complete batches of apprentices, at seven years per apprenticeship.[2]

Hulme sees Sturtevant's patent of 1611, accompanied as it was by a description of the invention in the form of a 'treatise of Metallica', as introducing the patent specification, although the specification was not revived until nearly a century later with Nasmith's patent.[3] Davies disputes the prominence given by Hulme to Sturtevant's treatise in the history of the specification. He agrees with Hyde Price that to use the title of 'the first specification' for the 'treatise of Metallica' would be disproportionate. Its contents do not reveal the exact nature of the inventions and disclosure is not its real object. The treatise is better seen as a prospectus, for Sturtevant was above all things an advertiser who was promoting his own wares.[4] Whether Sturtevant's patent can be seen as enrolling the first specification depends upon what the function of the specification is deemed to be at that time. Sturtevant's specification could be consistent with the function ascribed to it in the early period by Hulme: as a means to protect the patentee rather than as a means of instruction (see below). Yet even on Hulme's reading of the origins of the specification, it is still rather strange that if Sturtevant's patent did introduce the specification, there should be so few instances of it before Nasmith filed a written description a hundred years later.

Nasmith's patent of 1711 required the enrolling of a specification. The attention given to Nasmith's patent at the time would seem to indicate that this requirement marked a new departure in patent practice. Not only are there extraordinary references to the grant in the State Papers, but also the patent is set out at length in the Warrant Book.[5] Nonetheless, it has been argued that Nasmith's patent was not a sudden and startling development. The practice had arisen fairly early of either expanding the recitals in the patent to identify the nature of the invention and technique of making it, or of requiring the publication of the description expanding the recital.[6] Hulme sees these recitals as undoubtedly the precursors of the modern patent specification, but he considers that they

---

1 Hulme, "On the Consideration of the Patent Grant Past and Present" (1897), pp. 313-315 and Seaborne Davies, "The Early History of the Patent Specification" (1934), pp. 99-100.
2 Coke, *Third Institute*, p. 184.
3 Hulme, "On the Consideration of the Patent Grant Past and Present" (1897), p. 315.
4 Seaborne Davies, "The Early History of the Patent Specification" (1934), pp. 266-267.
5 *Ibid.*, p. 89.
6 Getz, "History of the Patentee's Obligations in Great Britain", (1964), pp. 78-79.

formed no part of the consideration of the grant.[7] However, disclosure did take the place of practice at some point in the eighteenth century, although when that point was has been the subject of academic controversy.

Hulme traces the requirement of compulsory disclosure back to 1716, but acknowledges that the uniform insistence upon the acceptance of this condition did not become part and parcel of patent practice until a much later date, which he considers to be about 1740.[8] Nasmith's patent did not signify the beginning of a consistent policy requiring the enrolment of a specification. Davies points out that although a patent grant of 1723 definitely stated that the patent would be void unless a specification were enrolled, the practice of including this provision does not seem to have become customary until about 1734.[9] The adoption of a condition requiring the enrolment of a specification appears to have been piecemeal.

4.1.1   Why Did the Doctrine of Patent Specification Arise in the Early Eighteenth Century?

There are no definitive answers as to why the doctrine of patent specification arose in the early eighteenth century, but there are certain indicators. As noted in the previous chapter, Van Zijl Smit points out that the subject matter of patents had started to change in the early eighteenth century: rather than being granted for the encouragement of whole new industries, they increasingly concerned new techniques. Inventions had become more technical. The search for technical solutions to specific problems meant that the subjects for which patents were required became more narrowly circumscribed and accurate definitions of the patent became more important.[10] Along the same lines, Adams and Averley argue that filing plans must have become increasingly necessary because many inventions were improvements to existing manufactures, rather than entirely new manufactures. In the industrial climate of the eighteenth century, Coke's prohibition on improvements was untenable. The removal of the prohibition on improvements, as the subject matter of a patent, was accepted by the courts in the wake of *Morris v. Bramson* 1776, but Adams and Averley point out that the actual practice seems to have significantly anticipated an actual decision to this effect.[11] MacLeod considers that the specification was introduced to make discrimination between superficially similar inventions easier.[12]

---

7   Hulme, "On the Consideration of the Patent Grant Past and Present" (1897), p. 317.

8   Hulme, "On the History of Patent Law in the Seventeenth and Eighteenth Centuries" (1902), p. 283.

9   Seaborne Davies, "The Early History of Patent Specification" (1934), pp. 89-90.

10   Van Zijl Smit, *The Social Creation of a Legal Reality: A Study of the Emergence and Acceptance of the British Patent System as a Legal Instrument for the Control of New Technology* (1981), p. 90.

11   Adams and Averley, "The Patent Specification: The Role of Liardet v Johnson" (1986), p. 161.

12   MacLeod, *Inventing the Industrial Revolution: the English patent system, 1660-1800* (1988), p. 51.

Getz suggests that at least part of the explanation for the move to the specification might be found in the economic condition of England at the time the change took place. The economic problems confronting the Tudors and Stuarts were different. What was now required was not the establishment of skills formerly absent, but the diffusion of skills amongst a wider community.

> "Greater scientific and technical knowledge and a higher level of culture had rendered the old techniques of instruction in new methods either obsolete or inefficient. A more rapid and wide-spread diffusion of skills could clearly be more efficiently achieved by publishing full details of the invention than by requiring the patentee to employ a specified number of Englishmen in working it."[13]

4.1.2   Who Was behind the Instigation of the Specification?

Given this shift from introducing whole industries to introducing items of technology, in whose interest was a system requiring the filing of a patent specification? Historians have put forward various theories to explain why the crown substituted the obligation on the patentee to practice the industry for one demanding a formal, written disclosure of the invention. There are historians who argue that the specification came into existence because the patentees wanted it; it was a means of making the patent grant more secure. Others argue that the filing of a specification was neither suggested by the patentees nor in their interest. The specification was imposed upon reluctant patentees by the crown as a means of securing the secrets of the invention for the public after the termination of the monopoly.

Hulme argues that the institution of the specification arose at the suggestion and for the benefit of the patentee. When Sturtevant applied in 1611 for the exclusive right to use certain inventions, he had handed in a treatise with his application, the 'treatise of Metallica'. At the end of the 'treatise of Metallica', Sturtevant gave his reasons why he had appended the treatise: that it would be clear that the inventions were new and his own, and that they were different from other men's inventions. This concern for the security of the invention and the fear of piracy reoccurs in Nasmith's patent. In the patent roll, it states that Nasmith does not think it safe to mention in what the new invention consists until he has obtained the letters patent, but thereafter he will put it in writing and enrol it in the Court of Chancery. Hulme sees this concern as the reason behind the revival of the specification.[14]

As noted above, Davies is sceptical of Hulme's theory that Sturtevant's patent introduced the specification. He does, however, consider that Hulme's deduction that the practice of

---

13 Getz, "History of the Pantentee's Obligations in Great Britain" (1964), p. 81.
14 Hulme, "On the Consideration of the Patent Grant Past and Present" (1897), pp. 315-317.

enrolling a specification arose at the suggestion and for the benefit of the grantee to make the grant more certain is a tenable hypothesis. He puts forward several arguments which he considers strengthen Hulme's assertion. Why, if the crown rather than the patentee had insisted upon a specification, is it only in a patent grant of 1723 that there is a definite statement that the non-enrolment of a specification would void the grant? Furthermore, that rule does not appear to have been enforced for many years after 1723. There is also a letter in the State Papers addressed to the secretary of state, written a year before Nasmith's petition, raising the matter of the dangers of piracy to which inventors were exposed before the patent grant was made.[15]

Noting Davies' endorsement of Hulme's view, MacLeod's response to the question 'Why was specification introduced' is: "It was certainly not for the purpose of disseminating inventions by disclosure." She considers it more likely, however, given the wording of specification clauses in numerous patents and law officers' reports, that it was introduced at the government's initiative. Although there was no system of examination, there had been disputed applications for patents, which had required investigation by the law officers, and the specification offered a mechanism for knowing exactly what had been patented. When the Attorney-General, Philip Yorke, replied to a patentee in 1731, granting him an extension of time in which to file his specification, Yorke remarked: "in regard his enrolment of the said description of his machine was intended only for his benefit, by securing to him with greater certainty his said invention." Specification could save the patentees trouble later if their title was challenged or their patent infringed. "Specification offered a mechanism whereby the system could be self-policing and the law officers be spared much tedious investigation."[16]

The contention that the specification came into existence at the behest of, and for the benefit of the patentee, is firmly rejected by Adams and Averley. In their opinion, the best support for Hulme's argument is the wording of Nasmith's patent, but as Davies had already pointed out, it is dangerous to place too much emphasis on the exact language of historical documents. While there appears to be no direct evidence as to the origins of the practice, they consider that there are two facts which both Hulme and Davies overlooked. One is that there is a time stipulated in the proviso for the filing of the specification, and that time varies from patent to patent throughout the century, and the second is that the filing of drawings and plans of mechanical inventions becomes increasingly common from about 1741.[17]

Adams and Averley suggest that a time limit to enrol the specification was required from the outset. They consider that the variations in times stipulated in different patents

---

15 Seaborne Davies, "The Early History of Patent Specification" (1934), pp. 90, 92.
16 MacLeod, *Inventing the Industrial Revolution: the English patent system, 1660-1800* (1988), pp. 51-53.
17 Adams and Averley, "The Patent Specification: The Role of Liardet v Johnson" (1986), p. 159.

for filing a specification, ranging from one month to six, is evidence against the introduction of the specification being initiated by the patentees. If the patentees had initiated the move, a uniform time would have been fixed.[18] However, they do not explain why a uniform time would have been more favourable to the patentees. A mandatory, fixed time limit could, after all, be considerably less favourable to patentees than a more flexible time limit, a time limit adapted to a particular situation and found to be reasonable by both parties. Indeed, Adams and Averley remark that the variable times look like a bargain was struck between the crown and the patentees.[19] They then pose what they consider to be the more important question: why would the patentees have wished to impose a time limit at all?[20] Without historical evidence, any answer to that question would have to be speculation. However, if there were no time limit, the whole system of specification would fail. The failure of a specification system would not be in the interests of a patentee if a specification were seen as an evidential document, enabling a patentee to prove an invention was his own and to protect it against piracy. It was in the patentee's interest to make sure the specification was in place within a reasonable time after the patent grant had been issued.

Was the enrolment of a specification in the interests of the patentees? Pointing to the vagueness of the specifications enrolled throughout the eighteenth century, specifications that in no way could have enabled those skilled in the art to carry out the invention, Adams and Averley conclude that "enrolment was always a requirement imposed upon persons often reluctant to disclose their inventions". Why would these specifications be vague and evasive if patentees were trying to make their patent grants more certain?[21] The answer to that is: it depends what kind of certainty the patentees were looking for. The vagueness of specifications is not proof that the enrolment of a specification was imposed upon patentees rather than endorsed by them or that the existence of even a rudimentary specification was not in the interests of the patentee. Adams and Averley are presuming that if it had been the patentee who had instituted the enrolment of a specification, the patentee would only consider his patent to be safe if the specification was sufficiently clear to enable another to make the invention. An examination of early specifications has shown that there was no settled notion as to what the specification should include. A large number of these early specifications are mere outlines of the inventions from which no one could learn the technical details.[22] The format of the specification had yet to be developed. Furthermore, this early lack of sufficient technical detail to enable another to make the invention does not discount the theory that the specification arose at the patentee's suggestion and for his benefit. It makes sense if the aim of the patentees in instituting the specification was

---

18 *Ibid.*
19 *Ibid.*
20 *Ibid.*
21 *Ibid*, pp. 160-161.
22 Seaborne Davies, "The Early History of Patent Specification" (1934), p. 90.

not first and foremost to hand on their knowledge but to protect their own interests by only providing sufficient pointers to identify their invention.

From what can be gleaned from Sturtevant's patent and Nasmith's patent, it appears that patentees were anxious to secure their own position. Some form of registered, written documentation which could be instrumental in proving that the invention was his and not that of another would be advantageous if the patentee needed to defend his patent against piracy. What was important to the patentee was to write down his invention in such a way that the invention was protected as the patentee's own creation while limiting the information which would enable another to steal that invention. Drafting the specification in this way would persist well into the eighteenth century. One high-profile example will serve to illustrate the point. When Watt's first patent was granted in 1769, he was given four months to file a specification. Finding the drafting of the specification difficult, he took the advice of his friend, Dr. Small, which was as follows: "as to your principles we think they should be enunciated (to use a hard word) as generally as possible, to secure you as effectually against piracy as the nature of your invention will allow."[23] This was the benefit of the specification from the patentee's perspective: 'to secure you as effectually against piracy as the nature of your invention will allow'.

The second objection made by Adams and Averley is that the filing of drawings and plans of mechanical inventions becomes increasingly common from about 1741. They consider this to be consistent with the view that the function of the specification to instruct the public long preceded the case of *Liardet v. Johnson* 1778 (see below).[24] That the filing of drawings or plans becomes common from the 1740s, does not indicate that instructing the public was the aim of the specification from the outset. It could be argued that filing drawings was an initiative of the patentee, a natural progression if his aim was to make his patent grant more secure. As Adams and Averley point out, when patents were being increasingly granted for improvements to existing manufactures, it became necessary for patentees to give more detail to distinguish their own invention from what existed before.[25] There is no evidence to indicate that the crown imposed the requirement of filing drawings or plans upon patentees. It is interesting to note in this context what Rooke, J. said in *Boulton & Watt v. Bull* 1795:

> "if they [the jury] can understand it without a model, I am not aware of any rule of law which requires a model or a drawing to be set forth, or which makes void an intelligible specification of a mechanical improvement, merely because no drawing or model is annexed."[26]

---

23 Davenport, *James Watt and the Patent System* (1989), p. 14.
24 Adams and Averley, "The Patent Specification: The Role of Liardet v Johnson" (1986), p. 161.
25 *Ibid.*
26 *Boulton & Watt v. Bull* 1795, 2 H. Black 480.

The origins of the patent specification need not be formulated in terms of antagonistic interests. The specification could have initially developed as a cooperative endeavour, as both patentees and the crown could see a form of written disclosure as being in their own best interests. The patentees wished to secure their invention from piracy. An enrolled document with sufficient detail to make the invention identifiable as their own would be useful. The time limit in which this specification was to be filed was flexible, and therefore probably subject to negotiation between the parties. The crown supported the enrolment of a specification possibly because the law officers saw it as a more effective way of distinguishing between inventions, and hence a saving of their time, but also because it was a way of ensuring that the benefit of innovative techniques would not be lost to the public at the end of the period of monopoly. That aspect was reflected in the early patent recitals; that the working and practice of the invention was "to secure the memory of this invention" and "to make certain that the knowledge of it should remain known to our people".[27] In passing, Adams and Averley do actually mention the advantages of the specification for both parties. They admit that: "No doubt enrolment could be helpful to inventors themselves in assisting them in asserting their patent rights against infringers and the idea of some form of enrolment may have gained currency among them." They also point to the interest of the law officers in requiring enrolment where they saw fit because they had become dissatisfied with the dissemination of information about inventions.[28] The importance of preserving the knowledge of the invention after the patent had expired does not necessarily imply that once the filing of a specification became more common the law officers would have seen the specification as a replacement for the earlier form of consideration: working the invention and training apprentices in the art. There is no strong evidence to indicate that in the period before the common law courts took over from the Privy Council either the patentees or the law officers saw the specification as fully replacing the older obligation.

The function of the specification would not be tested in the courts until later in the century. Only a few patent disputes were heard in the early eighteenth century and when the common law courts took over after the mid-eighteenth century there was little in the way of precedent. In the latter part of the eighteenth century it became very clear that the common law courts considered the function of the specification to be to teach others to make the patented invention at the expiration of the monopoly period. As this accords with the crown's interest of information dissemination, the approach adopted by the courts could be read as evidence that the specification originated at the initiative of the crown. However, how the courts would interpret the purpose of the specification in the latter part of the eighteenth century cannot be taken as evidence as to the origins of the specification

---

27   Seaborne Davies, "The Early History of Patent Specification" (1934), p. 99, quoting recitals in patents to Synerston (1573) and the New Art Society (1575).
28   Adams and Averley, "The Patent Specification: The Role of Liardet v Johnson" (1986), p. 160.

in the early years of the eighteenth century. The introduction of a specification need not be read in terms of a conflict. The interests of both parties were not identical, but both had reasons to support the implementation of the specification. There is no reason to suppose that in its pre-modern form the specification was necessarily an imposition forced upon reluctant patentees by the crown.

4.2   THE INTERPRETATION OF THE PATENT SPECIFICATION BY THE JUDGES

From the mid-eighteenth century onwards, the forum for patent disputes became the common law courts. The attitude of the common law courts towards the specification changed over the period examined in this study. In the very early years of the jurisdiction of the common law courts in patent disputes, the specification may not have been quite the determining factor it later became. In the latter part of the eighteenth century, the insufficiency of the specification would be the most frequently cited ground to determine that a patent was invalid. As was seen in chapter 3, there were judges who advocated a literal reading of the Statute of Monopolies and those who adopted a more purposeful approach. Similarly, with respect to the interpretation of the specification, there were different schools of thought within the judiciary. There were judges who considered that it was the task of the court to subject the specification to a strict, literal interpretation. There were others who considered that the specification was sufficient if it had effectively communicated the instructions to make the invention, regardless of possible minor defects. It is this latter approach, rather than the strict literal approach, which would become predominant in the 1830s.

4.2.1   The Function of the Specification

In *R v. Arkwright* 1785, Buller, J. explained the function of the specification to the jury as follows:

> "Upon this point it is clearly settled as law, that a man, to entitle himself to the benefit of a patent for a monopoly, must disclose his secret, and specify his invention in such a way, that others may be taught by it to do the thing for which the patent is granted; for the end and meaning of the specification is, to teach the public, after the term for which the patent is granted, what the art is; and it must put the public in possession of the secret in as ample and beneficial

a way as the patentee himself uses it. This I take to be clear law, as far as it respect the specification."[29]

Buller had apparently no doubt in 1785 that the function of the specification was to teach the public, and that this was not a new principle of law but was at this time already settled law. This reading of the purpose of the specification made its way into legal literature in his general treatise, *An Introduction to Law relative to Trials at nisi prius*:

> "Whether the specification is sufficient to enable others to make it up. The meaning of the specification is, that others may be taught to do the thing for which the patent is granted; and if the specification is false, the patent is void; for the meaning of the specification is, that after the term the public shall have the benefit of the discovery."[30]

Yet had the common law courts always considered that instructing the public was the function of the specification?

As noted above, Hulme argued that the instruction of the public was not the original function of the specification at all. The practice of enrolling a specification was put forward by the patentees to make their patents more certain; it was only later that a change in the function of the specification took place. Hulme pinpointed a specific moment when the older doctrine of working the manufacture and personal instruction finally gave way to the new doctrine of written disclosure. He argued that the turning point in this process was the landmark case of *Liardet v. Johnson* 1778, heard by Lord Mansfield. *The Morning Post*, which reported upon the hearing of the case in February 1778, quoted Lord Mansfield as follows:

> "The third point is whether the specification is such as instructs others to make it. For the condition of giving encouragement is this: that you must specify upon record your invention in such a way as shall teach an artist, when your term is out, to make it – and to make it as well as you by your directions; for then at the end of the term, the public have the benefit of it."[31]

This was evidence, according to Hulme, that "the doctrine of the instruction of the public by means of the personal efforts and supervision of the grantee was definitely and finally laid aside in favour of the novel theory that this function belongs to the patent specification".

---

29 Arkwright, *The Trial of a Cause instituted by Richard Pepper Arden, Esq* (1785), p. 172.
30 Francis Buller, *An Introduction to the Law relative to Trials at nisi prius*, (fifth ed.) London 1790, p. 76.
31 Hulme, "On the History of Patent Law in the Seventeenth and Eighteenth Centuries" (1902), p. 285.

More specifically, it was the case of *Liardet v. Johnson* that "invested the patent specification with a character and function totally distinct from that with which it had been originally introduced". Hulme described it as an "irony of fate" that the specification now became the means of instructing the public rather than an instrument to make the patent grant more certain for patentees.[32]

The significance assigned to the case of *Liardet v. Johnson* by Hulme seems to have been later generally accepted. In his *A History of English Law*, Holdsworth considered that it was the common law courts which were responsible for the new view that the consideration for the patent grant was the written disclosure of the invention contained in the specification. Following Hulme, Holdsworth maintained that it was Lord Mansfield in the case of Liardet who laid down that the consideration for the patent was not undertaking to instruct by working the invention, but the disclosure of the invention in the specification.[33] This theory has made its way into more modern works such as those of Van Zijl Smit and Dutton.[34]

However, this reading of the role of *Liardet v. Johnson* has been challenged by Adams and Averley. Assuming that the enrolment of a specification was required of patentees from the outset, that would suggest that the function of the specification had always been the dissemination to the public of information about the invention. Therefore, the doctrine that the function of the specification was to instruct the public long preceded *Liardet v. Johnson*: the older doctrine of instruction by personal efforts and supervision had simply fallen into disuse and was not explicitly abolished in *Liardet v. Johnson* or in any other known case. Furthermore, if the case were so significant why has it been virtually ignored?[35]

Had the older doctrine of working the manufacture and instruction by personal efforts and supervision long fallen into disuse? As the incorporation of a provision requiring the filing of a specification seems to have developed in a piecemeal manner, the obligation to work the invention would not have been immediately and entirely abandoned directly after Nasmith's patent. Indeed, the fact that the requirement to file a specification did not become commonplace until some twenty or more years after Nasmith's patent would seem to indicate a transitional phase during which the obligation to work the invention was only gradually giving way to the duty to disclose in a written form.

Even though the enrolling of a specification appears to have become commonplace before the mid-eighteenth century, this does not necessarily mean that in practice personal supervision had now given way to disclosure. In 1750 there were probably 102 patents in

---

32 Hulme, "On the Consideration of the Patent Grant Past and Present" (1897), pp. 317-318.
33 Holdsworth, *A History of English Law* (1964), vol. XI, pp. 427-428.
34 Van Zijl Smit, *The Social Creation of a Legal Reality: A Study of the Emergence and Acceptance of the British Patent System as a Legal Instrument for the Control of New Technology* (1981), pp. 90-91; Dutton, *The patent system and inventive activity during the industrial revolution 1750-1852* (1984), p. 75.
35 Adams and Averley, "The Patent Specification: The Role of Liardet v Johnson" (1986), pp. 158, 161-162.

force. That number rose gradually and by the time *Liardet v. Johnson* was heard in 1778, there were 384.[36] As the figures indicate, patents were not widespread and whole areas of commerce were still unaffected by patents in the mid-eighteenth century. As MacLeod points out, governments had resisted patents that might interfere with the supply of necessities and the guilds had opposed the issuing of patents that might interfere with the livelihood of established craftsmen. It was only after the mid-eighteenth century, when the guilds loosened their notoriously tight reins that individuals in industries like instrument making turned to patent protection.[37]

Handing down the secrets of an invention by means of personal instruction to apprentices must still have been common well into the eighteenth century. The older way may have persisted even in industries where patents were more common. On the other hand, if the obligation on patentees to work the manufacture and supervise the instruction of others had become out of step with commercial life, then it would be in keeping with Mansfield's decision-making to recognise that factor in his judgment. As Fifoot noted, Mansfield would not allow an antiquated dogma to "sterilize the fruits of modern enterprise".[38]

In this context, and the importance which Mansfield's decision may have had, it is very interesting to note the wording used in the Act of Parliament of 1776, which extended Liardet's patent of 1773. The Act first recited the grant of the letters patent and then further recited the grounds for the request. This included the following:

> "And whereas, if the term is not enlarged, the same narrow plan must be continued, *a general plan of erecting works and training men all over the kingdom, which is necessary if the use of the cement is to be universal,* cannot upon so short a prospect be undertaken..."[39]

These words would seem to refer to the older doctrine. Reference is made to working the invention ('a general plan of erecting works') and the personal instruction of others ('training men all over the kingdom'). What is stressed in this recital in the Act is that: "training workmen and erecting works is difficult and expensive."[40] Liardet obtained the extension of his patent that he required, for a period of eighteen years, and was given four months in which to enrol the specification. Patentees may not necessarily have seen enrolling a specification and the older doctrine of working the invention and personal

---

36 Statistics produced by Mitchell and Deane cited in Dutton, *The patent system and inventive activity during the industrial revolution 1750-1852* (1984), Appendix C.

37 MacLeod, *Inventing the Industrial Revolution: the English patent system, 1660-1800* (1988), pp. 112-113.

38 Fifoot, *Lord Mansfield* (1977), p. 216.

39 Liardet's patent, 16. Geo. III c. 29, in 1 WPC 52 [my italics].

40 *Ibid.*

supervision as mutually exclusive. This may indicate that patentees saw the specification primarily as a means of protecting their inventions; the duty to work the invention and supervise others was still the consideration for the patent grant. As the recital in Liardet's private Act seems to suggest, the older doctrine may in practice have lingered on into the 1770s. If that is the case, the older doctrine may not have entirely fallen into disuse, as Adams and Averley contend.

Furthermore, there are indications that in the very early days of the common law courts' jurisdiction it was not clear that a specification which described the invention but would have been insufficient to instruct the public would necessarily render that patent void. The trials of Dollond's patent heard in the 1760s point in that direction. Dollond's case appears to be the first major patent case heard by the common law courts after the Privy Council ceded its jurisdiction. John Dollond had been granted a patent in 1758 for making achromatic lenses. His son, Peter Dollond, brought twelve actions against seven different opticians for the infringement of the patent granted to his father. He won them all. Sorrenson's research has shown that several cases were heard in King's Bench, before Lord Mansfield, in the early 1760s.[41] The action Dollond brought against James Champney, which was heard before Lord Camden in Common Pleas in 1766, was not, therefore, the first or only trial of this cause.

As noted in chapter 3, the Dollond case was not decided upon the specification, but as to whether Dollond was the true and first inventor. It was deemed that he was the first inventor because he was the first to bring the invention into the open. The specification seems to have hardly played a role in the decision. The issue of the specification's inadequacy had been raised by several of the defendants, but the courts had not seemed concerned. James Champneys argued that: "such new invention must consist … in the particular formation of the convex and concave glasses and the mediums and substances … in which particulars the said pretend Specification is totally silent." Similar language concerning the deficiency of the specification was used by other defendants in the various Dollond actions: Watkins, Smith, Eastland and Steadman.[42] This inattention by the courts to the sufficiency of the Dollond specification is remarkable, given the later emphasis placed by the courts upon the specification. The Dollond specification was vague. It provided no diagrams, nor any indication of the materials used or the mathematical figure of the lenses. Indeed, Sorrenson argues that it was because the patent's lack of clarity did not seem unduly to worry the courts that the defendants in these actions put forward an alternative line of

---

41 Sorrenson, "Dollond and Son's Pursuit of Achromaticity 1758-1759" (2001), pp. 40, 43. Peter Dollond refers to Lord Mansfield's instructions to the jury in "An Answer to a Paper Presented to the Royal Society by Mr. Jesse Ramsden Relating to the Invention of the Achromatic Telescope".

42 *Ibid.*, 41-42, fn 44 on p. 53.

defence: not Dollond but Dr. Hall was the original inventor of the lens and therefore Dollond was not the first and true inventor.[43]

If Dollond's specification did not contain sufficient detail to enable another to make the patented lenses, then presumably the patent could have been set aside if disclosure in the sense of instructing the public was the overriding consideration. Yet the judges had not taken up the challenge to the sufficiency of Dollond's patent specification. Its sufficiency does not seem to have been questioned, either by Mansfield in King's Bench or by Camden in Common Pleas. The imprecision was not even mentioned as a deciding factor in the surviving accounts of the verdicts.[44] It may indicate that at this early stage, the importance of 'working' an invention and bringing it into public use was still the most significant factor.

The other objection made by Adams and Averley to Hulme's theory was that if *Liardet v. Johnson* was the landmark case Hulme argues it was, why was it not treated as a significant precedent? They have what appears to be compelling evidence to support their argument. Buller does not refer to *Liardet v. Johnson* in *Turner v. Winter* 1787 (a case that deals at length with the demands of the specification) nor does he correctly record the outcome of the case in his *Nisi Prius* book; a number of later authorities mistakenly identify *Liardet v. Johnson* as the case of the trusses (*Liardet v. Johnson* concerned the composition of cement, not steel trusses); it is not dealt with as a seminal case in either Collier or Godson; and the only law report of *Liardet v. Johnson* in a series concerns the Chancery proceedings in 1780. If *Liardet v. Johnson* were of central importance, why was it not better recorded?[45]

That the Liardet case was not officially reported does not in itself indicate that the case was unimportant. *Morris v. Bramson* was never fully reported. None of the trials of Dollond's patent was reported. Dollond's case is known primarily because it was referred to by judges in other cases. Yet both *Morris v. Bramson* and Dollond were significant cases. Furthermore, the Liardet case did attract public attention, a fact acknowledged by Adams and Averley. The case was reported in quite some detail in the newspaper. That indicates that the case was, at least to some extent, newsworthy.

However, what appears to weaken Hulme's reading of the Liardet case, as a landmark case, is that when the case is cited in legal literature it is confused with another case: that of the steel trusses. The Dollond case, although unreported, did not suffer a similar fate and is referred to correctly in subsequent case law and legal treatises. The same can be said of *Morris v. Bramson*. Yet Mansfield's own colleague, Francis Buller, apparently incorrectly records the outcome of the case in his general treatise, *An introduction to law relative to trials at nisi prius* 1790, according to Adams and Averley. The reason they give is that Buller's version is evidently based on the defendant's pamphlet.[46]

---

43   *Ibid.*, p. 42.
44   *Ibid.*, p. 41.
45   Adams and Averley, "The Patent Specification: The Role of Liardet v Johnson" (1986), pp. 165-167.
46   *Ibid.*, p. 165.

Much of the confusion concerning *Liardet v. Johnson* seems to stem from Buller's entry of the case in his *Nisi Prius* book, and it is this entry to which the reporters of the case of *Turner v. Winter*[47] and *Harmar v. Playne* refer (see below). The reference to *Liardet v. Johnson* 1778 is made in the margin in this book. Not all references to cases are made in the margin. *Morris v. Bramson* 1776, for example, appears in the full text.[48] The paragraph next to the Liardet reference in the margin reads:

> "The general questions on patents are, 1st, Whether the invention were known and in use before the patent. 2nd, Whether the specification is sufficient to enable others to make it up. The meaning of the specification is, that others may be taught to do the thing for which the patent is granted; and if the specification is false, the patent is void; for the meaning of the specification is, that after the term the public shall have the benefit of the discovery."[49]

The points raised here comply with the subject matters dealt with in the Liardet case, as revealed by the newspaper reports and pamphlets. The confusion is caused by the two paragraphs which follow and which are placed between quotation marks. The first paragraph refers to the patent for trusses, which Lord Mansfield held void for omitting a material element. The second paragraph explains that inventions can be of various kinds; some are based on reasoning and others are lucky discoveries, such as a man discovering water tabbies by spilling on the floor.[50]

Adams and Averley impute Buller's wrongly recorded outcome of the Liardet case to his use of the defendant's pamphlet. There is an alternative explanation. Buller was not mistaken about the outcome of the Liardet case (which was found in favour of the patentee); what he was recording here was the outcome of the trusses case. Buller made a summary of Lord Mansfield's instructions to the jury in the first hearing of the Liardet case in his trial notes. In those notes he records that Lord Mansfield said:

> "Some [inventions] depend on the result of figuring, others on mechanism, etc. But there are others that depend on no reason a priori, no theory, but lucky discovery.
> Water tabbies [were] discovered by means [of] spilling on the floor."

> "The meaning of the specification is that others may be taught to do a thing for which the patent is granted, & if the specification [is] false, the patent is

---

47   *Turner v. Winter* 1787, 1 T.R. 608 fn (a).
48   Buller, *An Introduction to the Law relative to Trials at nisi prius* (1790), p. 77.
49   *Ibid.*, p. 76.
50   *Ibid.*

void, for the meaning of the specification is that after the term [of the patent] the public shall have the benefit of the discovery.

In a patent for trusses for ruptures, the patentee omitted what [was] very material for tempering steel, which was rubbing it with [?]& for want of that, I held it void."[51]

If the entry in his *Nisi Prius* book is read simply as referring to points raised in the Liardet case, Buller makes no mistake. However, from the way in which these paragraphs are set out it can be seen how later lawyers, like Godson, thought that the Liardet case was the case of the steel trusses and therefore Mansfield had found against Liardet.

As Adams and Averley concede,[52] the case of *Liardet v. Johnson* does not seem to have been subsequently entirely ignored. *Liardet v. Johnson* is quoted in *Harmar v. Playne* 1809 as the authority for stating the purpose of the specification. According to Davies's compilation of patent cases, Lord Ellenborough cited Lord Mansfield in the case of *Liardet v. Johnson* as follows:

"And when Lord Mansfield said (in the case of Liardet *v.* Johnson) that the meaning of the specification was, that others might be taught to do the thing for which the patent was granted, it must be understood to enable persons of reasonably competent skill in such matters to make it." [53]

This version of the reference appears in *Harmar v. Playne* in Carpmael's patent reports. Carpmael used as his sources for the report of the case Davies's Patent Cases and East's report.[54] In East's report, the reference to Liardet appears in a footnote to the Harmar case. The footnote states: "*Liardet v. Johnson*, sittings at Westminster after Hilary 1778, Bull. Ni Pri. [76]."[55] East, having first cooperated with Durnford to produce the Term Reports of King's Bench cases 1785-1800, stayed on as the court reporter for cases in King's Bench between 1801-1812. East enjoyed a very high reputation for the quality of his reports.[56] This would seem to support Hulme's contention: if *Liardet v. Johnson* was not the authority why was it being cited nearly thirty years later by Lord Ellenborough?

However, does this reference in *Harmar v. Playne* justify Hulme's assertion that *Liardet v. Johnson* was *the* precedent for this principle? In a letter written by Bramah and sent to Eyre, C.J., Mansfield is said to have "cited an instance where there was in the specification

---

51 Oldham, *The Mansfield Manuscripts and the growth of English law in the eighteenth century* (1992), pp. 753-754.
52 Adams and Averley, "The Patent Specification: The Role of Liardet v Johnson" (1986), p. 166.
53 DPC 318-319.
54 *Harmar v. Playne* 1809, 1 CPC 264, sources p. xiv.
55 *Harmer v. Playne* 1809, 11 East 107-8 in 103 ER 945 fn (a)1.
56 Holdsworth, *A History of English Law* (1964), vol. XII, p. 116.

such an omission as must have been fatal to the patent had it ever been contended in a court of law". The example was that of Dr. James's fever powders, where only the ingredients were mentioned, but not the proportion or quantity.[57] A similar statement appears in a pamphlet giving a verbatim report of Lord Mansfield's address to the jury in the *Liardet v. Johnson* case. In this address, Mansfield refers to earlier cases, including that of Dr. James's fever powders, as follow:

> "But if, as Dr. James did with his powders, the specification of the composition gives no proportions, there is an end of his patent, and when he is dead, nobody is a bit the wiser... I have determined in several cases here [in King's Bench] that the specification must state, where there is a composition, the proportions; so that any other artist may be able to make it, and it must be a lesson and direction to him by which to make it. If the invention be of another sort, to be done by mechanism, they must describe it in a way that an artist must be able to do it."[58]

If the purpose and the requirements of the specification had been formulated by Lord Mansfield, as he indeed states, in cases heard earlier than that of *Liardet v. Johnson*, the Liardet case would then be less remarkable. It would merely have followed in the wake of these earlier decisions.

Hulme, however, denies Mansfield's version of events. In referring to Dr. James's specification as giving no proportions: "Either the learned judge's memory was at fault or he was trying to invest his new doctrine of the function of the patent specification with a semblance of established practice." For Dr. James's specification had specified the proportions – thirty parts of antimony to one of mercury. While Hulme acknowledges that James prefaces the prescription with a warning that the strength of the mercury powder is liable to vary with the skill of the operator, in 1747 chemical operations were very imperfectly understood and the caution was a proper one. Hulme concludes:

> "It is clear that in 1753 Lord Mansfield formed an unfavourable opinion of the validity of James's patent – probably on good grounds; for the doctor's reputation was not of the highest. But James's specification lends no support to the new legal doctrine, and it is probable Lord Mansfield antedated his own law by some twenty years."[59]

---

57 *Liardet v. Johnson* 1778, 1 WPC 54 fn (e).
58 Hulme, "On the History of Patent Law in the Seventeenth and Eighteenth Centuries" (1902), p. 285.
59 Hulme, "Privy Council Law and Practice of Letters Patent for Invention from the Restoration to 1794" (1917), p. 194.

As the Dollond case indicates, the specification, as a means of instructing the public, may not have been an explicit requirement from the outset of the jurisdiction of the common law courts. However, the importance which Hulme ascribes to *Liardet v. Johnson* requires him to conclude that Mansfield made no statements concerning the need for the specification to be "a lesson and direction to him by which to make it" in any of those 'several cases' Mansfield states he heard in King's Bench prior to the Liardet case. In order to maintain the pivotal importance of the Liardet case, Hulme has to accuse Mansfield not only of a misreading of an older case heard by the Privy Council, but also of projecting his new legal doctrine backward.

It is difficult to know which are the 'several cases' to which Mansfield refers, as not all cases were officially reported. The case of *Yerbury v. Wallace* 1768, for example, was only reported in the *London Gazette* of 17 December. In that case the specification had played a role: the plaintiff was nonsuited because the true nature of his invention was not given in his "description" of it "pursuant to his patent".[60] From Mansfield's trial notes of some of these earlier cases, it is not possible to deduce whether Mansfield made specific statements concerning the function of the specification. In Buller's trial notes of the Liardet case, it is evident that the steel trusses case had been heard by King's Bench before the Liardet case and that Mansfield had dealt with the specification in that case: he had held the patent to be invalid because the patentee had omitted a material piece of information.[61] Finding a patent void for the withholding of material information is a strong indicator that Mansfield considered the primary function of the specification to be the instruction of the public.

When the common law courts assumed jurisdiction in patent validity cases, it is quite probable that there was a transitional phase in which the requirements and the role of the specification had to be established more definitively. It is also possible that, in this phase, the filing of a specification was not necessarily seen by patentees as a replacement of the obligation to work the invention. *Liardet v. Johnson* certainly made it clear that that the purpose of the specification was to instruct the public. Whether *Liardet v. Johnson* was chronologically the very first case in which such a statement had been made is more debateable. As in the eighteenth century not all cases were reported, and some that were reported were not reported fully, it is possible that Mansfield, as he contended, had indeed already made a statement concerning the function of the specification at an earlier occasion than that of *Liardet v. Johnson*. It may have been made in the steel trusses case, but that case was not reported and even the name cannot be ascertained with total certainty. Hulme thought the case of the steel trusses was probably concerned with Brand's patent. The date of that trial is not known but if the patent at issue was Brand's patent, the patent was dated 1771. It could, therefore, have been Brand's patent that was the steel truss case referred to

---

60 Oldham, *The Mansfield Manuscripts and the growth of English law in the eighteenth century* (1992), p. 733.
61 *Ibid.*, p. 754.

in *Liardet v. Johnson* in 1778. Hulme even concedes: "it is probable that it was in this case that Lord Mansfield first applied his doctrine of the patent specification."[62] Given the somewhat random nature of the reporting, it would seem unwarranted to claim categorically that the Liardet case was the landmark case which marked the end of the older doctrine. However, it was at least a case with a name, which had specifically dealt with the purpose of the specification. It may have been cited in *Harmar v. Playne* by Lord Ellenborough in the King's Bench in 1809 not because it was historically *the* precedent, but simply because it was the only named, available precedent.

4.2.2   The Instruction of "the Public"

If the function of the specification was to instruct the public, who did the courts consider to be "the public" for this purpose? In his address to the jury in *Liardet v. Johnson*, Mansfield referred to the public in terms of "an artist": "you must specify upon record your invention in such a way as shall teach an artist".[63] In Buller's notes on the second Liardet trial, he records that Mansfield: "left to the jury 1st, on all objections made to exactness, certainty and propriety of the specification, & whether any workman could make it by [the specification]."[64] This kind of language was imprecise: could more be expected of an 'artist' than 'any workman'?

This point was raised by Sergeant Adair, representing Arkwright in *Arkwright v. Nightingale* 1785: "If an ingenious mechanic were to make a new invention in clocks or watches, it would not be incumbent upon him to make a specification intelligible to a common cobbler."[65] Clarification was given in answer to this point by Lord Loughborough. The specification should be:

> "intelligible that those who are conversant in the subject are capable of understanding it, and of perpetuating the invention when the term of the patent is expired. The clearness of the specification must be according to the subject-matter of it; it is addressed to persons in the profession having skill in the subject, not to men of ignorance; and if it is understood by those whose business leads them to be conversant in such subjects, it is intelligible."[66]

---

62 Hulme, "Privy Council Law and Practice of Letters Patent for Invention from the Restoration to 1794" (1917), p. 192.
63 Hulme, "On the History of Patent Law in the Seventeenth and Eighteenth Centuries" (1902), p. 285.
64 Oldham, *The Mansfield Manuscripts and the growth of English law in the eighteenth century* (1992), p. 756.
65 *Arkwright v. Nightingale* 1788, 1 CPC 40.
66 *Arkwright v. Nightingale* 1 WPC 61-62.

In the *scire facias* proceeding against Arkwright, which followed the *Arkwright v. Nightingale* case, counsel for the crown agreed with Adair that the "disclosure need not be such as that a cobbler might thereby perform the work, but it ought to be so plain, that persons conversant in mechanics may understand it". This approach was confirmed by Buller, J. However, Buller held that a specification could still be insufficient even if such a person had found it intelligible. A specification was not sufficient only because a sensible mechanic would have enough understanding to remedy any defect in the specification. A man was not expected to use his own ingenuity to remedy a defect: the answer must be found in the specification.[67]

The principle that the specification was intended as a means of instructing one skilled in the art was quickly established. It was repeated by Buller in *Turner v. Winter* 1787.[68] In *Harmer v. Playne* 1809, Ellenborough used the example of a ploughman not being expected to be able to make a watch from a specification. He explained that the object of enrolling a specification was to enable "persons of reasonable intelligence and skill in the subject matter" to be able to tell from the specification what the invention was for and how it was to be executed.[69] In *Bovill v. Moore*, the level of ability expected of this person who was conversant in the subject was "common skill".[70] That a gifted inventor could understand the specification and carry it out was not the criterion. As Alderson, B. instructed the jury in *Morgan v. Seaward* 1836, having heard the testimony of the respected engineer Isambard Kingdom Brunel:

> "You ought to be satisfied that without any instructions a workman of ordinary and competent skill and knowledge would be able to do that. Mr. Brunel says 'I have read the specification, and I think I could construct by it a machine at any required angle without difficulty.' But whether Mr. Brunel could do it or not, is not the point. I dare say, Mr. Brunel, the inventor of the block machinery, could invent any thing of this sort the moment it was suggested to him, but that is not the criterion. The question is whether a man of ordinary knowledge and skill, bringing that ordinary knowledge and skill to bear upon the subject, would be able to do it."[71]

The criterion was not whether the judge could understand the specification. However, as will see below, the judge's own ability to understand the specification could play a role, particularly where the testimony of expert witnesses was contradictory.

---

67   Arkwright, *The Trial of a Cause instituted by Richard Pepper Arden, Esq* (1785), pp. 171, 172 and 178.
68   *Turner v. Winter* 1787, 1 T.R. 604.
69   *Harmer v. Playne* 1809, 1 CPC 263-264.
70   *Bovill v. Moore* 1816, 1 CPC 339.
71   *Morgan v. Seaward* 1836, 1 WPC 178-179.

4.2.3   The Requirement of Equal Benefit

The specification had to disclose not only how to make the invention, but how to make it in a way that would be as equally advantageous to the public as it had been to the patentee. Any instructions which would involve the public in more expense or more effort than necessary would be sufficient to hold the patent void. This requirement was made explicit by Buller in *Turner v. Winter* 1787: the public must have the same benefit as the patentee himself. In *Turner v. Winter*, Buller explained that if the specification instructed that more expensive materials were to be used than the patentee himself used, if the cheaper materials would be perfectly satisfactory, this would be a ground to declare the patent void. [72]

Full disclosure was a necessity; the public should know *all* that the patentee knew upon the subject. In *Wood v. Zimmer* 1815, the patentee slipped aqua fortis into the boiler, which dissolved copper more rapidly. However, there was no mention of aqua fortis in the specification. It was argued for the patentee that the omission of aqua fortis from the specification was irrelevant; it was not a necessary ingredient. The specification was sufficient to make the verdigrease. That submission was rejected by Gibbs, C.J. on the ground that "The law is not so". The specification must reveal the most beneficial manner to make the invention. It "must disclose the means of producing it in equal perfection, and with as little expense and labour as it costs the inventor himself". If anything was concealed which would be advantageous in carrying out the process, then the specification would be void.[73] Gibbs repeated this criterion in *Bovill v. Moore* the following year, stressing that a specification which enabled a workman to construct a machine, but not one that reflected the full extent of the patentee's knowledge at the time would not satisfied the law.[74]

It was also the duty of the patentee to show in his specification the most straightforward and easiest way to make the invention. In *Savory v. Price* 1823, heard in King's Bench by Abbott, C.J. (Lord Tenterden), an action for damages had been brought by the patentee for the infringement of his patent for a combination of neutral salt or powder, which was said to possess all the properties of the medicinal spring at Seidlitz, Germany. The objection made to the specification was that anyone reading the specification would imagine that complex processes must be carried out in order to produce the result. Abbott stated:

> "It is the duty of any one to whom a patent is granted, to point out in his specification the plainest and most easy way of producing that for which he claims a monopoly; and to make the public acquainted with the mode which he himself adopts. If a person, on reading the specification, would be led to suppose a laborious process necessary to the production of any one of the

---

72   *Turner v. Winter* 1787, 1 T.R. 607.
73   *Wood v. Zimmer* 1815, 171 ER 161.
74   *Bovill v. Moore* 1816, 1 CPC 339.

ingredients, when in fact, he might go to a chemist's shop and buy the same thing as a separate simple part of the compound, the public are misled. If the results of the recipes, or of any one of them, may be bought in shops, this specification, tending to make people believe an elaborate process essential to the invention, cannot be supported."[75]

Full disclosure also meant that the public should not be induced to make experiments which the patentee knew would fail. *Crompton v. Ibbotson* 1828 concerned a patent for drying and finishing paper. The patentee had found, after repeated trials, that nothing served the purpose except the cloth described in the specification. However, in the specification he had stated that the cloth might be made of any suitable material, and merely that he preferred the particular kind mentioned in the specification. Lord Tenterden considered that other persons could be misled by the terms of the specification. Its reference to 'any suitable material' could lead them to make experiments, although it was clear that the patentee in this case knew wool, linen and cotton would not do. The public, therefore, had not the full and entire benefit of the invention. As Justice Bayley pointed out, it was "the bounden duty of a patentee to make a full disclosure to the extent of his knowledge".[76] Lord Lyndhurst explained the law on this point in the following terms: "It is a principle of patent law, that there must be the utmost good faith in the specification."[77]

4.2.4 The Wording of the Specification

By the mid-eighteenth century, the specification was still a relatively new instrument. Patentees did not know exactly what would be required of them by the courts. With no recent experience in patent cases, it is very likely that the courts themselves did not at that stage have an entirely clear concept of what should be in the specification. Furthermore, the importance of actually bringing an invention into use may, at first, still have been uppermost. When, however, the purpose of the specification was deemed to be the instruction of the public, the wording of the specification had to be read in that context.

By the time Buller heard *Turner v. Winter* in 1787, he apparently felt able to declare: "Many cases upon patents have arisen within our memory, most of which have been decided against the patentees upon the ground of their not having made a full and fair discovery of their inventions."[78] Ashhurst, J. in *Turner v. Winter* stressed that it was the responsibility of the patentee to provide a specification "in the clearest and most

---

75 *Savory v. Price* 1823, 1 CPC 432.
76 *Crompton v. Ibbotson* 1828, 1 CPC 462.
77 *Sturtz v. De la Rue* 1828, 1 CPC 469.
78 *Turner v. Winter* 1787, 1 T.R. 606.

unequivocal terms of which the subject is capable". Any "unnecessary ambiguity affectedly introduced into the specification, or any thing which tends to mislead the public" would render the patent void.[79] In *Turner v. Winter*, Buller had considered that a strict interpretation of the patent specification was mandatory: "Slight defects in the specification will be sufficient to vacate the patent."[80] This approach was queried by Watt's counsel in *Boulton and Watt v. Bull* 1795, who argued that Dollond's patent specification had not been sufficient. There had been no mention of any mechanism, nor the degrees of curvature of the glasses. Buller had apparently found it expedient to dismiss the point made by Watt's counsel by stating: "the [Dollond's] specification properly stated the method of making those glasses."[81] The strict approach to the specification propounded by Buller persisted into the nineteenth century. For example, Dallas, C.J., citing Buller in *Turner v. Winter* as an authority, had alluded to "the strictness with which, on the point of discovery, patents must be construed" in *Hill v. Thompson* 1818.[82] Later, Dallas made this point abundantly clear in *Campion v. Benyon* 1821: "If the instrument contains any ambiguity on a material point, that is a ground on which it may be avoided altogether."[83]

Grammatical irregularities in the specification could be sufficient to set a patent aside. In *Bainbridge v. Wigley* 1810, a patent had been awarded for an improvement to the English flute, to render fingering easier and to produce notes not produced before. It was set aside by Lord Ellenborough because only one musical note had been produced, and the patent had stated a plural: 'new notes'. It was voided despite the fact that witnesses considered that the instrument had been greatly improved.[84] In *R v. Metcalf* 1817, similar grammatical niceties saw the annulment of a patent for a tapering hairbrush because, according to Lord Ellenborough:, "Tapering means gradually converging to a point. According to the specification, the bristles would be of unequal length, but there would be no tapering to a point, which the title of the patent assumes."[85] This grammatical approach was specifically endorsed by Dallas in *Campion v. Benyon*:

"It is agreed that the instrument is not altogether a subject of legal, but in some degree grammatical construction; for, if the instrument be chargeable with grammatical ambiguity, it cannot give that clear description which every man who reads may understand."[86]

---

79 *Ibid.*, 605.
80 *Ibid.*, 608.
81 *Boulton and Watt v. Bull* 1795, 2 H. Black 459, 487.
82 *Hill v. Thompson* 1818, 1 WPC 249.
83 *Campion v. Benyon* 1821, 129 ER 1186.
84 *Bainbridge v. Wigley* 1810, 1 CPC 273.
85 *R v. Metcalf* 1817, 1 CPC 393.
86 *Campion v. Benyon* 1821, 129 ER 1186.

This literal reading of the specification seems to have been at odds with the terms of the patent grant itself. A familiar clause in patent grants stated that these instruments should be favourably construed at law "not withstanding the not full and certain describing the nature and quality of the said invention, or of the materials thereunto conducing and belonging". As Hulme noted: The courts of law "were thereby directed to observe the plain intention of the Royal Warrant and to disregard any technical flaws which might have crept into the recitals of these grants, due to unintentional misrepresentation on the part of the applicants".[87] However, it would appear that once the courts had determined that the primary aim of the specification was to instruct the public, they would not exempt the patentee from that duty, regardless of any such proviso in the patent grant.

It was this strict, literal way of reading the specification which caused the most dissatisfaction amongst patentees. The judges appeared to them to be overly concerned with the wording rather than with the substance of the specification. The testimony given before the Select Committee 1829 reflects this irritation. William Newton, a patent agent, stated that the most frequent ground for setting aside a patent in the past had generally been for some trifling fault in the specification: "it is more frequently overturned upon some little point, or upon some legal question; it is very seldom that the merits of the question are gone into in court; if there is any faulty point, they take hold of that first." This was a sentiment echoed by Joseph Merry, a ribbon manufacturer. Merry complained that the judges required the specification to be too detailed; a trifling inadequacy, not of the least importance would avoid the patent. Isambard Brunel's testimony illustrates that an engineer may have had rather different ideas than a lawyer concerning what constituted a sufficient specification:

> "I took out a patent for an improvement, and I specified the thing altogether; I could not maintain my action, because I was told I ought to have specified and defined what preceded, and what was my improvement; *now, every body could know what existed before*, and they might have used it, but it was very hard for me to lose the patent because that was not exactly specified according to the law." [88]

It was this rigorous approach to the specification that has led some historians to typify judicial behaviour towards patents as 'hostile'. The question which needs to be answered is: why did some judges consider that the specification had to be subjected to a strict interpretation? It is contended below that it depended upon the context in which they read the patent specification.

---

87 Hulme, "On the Consideration of the Patent Grant Past and Present" (1897), p. 313.
88 *Select Committee Report 1829*, pp. 39, 76, 88 [my italics].

4.2.4.1   The Patent Specification Read within the Context of a Monopoly Grant

From the cases, one factor comes clearly to the fore: for some judges, the specification had to be read strictly because the patent awarded a monopoly to its recipient. The patent as a monopoly will be examined in chapter 5. As will be seen in chapter 5, it was a matter of debate in legal circles whether the monopoly was a construction against the common law. With respect to statutory law, the Statute of Monopolies itself actually prohibited monopolies. A patent for a new invention was one of the few exceptions to this general prohibition: the Statute of Monopolies allowed the imposition of a monopoly for fourteen years. In the light of the general prohibition on monopolies, it would seem that some judges considered that great care had to be taken to ensure that the patentee had fulfilled the legal requirements for the grant of a monopoly. That a monopoly should be approached with caution was very evident in Ashhurst, J.'s judgment in *Turner v. Winter* 1787:

> "I think that, as every patent is calculated to give a monopoly to the patentee, it is so far against the principles of law, and would be a reason against it, were it not for the advantages which the public derive from the communication of the invention after the expiration of the time for which the patent is granted."[89]

Some thirty years later, the same reservation concerning monopolies was still being voiced. A very outspoken Dallas, C.J. said in *Campion v. Benyon*, heard in the Court of Common Pleas in 1821:

> "With respect to patents, every patent being a monopoly, that is, an infringement of public right, and having for its object to give the public warning of the precise extent of the privilege conferred on the patentee, the Court (without going into the controversy whether it is politic that such privileges should be conferred or not) is bound to require that such warning should be clear, and accurately describe what the inventor claims as his own."[90]

For some judges, this legally permissible 'infringement of public right' apparently had to be monitored closely.

Even if the judge acknowledged that the invention was beneficial to the public, if there were any defects in the specification, the patent could still be set aside. Gibbs, C.J. in *Bovill v. Moore* 1816 explained why:

---

89   *Turner v. Winter* 1787, 1 T.R. 605.
90   *Campion v. Benyon* 1821, 129 ER 1186.

"But although it is beneficial for the public, and may, in this respect, be new; yet if the plaintiff has in this specification asserted to himself a larger extent of invention than belongs to him, – if he states himself to have invented that which was well known before, – then the specification will be bad, because that will affect to give him, through the means of this patent, a larger privilege than could legally be granted to him."[91]

It did not matter that no moral blameworthiness was involved. This was made clear in an exchange between Gibbs and a juryman during his instructions to the jury in *Bovill v. Moore*. The juryman pointed out that a defect in the specification might have been inadvertent, and not fraudulent. Gibbs replied: "Certainly; and if it was inadvertent, if he actually knew, and meant to practice that mode, and inadvertently did not state the whole in his specification, he must answer for his inadvertence."[92] The point was raised by the Select Committee investigating patents in 1829. The Committee asked a witness: is it ever considered by the court whether mistakes in the specification were unintentional; or is it taken for granted that any mistakes in the specification are fatal? The witness answered that he had always found any mistakes to be fatal to the patent.[93]

4.2.4.2 The Patent Specification Read within the Context of Protecting the Public against Monopolies for Fraudulent Patents

Buller, J. in *Turner v. Winter* 1787 had announced that where a patentee had made a fair disclosure, he had a strong bias in his favour "because in that case he is entitled to the protection which the law gives him". However, if a patentee had attempted to evade a fair disclosure: "the court ought to look with a very watchful eye to prevent any imposition on the public."[94] The fear that a patentee could have obtained his monopoly by fraud also seems to have been considered as a justification for the strict, literal approach to the patent specification. The 'watchful eye' function of the court may have been an overriding factor in the way some judges read the specification.

The fear of fraud in the specification was not ungrounded. As noted above, the interest of the patentee was to protect his invention rather than ensure another could make it at the expiry of the patent. This would, for example, appear to be the case with respect to Arkwright's second patent, which was revoked in *R v. Arkwright* 1785. In an earlier trial, Arkwright acknowledged that he had omitted to give so full and particular a description of his inventions in his specification as he would otherwise have done, the reason being his concern that his inventions, which were of national importance, would be sought after

---

91 *Bovill v. Moore* 1816, 1 CPC 341.
92 *Ibid.* 348.
93 *Select Committee Report 1829*, p. 76.
94 *Turner v. Winter* 1787, 1 T.R. 606.

by foreigners.[95] That reason had carried little weight in the subsequent *scire facias* proceeding. Not even some other patentees believed Arkwright's contention that his intention was to keep his invention from the French, but not to obscure his specification for an Englishman. In a letter to Watt, Boulton noted that Watt's "ingenious and amiable friend R. Arkwright" had "entered a specification that no man can understand". In a later letter to Watt, Boulton was even more blunt: "Surely, you cannot think it just that any tyrant should tyrannise over so large a manufactory by false pretences. He had no shadow of right and the judge and the whole court were unanimous that no mention was made in his specification of the thing or principle that was there in dispute."[96] (Boulton's sermon is perhaps misplaced, given the way in which Watt's own specification had been drafted! See paragraph 4.1.2).

In several of the testimonies given by witnesses before the Select Committee 1829 the reluctance of patentees to disclose their inventions was acknowledged. Francis Abbott had no doubt that a great deal was "put into specifications to mystify them, to obscure the transaction as much as possible". The aim was to enable the patentee to keep his invention from the public. Benjamin Rotch, who appeared regularly as counsel in patent cases, stated: "my experience tells me that, in three cases out of four, it is the main object of the patentee to deceive the public if he can, and nothing but the dread and fear of losing his patent altogether keeps him constantly from imposing on the public a false description." Samuel Clegg, an inventor who had defended his patent for a gas meter in King's Bench, also recognised that some specifications were drawn with the "view of misleading the public"; indeed many specifications were enrolled that were totally different from the real thing for which the patent had been taken out.[97] Enrolling a specification which was different from the terms of the patent grant, was the reason why the courts had to read the specification in conjunction with the patent grant itself. The court had to be alert to discrepancies between the patent title and recitals, and the specification. As Abbott explained in *R v. Wheeler* 1819:

> "the patent must not represent the party to be the inventor of one thing, and the specification show him to be the inventor of another; because, perhaps, if he had represented himself as the inventor of that other, it might have been well known that the thing was of no use, or was in common use, and he might not have obtained a grant as the inventor of it."[98]

---

95 Arkwright, *The Trial of a Cause instituted by Richard Pepper Arden, Esq* (1785), p. 100.
96 Boulton and Watt MSS 24.7.1781, Parcel D, B.R.L., and 7.8.1781 Parcel D, B.R.L., cited in Dutton, *The patent system and inventive activity during the industrial revolution 1750-1852* (1984), p. 76.
97 *Select Committee Report 1829*, pp. 66, 96, 107.
98 *R v. Wheeler* 1819, 106 ER 395.

It is, of course, possible that some judges exaggerated the need for the 'watchful eye'. However, as argued in chapter 2, to describe these judges as hostile or prejudiced against patents is to apply emotive terms and is misplaced. The fact that some judges rejected a specification because of a detail in the wording does not in itself prove the accusation of hostility or prejudice. Was, for example, Ellenborough showing hostility or prejudice against patentees because of his insistence on grammatical accuracy in the specification? Such an accusation would only hold up if it could be proved that Ellenborough reacted less sternly in cases where the litigants or defendants were not patentees. Yet that would not appear to be the case.

Ellenborough was known for his great tendency to severity. For example, he pronounced the marriage of an illegitimate minor to be invalid even though she had her mother's permission (her father was dead), had been married in the church by an ordained priest and the couple had lived together as man and wife for many years. The reason for the decision was because the Court of Chancery had not appointed a guardian to the minor to consent to the marriage. Campbell, commenting upon this case, was of the opinion that Ellenborough's nature was stern and that it was not a problem for him to give a judgment that others would have found painful. Indeed, Ellenborough would have rejoiced in an opportunity to show that he was "not diverted by any weak sympathies from the upright discharge of his duty".[99] Ellenborough's stern code of morals also led him to abominate anything that savoured of fraud.[100] James Scarlett, who would later become Lord Abinger the Chief Baron of the Court of Exchequer, explained how he had manipulated this facet of Ellenborough's personality when he was an advocate: "His mind was naturally suspicious of fraud. ...The safest course with him, was so to state the case as not to appear to rely strongly upon the presumption of fraud, and to keep back the facts that chiefly tended to prove it. When these facts came out in evidence they never failed to produce all the effects which they deserved to have."[101]

These characteristics may very well have affected Ellenborough's attitude to the patent specification. From the case of Tennant's patent 1802, a patent which Ellenborough described as "a scandalous patent", it is clear that Ellenborough was alert to the possibility of fraudulent specifications. In his address to the jury in that case, Ellenborough said that he knew from his time as Attorney-General that there were shameful abuses in patents.[102] Given his stern moral code and that "his mind was naturally suspicious of fraud", even the most minor defects may have been sufficient for him to reject the specifications in such cases as *Bainbridge v. Wigley* 1810 and *R v. Metcalf* 1817. Ellenborough was not singling out patents for special treatment; his general approach was strict and rigorous.

---

99   Campbell, *The Lives of the Chief Justices of England* (1874), vol. IV, pp. 221-222.
100 Holdsworth, *A History of English Law* (1964), vol. XIII, p. 505.
101 *Ibid.*, vol. XV, pp. 470-471.
102 Collier, *An Essay on Patents for new Inventions* (1803), p. 182.

Nor would it appear that Ellenborough was against the interests of the patentee per se. For example, in *Huddart v. Grimshaw* 1803, he would not only find for the patentee but also acknowledge that patents were important. In that case, Lord Ellenborough stated that patents were "a species of property highly important, as it respects *the interests of the individual*, and with him also the interests of the public".[103] In *Harmar v. Playne* 1809, Ellenborough would once again find for the patentee and show a flexibility of approach which would appear out of keeping with the strict, literal approach in *Bainbridge v. Wigley* 1810. The determining factor in these cases seems to have been what Ellenborough considered to make a specification misleading rather than any specific 'hostility' towards patentees.

In *Harmar v. Playne*, a patent had been granted for a machine for the manufacture of woollen cloths. A few years later, another patent was granted to the same man for improvements to that machine. The defendant, accused of having infringed the patent, contended that the specification enrolled for the second patent was invalid. The objection was that the second specification had not distinguished between the original machine and the improvements; it had described the whole machine in its improved state without individually explaining the improvements. It was argued for the patentee that had the second specification only stated the improvements, without reference to the original machine, the second specification would have been unintelligible. The second patent referred to the first. A specification could refer to other public instruments. By comparing the two specifications, it would have been apparent to anyone what were the old parts and what were the new. Lord Eldon, hearing this case in Chancery upon the application for an injunction, considered this an inappropriate means of drafting a specification. He argued that no man on reading the second specification would realize that two patents had been issued, one for the original machine and the other for the improvements to that machine.[104]

However, when the case was heard in King's Bench, Lord Ellenborough arrived at a different conclusion concerning the second specification. He acknowledged his initial reservations, but decided that the trouble and labour of comparing the former specification with the latter would be as great if the patentee had only described in the latter the precise improvements upon the former machine.[105] Ellenborough even accepted that:

> "It may not be necessary, indeed, in stating a specification of a patent for an improvement, to state precisely all the former known parts of the machine, and then to apply to those the improvement: but, on many occasions, it may be sufficient to refer generally to them."[106]

---

103 *Huddart v. Grimshaw* 1803, 1CPC 225 [my italics].
104 *Harmar v. Playne* 1807, 1 CPC 259-260.
105 *Harmar v. Playne* 1809, 1 CPC 268.
106 *Ibid.*, 264.

And:

> "Reference, indeed, must often be necessarily made in these cases to matters of general science, or the party must carry a reasonable knowledge of the subject matter with him, in order clearly to comprehend specifications of this nature."[107]

The test for Ellenborough was:

> "Whether this mode of making the specification be not calculated to mislead a person looking at it."[108]

Ellenborough was looking for fraud. Apparently, he drew the conclusion in the Harmar case that it was not 'calculated to mislead'.

However, Ellenborough seems to have insisted that what was actually stated had to be correct. In *Bainbridge v. Wigley*, heard the following year, Bainbridge had made a misleading statement by promising new notes for the flute when only one new note had been produced. Ellenborough considered that the consideration which had induced the grant of patent failed, as "it was granted on the faith that the patentee had truly stated the grounds on which he claimed that exclusive privilege".[109] Similarly, in *R v. Metcalf* in 1817, if a brush was described as tapering, which did not converge to a point, the description was defective. All the patentee had actually produced was not a tapering brush but only a brush with bristles of an unequal length.[110] Whether the descriptions of the inventions in these two cases were '*calculated* to mislead' is debateable. It was apparently sufficient for Ellenborough if he considered that the *effect* was to mislead. An inaccurate specification could not be the basis for a grant of patent. By inducing a wrongful grant of patent, a fraud had therefore been perpetrated on the crown.

4.2.4.3 The Patent Specification Read within the Context of the Contractual Approach

Some judges interpreted the specification within the context of a contractual transaction. The analogy with a contractual transaction in private law, between individuals, provided judges with a set of tools for analysing the patent specification. One judge who applied this analogy was Lord Mansfield. At first sight, this may not appear to be the case. Lord Mansfield has recently been accused of wielding the specification "as a somewhat blunt

---

107 *Ibid.*, 268.
108 *Ibid.* 264.
109 *Bainbridge v. Wigley* 1810, 1 CPC 273.
110 *R v. Metcalf* 1817, 1 CPC 393.

instrument for annulling a patent".[111] This too is the implication of counsel's address to Lord Eldon in the Chancery hearing of *Harmar v. Playne* 1807. The counsel (Mr. Holroyd) brought to Lord Eldon's attention in that case that when Eldon had been Lord Chief Justice he had "controverted the opposite opinions, both of Lord Mansfield and Mr. Justice Buller" by putting the question whether a mechanist could make the machine from the description given, and considering the case of a patent "not in the light of monopoly, as it had before been put by the judges, but as a bargain with the public".[112]

However, as Oldham points out, in contrast to other areas of law, in no case does Mansfield express impatience or disapproval of the idea of patents.[113] Indeed, quite the reverse. Mansfield had instructed the jury, in his address in the Liardet case 1778, to avoid two extremes. The inventor should not be deprived of the benefit of his invention for the sake of the public; nor should men get monopolies for what was in use, and in the trade, at the time they applied for the letters patent. A patent monopoly was only "a prejudice to every man in the trade" if the invention were not new.[114] According to Buller's trial notes of the first Liardet trial, Mansfield told the jury that it was "of vast consequence to the public that there should be an inducement to men to make discoveries of arts and inventions of various kinds".[115] This casts some doubt on the assertion that Mansfield was using the specification as a blunt instrument to annul a patent. Nor should it be forgotten that Mansfield actually found for the patentee in the case of *Liardet v. Johnson* (and not for the defendant, as was later wrongly reported by Carpmael and Webster). Mansfield was drawing upon the idea of a contract to analyse the nature of the patent grant and the rights and obligations of both parties: the patentee and the public. Oldham considers that it was this contractual framework which led Mansfield to emphasise the content of the patent application and the patent specification in assessing whether there had been any patent infringement.[116]

Lord Eldon was a more outspoken advocate of placing the specification within a contractual framework, rather than placing the emphasis on the monopoly aspect of the patent grant. Lord Eldon heard the case of *Cartwright v. Amatt* in 1800, when he was the Chief Justice of the Court of Common Pleas. As noted above, in examining whether the machinist could make the machine from the description in the specification, Eldon considered that a patent should not be seen in the light of a monopoly, but as a bargain with the public. Therefore the patent should be construed upon the same principle of good faith

---

111 Hewish, "From Cromford to Chancery Lane: New Light on the Arkwright Patent Trials" (1987), p. 80.
112 *Harmar v. Playne* 1807, 1 CPC 257.
113 Oldham, *The Mansfield Manuscripts and the growth of English law in the eighteenth century* (1992), p. 736.
114 Hulme, "On the History of Patent Law in the Seventeenth and Eighteenth Centuries" (1902), pp. 285, 287.
115 Oldham, *The Mansfield Manuscripts and the growth of English law in the eighteenth century* (1992), p. 753.
116 *Ibid.*, p. 731.

that regulated all other contracts; and therefore if the description was such that the invention could be communicated to the public, the statute was satisfied.[117]

By analysing the specification in practical terms – quite simply, could the public understand it or not – Lord Eldon had rejected the strict interpretation of the specification. Linguistic niceties were not relevant: the patentee had provided good consideration for his contract with the public if the specification effectively communicated to the public the nature of the invention. What is interesting, however, is Eldon's insistence upon good faith in the contractual relationship between the patentee and the public. Given the way in which contract law developed in England over the course of the nineteenth century, this reference to the principle of good faith as regulating contracts seems misplaced. It was not that good faith was to be totally eradicated in English law as a factor in contractual transactions, for example, contracts of insurance remained *uberrimae fidei* and fraudulent statements which induced contracts could result in a contract being set aside. Nonetheless, as the nineteenth century progressed, the concept of good faith would become linked to certain types of transactions rather than as a basic, general principle applicable to all contractual transactions. Even at the beginning of the twenty-first century, as Furmston noted (in his revision of the classic contract law textbook by Cheshire and Fifoot), the role of good faith was minimal:

> "Do the parties owe each other a duty to negotiate in good faith? Do the parties, once the contract is concluded, owe each other a duty to perform the contract in good faith? Until recently, English lawyers would not have asked themselves these questions, or, if asked, would have dismissed them with a cursory 'of course not'."[118]

In the eighteenth century, however, Lord Mansfield did bring the moral aspect of a contractual transaction to the fore in several cases in which the doctrine of consideration was discussed. In the case of *Pillans v. Van Mierop* 1765, Mansfield contended that: "In *commercial* cases amongst merchants, the want of consideration is *not* an objection." This assertion was based on the ground that a *nudum pactum* did not exist in the Law Merchant and that consideration went to evidence only. A lack of consideration was not an issue if the agreement had been put in writing.[119] This case is of interest here because one element upon which Mansfield built his argument was fair dealing. Van Mierop had agreed in a letter to accept a bill of exchange drawn on him by the plaintiff, but he later refused to honour the transaction due to the bankruptcy of the plaintiff's client. Mansfield argued

---

117 *Cartwright v. Amatt* 1800 was not reported, but was cited in several cases. It was cited by counsel to Lord Eldon himself in *Harmar v. Playne* 1807, 1 CPC 257.
118 Cheshire, Fifoot and Furmston, *Law of Contract*, London 2001, p. 28.
119 *Pillans v. Van Mierop* 1765, 3 Burr 1669.

that when Van Mierop had written to Pillans agreeing to "give the bill due honour" the defendant was in effect accepting it and Van Mierop could not afterwards retract: "It would be very destructive to trade, and to *trust in commercial dealing*, if they could."[120] Wilmot, J., agreeing with Mansfield, referred in his argument in the Pillans case to Roman law and the works of Grotius and Pufendorf. He argued that if an agreement was entered into upon deliberation and reflection, as would be shown by writing or other formalities, such promises were binding and the agreement would not fail for lack of consideration. The importance of integrity in commercial dealings was underlined by Wilmot: "*Fides servanda est*" (faith must be kept) was "for the convenience of trade and commerce."[121]

Lord Mansfield did not restrict his good faith reasoning to commercial cases between merchants. In *Hawkes v. Saunders* 1782, a legacy had been bequeathed to the plaintiff and the defendant was the executrix. Lord Mansfield stated:

"Where a man is under a legal or equitable obligation to pay, the law implies a promise, though none was ever actually made. *A fortiori*, a legal or equitable *duty* is a sufficient consideration for an actual promise. Where a man is under a moral obligation which no court of law or equity can enforce, and *promises*, the honesty and rectitude of the thing is a consideration…though the promise gives a compulsory remedy where there was none before, either in law or equity, yet as the promise is only to do what an honest man ought to do the ties of conscience upon an upright mind are a sufficient consideration."[122]

In the same case, Buller, J. declared:

"The true rule is, that wherever a defendant is under a moral obligation, or is liable in conscience and equity to pay, that is a sufficient consideration."[123]

---

120 *Ibid.*, 1669-1670 [my italics].

121 *Ibid.* 1670-1672. In the context of the arguments made here, the classic work of the Dutch scholar Meijers is of interest. Meijers examined the doctrine of consideration in the common law and the requirement of *causa* (the motive or purpose for the agreement) found in Roman and canon law. Looking at the work of Hugo de Groot, he remarked that De Groot does not mention the requirement of consideration but does require that the contract is reasonable. Whether a judge would uphold a contract would depend not on consideration but upon whether, taking the law, morals and fairness into account, the agreement was reasonable. See *Verzamelde Privaatrechtelijke Opstellen: Derde Deel Verbintenissenrecht*, Leiden 1955, p. 310. Given Lord Mansfield's familiarity with the writings of Natural Lawyers, as well as his knowledge of Scottish law with its civilian tradition, civilian principles may have influenced his approach to the law of obligations.

122 *Hawkes v. Saunders* 1782, 1 Cowper 290. The case was reported out of chronological order by Cowper and placed under *Atkins v. Hill* 1775, as that case also dealt with the meaning of consideration.

123 *Ibid.*, 294.

The importance of a promise, of honesty and the "ties of conscience" are stressed here. Mansfield advocated good faith in contracts in general. In *Bexwell v. Christie* 1776, he had stated: "The basis of all dealings ought to be good faith."[124]

The approach of Mansfield's King's Bench to the doctrine of consideration as put forward in *Pillans v. Van Mierop* 1765 would, within little more than a decade, be firmly rejected in *Rann v. Hughes*. In this case, heard by the House of Lords in 1778, Skynner, C.B. stated:

> "It is undoubtedly true that every man is by the law of nature, bound to fulfil his engagements. It is equally true that the law of this country supplies no means, nor affords any remedy, to compel the performance of an agreement made without sufficient consideration."[125]

Nonetheless, as Ibbetson points out, the result of *Pillans v. Van Mierop* would stand, leaving mercantile letters of credit as another special exception to the doctrine of consideration.[126]

It is against this background that Lord Eldon's assertion in 1800, that the patent specification should be construed upon the same principle of good faith that regulated all other contracts, should be seen. It would seem that for judges like Eldon, Mansfield's contention that 'the basis of all dealings ought to be good faith' had not disappeared as a frame of reference. With respect to patents, good faith required the patentee to draft a patent specification which constituted a fair disclosure of the invention; anything else was a fraud on the public. In turn, if the specification had been drafted in good faith and there was a fair disclosure of the invention, the requirement of communicating the invention to the public had been satisfied. Noting the case of *Cartwright v. Amatt* in the 1823 version of his treatise, Godson considered that the opinion of Lord Eldon had generally been adopted: "that as the disclosure of the new invention is the equivalent for which the grant is obtained, letters patent come within that general rule, by which, when a valuable consideration is given, the grant is to be construed strictly in favour of the grantee."[127]

Lord Eldon's principle in *Cartwright v. Amatt* 1800 was cited in various proceedings over the years. It was cited before him in the Chancery proceedings of *Harmar v. Playne* 1807, but also by counsel in King's Bench in *Minter v. Williams* 1835.[128] In the Chancery hearing of *Sturtz v. De la Rue* 1828, Lord Lyndhurst clearly had Eldon's formulation in mind when he stated: "It is a principle of patent law, that there must be the utmost good

124 *Bexwell v. Christie* 1776, 1 Cowper 396.
125 *Rann v. Hughes* 1778, 7 T.R. 350.
126 D.J. Ibbetson, *A Historical Introduction to the Law of Obligations*, Oxford 1999, p. 206.
127 Godson, *A Practical Treatise on the Law of Patents for Inventions and of Copyright* (1823), pp. 157-158.
128 *Harmar v. Playne* 1807, 1 CPC 257, *Minter v. Williams* 1835, 1 CPC 648.

faith in the specification. It must describe the invention in such a way, that a person of ordinary skill in the trade shall be able to carry on the process."[129] Even beyond the period under consideration in this study, reference was still being made to Eldon's principle in patent cases, a principle described by Alderson, B. in *Nielson v. Harford* 1841 as: "That is the principle which must be taken to be the sound principle."[130]

4.2.4.4   The Diversity of Approach

The case law of the latter part of the eighteenth century and the early nineteenth century undeniably shows that the doctrine of strict interpretation had its judicial supporters. In his treatise on patents in 1823, Godson commented:

> "The courts of law have ever looked with jealousy on the specification, lest the bargain between the public and the inventor, as Lord Eldon called it, should be too much in favour of the patentee; and hence more questions have arisen upon it in the courts of law than upon any other part of the grant, and more patents have been declared void on this than on any other ground."[131]

The doctrine of strict interpretation was based on the premise that the interest of the public was of far greater significance than the interest of the patentee. The priority was to protect the public from fraudulent or inaccurate claims; such patents imposed an unwarranted monopoly, which was a violation of the rights of the public.

Dutton argues that this strict attitude changed: from the mid-1830s the law, as applied by the courts, became both more certain and more favourable to patentees. He notes that this change was summed up precisely by Baron Parke in the 1841 case of *Neilson v. Harford*: "within the last ten years or more the courts have not been so strict in taking objection to the specification; and they have endeavoured to hold a fair hand between patentee and the public."[132] Godson contended in his treatise of 1823 that while the treatment of the specification had formerly been subjected to a narrow interpretation, extending no further than the literal meaning of its terms, "patents now receive a construction more in favour of the grantee than they formerly did".[133] Godson's opinion indicates that a shift was discernable before 1823.

Even in the eighteenth century, it is clear that not all judges adhered to a doctrine of a strict interpretation. As already noted in chapter 3, several of the judges in *Boulton and*

---

129 *Sturtz v. De la Rue* 1828, 1 CPC 469.
130 *Nielson v. Harford* 1841, 1 WPC 341.
131 Godson, *A Practical Treatise on the Law of Patents for Inventions and of Copyright* (1823), pp. 101-102.
132 Dutton, *The patent system and inventive activity during the industrial revolution 1750-1852* (1984), pp. 69, 78.
133 Godson, *A Practical Treatise on the Law of Patents for Inventions and of Copyright* (1823), pp. 156, 158.

Watt v. Bull were not prepared to reject Watt's specification purely upon the wording. Watt's specification referred to a 'method'. Even though, with the exception of Eyre, the judges doubted whether a method could be the subject of a patent, they were prepared to accept 'method' as a broad term or see this word usage as a verbal inaccuracy, which they would overlook. Another objection that had been made by the defendant in this case was that the specification had not stated to what extent the consumption of steam would be lessened by the invention. That objection was dismissed by Eyre:

> "but the method does not profess to ascertain this: it professes to lessen the consumption; and to make the patent good, the method must be capable of lessening the consumption to such an extent, as to make *the invention useful.* More precision is not necessary, and absolute precision is not practicable."[134]

If the case law before 1830 is analysed, it becomes apparent that there always had been a diversity of approach within the judiciary. Occasionally, this diversity of opinion was referred to in court. One example is the comment made by Lord Eldon in *Beaumont v. George* 1815. He was of the opinion that patentees had been "rather hardly dealt by", though he knew there were some "sound opinions at variance with his own" in that respect.[135] Given Eldon's assertion that patents should be read in terms of a contractual relationship, he was perhaps alluding to those who preferred to place the patent grant within the context of a monopoly. What mattered to those judges, like Lord Eldon, was whether the specification, taken as a whole, was clearly intended to communicate the nature of the invention to the public. Rather than subjecting the specification to a strict, literal reading, a balance had to be struck between the interests of the public and the interests of the inventor.

Campion v. Benyon 1821 is an interesting case because the dual approach is revealed here, even though the judges reached the same conclusion. What the judgments indicate is that where the patent is viewed primarily as imposing a monopoly, the interests of the public will be uppermost, whereas if the patent is framed within a contractual structure there is more room to take the interests of the patentee into account. Campion had taken out a patent "for an improved method of making sail cloth without any starch whatever". Taking the title, patent and specification together, the court considered that it was difficult to say whether the word 'whatever' referred to the total exclusion of starch or to a description of a kind of sailcloth which had been improved. The advantage of excluding starch had already been discovered and made public. It was held that the patent was void as it claimed, in addition to what the patentee had discovered, the discovery of something

---

134 *Boulton & Watt v. Bull* 1795, 2 H. Black 498.
135 *Beaumont v. George* 1815, 1 CPC 303-304.

already made public.[136] The emphasis for Dallas in reaching this decision, as noted above, was that every patent is a monopoly, "that is, an infringement of public right". It is within this context that Dallas argues that grammatical ambiguities are sufficient to set aside a patent, as they stand in the way of a clear description. This justifies the strict interpretation. Parke, J., in that case, also upheld the importance of a clear, unambiguous specification to prevent the public being barred from using something that was already in the public domain. However, the observations Parke makes are far more reminiscent of Eldon's contractual approach than Dallas's monopoly orientated, literal approach:

> "There can be no doubt that ingenious men, who incur labour and expense in the production of inventions advantageous to the public, have a fair claim to be indemnified by the exclusive privilege of a patent. But on the other hand, it is important that the public should have the means of turning such inventions to account, after the inventor has been satisfied for his trouble; and it is for this reason, among others, that every patent ought to contain a clear statement of what the party has accomplished."[137]

The literal interpretation of the specification was on the wane in the Court of King's Bench under Lord Tenterden. The wording was a factor, but not the only factor. In *Brunton v. Hawkes* 1820, Tenterden stated: "If a drawing, or figure, enables workmen of ordinary skill to construct the improvement, it is as good as any written description."[138] A similar sentiment was expressed in *Bloxam v. Elsee* 1825. In that case, Gamble had taken out a patent in his own name but acting as a trustee for Didot, who was a Frenchman, as at the time France was at war with Britain. Tenterden was not prepared to reject the specification simply on the grounds that certain French words had been used. An inventor was not tied down to words only in his specification, and if the words and drawings explained the other sufficiently to enable a skilled mechanic to perform the work, the specification was sufficient.[139]

In *Crossley v. Beverley* 1829, Tenterden was more explicit as to his reservations concerning the strict doctrine approach to the specification. In that case he said:

> "It is a hard case to set aside the whole patent because there is some little matter in it which is not quite right. It is a hard case, and therefore one ought to see that the objection is applicable."[140]

---

136 *Campion v. Benyon* 1821, 129 ER 1184.
137 *Ibid.* 1186.
138 *Brunton v. Hawkes* 1820, 1 CPC 410.
139 *Bloxam v. Else* 1825, 1 CPC 437.
140 *Crossley v. Beverley* 1829, 1 WPC 108.

Nor was he prepared to discount the patent in that case because improvements had been made between applying for the patent and enrolling the specification. Tenterden did not see why time was allowed for the specification unless this was to permit the invention to be brought to the greatest degree of perfection. He saw no objection to the patent.[141] What Godson found particularly noteworthy about the Crossley case was that no direction had been given in the specification concerning a condenser, which is a necessary part of every gas apparatus. Tenterden saw no reason to vacate the patent on that ground: a workman who is capable of making a gas apparatus would know that he must put in a condenser.[142] An interesting remark was made by Littledale, J. when the Crossley case came before King's Bench again in 1830 (this time it was heard on a motion from the defence counsel for a nonsuit). Littledale acknowledged that it had been held in previous cases that if a man applied for a patent for two things or more, and he was not the inventor of one of them, or there was some objection to one of them, the whole was void because the patentee was considered to have made an unfair representation to the crown. Littledale's response was:

> "That, however, appears to me to be only a technical rule, which has been intended to prevent frauds in obtaining patents, or for some other reason, but it is merely a technical rule, and there is no reason why it should be carried further than it has been."[143]

In *Hullett v. Hague* 1831, it would seem that Tenterden was taking even more distance from the literal approach when he declared: "I cannot forbear saying, that I think a great deal too much critical acumen has been applied to the construction of patents, as if the object was to defeat and not to sustain them."[144]

Indeed, there were those who thought the court, in particular Lord Tenterden's King's Bench, had become too liberal in its interpretation of the specification. William Newton, the patent agent, responded as follows to the question of the Select Committee hearing on patents in 1829:

> Question: Have not the courts of late construed the specification as liberally as possible? – Yes, they have lately taken rather too liberal a construction, and they have sometimes considered what the specification never intended.[145]

---

141 *Ibid.*, 1830, 1 WPC 117.
142 Godson, *Supplement to A Practical Treatise on the Law of Patents for Invention* (1832), p. 29.
143 *Crossley v. Beverley* 1830, 1 WPC 118.
144 *Hullett v. Hague* 1831, 109 ER 1183.
145 *Select Committee Report 1829*, p. 76.

In his testimony before the same committee, the inventor Samuel Clegg was asked whether he was aware that the judges differed in their interpretation of the law, to which he responded: "Yes; I think the present Lord Chief Justice [Tenterden] is very favourable to the law of patents; and I think a patent is much more secure while he presides, than it was with his predecessors."[146] Clegg makes a link between a more favourable approach to patentees and a more liberal interpretation of the patent specification. He had good reason to do so, given that it had been his patented invention which had been defended in *Crossley v. Beverley*.

Godson considered in 1832: "It is worthy of observation that the tide has turned in favour of patentees, and that the judges of the present day make every reasonable intendment in favour of the patentee."[147] By the early 1830s, the literal approach to reading the specification was being discarded. The following examples of judicial statements illustrate this shift:

In *Haworth v. Hardcastle* 1834, heard by Tindal, C.J. in the Court of Common Pleas, Tindal stated:

> "There can be no rule of law which requires the Court to make any forced construction of the specification…; on the contrary, such construction ought to be made as will, consistently with the fair import of the language used, make the claim of invention co-extensive with the new discovery of the grantee of the patent."[148]

In response to the defence counsel in *Russell v. Cowley* 1834 citing *Macfarlane v. Price*, a case decided by Lord Ellenborough in 1816, Lyndhurst, C.B. intimated that that had been an extreme case and said:

> "if you take the whole instrument together, and the ordinary knowledge which persons have previously of that, and it is quite clear what is claimed, it is sufficient."[149]

The other judges in *Russell v. Cowley*, heard 1834-1835, voiced similar opinions. Parke, B.:

---

146 *Ibid.*, 96.
147 Godson, *Supplement to A Practical Treatise on the Law of Patents for Invention* (1832), pp. 51-52.
148 *Haworth v. Hardcastle* 1834, 131 ER 1091.
149 Fn to *Macfarlane v. Price* 1816, 1 CPC 311.

"I think we ought to read this patent without a disposition to upset it, which has been too frequently the case in many instances on such subjects, that we ought to read it fairly, in order to understand what the meaning of the patentee is.... the fruits of a very ingenious invention will be secured to the person deserving it."[150]

"In the construction of a patent, the Court is bound to read the specification so as to support it, if it can fairly be done."[151]

Alderson, B.:

"we ought not to be understood to deprive people of advantages which their own ingenuity and talents entitle them to receive; we ought to give them a fair and candid construction, certainly not by any means being astute to pick holes in their specifications."[152]

In *Derosne v. Fairie* 1835, Lord Abinger in the Court of Exchequer remarked:

"One would not be disposed, from any obscure word in the specification, which might be interpreted in favour of the plaintiff taking it altogether, to deprive him of his patent".

The jury had to be satisfied that:

"the plaintiff meant fairly to communicate, and has fairly communicated, satisfactorily to the world engaged in this sort of trade, what his object was."[153]

In the Derosne case, Abinger even found that the fact the word 'improvements' was being relied on in the plural as of no consequence because "the plaintiff may mean every part of his process to be treated as an improvement, forming together a series".[154] The doctrine of the strict approach to the specification was being set aside in the 1830s. As Alderson, B. said in *Morgan v. Seaward* 1836:

---

150 *Russel v. Cowley* 1834, 1 CPC 561.
151 *Ibid.*, 1835, 149 ER 1335.
152 *Ibid.*, 1834, 1 CPC 562.
153 *Derosne v. Fairie* 1835, 1 CPC 683.
154 *Ibid.*, 1 WPC 162.

"The public, on the one hand, have a right to expect and require that the specification shall be fair, honest, open and sufficient; and on the other hand, the
patentee should not be tripped up by captious objections which do not go to
the merits of the specification."[155]

This contractual approach to the reading of the patent specification would predominate
for the rest of the period under consideration. It is not coincidental that the gradual demise
of the literal approach to construing the specification coincided with a shift in attitudes
towards the monopoly grant (see chapter 5).

4.3   Understanding the Patent Specification

The patentee owed a duty to the public to disclose his invention fairly and fully in the
patent specification. The specification had to reveal a new invention, or an improvement;
it could not claim more than had actually been invented by the patentee and it had to be
sufficient to enable a reasonably skilled and competent workman conversant with the
industry concerned to make it. The legal profession was increasingly required to deal with
patent specifications that could have as their subject matter complex technical and chemical processes. This mandated an interaction between very different professional communities: the legal community on the one hand and the technical and scientific communities
on the other. Their languages were different. The patentees brought to their patent titles
and specifications a language based upon the concepts of physical science: they spoke of
principles and methods and processes. The concern of the judges was whether the subject
matter of the patent conformed to the legal requirements of a 'new manufacture' under
the Statute of Monopolies. Principles, methods and processes had to be assessed within
that particular legal context. The frames of reference of these professional communities
were quite simply different. It was a point raised before the Select Committee on Patents
for Invention in 1829: that the "natural tendency" of the judge and counsel was to "decide
the case before them on a point of law, that being a subject with which they are familiar,
rather than on the practical parts of the specification".[156]

Leaving the interpretation of the specification to men not specifically conversant with
science and technology was one of the major complaints aired during the Select Committee
hearing on patents in 1829. William Newton, the patent agent, was forthright in his criticism: "I really do not consider that the judges are the most competent men to decide such
points, and certainly juries are not the most competent men to consider them."[157] Newton

---

155 *Morgan v. Seaward* 1836, 1 WPC 174.
156 *Select Committee Report 1829*, p. 45.
157 *Ibid.*, p. 72.

was one of several witnesses who suggested that patent cases should not be heard by the common law courts, but by a special tribunal consisting of lawyers and scientific men. This was endorsed by the patentee Charles Few, who considered that such a commission was necessary because a jury very frequently knew "nothing about what they try". When asked whether the decision of a tribunal of this type would give general satisfaction, he responded "I am not sure that it would, but it would be more sensible than the present one" for "I am sure the present mode never can give satisfaction". Ribbon, a manufacturer, thought that the whole system of a specification was not a good idea. He considered that it would be better to send an identical machine to a board for examination, although he accepted that that was not feasible with respect to chemical processes. The appointment of a scientific commission for deciding patent disputes would then be very desirable. John Millington, a professor of mechanics who had already appeared as an expert witness in several patent cases, including *R v. Fussel* 1826 and *Barton v. Hall* 1827, similarly thought that a commission would be preferable to the present system.[158]

The task of the common law judge in patent cases was, during the period under consideration, particularly demanding because the English patent system had no place for the examination of inventions before their enrolment. The patent petition was handed to one of the law officers, and if the report of the law officer was favourable the patent would be granted and the specification enrolled. The report was a formality. There are indications that the system was administered by the law officers in the most cursory way.[159] The court was, therefore, in the absence of a contended patent petition, the first body to examine the invention in any detail.

There was an inherent contradiction as to what was required from the judge with respect to the specification. The courts considered that a specification was sufficient if a man of reasonable skill and knowledge of the craft could make the invention. It was irrelevant whether the judge himself could understand the specification instructions. As Buller noted in his trial notes of the *Liardet v. Johnson* case:

> "No witness has been asked, nor does it appear that the cement can be made up by the trade from the directions contained in the Specification. If it can be made by the trade from these directions, the patent will be good, *though not intelligible to us.*"[160]

This was acknowledged by Abbott, C.J. in *R v. Fussel* 1826. Fussel had taken out a patent for 'an improved method of heating woollen cloth for the purpose of giving it a lustre in

---

158 *Ibid.*, pp. 47, 89, 101.
159 Adams and Averley, "The Patent Specification: The Role of Liardet v Johnson" (1986), p. 160.
160 Oldham, *The Mansfield Manuscripts and the growth of English law in the eighteenth century* (1992), p. 753 [my italics].

dressing'. This process involved rolling the cloth upon a hollow roller or rollers "so contrived as to receive or enclose the list or forrel". The objection was that the nature and construction of these hollow rollers could not be understood from the specification. Abbott admitted that he had "not the least notion what it is". However, he acknowledged:

> "But I have great difficulty in saying that I can take upon myself to determine it, because, if persons acquainted with the manufacture would say that there would be no difficulty in saying how the roller could be contrived, that would be sufficient."

If simply mentioning 'so contrived as to receive or enclose the list or forrel' was sufficient:

> "*though I do not understand it*, the specification may be good."[161]

The test of sufficiency was a matter of fact to be determined by the jury. It was not determined by whether the judge had understood the instructions in the specification. Nonetheless, this did not exempt the judge from having to understand the essentials of the specification. It was the court which determined the meaning of the specification, the court which told the jury what the specification had said, although it was the jury which determined whether what the specification had said was sufficient.[162] The meaning of the specification was, therefore, a matter of law and distinct from whether a specification was intelligible and sufficient. However, if it were the task of the judge to tell the jury what the specification had said, this could hardly be accomplished if the judge had not understood the specification at all.

4.3.1   Directing the Jury

The judge had to direct the jury as to the meaning of the specification and the evidence given by witnesses. With respect to directing the jury upon the evidence, in the face of contradictory witness testimony, the judge could focus upon the credibility of the witnesses rather than the scientific content of the specification itself. In *Arkwright v. Nightingale* 1785, Lord Loughborough's directions to the jury rested upon one short point: "simply whether you believe five witnesses who have sworn to a positive fact." Five witnesses had alleged that they had been able to make the machine from Arkwright's specification. The only question Loughborough, therefore, directed the jury to consider was whether these five had done what they contended (made the machine) or whether they had committed

---

161 *R v. Fussel* 1826, 1 CPC 451-452 [my italics].
162 Weber's footnote to *Hill v. Thompson* 1817, fn (h) describing *Nielson v. Harford* 1841, 1 WPC 237.

perjury.[163] The less impartial a witness was, the more it would affect his credibility. For example, one of the witnesses in *R v. Arkwright* was a partner in a mill with Arkwright's son. Buller accepted that the witness was still competent to give evidence, as he had no legal right in the patent, but noted it was an objection to his credibility.[164]

Not all the witnesses called to give evidence were those who had been directly involved in the working of the invention. The role of expert witnesses, those acknowledged for their scientific skills, became of increasing importance. When addressing the jury, judges had to sum up the testimony of the expert witnesses called by both sides. The problem was, as Alderson, B. noted in his address to the jury: "You may have a great difference of opinion among scientific men on a question relating to science" as "They come to state to you not matters of fact, but matters of opinion".[165] The high status of certain expert witnesses may have influenced the opinion of some judges. James Watt, astute as ever, was careful in selecting his expert witnesses. In his letter to Professor Robinson, asking him to come down from Scotland to appear as a witness on his behalf, Watt wrote: "I shall only say that such appearance could not fail to be of great service to us, from your character, your Station, your Science and your knowledge of the invention."[166] The status of the plaintiff's witnesses seems to have influenced Denman, C.J. in the *Cochrane v. Braithwaite* case, heard before him in 1832. He said:

> "Several of the defendant's witnesses gave the opinion that the apparatus con-
> structed in the manner of the plaintiff's specification would not work, but I do
> not think any mere opinion of this sort is to be put in competition with the
> positive testimony of such men as Brunel, Bramah, Birkbeck, Turrell and
> Partington who all swore they had actually seen the plaintiff's apparatus
> work."[167]

The writers of *The Mechanics Magazine* 1833 pointed out that whether these respected engineers had seen the plaintiff's engine working or not was beside the point. All their testimony amounted to was: "that they saw an engine at work, which they were *told* and *understood* was constructed in the manner specified by the plaintiffs."[168]

Well-known engineers like Brunel and Bramah were sought after as witnesses. Brunel, for example, appears as an expert witness in various cases. In *Jones v. Pearce* 1832 he appeared for the plaintiff. Scarlett, counsel for the plaintiff in that case, opened by

---

163 *Arkwright v. Nightingale* 1785, 1 WPC 64.
164 Arkwright, *The Trial of a Cause instituted by Richard Pepper Arden, Esq* (1785), p. 128.
165 *Morgan v. Seaward* 1836, 1 WPC 183.
166 Robinson and McKie, *Partners in Science: James Watt & Joseph Black* (1970), Letter 162, p. 231.
167 *Cochrane v. Braithwaite* 1832, 1 CPC 501.
168 "Cochrane *v.* Braithwaite", *The Mechanics Magazine, Museum, Register, Journal and Gazette* 19 (1833), pp. 253-254.

announcing "he should call as witnesses persons of known genius and scientific knowledge, who would prove the novelty of the plaintiff's invention". Brunel's testimony in that case was reported in some detail in *The Times*, his opinion being that the invention was original in its application. The jury, apparently after only a short deliberation, found for the plaintiff.[169] If Brunel was appearing as a witness, the opposing party was well advised to have its own high status expert. In *Russel v. Cowley* 1834, when Brunel appeared for the plaintiff, Bramah was called for the defendants. Such was the status of Brunel that when Brunel appeared as a witness in *Morgan v. Seaward* 1836, Alderson, B., as noted above, had to remind the jury that the point was not whether Brunel could understand the specification, but whether a man of ordinary knowledge and skill could. The potential influence of a high status expert witness was a reason why, according to one of the witnesses before the Select Committee hearing on patents in 1829, the defence of a patent was one of the most expensive kinds of defence. "It has", he remarked, "become the fashion of late to subpoena a number of eminent scientific men."[170] It was a 'fashion' that would continue.

4.3.2   The Specification as a Text

One familiar tool the judge had at his disposal in order to direct the jury as to the meaning of the specification, was to subject the specification to a grammatical analysis. As noted above, Dallas had pointed to the importance of the grammatical interpretation of the specification and Ellenborough had found several patents void on the basis of a textual analysis. Grammatical tools were applied with respect to the specification in the case of *Hullet v. Hague* 1831. In *Hullet v. Hague*, the plaintiff had complained that his patent for certain improvements in evaporating sugar, which was also applicable to other purposes, had been infringed. It was necessary to compare the specification drafted for Kneller's patent and that of Knight and Kirk's patent (the patents had been assigned). Tenterden concluded that although the object of both patents was the same, the method of producing that object was different. He reached this conclusion based on a syntactical analysis of the Kneller's specification.

> "Now it was said that the words which immediately follow 'and this I do by
> means of pipes,' constituted a separate and distinct sentence from those which
> immediately preceded them... and had claimed the same invention as that
> described by Knight and Kirk in their specification. But we think that the words,
> 'and this I do by means of pipes,' etc, must, in conjunction with those which
> immediately precede them, be taken to form one entire sentence...Now the

169 *Jones v. Pearce* 1832, *The Times*, 28 June, p. 6; Issue 14890; col D.
170 *Select Committee Report 1829*, p. 14.

method described in Knight and Kirk's patent appears to us to be perfectly different."[171]

4.3.3   Examining the Technology

Linguistic analysis was not always sufficient in order to determine whether the invention described in the specification covered more than the patentee's own invention. That determination required the judge to have at least some understanding of the machinery or processes involved to enable him to make a comparison with any existing machinery or processes. It became common for the parties to produce models of their inventions in court to help explain their working and to distinguish their machinery from that of others. Nonetheless, directing the jury as to the meaning of the patent specification could be difficult.

    Bramah v. Hardcastle 1789, an action for infringing a patent for a newly constructed water closet, was one of the few cases where the jury's verdict was not in accordance with the directions of the judge. Bramah had constructed a water closet by applying the valves horizontally, so that they opened downwards and did not become obstructed by water and filth. The claim was not for the valves, but for their new horizontal application. Bearcroft, counsel for the defendant, insisted that wires passing through pipes was the only new part for which the plaintiff might have had a monopoly. By claiming a monopoly on the whole water closet, as if he were the inventor of the whole, the patent was therefore void. Erskine, counsel for the plaintiff, argued that it was a new invention, and Bramah's patent did not prevent anyone from placing a valve vertically as in the previous design. Lord Kenyon was for the defendant: "In my opinion, the stress of the cause mainly depends upon this, whether the thing granted by patent be entirely new. The conducting of the wire through the hollow tube, to prevent obstruction from frost, I admit is very ingenious and perfectly new, but it is not claimed by the patent." He added: "The question for your consideration is, whether in principle that is the same, whether the effect obtained of stopping the apertures is by the same means? Whether those means differ in shape or not, I think is not material." Kenyon concluded by telling the jury the patent was void, as the invention was not new, and that they should find for the defendant. The jury, however, clearly had a different view of the patent claim from Kenyon and found for the patentee. The verdict was not disputed.[172]

    In *Bovill v. Moore* 1816, the issue was whether Brown (who had assigned the patent to Bovill) had invented a new machine for lace making, because it was a new combination of parts, or whether it was only an improvement of an earlier lace-making machine which had been patented by Heathcoat in 1809. If the latter were the case, and the specification

---

171 *Hullett v. Hague* 1831, 109 ER 1183.
172 *Bramah v. Hardcastle* 1789, 1 CPC 170-172.

had not differentiated between the former machine and the new invention, the patent
would be void. To decide upon this issue, it was necessary to understand whether Brown's
machine was, up to a certain point, the same as Heathcoat's machine. Gibbs, C.J., having
come to the matter of whether the specification claimed too much, admitted in his address
to the jury that: "I understand the case better now than I did in the outset, though I cannot
say that I understand it in a way so satisfactory to myself as I could wish."[173] Possibly this
was why Gibbs put the question of whether the patent claimed too much to the jury in
Bovill v. Moore (see chapter 1).

The case of *Cochrane v. Braithwaite* illustrates how two judges could understand the
technology set down in a specification in different ways. *Cochrane v. Braithwaite* was a
case involving the infringement of a patent for boilers for steam engines. The whole
question turned on what was the proper construction to be put on part of the plaintiff's
specification. When the case came before Denman, C.J. in 1832, he would openly disagree
with Lord Tenterden, who had previously heard the case. Tenterden had nonsuited the
plaintiff because he considered that the valve at the extremity of the flue was the essential
feature of the plaintiff's invention, and that as the defendant did not use a valve, it could
not be said that the two machines were similar. Denman, however, had a very different
idea of the working of the invention:

> "but I do not consider such a valve as an indispensable condition of the plain-
> tiff's invention, and such was the opinion of the court when a new trial was
> directed... All that seems indispensable is, that the required resistance, the
> necessary degree of compression, should be produced, and if that could be
> obtained by narrowing the outlet as well as by a weighted valve, I think such a
> mode of effecting the object must be held as being covered by the words "any
> other known means of producing any required resistance".[174]

It is interesting to note that the authors of the popular *The Mechanics Magazine* disagreed
with Denman's analysis of the working of the invention. The magazine found Denman's
interpretation "very much at variance with common sense". In their opinion, the resistance
meant here was plainly resistance to the rising of the plate or valve, and not such resistance
as might be produced by a narrowing of the flue. Indeed: "From the beginning of the
specification to the end, there is not a single expression which indicates that the plaintiffs
ever contemplated the narrowing of the flue as a means of compression." They considered
that Lord Tenterden was right in holding that if the plate or valve was taken away, that
was an end to the peculiar means of compression, for which the plaintiffs had taken out

---

173 *Bovill v. Moore* 1816, 1 CPC 340-341.
174 *Cochrane v. Braithwaite* 1832, 1 CPC 500-501.

the patent, and would be an end to the question of infringement. They noted that Tenterden's analysis had also been in conformity with that of Lord Lyndhurst (who had heard the case in 1830 as an application for an injunction). Denman's opinion, and the subsequent verdict of the jury in accordance with his directions, was "at palpable variance with evidence adduced".[175]

As to which judge had understood the invention the best, it is interesting to note that although Campbell described Abbott as remaining "a stranger to the exact sciences" throughout his life, the same cannot be said of Lord Lyndhurst. Lyndhurst had given his opinion upon the working of the invention when the application had been made for the injunction (to the irritation of Denman, according to the article in *The Mechanics Magazine*). Lyndhurst's opinion perhaps carries more weight than that of Denman as Lyndhurst had studied mathematics and chemistry, as well as classics, and he maintained his interest in mechanical scientific inventions until the end of his life. Lord Denman seems to have distinguished himself at Cambridge primarily because of his literary ability.[176]

Lord Lyndhurst was certainly not adverse to giving his opinion on a specification. In *Beeston v. Ford* 1829, Lyndhurst had had to decide whether to revive an injunction. While pointing out that deciding the validity of a patent was not his province, in his capacity as chancellor of the Court of Chancery, nonetheless he did express his misgivings concerning the specification. He considered that the specification included a new and an old machine, and doubted whether the invention for constructing the covers to boilers was a new invention. An order for the speedy hearing of the case at common law was made.[177]

There were certainly occasions when the common law judge took it upon himself to reach a decision based on his own understanding of the technology and nonsuit the patentee. As explained in chapter 1, one ground for a nonsuit was if the judge considered there was insufficient evidence to substantiate a prima facie case and the case was dismissed at that point. One such case was *Barton v. Hall*, heard 1827-1828, which was an action for the infringement of Barton's improvement in metallic pistons for steam engines. In that case, the models of several pistons were produced and inspected by Lord Tenterden. Having examined them, he was of the opinion that the piston used by the defendants was different from that described in the plaintiff's specification and directed that the plaintiff should be nonsuited.[178] This was described by Godson as the judge "taking on himself" to decide that the pistons were not the same invention as that described in the plaintiff's specification.[179] Whether Tenterden was right in that opinion seems to have attracted some

---

175 "Cochrane v. Braithwaite", *The Mechanics Magazine*, pp. 253-254.

176 Campbell, *The Lives of the Chief Justices of England* (1874) vol. IV, p. 319 and Holdsworth, *A History of English Law* (1964), vol. XVI pp. 5, 11, vol. XV, p. 395.

177 *Beeston v. Ford* 1829, 1 CPC 492.

178 *Barton v. Hall* 1827-8, 1 HPC 925/5 RA 120.

179 Godson, *Supplement to A Practical Treatise on the Law of Patents for Invention* (1832), p. 65.

attention. Even several years after that decision, *The Mechanics Magazine* of 1834-835 devoted several pages to the matter of Barton's pistons. An engineer, Mr. W. Baddeley, provided diagrams of both Barton's pistons and Heaton's pistons so that readers could form their own opinion as to their similarity.[180]

Men of science were often critical of the judge's ability to understand the science laid down in the specification. In his testimony before the Select Committee on patents 1829, John Taylor May complained that "the great evil is having to defend your patent in a court of law, if there is any infringement" and one of the reasons why it was a 'great evil' was because "it is very often exceedingly difficult to make even the judge understand". He cited the example of the Crossley case, which was for a gas meter: "the principle was well detailed, but the particulars of the application were exceedingly difficult for persons not scientific to understand; it occupied the court a great deal of time, but the principle of the patent was quite clear to all scientific men."[181] It was an opinion shared by a number of other witnesses heard by the Select Committee. Less prominence was given by these witnesses, however, to the fact that the scientists themselves often disagreed with each other. As noted above, both the patentee and the alleged infringer could usually find eminent men of science to act as expert witnesses to support their interpretation of the specification. Godson, although an advocate of patent law reform, had no desire to remove the common law judge from patent cases: judges decided matters connected to every walk of life, so they might as well decide what was an infringement of a patent.[182]

4.4 Summary

Before the mid-eighteenth century, the patent specification had become a settled aspect of patent procedure. Patentees would enrol a specification describing the nature of their invention within a certain period of time after the grant of patent. This form of disclosure would replace the previous obligation on patentees to work the invention and to supervise the instruction of others in its practice. Whether the enrolling of a specification was initiated by the crown or by the patentees themselves is a matter of scholarly debate. It is contended here that in the early eighteenth century the enrolment of a specification was in the interests of both parties, although those interests were not identical. The specification was of use to a patentee against an infringer as it could identify an invention as the patentee's own invention, while giving the crown the opportunity to ensure that the working of the invention would not be lost to the public at the expiration of the monopoly period. That

---

180 "Barton's improved metallic pistons", *The Mechanics Magazine, Museum, Register, Journal and Gazette* 22 (1834-1835), pp. 38-39.
181 *Select Committee Report 1829*, pp. 12-14.
182 Godson, *Supplement to A Practical Treatise on the Law of Patents for Invention* (1832), p. 63.

the common law courts would determine that the purpose of the specification was to instruct the public does not make it a foregone conclusion that the enrolling of a specification was, from the outset, forced upon reluctant patentees by the crown.

This division of scholarly opinion concerning the origin of the specification has affected the way in which the case of *Liardet v. Johnson* has been interpreted. In *Liardet v. Johnson* 1778, Lord Mansfield stated that the function of the specification was to instruct the public. Hulme argues that the case marked a radical departure: before this case, the specification had been a means for the patentee to secure his invention. Adams and Averley, on the other hand, contend that the specification had, from the outset, the function of instructing the public. They dispute that the case of *Liardet v. Johnson* was a landmark case, either in the sense that it marked a change in the function of the specification or in the sense that it set the precedent which stated that the role of the specification was to instruct the public.

It is argued in this study that, for some years after the mid-eighteenth century, working the manufacture and instruction by personal effort and supervision had probably not been entirely displaced by the concept of disclosure in a specification. The success of Dollond's patent actions in the common law courts, despite a vague specification, indicates that the courts may not immediately have discarded working the invention for the requirement of instructing the public. *Liardet v. Johnson* may not have been chronologically the very first case to state that the role of the specification was to instruct the public. Not all patent cases were reported or fully reported. Nonetheless, it did service as a precedent. The common law courts would formalise that the function of the specification was to disclose the invention in such a way that others could be taught to make the invention. The specification had to be sufficient to instruct a man of common skill who was conversant with the subject matter. It also had to enable the public to make that invention as advantageously as the original inventor.

The way in which the wording of the specification would be interpreted by the court depended upon whether a strict, literal approach was applied or a more liberal, contractual approach. The strict, literal approach justified setting the patent aside even for a slight defect. With respect to the contractual approach, the criterion was simply whether the nature of the invention had been effectively and fairly communicated and not whether there were minor shortcomings in the description. The approach adopted seems to have depended upon the context in which the judge placed the patent grant: whether he saw the patent grant primarily in terms of a monopoly; whether the task of the judge was to be ever watchful in patent cases to protect the public from a monopoly obtained fraudulently; or whether the specification was read in terms of a contractual relationship between the patentee and the public, which acknowledged rights and obligations on both parties. The diversity of approach within the judiciary was already evident in the eighteenth century. However, by the 1820s, it became apparent that the strict, literal interpretation of specifications was on the wane. By the 1830s the criterion had become that of the more liberal approach: whether the patentee had made a fair and effective communication. Specifications would not be set aside on the basis of minor defects.

Throughout the period under consideration, one of the challenges confronting judges was to understand the scientific explanation of the invention set out in the patent specification. It was not a legal requirement that the judge could understand from the specification how the invention was to be made, only that a man skilled in the craft could understand it. However, there was a catch: if a judge did not have an understanding of the essentials of the invention, it became very difficult for him to direct the jury as to the meaning of the specification or on witness testimony. During this period, it was not always entirely clear what were matters of fact to be left to the jury to decide and what were matters of law to be decided by the judge. It is possible that, on occasion, a judge found it more convenient to consider a matter one of fact rather than of law and allow the jury to decide the point. The role of expert witnesses was becoming increasingly important, and the status of certain expert witnesses may have swayed some of the judges.

5   The Patent Monopoly: Factors Affecting the Attitude of Judges to the Monopoly Grant for Patents for Invention

As already noted in chapter 4 on the interpretation of the specification, the fact that a patent awarded a monopoly of fourteen years to the inventor (with the potential for a further extension) may have affected the way in which some judges read the specification. In this chapter, a more detailed examination is made of factors, connected to the awarding of a monopoly, which may have influenced the way in which judges viewed the grant of a monopoly for a patent for invention.

The first of these factors is the negative association of the word 'monopoly': the negative association was linked to the abuse of monopolies in the past. Other factors examined here are the presumption that a monopoly was against the common law, or natural law, that monopolies were harmful to society or were contrary to religious dictates. Furthermore, the social position of inventors and the power of vested interests may also have played a role. Indications of these factors are to be found in contemporary legal treatises and in various types of case reports: in the reports of patent cases themselves, in copyright cases and in case reports dealing with other forms of monopolistic practice.

5.1   The Patent as a Monopoly: The Negative Association

There is disagreement between historians as to the interpretation of royal policy with respect to the granting of patents under Elizabeth and James I. On the one hand, there are those who argue that the patent grants of Elizabeth and James I should not be seen purely in terms of "a tale of nepotism and abuse resulting in the triumph of Parliament in 1624 – the Statute of Monopolies", but that patents had also been used as a policy device. Tudor and Stuart governments aimed at three significant policy objectives: an increase in employment levels, an increase in foreign trade and the better regulation of industries.[1] On the other hand, there are those who totally reject the theory that Tudor policy was concerned with social or economic welfare; there was no considered policy of protecting English industry or furthering English trade.[2] The latter view has been argued to be too

---

1   Dent, "Patent Policy in Early Modern England: Jobs, Trade and Regulation" (2006), pp. 71-72.
2   For example, Hill cited in Van Zijl Smit, *The Social Creation of a Legal Reality: A Study of the Emergence and Acceptance of the British Patent System as a Legal Instrument for the Control of New Technology* (1981), p. 65.

extreme. While there were certainly abuses of monopolies, including monopolies on such basic necessities as salt, monopolies were also used to encourage the introduction of new industries. By setting up these new industries, products that had once had to be imported could now be manufactured domestically. Patents for new industries were issued in a significant number of spheres of economic importance in the period 1560-1640.[3]

Whether patents had been used primarily as policy devices or simply as a means of enhancing royal revenues is not the issue here. What is significant is that in the eighteenth century, the word 'monopoly' was tainted. Rightly or wrongly, the granting of patents under Elizabeth and James I was not commonly associated with a policy aimed at social and economic progress, but with the more obvious forms of monopolistic abuse of the royal prerogative. That association had only been reinforced by the policies of Charles I. Charles I became infamous for his use of monopolies as financial expedients to augment the crown's income. Various commodities, like salt and soap, became subject to monopolies. So severe did the popular aversion to patents become under Charles I that patents had been recalled in 1640 by parliament, in response to a general outcry against monopolies. As MacLeod notes, monopolies had entered popular mythology as a major cause of the Civil War. The popular distrust of monopolies would persist: "'Monopoly' had become, more than ever, an emotive word, and it retained its pejorative force long after 1660."[4]

This is the framework for the historical references to the monopoly in Blackstone's *Commentaries*. He describes how monopolies "had been carried to an enormous height" during the reign of Elizabeth I, how Edward Coke had complained about them at the beginning of the reign of James I, and how these monopolies had been "in great measure" remedied by the Statute of Monopolies.[5] Blackstone is highly critical of James I, alluding to the "unreasonable and imprudent exertion of what was then deemed to be prerogative". The king's push towards absolute power "awakened the sleeping lion" and the leaders, aware of popular feeling, opposed it. One of the "little victories" of these leaders, Blackstone noted, was their stand against monopolies. Unfortunately, James' successor, Charles I, by straining his prerogative "beyond the examples of former ages", would leave popular leaders "fired with resentment for past oppressions".[6]

In the eighteenth century, those who wished to justify patents for invention, and the monopoly which such a patent bestowed, could not ignore the historical context in which monopolies were viewed. It was acknowledged by W. Kenrick, in his well publicised *An Address to the Artists and Manufacturers of Great Britain* published in 1774, when he stated

---

3   *Ibid.*, p. 65.
4   MacLeod, *Inventing the Industrial Revolution: the English patent system, 1660-1800* (1988), p. 16.
5   Blackstone, *Commentaries on the Laws of England* (1793), IV, p. 159.
6   *Ibid.*, IV, pp. 435-437.

that these old style abuses "had thrown on the word an odium, continued to this very day".[7]
When Collier wrote the first treatise on patents for invention, which appeared in 1803,
the public distaste for monopolies was apparently still such that Collier considered it necessary to begin his treatise by justifying monopolies for patents for invention. A monopoly
for a new invention could not be compared to the "pernicious grants of monopolies", that
had been so extensive under Elizabeth, where "private interest threatened the extinction
of public prosperity".[8] Richard Godson published his treatise on patents for invention in
1823. In one respect, little appears to have changed over the twenty-year period separating
Collier's treatise from that of Godson's: Godson, like Collier, begins his treatise with the
subject of monopolies and, like Collier, Godson feels obliged to justify the monopoly grant
of a patent for invention:

> "For although they are monopolies, yet they are very limited ones; and are as
> beneficial in their effects, both to the inventors and to the community, as the
> old kind were detrimental to the best interests of the state."[9]

That judges were aware of the controversial nature of the monopoly grant for patents for
invention can be deduced from statements made by judges in court. In *Turner v. Winter*
1787, Buller, J. remarked: "How far that law, which authorises the king to grant patents,
is politic, it is not for us to determine."[10] More than thirty years after Buller's comment in
Turner v. Winter, Chief Justice Dallas in *Campion v. Benyon* 1821 makes a similar comment.
Dallas states that he will give his judgment: "without going into the *controversy* whether
it is politic that such privileges should be conferred or not".[11] This again suggests enduring
resistance to the granting of patent monopolies. Such reservations were quite possibly to
be found within the ranks of the judiciary. A certain distain for monopolistic practices
could have been reinforced by several factors, one of which was the supposition that
monopolies were actually contrary to the common law.

5.1.1   The Monopoly as against the Common Law

Whether a patent was a form of property recognised at common law is a question which
will be addressed in chapter 6. What is examined here is one particular aspect of that patent

---

7   W. Kenrick, *An Address to the Artists and Manufacturers of Great Britain; respecting an Application to Par-
     liament for the farther Encouragement of new Discoveries and Inventions in the useful Arts*, London 1774,
     p. 60.
8   Collier, *An Essay on Patents for new Inventions* (1803), p. 16.
9   Godson, *A Practical Treatise on the Law of Patents for Inventions and of Copyright* (1823), p. 43.
10   *Turner v. Winter* 1787, 1T.R. 606.
11   *Campion v. Benyon* 1821, 129 ER 1186 [my italics].

grant: the monopoly. Was the common law opposed to monopolies and hence to the monopoly grant awarded by patent?

Several cases on monopolies were heard in the common law courts early in the seventeenth century. In *Darcy v. Allin* 1602, the famous 'Case of the Monopolies', the court held a patent for the sole making and selling of playing cards to be void. The reports of this case do not disclose the judicial reasoning, but only the arguments of counsel. There are certain differences in emphasis between Coke's report of this case and that of Noy. Coke focuses on the patent being against the common law.[12] Coke's report records the argument: "All trades, as well mechanical as others, which prevent idleness...are profitable to the commonwealth, and therefore the grant to the plaintiff to have the sole making of them is against the common law." Noy, however, records the argument: "all patents made for the general good of the realm may restrain some subjects in their particular trade lawfully." In other words, a monopoly for the common good was not void. Furthermore: "I will show you how the Judges have heretofore allowed of monopoly patents, which is, that where any man by his own charge and industry, or by his own wit or invention doth bring any new trade into the realm."[13] The report, in law French, of *Taylors de Ipswich v. Sherring* 1615 shows a similarity to Noy's treatment of the subject of monopolies. In this case, the common law court recognised that the king could grant a patent for a new invention for a reasonable time. The judgment at 5 gives the common law view on this point: "*Mes lou nest ascun novell invention, le Roy per son patent ne polt hinder ascun trade.*"[14]

It is possible that the idea that the common law had *always* been against monopolies per se arose in response to mounting resentment concerning the abuse of monopolies. It was in response to the Case of the Monopolies and in an attempt to win the support of his subjects that James I had produced his *Book of Bounty* in 1610. It was a declaration against monopolies: monopolies were against the laws of the realm and therefore he expressly commanded that no suitor move the king to grant any of them.[15] In practice, James I continued to grant monopolies, despite his assertion in the *Book of Bounty*. The campaign against monopolies in the seventeenth century owed much to one man in particular: Sir Edward Coke. Before he rose to pre-eminence as the Chief Justice of the Court of Common Pleas and later as the Chief Justice of King's Bench, Coke had been a law officer and in this capacity he had represented the plaintiff in *Darcy v. Allin*. It was also Coke, together with Noy, who had introduced the unsuccessful monopolies bill in 1621.[16] Coke set out his

---

12 Dent, "Patent Policy in Early Modern England: Jobs, Trade and Regulation" (2006), p. 81.

13 *Darcy v. Allin* 1602, 11 Co Rep 86a and Noy 178, 182.

14 *Taylors de Ipswich v. Sherring* 1615, 1 Roll. R. 4, ["My law is no new invention, the king may not hinder trade by his patent."] cited in Harold G. Fox, *Monopolies and Patents: a Study of the History and Future of the Patent Monopoly*, Toronto 1947, p. 86.

15 *Book of Bounty*, reproduced in the appendix of Fox at p. 332.

16 Boehm, *The British Patent System I* (1967), pp. 17-18.

opinion on monopolies very clearly in his *Institutes*: monopolies are against the law. He states this repeatedly:

"all grants of monopolies are against the ancient and fundamental laws of this kingdom."

"That monopolies are against the ancient and fundamental laws of the realm"

"but the use of a monopoly is contrary to the ancient and fundamental laws of the realm, therefore the use of a monopoly is punishable by law." [17]

Historians have interpreted this assertion in the *Institutes* in a variety of ways. There are those who argue that this statement is Coke projecting his own opinion backward. The assertion was an "invention", or represented nothing more than economic and political propaganda rather than the law;[18] that to represent the common law as abhorring monopolies from time immemorial would be a mistake, as the early attacks in the common law courts on crown monopolies are best explained as a constitutional struggle between crown and parliament.[19] Getz, however, argues that whether Coke was restating the common law or merely erecting his private prejudices into legal principles is of no importance in one respect: "by the time the patent system had become a regular feature of the English commercial scene, or shortly thereafter, the common law had become hostile to monopoly."[20]

Coke's statement appears absolute: *all* grants of monopolies are against the ancient and fundamental laws of the realm. However, Coke acknowledges that, as monopolies are against the ancient and fundamental laws of the realm, it is therefore necessary to define what a monopoly is. Coke's definition of a monopoly leaves a little more room for manoeuvre.

"A monopoly is an institution, or allowance by the king, by his grant, commission, or otherwise to any person or persons, bodies politique or corporate, of or for the sole buying, selling, making, working, or using of any thing, whereby any person or persons, bodies politique or corporate, are *sought to be restrained of any freedom, or liberty that they had before or hindered in their lawful trade.*"[21]

---

17   Coke, *Third Institute*, p. 181.
18   Letwin and Wagner respectively, cited in Getz, "History of the Patentee's Obligations in Great Britain" (1964), p. 65.
19   M.J. Trebilcock, *The common law of restraint of trade: a legal and economis analysis*, Toronto 1986, p. 12.
20   Getz, "History of the Patentee's Obligations in Great Britain" (1964), p. 67.
21   Coke, *Third Institute*, p. 181.

If these persons, or institutions, were not restrained in the exercise of a freedom or liberty that they had had before, or were not hindered in their lawful trade, then according to Coke's definition there would be no monopoly. In his study of the history of patents, Fox argued that it was evident from Coke's own definition of monopoly that the term only included those monopolies that on the authority of *Darcy v. Allin* were against the common law.[22] Yet Getz makes a valid point. Even if Coke had indicated that not all restrictions on trade were against the common law, that there was a distinction between monopolies that were valid at common law and those that were not, it was a nicety that was certainly not perceived by all members of the judiciary in the eighteenth century. In the eyes of some judges, any form of monopolistic practice was against the common law, whether that practice involved invention, literary works or basic commodities.

One of the arguments put forward against copyright was that it was a monopoly and hence against the common law. Several examples serve to illustrate the point here. Yates drew a comparison between patents and copyright in *Tonson v. Collins* 1762. (At the time, Yates was acting in his capacity as counsel in *Tonson v. Collins*, but he seems to have held the same opinion when he became a judge.) He argued that a patent for a new invention was only allowed as a temporary privilege. The very fact that a patent was *granted* was proof that independent of these grants "the grantees could have no monopoly". The claim for perpetual copyright "tends to a monopoly, is contrary to the provisions of the legislature, or the good of the community". "The author can claim no privilege by common law", as copyright was a "temporary indulgence" allowed by statute.[23] Lord Camden, in the copyright case of *Donaldson v. Beckett* 1774, similarly declared that there was no real difference between inventors and authors, and as inventors had "no such right at common law, which declares it a monopoly" the same was true for authors.[24] Baron Perrot, in the Donaldson case, also rejected the claim that copyright existed at common law because the claim in that case "was neither more nor less than a claim for a monopoly, and *all* monopolies were odious to the common law".[25]

Any conduct involving raising the price of basic commodities was seen as a particularly abhorrent form of monopolistic practice. There are indications that the common law courts in the eighteenth century were opposed to cartel forming; in several cases business combinations were indicted as criminal conspiracies.[26] There were specific offences dealing with monopolistic practices affecting victuals: forestalling, engrossing and regrating. A forestaller altered the current value of commodities (by buying up produce on the way to market, dissuading persons from bringing their goods to market, or persuading them to increase

---

22 Fox, *Monopolies and Patents: a Study of the History and Future of the Patent Monopoly* (1947), p. 89.
23 *Tonson v. Collins* 1762, 1 W. Black 339-340.
24 William Cobbett, *Parliamentary History of England*, vol. 17, London 1813, col. 999.
25 *Ibid.*, col. 983 [my italics].
26 Trebilcock, *The common law of restraint of trade: a legal and economic analysis* (1986), p. 12.

the price); an engrosser bought up a whole commodity with the intent to sell it at an unreasonable price; and a regrater bought up commodities and sold them at a profit in the same place or within four miles. When the old penal statutes on forestalling, engrossing and regrating were repealed in 1772, legal controversy ensued. There were those on the bench who considered that, even if these offences had been given an early statutory form, they were in essence common law offences and hence the common law remained unaltered. This standpoint is testimony to the strength of their conviction that the common law was intrinsically opposed to monopolistic practices.

Lord Kenyon was adamant that, as the common law saw forestalling, engrossing and regrating as offences, it did not matter that the statutes had been repealed. In the trial of *R v. Rusby* 1800, a case on regrating corn which was covered in some detail by *The Times*, Lord Kenyon stated: "there is no doubt now but that the Common Law provides, and wisely provides, for the three offences called forestalling, engrossing and regrating."[27] In *R v. Waddington*, a case heard before Lord Kenyon that same year, Waddington was convicted for forestalling hops, with intent to enhance the price. Kenyon was not alone in his opinion that these practices were common law offences. Grose, J., in the Waddington case, dismissed the idea that:

> "the Legislature of a great and populous kingdom, ever anxious to provide for the most necessitous objects in it, should have intended by this statute [of 1772] to have taken from the lower and middling classes of men that security against the unnecessary high price of provisions, which the common law intended to give them."[28]

Just how controversial the matter was is apparent from the speeches in *R v. Waddington*. Edward Law (the future Lord Ellenborough) argued on behalf of the defendant in that case that the greater part of the old laws had been repealed. He based this argument not only upon the statute abolishing the old penal statutes, but also upon case law. It is interesting to see whose cases he cited. One was decided by Eyre, who had apparently determined in *Williams v. Watkins*, an action brought upon one of the old statutes for forestalling cattle going to Smithfield market, that there was no such offence. The other case cited was decided by Lord Mansfield. In that case, Law argued that Mansfield had compelled a bargain for hops to be fulfilled, although the maker of the bargain was beyond all doubt an engrosser and, therefore, had engrossing this article been contrary to the law, the contract would

---

27   *R v. Rusby* 1800 *The Times Law Report*, July 5, 1800, Issue 4839 p. 3, col A.
28   *R v. Waddington* 1800, 102 ER 65. The two hearings of the case in January and February 1800 were reported by East (102 ER 56 and 65). It was also reported in *The Counsellor's Magazine*. The date on the title page of *The Counsellor's Magazine* is 1796, but it contains cases up to and including 1801. *The Counsellor's Magazine* report is similar to East's reports, but contains some other details.

have been void. Apparently such was the sensitive nature of this issue that Lord Kenyon was moved to remark that he "deplored" that the defence had "though necessary to pollute the grave, and insult the ashes, of so great and good a man as Lord Mansfield".[29]

These grain cases may have concerned forms of monopolistic practice that had nothing to do with patents for invention, but the strength of judicial feeling evident from the case reports is telling. That strength of feeling is relevant to patents for invention because monopolies, forestalling, regrating and engrossing tended to be classed together. This is the case in two eighteenth century standard works: that of Blackstone in England and Forbes in Scotland. In Forbes *Institutes of the law of Scotland*:

> "A monopoly… is the engrossing by one or more persons combined together, the whole sale of any kind of goods, in order to raise the price of them, and that none may gain but they. Or an allowance by the king to any person or persons of the sole buying, selling, making, working or using of any thing or known trade, whereby others are sought to be restrained from any freedom they had before."

Forbes then points out that an exception is made under the Statute of Monopolies 1624, allowing the king "for the public good" to "grant the sole use of any profitable new invented art, or first brought into the realm by the grantee" for a period in compliance with the Statute.[30]

In Book IV of his *Commentaries on the Laws of England*, under the heading 'Of Offences Against Public Trade', Blackstone explains the offences of forestalling, regrating and engrossing in paragraphs 6, 7 and 8, and monopolies are dealt with in paragraph 9. He says of monopolies:

> "Monopolies are much the same offence in other branches of trade, that engrossing is in provisions: being a licence or privilege allowed by the king for the sole buying and selling, making, working or using of any thing whatsoever; whereby the subject in general is restrained from that liberty of manufacturing or trading *which he had before*."[31]

In the same paragraph, he notes that the Statute of Monopolies had declared such monopolies to be contrary to law and void, with certain exceptions (which Blackstone points out included patents "to the authors of new inventions").[32]

---

29 *The Counsellor's Magazine*, pp. 277-278, 284.
30 William Forbes, *The Institutes of the Law of Scotland*, vol. 2, Edinburgh 1722-1730, Book IV, 10 iii p. 189.
31 Blackstone, *Commentaries on the Laws of England* (1793), IV, 158-159 [my italics].
32 *Ibid.*, 159.

Blackstone draws the comparison here between monopolies for buying, selling, making, working or using something with practices like engrossing victuals. Patents for inventions are listed as an exception, but nonetheless, they seemed to be tainted by association. From Blackstone's description of a monopoly it becomes clear why Kenrick, Collier and Godson were at such pains to stress that a patent for invention was different: it did not restrain 'from that liberty of manufacturing or trading *which he had before.*' The invention brought something into society which had not existed before, and it was, therefore, not the sort of monopoly to which Coke and Blackstone had referred.

Kenrick, in his 1774 publication, sought to distinguish the monopoly awarded by the patent grant for a new invention from former monopolistic abuses. He contended that the exclusive privilege granted to the patentee of a new invention was of a quite different nature:

> "The first difficulty, that presents itself against the granting an exclusive privilege to the authors of new inventions in the useful arts, is the general one of establishing *monopolies*; which are supposed to have the pernicious effect of enriching a *few*, and depriving a *multitude* of the means of subsistence; of enhancing the price of the manufactures monopolized; and thence of course proving injurious to domestic economy and foreign commerce."

> "As to monopolies, it is an odious word without a determinate meaning. In its legal sense, as defined by Hawkins, Blackstone and others, it has no proper reference to new inventions in the useful arts."

> "It is plain that the subject is *not* so restrained by any exclusive privilege granted to the author of a new discovery, produce, invention or species of *manufacture*, which the subject in general COULD NOT manufacture, and in which of course he DID NOT *trade* before."[33]

Collier too argued, in his patent treatise of 1803, that the old style monopoly described by Coke as against the ancient and fundamental laws of the realm was not a description of monopolies allowed under the Statute of James I. He made a distinction between the general character of monopoly grants before the Statute of Monopolies and after the Statute of Monopolies. The old "pernicious system" had been "wholly destroyed" by the Statute.

---

33   Kenrick, *An Address to the Artists and Manufacturers of Great Britain, respecting an Application to Parliament for the farther Encouragement of new Discoveries and Inventions in the useful Arts* (1774), pp. 44-46.

"Thus monopoly, in the more enlarged sense, may extend to a trade already in existence, in the more confined, applies merely to a new invention. In the former case it is the exclusion of all others from what the public was already in the possession, and the practice of, until the monopoly was sanctioned. In the latter, it is taking nothing from the public which it before possessed and practiced. The first is a violation of public right, and is nothing less than legalised plunder – the last is an equitable reward to ingenuity, and, under proper restrictions, is abundantly conducive to the general good." [34]

Collier stressed that times had changed. He expressed dissatisfaction with the way Grotius had dealt with the subject of monopolies in *De Jure Belli ac Pacis:* "The learned Grotius has examined the question, if every species of monopoly be a violation of the natural rights of mankind: but on this subject he has not attended with his usual accuracy to the facts by which he would illustrate his principles." Grotius had argued that the sovereign may sometimes permit individuals to enjoy the right of an exclusive sale of certain articles, and the examples given had been Joseph's monopoly and the city of Alexandria. Monopolies in former times, argued Collier, had had a uniform character: "they were an agreement between the reigning power and certain individuals to deprive the people of their natural rights." However, that was before "the ingenuity of man was directed to the increase of the necessaries and comforts of life, by rendering science and philosophy extensively sub-servient to the purpose of commerce". [35]

Davies too introduced his compilation of patent cases, published in 1816, by observing that monopolies for new inventions were not like the old style monopolies:

"this mode of encouraging ingenuity seems calculated to produce its effect, without violating any principle of commerce or of justice; because the reward is exactly proportioned to the merit and utility of the invention...It takes nothing from the public of which they were before in possession; while it tends greatly to promote the general interest of the community." [36]

Godson, in Book I of his treatise, began by pointing out that forestalling, engrossing and regrating were offences meant to contend with the malpractices of subjects, to deter "the monopolists among the people". With respect to the common law and patents for invention, Godson comments that the common law had interpreted the grants made by the crown with "the greatest strictness". Yet even by that law, he notes, the king had the power of

---

34 Collier, *An Essay on Patents for new Inventions* (1803), pp. 2, 19.
35 *Ibid.*, pp. 2-3, 7-8.
36 Davies, *A Collection of the Most Important Cases respecting Patents of Invention* (1816), p. 6.

conferring on the inventor of any useful manufacture or art the exclusive power of using or vending it for a reasonable time. This is presumably his reason for declaring that the Statute of Monopolies was merely declaratory of the common law: patents for invention had never fallen under the same category as forestalling, engrossing and regrating. However, in Godson's opinion, the crown had failed to give sufficient encouragement to inventors, and in this respect the Statute of Monopolies marked a watershed:

> "This statute has always been considered as merely declaratory of the common law prerogative of granting patents: but the acknowledged power of the crown was so seldom exerted in favour of the inventor of a useful manufacture, that the legislature was compelled at once to put an end to the licentious and grievous monopolies, and to hold out encouragement to the ingenious artist."

Godson considered that the necessity of some legal provision to secure a reward to those who would exert their abilities, employ their time, and spend their money in the production of something new and useful to the community, was apparent to every one.[37] Like Collier, he saw the monopoly granted in conjunction with a patent for invention as a separate species of monopoly.

Not all judges seem to have been convinced that the monopoly awarded for a patent for an invention was a quite distinct species of monopoly. A monopoly was a monopoly and as such against the principles of the common law. For example, in *Turner v. Winter* 1787, Ashhurst, J. considered that patents, because they gave a monopoly to the patentee, were "against the principles of law"; the only justification for them was that the inventor's knowledge would be available to the public upon the expiry of the patent.[38] Lord Kenyon was adverse to any form of monopolistic behaviour that he considered would oppress the lower ranks of society. That included patents for inventions: the duty to protect "the lower orders of men from patents" had caused him to declare in *Hornblower v. Boulton and Watt* 1799 that he was "not one of those who greatly favour patents".[39]

However, there are indications that some judges did make a distinction between monopolies for patents for invention and other types of monopolies. It was brought to the fore in chapter 4 that not all judges emphasised the monopolistic nature of the patent grant; a patent for new inventions could be placed within a contractual framework. Lord Mansfield may have considered the contractual format to be appropriate because the monopoly to a patentee was distinct from monopolies on existing products; if an invention

---

37   Godson, *A Practical Treatise on the Law of Patents for Inventions and of Copyright* (1823), pp. 7, 43-45.
38   *Turner v. Winter* 1787, 1 T.R. 605.
39   *Hornblower v. Boulton and Watt* 1799, *The Times*, 26 January 1799, Issue 4393; p. 3; col. C.

was novel it did not take away any public right that had existed before. As noted in chapter 4, in his address to the jury in the case of *Liardet v. Johnson*, Mansfield had said:

> "...that in all patents for new inventions, if not really new discoveries, the trade must be against them; for if it is *an old thing* it is a prejudice to every man in the trade; it is a monopoly."[40]

This sounds like Mansfield is contrasting the reward to the patentee for a new invention with a monopoly for an 'old thing'; it is only the monopoly for the 'old thing' which is 'a prejudice to every man in the trade'.

Indeed several judges drew the distinction explicitly between patent rights and monopolies. One was Lord Chief Justice Eyre in *Boulton and Watt v. Bull* 1795:

> "Patent rights are no where, that I can find, accurately discussed in our books. Sir Edward Coke discourses largely, and sometimes not quite intelligibly, upon monopolies in his chapter of monopolies 3 Inst. 181. But he deals very much in generals, and says little or nothing of patent rights, as opposed to monopolies."

He then refers to several early cases (including *Darcy v. Allin* and Bircot's case) and remarks:

> "There is also a case in Godbolt, and there are a few others condemning particular patents, which were beyond all doubt *mere monopolies*."

At the end of his judgment in *Boulton v. Bull*, Eyre says:

> "for let it be remembered, that though monopolies in the eye of the law are odious, the consideration of the privilege created by this patent, is meritorious because, to use the words of Lord Coke, 'the inventor bringeth to and for the commonwealth a new manufacture by his invention, costs and charges'."[41]

Describing monopolies as 'odious' echoes Coke's sentiments in the third part of his *Institutes* (p. 181). Yet from these comments, it would seem that Eyre, while considering that monopolies are against the law, sees the reward for a patent as something quite distinct from 'mere monopolies'. The 'consideration' for the grant is a new manufacture. It is the

---

40 Hulme, "On the History of Patent Law in the Seventeenth and Eighteenth Centuries" (1902), p. 287 [my italics].

41 *Boulton and Watt v. Bull* 1795, 2 H. Black 491, 500 [my italics], Henry Blackstone's footnote indicates the case reported in Godbolt is the Clothworkers of Ipswich case.

same argument put forward by Kenrick, Collier and Godson: a patentee of a new invention takes away nothing that was there before. Hence, to use Eyre's words, the consideration for a patent for a new invention is not a 'mere monopoly'. In that same vein, Lord Eldon as already noted in chapter 4, unequivocally rejected the notion that a patent should be seen in the light of a monopoly, for it was a bargain with the public and hence the patent specification was of a contractual nature.[42]

In this context, it is interesting to note the speech made by John Campbell, the future Lord Chief Justice of the Queen's Bench, in the case of *Cornish v. Keene* 1837. At that time, Campbell was appearing in his capacity as Attorney-General, representing the patentee. He stated:

> "Gentlemen, monopolies, strictly speaking, in the proper sense of the word, are detestable things; and I am happy to say, they have not existed in this country for a period of two hundred years; but how great is the difference between monopoly and giving reward to ingenuity, skill, industry, and perseverance."[43]

It is an interesting speech for two reasons. Firstly, the Attorney-General, in addressing both judge and jury, apparently still felt he had to deal with the negative associations connected to monopolies. Secondly, the argument that the reward granted to a patentee was something quite distinct from the old style 'detestable' monopoly was one that was being taken up now by the senior law officer.

5.1.2   The Monopoly from the Economic Perspective

One of the main arguments of Dutton's work is that a change took place in the attitude of judges towards patents for invention sometime in the early 1830s: "Judges' attitude to patents changed because they now accepted that inventions led to prosperity and economic growth." Dutton endorses Robert Macfie's suggestion that the 'history of patents is one of continually relaxing aversion on the part of the Courts of Law'; the process was a slow one but much of the change took place between 1830 and 1840.[44] This would imply a judicial acceptance of monopolies for patents for invention during that decade. Whether patents actually are stimulants for economic growth was not the issue addressed by Dutton; nor is it the issue here. From the perspective of this study, the relevant issue is whether the

---

42   *Harmar v. Playne* 1807, 1CPC 257.
43   *Cornish v. Keene* 1837, 2 CPC 352.
44   Dutton, *The patent system and inventive activity during the industrial revolution 1750-1852* (1984), pp. 79, 81.

judges in the 1830s had come to the conclusion that monopolies for invention were good for economic growth.

In the eighteenth century, it was commonly considered that the function of the common law, in prohibiting monopolistic practices, was the protection of the poorer members of society. An outspoken proponent of this duty was Lord Kenyon. In *R v. Waddington* 1800, a case concerned with enhancing the price of hops, Kenyon stated:

"It was the peculiar policy of this system of laws to provide for the wants of the poor labouring class of the country. If humanity alone cannot operate to this end, interest and policy must compel out attention to it…It is our duty to take care that persons in pursuing their own particular interests do not transgress those laws which were made for the benefit of the whole community."[45]

When Grose, J. delivered the sentence of the court *in R v. Waddington*, the sentiments that he expressed were not different from those already expressed by Kenyon. Grose commented:

"those who can feel for the misery of the lower classes of human beings, would think and speak differently; for they would see how important it is to society, that those who abound in riches, shall not be allowed to employ them to the oppression of the poor, for the gratification of their own avarice."[46]

One of the most influential economists of the day, Adam Smith, shared Kenyon's dislike of monopolies in general. In his *Lectures on Jurisprudence*, Smith states: "All monopolies in particular are extremely detrimental."[47] However, Smith had different ideas from Kenyon as to what constituted a detrimental monopolistic practice. The effect of monopolies was dealt with in some detail by Smith in *The Wealth of Nations*:

"In every country it always is and must be the interest of the great body of the people to buy whatever they want of those who sell it cheapest. The proposition is so very manifest, that it seems ridiculous to take any pains to prove it; nor could it ever have been called in question, had not the interested sophistry of merchants and manufacturers confounded the common sense of mankind."

---

45 *R v. Waddington* 1800, 102 ER 62.
46 *R v. Waddington*, *The Counsellor's Magazine*, p. 296.
47 Adam Smith, *Lectures on Jurisprudence*, reprint of Oxford University Press 1978 ed., Indianapolis 1982, Report of 1762-3 ii, 33 p. 83

"But in the mercantile system, the interest of the consumer is almost constantly sacrificed to that of the producer… the former is obliged to pay the enhancement of price which this monopoly almost always occasions."[48]

However, in *The Wealth of Nations*, Smith rejected the belief that forestalling and engrossing were to be feared:

> "The popular fear of engrossing and forestalling may be compared to the pop-
> ular terrors and suspicions of witchcraft. The unfortunate wretches accused of
> this latter crime were not more innocent of the misfortunes imputed to them,
> than those who have been accused of the former… The law which should restore
> entire freedom to the inland trade of corn, would probably prove as effectual
> to put an end to the popular fears of engrossing and forestalling."[49]

That was most certainly not Lord Kenyon's opinion. In *R v. Waddington* 1800, Kenyon had announced that, as the policy of the old system of laws (on forestalling, engrossing and regrating) had been called into question, he had "endeavoured to inform myself as much as lay in my power, and for this purpose I have read Dr. Adam Smith's work". However, Kenyon made it clear that he favoured those writers who had supported "our ancient system of jurisprudence, the growth of the wisdom of man for so many ages".[50] Kenyon took the opportunity in *R v. Rusby* 1800 to express how misguided he considered Smith's view to be. Rusby was a corn merchant who had been indicted for regrating, for having sold oats on at a higher price than he had bought them in the Corn Exchange. In his address to the jury in *R v. Rusby*, also reported at length in *The Times* newspaper, Kenyon states:

> "I wish the life of Dr. Adam Smith, who is a great name in the country, had
> been prolonged – there is a loss of part of the public stock, when a virtuous
> and good man dies. I wish we could have had that sagacious author here to
> have heard this transaction as it has been laid open by the witnesses, and then
> to have tell us whether forestalling, engrossing and regrating were as imaginary
> as witchcraft."[51]

---

48 Adam Smith, *An inquiry into the nature and causes of the wealth of nations*, Cannan online ed., London 1776, vol. 1, Book IV, iii, 39; vol. 2, IV, viii, 49.
49 *Ibid.*, vol. 2, Book IV, *v.*, 65.
50 *R v. Waddington* 1800, 102 ER 62.
51 *R v. Rusby* 1800, *The Times Law Report*, 5 July 1800, Issue 4839, p. 3, col A.

Although Kenyon's stance was at the time popular with the public, it was already starting to be outdated by the time parliament revoked the old penal statutes on forestalling, regrating and engrossing. A Committee of the House of Commons had reached the conclusion that the laws on forestalling, engrossing and regrating were harmful, as preventing 'free trade' had actually increased the price of provisions. It was an argument Edward Law had brought to the fore in *R v. Waddington*, adding that "To talk of preventing forestalling was absurd, they were all forestallers, they lived by forestalling, and were daily fed by its produce".[52] However, his submission had not convinced Kenyon. Campbell would later remark of Kenyon, rather condescendingly: "The notion that the price of commodities is regulated by the proportion between the supply and the demand, he thought was only fit to be entertained by democrats and atheists. These sentiments were at the time highly popular, and contributed to raise his reputation as a great judge." Reviewing the cases of Waddington and Rusby, Campbell found it shameful that most of the puisne judges had aligned themselves with Kenyon in the "hallucination of the King's Bench".[53]

Kenyon seems to have associated monopolies in general with the abuse of the poor, rather than as a potential means to improve the prosperity of society. Kenyon's dislike of monopolies, as being pernicious to the lower orders, may have coloured his vision of patents for invention. In *Hornblower v. Boulton and Watt* 1799, Kenyon conceded that "in many instances", and certainly in the case of Watt's invention, the public did receive a benefit from patents. Nonetheless, patents may have caused more harm than good: "yet on striking the balance upon this subject, I think that great oppression is practised on inferior mechanics by those who are more opulent."[54]

In this respect too, Kenyon disagreed with the analysis advanced by Smith. Whereas Smith considered most exclusive privileges to be prejudicial to society, this was not the case with privileges granted for patents or for copyright. These, Smith considered, "are harmless enough". Concerning patents for inventions he states:

> "Thus the inventor of a new machine or any other invention has the exclusive privilege of making and vending that invention for the space of 14 years by the law of this country, as a reward for his ingenuity, and it is probable that this is as equal an one as could be fallen upon. For if the legislature should appoint pecuniary rewards for the inventors of new machines etc, they would hardly ever be so precisely proportioned to the merit of the invention as this is. For here, if the invention be good and such as is profitable to mankind, he will

---

52 *R v. Waddington* 1800, *The Counsellor's Magazine*, p. 277.
53 Campbell, *The Lives of the Chief Justices of England* (1874), vol. IV, pp. 130-132.
54 *Hornblower v. Boulton and Watt* 1799, 8 T.R. 98.

probably make a fortune by it; but if it be of no value he also will reap no benefit."[55]

Within legal circles, there were those who were prepared to take the role of the market into account. Willes, J., in the copyright case of *Millar v. Taylor* 1769, considered that the "easiest and most equal way" of encouraging "letters, and the painful researches of learned men" was to secure to these men a property in their own works, for "sooner or later, the reward will be in proportion to the merit of the work".[56] Lord Mansfield adopted the same approach with respect to patents for inventions. In his address to the jury in the *Liardet v. Johnson* case 1778, Mansfield said: "It is not material to try the exact excellence of a composition; if the composition is good for nothing the plaintiff gets nothing and nobody gains by it... For if it is new and good for nothing, nobody will make use of it."[57] The same point was brought up by Arkwright's counsel in *R v. Arkwright* 1785: "the reward is proportioned exactly to the ingenuity: if his invention is worth nothing, he will derive no profit to his family; if ingenious, and valuable to the public, he will derive an adequate profit during the time, and the public would receive the benefit in reversion."[58]

These are arguments of utility; if the invention were not useful there would be no reward, if it were useful then the reward would be proportionate to its utility. This too was Jeremy Bentham's justification of the patent system: the utilitarian ground of efficiency.

> "With respect to a great number of inventions in the arts, an exclusive privilege is absolutely necessary, in order that what is sown may be reaped... An exclusive privilege is of all rewards the best proportioned, the most natural, and the least burthensome. It produces an infinite effect, and it costs nothing. 'Grant me fifteen years,' says the inventor, 'that I may reap the fruit of my labours; after this term, it shall be enjoyed by all the world.' Does the sovereign say, 'No, you shall not have it,' what will happen? It will be enjoyed by no one, neither for fifteen years nor afterwards: everybody will be disappointed inventors, workmen, consumers everything will be stifled, both benefit and enjoyment."[59]

As Van Zijl Smit points out, while Bentham conceded that a patent was a grant of monopoly, its effect was different. Whereas other monopolies caused some products not to be produced, patents for invention encouraged the manufacture of newly invented products. If patents increased "the general stock of wealth" then a reward for "industry and genius and

---

55   Smith, *Lectures on Jurisprudence* (1982), Report of 1762-1763, ii. 31 p. 83.
56   *Millar v. Taylor* 1769, 4 Burr 2335.
57   Hulme, "On the History of Patent Law in the Seventeenth and Eighteenth Centuries" (1902), p. 286.
58   Arkwright, *The Trial of a Cause instituted by Richard Pepper Arden, Esq* (1785), p. 106.
59   Jeremy Bentham, *A Manual of Political Economy*, Bowring (ed.), vol. 3, Edinburgh 1843, 3, s.23 *v.* p. 71.

ingenuity, is proportionate and essentially just".[60] In this reading of patents for invention, there was no place for a negative connotation. An unsuccessful patent would cost the public nothing, whereas a successful patent would reward both inventor and the public. When Collier wrote his treatise on patents for invention in 1803, he framed monopolies for invention within the context of public utility:

> "Perhaps the correct way to determine the justice of a monopoly, is by referring to the foundation of that virtue, to examine whether the monopolist benefit himself by his superior knowledge, without injury to others."

> "If the eloquent Hume be correct, 'that public utility is the sole origin of justice, and that reflections on the beneficial consequences of this virtue are the sole foundations of its merit,' the justice of a monopoly, which falls under this class, will not be disputed."[61]

The utilitarian argument of the classical economists was widely disseminated in the late eighteenth-early nineteenth century. With respect to patents for invention, a utilitarian approach took the sting out of the monopoly controversy: put in this framework, the patent monopoly was essentially a "harmless" practice.

Yet even if the practice of granting a monopoly for a new invention were not detrimental to the public, could a patented invention actually increase not only the inventor's prosperity, but also that of the country? Dutton argues that the practice of relating patented inventions to economic growth, although not entirely a nineteenth century phenomenon, was not widespread in the eighteenth century. It is only in the early nineteenth century that a shift in judicial attitudes takes place and the beneficial effect of patents for inventions for the country are acknowledged: "the question of relating patented inventions to economic growth had by the 1830s secured legal footing."[62] However, it should be borne in mind that not all patent cases were reported in the eighteenth century, and even some of those that were reported, were not reported fully. Even with this limitation, as Dutton concedes, there are clear indications that well before the 1830s some judges had coupled a successful invention to the increase in the wealth of a country, and that consequently an inventor should be rewarded. For example, Eyre in *Boulton and Watt v. Bull* 1795 had said:

---

60   Van Zijl Smit, *The Social Creation of a Legal Reality: A Study of the Emergence and Acceptance of the British Patent System as a Legal Instrument for the Control of New Technology* (1981), pp. 105-106.

61   Collier, *An Essay on Patents for new Inventions* (1803), pp. 4-5, fn p. 5.

62   Dutton, *The patent system and inventive activity during the industrial revolution 1750-1852* (1984), pp. 79-80.

"The advantages to the public from improvements of this kind, are beyond all calculation important to a commercial country, and the ingenuity of artists who turn their thoughts towards such improvements, is in itself deserving of encouragement."[63]

Several years later, when Watt's patent was the subject of the action in *Hornblower v. Boulton and Watt* 1799, Ashhurst was of the opinion that:

"Every new invention is of importance to the wealth and convenience of the public; and when they are enjoying the fruits of an useful discovery, it would be hard on the inventor to deprive him of his reward."[64]

Collier, in the first legal treatise on patents for invention in 1803, was already convinced that:

"this poison of the state has been deprived of all its pernicious ingredients, and has been converted into a nutritious aliment, applicable to the support of commercial prosperity."[65]

It was this school of though, which was certainly present within the ranks of the eighteenth century judiciary, that would predominate in the 1830s. If the invention increased the public wealth, the inventor should be rewarded proportionately. The patent for invention as a monopoly which infringed public rights, which took something away from the public that they otherwise would have had, did not fit within a utilitarian approach. A poor invention would not injure others; it would simply fail. A good invention would not injure others: it would bring benefits for both the inventor and the country.

5.1.3   The Monopoly as Contrary to Morality and Religion

The statements made by Lord Kenyon and Grose, J. in the monopoly case of *R v. Waddington* are very revealing. Kenyon speaks of the duty to protect the poor, labouring classes and Grose speaks of protecting the lower orders from oppression and avarice. Their stance against monopolies is identical to that of the theologians of the medieval Catholic

---

63 *Boulton and Watt v. Bull* 1795, 2 H. Black 494.
64 *Hornblower v. Boulton and Watt* 1799, 8 T.R. 99.
65 Collier, *An Essay on Patents for new Inventions* (1803), p. 12.

Church. The primary concern of these theologians was social justice rather than the operation of the economic system.[66]

In medieval times, the Catholic Church had been overtly against the practice of monopolies. The monopoly had been considered by the Catholic Church to be an immoral practice. Not only exacting interest on a loan but also raising prices by a monopoly had been condemned in the thirteenth century manual of St. Raymond as forms of usury. Well into the sixteenth century, any bargain in which one party gained more advantage than the other was regarded as usurious. There was a line that had to be drawn between enterprise and avarice. A man had a right to such wealth as was necessary to maintain his station in life, but not to more than that. Trade was legitimate, but it should be carried on for the public benefit, and the profits a merchant made should be no more than the wages of his labour. The merchant who bought goods in order that he could sell them dearer was to be justly condemned.[67]

It is beyond the scope of this study to examine the relationship between religion and the development of trade and commerce. Yet one point is of particular interest: had the old ethics with respect to usury and monopolies affected legal attitudes in the eighteenth century? In his *Commentaries*, Blackstone makes a distinction between usury and interest. With respect to usury, Blackstone examines the matter in some detail in Book IV. He states "Usury is an unlawful contract upon the loan of money, to receive the same again with exorbitant increase".[68] These were contracts where the level of interest exceeded the rates fixed by statute. With respect to interest, he presents both sides of the argument: those for and those against interest. As against, he puts forward the argument made by the "school divines" for interest being "contrary to the divine law both natural and revealed; and the canon law has proscribed the taking any, the least, increase for the loan of money as a mortal sin". The counter argument was that "moderate interest tends greatly to the benefit of the public, especially in a trading country". It is this counter argument which Blackstone himself endorses. He observes that in the "dark ages of monkish superstition and civil tyranny, when interest was laid under a total interdict, commerce was also at its lowest ebb". Only "when true religion and real liberty revived, commerce grew again into credit, and again introduced with itself its inseparable companion, the doctrine of loans upon interest". There is a major proviso: a distinction must be made between a moderate and an exorbitant profit: "to the former of which we usually give the name of interest, to the latter the truly *odious* appellation of usury." Demanding an exorbitant price is against conscience; a reasonable price is not immoral.[69]

---

66 Raymond De Roover, "Monopoly Theory Prior to Adam Smith: A Revision", *The Quarterly Journal of Economics* 65, no. 4 (1951), p. 495.

67 R.H. Tawney, *Religion and the rise of capitalism*, New York 1947, pp. 35, 37-38, 131.

68 Blackstone, *Commentaries on the Laws of England* (1793), IV, 156.

69 *Ibid.*, II, 453-455 [my italics].

Does Blackstone take the same liberal, pragmatic attitude towards monopolies? In the *Commentaries*, Blackstone simply points out that monopolies were declared against the law and void by the Statute of Monopolies, except for monopolies for patents for new inventions, printing, saltpetre, gunpowder, great ordnance and shot.[70] However, in *Tonson v. Collins* 1762, Blackstone had referred to a monopoly as "A very *odious* term" (see below). The use of the word 'odious' not only harks back to Coke's description of monopolies, but it is exactly the same adjective Blackstone used to show his disapproval of usury. That Blackstone accepted interest on loans at a moderate rate does not imply that he also condoned monopolies.

Is it possible that some members of the English judiciary may have had reservations concerning monopolies because of religious beliefs, or at the very least that monopolies were contrary to conscience? If so, this could have affected their attitude to patents because a monopoly was granted by a patent for an invention. Religious considerations were certainly used as an argument against monopolies by Coke, where a monopoly could take away a man's employment. In Coke's report of *Darcy v. Allin* 1602, it was claimed that the law of monopolies "agrees with the equity of the law of God, as appears in Deuteronomy cap 24, verse 6". That verse stated: "No man shall take the nether or the upper millstone to pledge: for he takes a man's life to pledge."[71] Coke argued, in his *Third Institute*, that to take away a man's livelihood was tantamount to taking his life: "the monopolist that takes away a man's trade, takes away his life." Coke made it very clear that this law was "grounded upon the law of God.": "Against these inventors and propounders of evil things, the Holy Ghost has spoken."[72] Noy's report of *Darcy v. Allin* also had a religious reference. It had been argued in that case that the letters patent made to the plaintiff were "contrary to the laws of God". Under the section 'Now to prove that it is against the law of God and man', Noy's report noted Thessalonians: "every man should live by labour." This "general ordinance of God" meant that: "it is as unlawful to prohibit a man not to live by the labour of his own trade … as to prohibit him not to live by labour."[73] As noted in chapter 3, in the early eighteenth century the prohibition of patents for inventions that could adversely affect employment, "that takes away a man's trade", was still considered good law. This type of labour-saving invention was deemed to fall under the 'generally inconvenient' clause in the Statute of Monopolies 1624. It was only towards the latter part of the eighteenth century that labour-saving machines were no longer considered by the courts to be 'generally inconvenient'.

To what extent religious sentiment had been instrumental in the prohibition of patents that would affect employment is difficult to determine. Religion and more worldly factors,

---

70   *Ibid.*, IV, 159.
71   *Darcy v. Allin*, 1602, 11 Co Rep. 86b, Coke, *Third Institute*, p. 181.
72   Coke, *Third Institute*, p. 181.
73   *Darcy v. Allin* 1602, Noy 174, 180.

such as economic considerations and the influence of vested interests, may have been intertwined. For some, religious considerations may have represented little more than convenient platitudes. For others, religion may have formed a more substantial motivation. As evident from the grain monopoly cases examined above, in the eighteenth century there were those on the bench who considered that the function of the common law, in prohibiting monopolistic practices, was the protection of the lower orders of society. The poor had to be protected against monopolies which would lead to the loss of their livelihood and other forms of monopolistic practices which would deprive them of the basic necessities of life. This evokes the concepts of social justice of the medieval theologians. It was part of an older vision of the role of the State, which Toynbee considered had lingered on. The medieval system conceived of the State as a religious institution. It was deemed the duty of the State to watch over the individual citizen in all his relations, to provide protection from force and fraud, and safeguard his spiritual well-being. Toynbee argues that this theory, and the policy of regulation and restriction which sprang from it, still affected English industry at the time Adam Smith was writing.[74]

Lord Kenyon was well known for his dislike of monopolistic practices and seems to have associated the duty of the courts to protect the lower orders with moral and religious values. In *R v. Rusby* 1800, a merchant had been accused of selling on oats at a higher price. As noted above, this case had been reported in some detail in *The Times*; the case must have been of general interest. Kenyon stressed in Rusby the importance of making sure the poor had the necessities of life: "humanity calls for it; the duties of religion call for it."[75] In *R v. Waddington*, which was heard that same year, the defendant was accused of forestalling, of having intended to resell a quantity of hops at an unreasonable profit. Kenyon brought the religious factor once again explicitly to the fore in that case:

"... to say the truth, it did appear to him, in the view he had, either of Law, or of Morality, or of Religion, a very heinous offence."

Kenyon added:

"and God forbid, that these things, which he has given us to be diffused and as generally divided among his creatures according to their wants, as may be, for the common benefit of all, should be hoarded up by a few, and rendered inaccessible to the many."[76]

---

74 A. Toynbee, *Lectures on the Industrial Revolution of the Eighteenth Century in England*, London 1916, VII p. 51
75 *R v. Rusby* 1800, *The Times Law Report*, 5 July 1800, Issue 4839, p. 3 col A.
76 *R v. Waddington* 1800, *The Counsellor's Magazine*, pp. 285-286.

The cases of Rusby and Waddington are cases on agricultural produce monopolies. Nonetheless, they may provide some insight into how the King's Bench under Kenyon viewed the monopoly awarded for a patent for invention. It is not contended here that Kenyon would purposefully set out to defeat a patent because of his aversion to monopoly. Kenyon and Grose, who both spoke out so clearly against a hops monopoly in the Waddington case, found in favour of Watt's patent, which was a case in which judicial opinion was divided. However, it is possible that Kenyon's religious and moral convictions concerning his duty to protect the lower orders of society was a factor that encouraged him to read patent specifications in a more restrictive manner. Kenyon was criticised for being unwilling to distinguish between patents and monopolies.[77] He certainly had a reputation amongst patentees for being prepared to set aside a patent on the slightest technicality.[78] Kenyon was unusually open concerning his personal opinion on these matters. As already noted, he had actually announced in court, in 1799 in the Hornblower case, that he was not in favour of patents precisely because he considered them as oppressive of the lower orders. As the cases of Rusby and Waddington show, he was quite prepared to express his religious and moral sentiments in connection with monopoly cases. There may have been other judges who shared Kenyon's attitude, but who were less outspoken in court than Kenyon.

There was another aspect of older religious doctrine which did not accord with new theories on economics, in particular those promulgated by Adam Smith. Catholic religious doctrine had rejected the pursuit of self-interest. Smith apparently felt the need to deal specifically with this point, arguing that the pursuit of self-interest was a natural reflex and was not necessarily harmful to the community:

> "The natural effort of every individual to better his own condition, when suf-
> fered to exert itself with freedom and security, is so powerful a principle, that
> it is alone, and without any assistance, not only capable of carrying on the
> society to wealth and prosperity, but of surmounting a hundred impertinent
> obstructions with which the folly of human laws too often incumbers its oper-
> ations."[79]

Smith's theory did arguably have a certain religious component, which was possibly a concession to the dominant Christian culture of the day - the idea of the providential, invisible hand. A man may intend only his own gain but he was often "led by an invisible

---

77 Hansard XV, 1833, p. 977 cited in Dutton, *The patent system and inventive activity during the industrial revolution 1750-1852* (1984), p. 77.

78 See, for example, the testimony of Francis Abbott in the *Select Committee Report 1829*, p. 64

79 Smith, *An inquiry into the nature and causes of the wealth of nations* (1776), vol. 2, IV,v. 82.

hand to promote an end which was no part of his intention".[80] Given the potential benefit to society of this pursuit of self-interest, Smith considered that State intervention was, on occasion, warranted to give adequate incentives in order to stimulate progress. For example, a temporary monopoly could be granted to merchants to establish a new trade when that required the merchants to take risk and encounter expense. This was "vindicated upon the same principles upon which a like monopoly of a new machine is granted to its inventor".[81] Lord Mansfield certainly seems to have understood that incentives offered by the State were necessary. Two years after Smith published his seminal *The Wealth of Nations*, Mansfield had told the jury in the Liardet case 1778 that it was "of vast consequence to the public that there should be an *inducement* to men to make discoveries of arts and inventions of various kinds".[82]

5.1.4   The Monopoly as Contrary to Natural Law

Treating the law of nature as a source of English law was conventional practice in the eighteenth century. Lieberman declares that: "Virtually every other eighteenth-century legal author who, like Blackstone, aimed his work beyond a purely professional audience likewise invoked natural law arguments." His examples include Edward Wynne, who stated that "the Law of Nature" had "ever been considered as part of the Common Law", and Richard Wooddeson, who saw Natural Law as the ultimate ethical foundation of law in England.[83] Indeed, not only was Natural Law deemed to be a source of the common law, it was also considered to be superior to the common law. As Ibbetson points out, an appeal to Natural Law could defeat traditional common law authorities. One instance is the case of *Omychund v. Barker* 1744 in which the young William Murray based his arguments on Natural Law reasoning, as expounded by Grotius and Pufendorf, to fly in the face of the common law authorities. Arguments from the writings of Natural Lawyers had provided a legally acceptable foundation for the overturning of long-standing common law rules. In the eighteenth century, Natural Law provided an acceptable basis for legal arguments.[84] The major works of the most prominent Natural Law philosophers, Grotius and Pufendorf, were available in England in the eighteenth century not only in Latin but also in English translations (the quotations below are taken from the eighteenth century translations of

---

80 *Ibid.*, vol. 1, IV, ii 9.
81 *Ibid.*, vol. 2, V, i, 119.
82 Oldham, *The Mansfield Manuscripts and the growth of English law in the eighteenth century* (1992), p. 753 [my italics].
83 Lieberman, *The province of legislation determined* (1989), p. 38.
84 Ibbetson, "Natural Law and Common Law" (2001), pp. 8-9.

these works). References to Grotius and Pufendorf are regularly to be found in the reports of cases[85] and are scattered throughout Blackstone's *Commentaries*.

Natural Law was conceived of as a set of rules accessible to men either by reason or by an innate moral sense. This gave Natural Law a secular dimension. It was a dimension alluded to by Grotius. In *The Rights of War and Peace* (*De iure belli ac pacis*), Grotius states:

> "And indeed, what we have now said would take place, though we should even grant, what without the greatest wickedness cannot be granted, that there is no God, or that he takes no care of human affairs."[86]

Natural Law did not depend upon divine revelation, but upon man's own reasoning or innate moral sense as to what was intrinsically right or wrong.

If Natural Law had an existence independent of God, did that mean that Natural Law was no longer associated with God's law? It is a question that is still addressed by modern scholars. Besselink contends, in his study on the work of Grotius, that Grotius's *etiamsi daremus* hypothesis cannot be a decisive argument for the alleged secularization of Natural Law. Grotius placed the emphasis upon the essential immutability of Natural Law, but he did not remove himself from the philosophical tradition which placed the origin of Natural Law in the Divine.[87] Ibbetson argues that Natural Law was secular, in the sense that it distanced itself from the tenets of revealed religion. The content of Natural Law was deduced from basic data about human nature: the desire for self-preservation or the need for co-operation or sociability to ensure human survival. However, Ibbetson does concede that "analytically God was essential to the theories, since it was only through Him that the rules could be said to obtain their foundations and their binding force".[88]

In the eighteenth century, whether Natural Law was secular or divine was a matter for debate. For example, John Edwards, in his *Theologia reformata* acknowledged the human dimension:

> "I do not deny that Natural Law may be styled Human, because it is seated in Human Minds, and issues from the Reason of Man".

---

85   For example, *Goss v. Withers* 1758, 2 Burr 688, 691, 692, 694, *Hamilton v. Mendes* 1761 2 Burr 1201, *Pillans v. van Mirrop* 1765, 3 Burr 1670.
86   Hugo Grotius, *The Rights of War Peace*, vol. 2, London 1715, Prol. para 11, p. 14.
87   Leonard F.M. Besselink, *Keeping Faith: a Study of Grotius' Doctrine of Natural Law*, Florence 1988, p. 200.
88   Ibbetson, "Natural Law and Common Law" (2001), p. 5.

However, he adds:

> "I take it in another Respect, viz. not as it is seated in Man; but as it proceeds from God, and I reckon the Law of Nature as Part of the Divine… The Natural Law in Man is the Participation of the Eternal Law which is in God."[89]

What is interesting is that in the *Commentaries*, possibly the most influential legal work of the eighteenth century, Blackstone puts forward an understanding of Natural Law that is not out of step with that propounded by John Edwards. Blackstone makes the connection between God and Natural Law explicit in the Introduction to his *Commentaries*. The law of nature was "dictated by God himself".[90] Blackstone stresses the importance of human reason, but also that human reason has its limitations. As every man knows "his reason is corrupt, and his understanding full of ignorance and error", and hence the necessity of the benign intervention of divine providence and the doctrines provided by revealed or divine laws, which are only to be found in the Holy Scriptures.

> "These precepts, when revealed, are found upon comparison to be really a part of the original law of nature, as they tend in all their consequences to man's felicity. But we are not from thence to conclude that the knowledge of these truths was attainable by reason, in its present corrupted state; since we find that, until they were revealed, they were hid from the wisdom of ages."

> "Yet undoubtedly, the revealed law is of infinitely more authenticity than that moral system, which is framed by ethical writers, and denominated the natural law. Because one is the law of nature, expressly declared so to be by God himself; the other is only what, by the assistance of human reason, we imagine to be that law."[91]

Blackstone, therefore, makes a distinction between the law of nature ordained by God and a moral system, referred to as the law of nature, which is an attempt by human reasoning to expound the law of nature. In his study of Blackstone's *Commentaries*, Boorstin ascribes an ulterior motive to Blackstone's tendency to "conservative affirmation": if a rational Science of Law was not to lead men to question the divinely-sanctioned existing order of society, the Science of Law would have to be a science that admired the Creator.

---

89 John Edwards, *Theologia Reformata: or the Body and Substance of the Christian Religion, comprised in Distinct Discourses*, vol. 2, London 1713, p. 279.

90 Blackstone, *Commentaries on the Laws of England* (1793), vol. I, Introd. 40.

91 *Ibid.*, Intro. 41-42.

"If the fundamentals of law came to be defined as 'what we all knew', the study
of society might cease to be an admiring science. The quest for legal principles
might become a perilous inquisition into the foundations of society."[92]

Blackstone also distinguishes between those rights that God and nature have established,
which are therefore called "natural rights", and those rights that are instituted by the state.
The legislature cannot destroy or abridge natural rights or make them stronger by declaring
natural rights to be the law of the land. The legislature only acts "in subordination to the
great lawgiver, transcribing and publishing his precepts". However, there are matters which
are deemed right or wrong, just or unjust according to the will of the legislator. These are
matters concerned with the welfare of society and the purposes of civil life. It is within this
context that Blackstone refers to monopolies:

"Thus our common law has declared, that the goods of the wife do instantly
upon marriage become the property and right of the husband: and our statute
law has declared all monopolies a public offence: yet that right and this offence
have no foundation in nature; but are merely created by the law, for the purposes
of civil society."[93]

Was Natural Law, whether considered either in the divine or secular sense, against
monopolies? Natural Law philosophers like Grotius and Pufendorf did devote attention
to such matters as a just price, usury and monopolies. In the chapter on contracts in *The
Rights of War and Peace*, Grotius notes that prices should reflect what was usually offered
or given for the goods. No more should be demanded by either party than what was just.[94]
With respect to monopolies, it would seem that Grotius considered that monopolies were
contrary to the law of nature in general, but not all monopolies violated the laws of nature.
Monopolies could be permitted by a sovereign power for a just cause and with a fixed
price. As an example, he gave the history of Joseph as a governor of Egypt. Grotius also
acknowledged that a *monopoly* could, in some cases, be established by private individuals,
provided they sell at a fair price. Combinations to raise the necessary articles of life to an
exorbitant rate, or all violent and fraudulent attempts to prevent the market from being
supplied, or to buy up certain commodities, in order to enhance the price, were "an
injustice" requiring "amends and a reparation".[95] Grotius did not, therefore, condemn *all*
monopolies as being against the law of nature. However, that seems to have been a point
that sometimes either got lost or was ignored. As noted above, Collier in his treatise on

---

92 Boorstin, *The Mysterious Science of the Law, An Essay on Blackstone's Commentaries* (1996), pp. 19, 25, 30.
93 Blackstone, *Commentaries on the Law of England* (1793), Introd. 54
94 Grotius, "The Rights of War and Peace" (1715), Book II, 12, xi and xiv.
95 *Ibid.*, Book II, 12, xvi.

patents seemed to be berating Grotius for seeing monopolies as a "violation of the natural rights of mankind".

As to Pufendorf, in his section on monopolies in *The Law of Nature and Nations* (*De Iure Naturae et Gentium*) of 1672, he explicitly addresses the issue of whether monopolies are against the law of nature. He notes: "'tis an odious name, and the laws of many states brand it grievously." Pufendorf points out that not all practices whereby only one person or country produces something fall under the category of monopoly. Yet even if there are 'several good reasons for the granting such a privilege", "Nor even then must the merchants be allowed to enhance the price of those things at their pleasure; for it is against reason to give an opportunity of scraping up exorbitant riches out the fortunes of the rest, when the public gets nothing by it." To be classed as a monopoly, the implication must be that "others too would sell the same, did not one Man engross the whole trade to himself". He considered, however, that a monopoly could not be established by private individuals. "The monopolies of private men are spurious and illegal, and do not depend upon rights and privileges, but are generally carried on by clandestine frauds and combinations."[96]

The moral dimension of the Natural Law position on monopolies had not dissipated in the eighteenth century. It was there, submerged beneath the rational arguments of the Enlightenment writers. A good example is Adam Smith. Smith argued that what is considered to be right or wrong is how it is perceived by the impartial spectator. The natural is connected with the rational. Norms and values are "natural or unnatural, arising from nature or being contrary to nature"; "nature and reason dictate; there are laws of natural reason".[97] Yet those laws, said Smith, that have been extorted by merchants and manufacturers to "support their own absurd and oppressive monopolies" may be said to be "all written in blood".[98] The emotive, moral context is clear. Smith may have been arguing that these 'absurd and oppressive monopolies' were against reason, but he too placed them in a moral context by the reference to them being 'written in blood'.

Even if the religious component is left out of Natural Law, if the law of nature is approached as a secular set of rules as to what is right and wrong rather than as divine rules, the interpretation of Natural Law could be highly unfavourable to how monopolies were perceived. If Natural Law was interpreted in a way that was analogous to the beliefs of the medieval catholic theologians, it could be used to reinforce the view that monopolistic practices were immoral. As noted above, Lord Kenyon bundled all these aspects together:

---

96 Samual Pufendorf, *The Law of Nature and Nation*, London 1749, Book V, 5, vii.
97 Knud Haakonssen, *The Science of a Legislator: the Natural Jurisprudence of David Hume and Adam Smith*, Cambridge 1981, p. 136.
98 Smith, *An inquiry into the nature and causes of the wealth of nations* (1776), vol. 2, Book IV, viii, 17.

"... to say the truth, it did appear to him, in the view he had, either of Law, or of Morality, or of Religion, a very heinous offence."

5.2   THE STATUS OF THE INVENTOR PATENTEE

The association of inventors with trade and industry may have done little to enhance the reputation of inventors in the eyes of some contemporaries in the earlier years of the Industrial Revolution. Adam Smith, for example, was highly critical of merchants and manufacturers. Several comments in *The Wealth of Nations* illustrate his distrust:

> "People of the same trade seldom meet together, even for merriment and diversion, but the conversation ends in a conspiracy against the public, or in some contrivance to raise prices."

The monopolizing spirit of merchants and manufacturers meant they: "neither are, nor ought to be, the rulers of mankind".[99] His distrust of merchant and manufacturers was one of the reasons he argued for free trade. The association of the inventor with manufacture was a reason that inventors were considered by some to be inferior to authors. Sherman and Bently contend that even in the nineteenth century a romantic idea of copyright prevailed: "The attitude adopted towards literary and artistic property is in marked contrast to the approach taken towards patents and designs which were seen to have clear connections with commerce and trade."[100] Those campaigning for better copyright protection also made unflattering comparisons between patentees and authors: inventions were more the product of manual labour than intellectual labour. Finally, there were religious and moral arguments which served to diminish the status of the inventor who chose to patent his invention.

5.2.1   The Comparison with Authors

Inventors, even if sometimes admired for their ingenuity, had not generally been as highly regarded in pre-industrial society as those who practiced other forms of creativity. Francis Bacon, for example, made an unfavourable comparison between men who had produced literary works and men who had made things:

---

99 *Ibid.*, vol. 1, I, x 82, IV, iii 38.
100 Sherman and Bently, *The Making of Modern Intellectual Property Law: The British Experience 1760-1911* (1999), p. 124.

"If, therefore, the invention of a ship was thought so noble, which carries commodities from place to place, and brings the remotest regions acquainted; how much more are Letters to be valued, which, like ships, pass through the vast ocean of time, and convey knowledge and inventions to the remotest ages."[101]

Books of learning, or of genius like the verses of Homer, were considered by Bacon to be more significant than things made by the hand of man. In the eighteenth century, there still seemed to be a higher regard in genteel society for those who expended their efforts upon literary works, rather than mechanical devices.

In this context, it is interesting to note a comment made by Wooddeson, professor of common law at Oxford, in his legal treatise which was published in 1792. In reviewing occupancy grounded on labour and invention as a means of acquiring property, Wooddeson turns his attention to both copyright and patents for invention. He remarks: "Of this kind the most distinguished and meritorious branch is called literary property."[102] Indeed, the whole theme of Kenrick's publication, which had appeared in 1774, was the discrimination suffered by those who practice the "useful arts" rather than the "polite arts". The "ignorant and indolent Great" failed to discern the difference between an inventor and a labourer, but rather blended the two together "and confound them indiscriminately with the refuse of mankind".[103] Kenrick attributed the differences in the legal protection offered to authors and that available to inventors to this prejudice.

How the patent was viewed by some members of the bench may have been affected by the arguments put forward by those who contended that copyright protection should be perpetual, not temporary like patent protection. It was incumbent upon those campaigning for authors to be treated differently at law than inventors to justify that inequality of treatment. This necessitated a distinction to be made between the fundamental nature of a literary work and that of an invention. The distinction hinged upon the amount of manual work as opposed to the amount of mental work that was involved. The amount of mental work in creating a machine was downplayed. Illustrative of this argument is Warburton's *A Letter from an Author* of 1747. Speaking of mechanical engines, Warburton considered:

"Now these partaking so essentially of the nature of *manual* works, the maker has no *perfect* right of property in the *invention*. For like a common utensil, it

---

101 Francis Bacon, *The philosophical Works of Francis Bacon, Baron of Verulam, methodized and made English, from the Originals... In three Volumes, by Peter Shaw*, vol. 1, London 1733, Preliminaries, sect.III, 72, p. 38.
102 Wooddeson, *A Systematical View of the Laws of England* (1792-1793), vol. 2, pp. 392-393.
103 Kenrick, *An Address to the Artists and Manufacturers of Great Britain; respecting an Application to Parliament for the farther Encouragement of new Discoveries and Inventions in the useful Arts* (1774), pp. 20, 30.

must be finished before it can be of use to himself; like that, its materials are its principal expense; and like that, a successful imitator must work with the ideas of the first inventor: which are all reasons why the property should terminate in the individual machine... that the constructor of a piece of mechanism has his property confined to the individual thing made; and the composer of a scholastic work has *his*, extended to the ideal discourse itself."[104]

Such, apparently, was the impact of Warburton's argument that it was specifically addressed by counsel in the copyright case of *Tonson v. Collins* 1761-1762. Thurlow, counsel for the defendant in the 1761 hearing, argued:

"He attempts a distinction between the labour of the head and of the hand. But in some machines the labour of the head is much greater than that of the hand."[105]

Blackstone, as counsel for the plaintiff in *Tonson v. Collins* in the 1762 hearing, argued that Warburton had successfully shown that the two, patents and copyright, were not comparable. He rejected the defendant's attempt:

"to compare intellectual inventions with such as are merely mechanical; they bear no comparison."[106]

Speaking of mechanical invention, Blackstone stated:

"Every man should be at liberty, to copy and imitate them at pleasure; which may tend to further improvements. However, a temporary privilege may be indulged to the inventor for a limited time, by the positive Act of the State, by way of reward for his ingenuity. This inconvenience will soon be over, and then the world will remain at its natural liberty."[107]

Copyright, according to Blackstone, was not to be treated as a monopoly:

"He [Yates, counsel for the defendant] has treated the present claim in the light of a monopoly. A very odious term. But what is a monopoly? An endeavour

---

104 William Warburton, "A Letter from an Author to a Member of Parliament", in *The Works of the Right Reverend William Warburton*, London 1811, vol. 12, pp. 410-411.
105 *Tonson v. Collins* 1761, 1 W. Black. 307.
106 *Ibid.*, (1762), 343.
107 *Ibid.*, (1762), 344 [my italics].

to appropriate to private use, what before belonged to all the world in common… But who can have a right to print another's composition … before he
pleases to publish it?"[108]

Blackstone was arguing here that the monopoly granted under a patent was of a quite different nature from the rights of an author. These statements in the Tonson case have to
be treated with caution. Like Yates, Blackstone was acting as counsel in *Tonson v. Collins*
and not as a judge, and his duty was to advance his client's case in the way he considered
best. It was in his client's interest to argue that copyright was recognised by the common
law, whereas, apparently patents were only a temporary privilege granted by a 'positive
Act of the State'. Nor was it useful for him to argue that a patent for a new invention also
did not 'appropriate to private use, what before belonged to all the world in common'.
However, there are indications that Blackstone did actually consider the monopoly for a
patent for invention in a fundamentally different light from the protection of literary works
and this was not simply the strategy adopted in the Tonson case. One indication is given
in his *Commentaries on the Laws of England*, a work in which he could be completely
neutral. In Book IV, chapter 12, 'Of offences against public trade', Blackstone deals with
monopolies and in that context mentions patents. He does not mention copyright. Furthermore, in his opinion as a judge in the copyright case of *Donaldson v. Beckett* 1774 he stated:

> "That the author of any literary composition, and his assigns, had the sole right
> of printing and publishing the Same in perpetuity, by the common law… That
> this right is not any way impeached, restrained, or taken away, by the statute
> 8th Anne."[109]

It would seem, therefore, that Blackstone may have considered the monopoly awarded by
a patent in terms of a temporary 'inconvenience' to 'natural liberty', but that was not how
he saw copyright.

5.2.2   The Public Good and Religious Doctrine

However, both authors and inventors suffered from the opinion, not infrequently voiced,
that the public good should be the aim of intellectual creativity, not private profit. Inventors
should be given sufficient means to enable them to carry out their work and to provide
them with a living, but their reward was the increase of knowledge. Within the scientific
community itself, there were those who voiced serious reservations about the practice of

---

108 *Ibid.*, (1762), 342.
109 *Donaldson v. Beckett* 1774, Cobbett, *Parliamentary History of England* (1813), vol. 17, col. 978.

patenting inventions. By the end of the eighteenth century there were many so-called philosophical societies spread throughout the country. In these societies men came together to discuss science and technology. These societies were strongly represented in the rapidly expanding urban centres; several of the most well-known provincial societies are the Manchester Literary and Philosophical Society and the Lunar Society in Birmingham. The main forum for the discussions and experiments of the Lunar Society was Matthew Boulton's Soho house. By the late eighteenth century, there was a widespread interest in applied science and many scientists had industrial interests and many industrialists were interested in science.[110]

Not all of these societies favoured the patenting of inventions. One of the most influential of these societies, the Society for the Encouragement of Arts and Manufacturers and Commerce, founded in 1754, was open in its disapproval of patents for inventions. It considered that patentees inhibited the spread of technological ideas. The Society offered premiums to those who were prepared to make their inventions freely available. Indeed its rules and orders, laid down in 1765, prohibited any person who had obtained a patent for applying as a candidate for any premium offered by the Society.[111] Kenrick was highly critical of the approach of the Society for the Encouragement of Arts and Manufactures: it may have been founded upon public-spirited principles but offering petty premiums was not an efficient means of encouraging invention. Little good was to be expected from such societies. Mankind as a whole, (and therefore by implication, not just inventors) needed to be stimulated to exert their private abilities for the public good. There were only a select few who would "devote their talents disinterestedly to the service of the public without regard to their private emolument".[112] There were, however, such men. For example, Clanny, Davy and Stephenson all produced safety lamps in the period 1813 to 1816 and all refused, in the interest of the miners, to take out patents for their devices.[113] Such altruistic behaviour cast a shadow upon other inventors who clung to their patent protection.

Jones's study of the Soho Manufactory brings to the fore the dilemma that patentees could face: genteel society subscribed to the free-flow of information, but that information when transformed to a technological use was in need of protection. Boulton and Watt were caught between two worlds: what was expected of educated men of substance and gentlemanly status and their desire to protect their cutting edge technology. Between 1767 and 1809 several thousand visitors came to Boulton's Soho Manufactory. Boulton and

---

110 A.E. Musson and Eric Robinson, *Science and Technology in the Industrial Revolution*, Manchester 1969, p. 188.

111 Van Zijl Smit, *The Social Creation of a Legal Reality: A Study of the Emergence and Acceptance of the British Patent System as a Legal Instrument for the Control of New Technology* (1981), p. 82.

112 Kenrick, *An Address to the Artists and Manufacturers of Great Britain; respecting an Application to Parliament for the farther Encouragement of new Discoveries and Inventions in the useful Arts* (1774), pp. 19, 27-28.

113 T.S. Ashton, *The Industrial Revolution 1760-1830*, Oxford 1968, p. 10.

Watt had to walk the line between the hospitality that was the due of their social equals and superiors and concealing sensitive information about such matters as a new prototype engine. Jones notes that Boulton and Watt continued to play the role of entrepreneurs in a cultural environment that was theoretically committed to the free-flow of information, but their sons, however, carried no such 'intellectual baggage'. As the nineteenth century began, the old culture of information exchange between gentlemen was being openly questioned.[114]

The tension between the public good and private interest was at times almost palpable in the courtroom. Adair, Arkwright's own counsel in *R v. Arkwright* explained to the jury:

> "If no benefit was to be derived to the inventor from the exercise of his ability and ingenuity, for the loss of his time, and the expenditure of his fortune, *who, do you believe, would be found sufficiently public-spirited, especially of that class from whence patents usually originate*; or what men, in the use of practical parts of the mechanics, would devote their time and labour for the benefit of the public, in a thing that the public were immediately to derive a benefit from; and for the sake of the public, to ruin themselves and families?"[115]

Most inventors were, according to this reading, men whose lowly social position made it necessary for them to put making money before the nobler goal of the public good. Adair had his reasons for making this statement; he was arguing that this was why the law granted an inducement to patentees to use their ingenuity. However, he must also have felt the need to convince the jury that inventors who had obtained a patent grant were not avaricious and mean-spirited men. It was simply that most inventors came from a class that could not afford to put noble goals like the public good before the more mundane duty of making a living.

However, the insinuation that patentees, like copyright holders, were men with baser motives is there in Lord Camden's speech in the copyright case of *Donaldson v. Beckett* 1774. The public good, not private profit should be the concern of inventors and authors, for "science and learning are in their nature *publici juris*, and they ought to be as free and general as air or water". For Camden: "Glory is the reward of science, and those who deserve it, scorn all meaner views."[116] Eyre, at that time Baron in the Court of Exchequer, apparently also had certain reservations. In the Donaldson case he stated:

---

114 P.M. Jones, "Industrial Enlightenment in Practice: Visitors to the Soho Manufactory 1765-1820", *Midland History Journal*, University of Birmingham, vol. 33, 1 Spring (2008), pp. 77, 83-85, 91, 96.
115 Arkwright, *The Trial of a Cause instituted by Richard Pepper Arden, Esq* (1785), p. 106 [my italics].
116 Cobbett, *Parliamentary History of England* (1813), col. 999-1000.

"That the thinking faculty was a gift with which all men were endowed; that
ideas produced by the occupation of a thinking faculty common to all, should
likewise be held common, and no more be deemed subject to exclusive appropriation than any other of the common gifts of nature."[117]

The public good was coming to the fore, in these arguments, as a reason to reject any other
interpretation than one in which the law provided temporary protection for intellectual
creations.

The idea that an invention should be made for the public good also had a religious
dimension. The inventor had no right to an intellectual creation if the creative insight was
not the inventor's in the first place. If the creative insight was a gift from God, then man
was simply his instrument. That meant the insight was given not for the profit of any one
individual, but for the common good. This belief was still common in the eighteenth century. Two publications, one from the middle of the eighteenth century and one from the
end, illustrate this view. Under the heading "The virtues and singular gifts... for the universal good and preservation of human society", one author pointed out that God bestows
different gifts on different men: "Some he endues with heroic virtues, to others he gives
the invention of arts and sciences."[118] George Huntingford, warden of St. Mary's College,
Winchester, sought to remind his public in 1795 that: "we too frequently forget that Being,
who is the author and giver of all abilities". He pointed to our tendency to want commen-
dation for our own attainments, but even if we have improved our faculties with application
and exercise "every man living is in the first instance indebted to Almighty God".[119]

There are indications that in the eighteenth century there was a move away from God
or Nature as the source of creation, with a greater emphasis being placed upon the individual
and his own efforts. Kant, in his famous essay *What is Enlightenment?* of 1784, saw
Enlightenment as man's release from his self-incurred tutelage, and encouraged his reader
to "Have courage to use your own intelligence".[120] MacLeod, noting that human agency
rather than Providence had taken centre stage for the thinkers of the Enlightenment, sees
the new secular understanding of invention as having ramifications for the patent system
and the wider question of how best to encourage invention. By the early nineteenth century,
invention was being recognised as the achievement of individuals. 'Use rights' might be
appropriate where the inventor was no more than God's agent, but more could be claimed

---

117 *Ibid.*, col. 972.
118 A.Z., *A New Essay on Divine Providence*, London 1755, p. 26.
119 George Huntingford, *Twelve Discourses on Different Subjects*, vol. 2, London 1795, pp. 79-80.
120 Immanuel Kant, "What is Enlightenment?" (1784), in Carl J. Friedrich (ed.), *The Philosophy of Kant: Immanuel
Kant's Moral and Political Writings*, New York 1949, p. 132.

by an inventor where God's role had been reduced to that of the supplier of the raw materials.[121]

Sherman and Bently place this shift within its legal context: they consider that there can be little doubt that over the course of the eighteenth century the "individual-as-creator" took on a more prominent role in law than had hitherto been the case. The language of legislation regulating differing forms of intellectual property, later in the eighteenth century, shows that the individual had become the focal point around which many legal concepts and rules which dealt with intangible property were organised.

> "In particular, it is clear that while God may have provided the starting blocks for the creative process, it was the contribution made by the author, engraver, designer or inventor who individualised the subject matter they worked with which the law protected."[122]

However, the strength of an older religious tradition should not be underestimated. It may have affected some sections of the judiciary in the eighteenth century. An indication can be found in the powerful speech of Lord Camden in the copyright case of *Donaldson v. Beckett* 1774. In that case, Lord Camden gave an opinion in his capacity as a member of the House of Lord, as he no longer sat on the bench. Nonetheless, Camden had been Lord Chief Justice in the Court of Common Pleas and Chancellor in the Court of Chancery. For Camden, there was a clear connection between genius and God. Science and learning was a gift from God:

> "They forget their Creator, as well as their fellow creatures, who wish to monopolize *his noblest gifts* and greatest benefits. Why did we enter into society at all, but to enlighten one another's minds, and improve our faculties, for the common welfare of the species? Those great men, those favoured mortals, those sublime spirits, who share that *ray of divinity which we call genius*, are *entrusted by Providence* with the delegated power of imparting to their fellow-creatures that instruction which heaven meant for universal benefit; they must not be niggards to the world, or hoard up for themselves the common stock."[123]

---

121 MacLeod, *Inventing the Industrial Revolution: the English patent system, 1660-1800* (1988), pp. 219-221.

122 Sherman and Bently, *The Making of Modern Intellectual Property Law: The British Experience 1760-1911* (1999), pp. 36, 46.

123 Cobbett, *Parliamentary History of England* (1813), col. 999 [my italics].

5.2.3   Privilege or Right?

MacLeod observes that before the mid-eighteenth century, patents were still regarded first and foremost as monopolies: the stigma of the royal prerogative lingered on.[124] Yet the patent would become not just a token of favour, a privilege granted by the royal prerogative, but an entitlement. Van Zijl Smit argues that the legal form of patents changed in the eighteenth century from a privilege granted in public law by the state to a *de facto* private right of a novel kind but analogous to a property right. In certain, defined circumstances, the inventor had a *right* to a patent. "While the wording of the actual grant continued to speak of a privilege granted by the Crown, the courts accepted that inventors had rights which could be embodied in a patent and enforced through it." It was this *de facto* recognition of a right to a patent which was enough to ensure a more liberal interpretation of patents in favour of the patentee.[125]

In the eighteenth century, there were certainly judges who spoke of a *right* to a patent. As noted above, Eyre specifically referred to 'patent rights' in *Boulton and Watt v. Bull*. Lord Loughborough in *Arkwright v. Nightingale* stated: "The law has established the *right* of patents for new inventions; that law is extremely wise and just."[126] In the nineteenth century, the courts would increasingly associate a patent with a right rather than with a privilege. Lord Eldon in *Beaumont v. George* 1815 complained that: "Great inconvenience to his Majesty's subjects must arise from the imperfect nature or doubtful interpretation of the *rights* of patentees."[127] Alderson, B. pointed out in *Minter v. Wells* 1834, if the patentee had shown that his invention was new, useful and the specification was sufficient, that was what was required "in order to establish his right".[128] If a patent was seen primarily in terms of a contract between the patentee and the public, rather than 'in the light of a monopoly', it was only logical that the relationship between the parties would be construed in terms of rights and obligations.

Over the period under consideration here, the view that inventors should have a right to enjoy a profit from an invention of use to society, rather than simply being compensated for the time and effort the invention had cost, became more commonplace. James Watt's experiments, which resulted in a vastly improved steam engine, did much to enhance the reputation of inventors. He was clearly admired by some of the judges who heard his patent infringement cases. In *Boulton and Watt v. Bull*, even Buller, who wished only to deliver his opinion "on the dry question of law", nonetheless remarked: "no man ought to envy them [Boulton and Watt] the profits which they have received: because the world has

---

124 MacLeod, *Inventing the Industrial Revolution: the English patent system, 1660-1800* (1988), p. 182.
125 Van Zijl Smit, *The Social Creation of a Legal Reality: A Study of the Emergence and Acceptance of the British Patent System as a Legal Instrument for the Control of New Technology* (1981), pp. 88, 98
126 *Arkwright v. Nightingale* 1785, 1 WPC 61 [my italics].
127 *Beaumont v. George* 1815, 1 CPC ii, 304.
128 *Minter v. Wells* 1834, 1 WPC 129.

undoubtedly derived great advantages from their ingenuity."[129] This, however, had not prevented Buller from deciding 'the dry question of law' against Watt's patent.

This change from the patent as a privilege to the patent as a right, may have taken somewhat longer to become the norm in the courts than Van Zijl Smit's chronology would indicate. The patent as a 'privilege' rather than a right would linger on into the nineteenth century. For example, Gibbs, C.J. consistently refers to the patent as a privilege.[130] Even if that usage could be dismissed as simply a reference to the vocabulary of the patent grant, there are indications that for some judges it meant more than that. One such instance is the judgment of Dallas, C.J. in the *Campion v. Benyon* case 1821 cited earlier. The only 'right' Dallas refers to in his speech is that a patent monopoly is "an infringement of a *public right*". The patent is a "*privilege* conferred on the patentee". It was only in the 1830s that it became commonplace for judges to read the patent specification in terms of rights and obligations (see chapter 4).

5.3   Vested Interests

In deciding upon the validity of patents, judges could be subject to outside pressure from differing fractions. That pressure could take the form of powerful manufacturing lobbies intent upon the revocation of a troublesome patent, and its imposition of an inconvenient monopoly. It could equally be in the form of pressure from the patentee and his backers to enforce the monopoly. Inventors often worked in association with entrepreneurs for whom a patent could represent a substantial financial investment, or a patent could have been assigned to one particular manufacturer. By the late eighteenth century, it was becoming a dictum that a patent was of little commercial value until it had been successfully defended in the courts.[131] Not surprisingly, there are no references to lobbying in the judgments, although there are sometimes indications of the interests involved in the case reports.

Collusive action by manufacturers to have patents set aside clearly prompted a number of cases. In Arkwright's case, an association of cotton manufacturers wished the crown to act against Arkwright's second patent. Hewish has discovered evidence of the unconventional way in which *R v. Arkwright* was commenced, "perhaps indicative of influence at high level". There is fairly conclusive evidence that the crown case to repeal Arkwright's second patent was already underway before the verdict in *Arkwright v. Nightingale* was known. Arkwright's counsel referred to "those behind the scenes, the movers and conduc-

---

129 *Boulton and Watt v. Bull* 1795, 2 H. Black 483.
130 *Wood v. Zimmer* 1815, 1 CPC 294 and *Bovill v. Moore* 1816, 1 CPC 334.
131 MacLeod, *Inventing the Industrial Revolution: the English patent system, 1660-1800* (1988), p. 73.

tors of this business".[132] Arkwright too had referred to this association in a document dated 1782, Arkwright's petition to parliament for an extension, which was read out in evidence in *R v. Arkwright*:

> "Without the assistance of Parliament, the late verdict threatens him with the most serious consequences; and truly alarming is the *association* against him, being formed of men of property, anxiously desirous of overbearing him at all events."[133]

Buller fully recognised the financial significance of Arkwright's patent. In his address to the jury, he commented that Arkwright must have been convinced that the former verdict was right or why else would he have given up on his patent for three and a half years, given that the invention "is lucrative to so enormous a degree as you have heard".[134] Whether the court was influenced by the cotton manufacturing lobbying is difficult to determine. Even if the prosecution had been prompted to take action by Arkwright's competitors, the evidence given in this case still provides reasonable grounds to doubt the validity of Arkwright's second patent.

Some years later, James Kay would also face opposition from the textile industry to his 1825 patent for the process of wet-spinning of flax. Initially, one firm in particular, Marshall and Co, refused to pay for Kay's invention. Marshall campaigned actively in Leeds to encourage the other manufacturers to resist the patent. They appear to have entered into a bond to contribute towards any expenses and to prevent private contracts with Kay. Marshall's persistence, together with the weight of the trade, brought down an invention which had made the boom in the early 1830s possible.[135] The strength of the opposition was recognised by Pollock, acting as counsel for the plaintiff. He described the defendants "of whom Mr. Marshall is at the head, are probably by name well known in this great county as a house of most extensive business, and as persons of the greatest wealth embarked in the commerce of this country". Pollock pointed out how much was at stake: the patent had nearly expired but "such is the importance of it, such is the value of it, that even at this late period the defendants have thought it worth their while to invade the patent".[136] Kay's patent was set aside by the House of Lords in 1841.

In the case of Watt's patent, there was strong opposition from mine proprietors, particularly in Cornwall. The proprietors of the Cornish mines did not want to pay Boulton

---

132 Hewish, "From Cromford to Chancery Lane: New Light on the Arkwright Patent Trials" (1987), pp. 82-83, 85-86.
133 Arkwright, *The Trial of a Cause instituted by Richard Pepper Arden, Esq* (1785), p. 102.
134 *Ibid.*, p. 177.
135 Dutton, *The patent system and inventive activity during the industrial revolution 1750-1852* (1984), pp. 189-192.
136 *Kay v. Marshall* 1836, 2 WPC 49.

and Watt's premium. In 1780, a movement was started to petition parliament to repeal the Act extending Watt's patent. There are also indications that Bull was supported by mine proprietors in his lawsuit against Boulton and Watt.[137] Eyre, C.J. referred in *Boulton and Watt v. Bull* 1795 to the magnitude of the interest involved, in particular to the mining industry. So vital had the engine become that "our mines cannot be worked without them".[138] Watt himself considered several of the judges hearing the case of *Boulton and Watt v. Bull* to be biased against them: "Justice Buller and Justice Heath against us (Cornwall and Devonshire own these gentlemen)."[139]

It was of vital importance to patentees and their backers to defend their patents in court. The development of an invention could necessitate a substantial investment; in some cases requiring inventors either to assign the patent or to take on partners to provide financial support. Patentees' applications to parliament, and later to the Privy Council, for an extension of their patents give some indication of the expenses that could be incurred in the commercial development of an invention. For example, in Joseph's Bramah's petition, to extend his 1784 patent, he states that the numerous machines and apparatus necessary for the production of locks and keys entailed such a capital outlay that he had not been able to realize a profit equal to 5%. He added: "Indeed so costly are the machines erected for making the locks, that no individual with a small capital could possibly undertake the business."[140] Arkwright entered into several partnerships to finance his spinning machinery. In requesting parliament to grant him an extension of his patent, he pointed out that: "He has induced men of property to engage with him to a large amount."[141] Watt too had a succession of investors: John Craig, John Roebuck and finally the successful Birmingham manufacturer, Matthew Boulton.

MacLeod distinguishes three broad categories of patentees: the amateur inventor, the professional inventor and the businessman. This last category came to dominate the patent system from 1760 onward. These businessmen inventors were artisans, manufacturers, millwrights or machine-makers interested mainly in patents which related to their own branch of business. They might devise an invention themselves or purchase an invention relevant to their business. It was a category that included men like Joseph Bramah and James Watt.[142] Schumpeter makes a distinction between invention and innovation: "The making of the invention and the carrying out of the corresponding innovation are, economically and sociologically, two entirely different things." Innovation was an economic process and a matter of business activity. The making of the invention and the correspond-

---

137 Cornish Record Office, volume 11, document AD 1583/11/102.
138 *Boulton and Watt v. Bull* 1795, 2 H. Black 495.
139 Robinson and McKie, *Partners in Science: James Watt & Joseph Black* (1970), Letter 155, p. 217.
140 Bramah, "The petition and case of Joseph Bramah, of Piccadilly, engineer, inventor of the patent locks for the security of life and property" (1798), p. 5.
141 Arkwright, *The Trial of a Cause instituted by Richard Pepper Arden, Esq* (1785), p. 102.
142 MacLeod, *Inventing the Industrial Revolution: the English patent system, 1660-1800* (1988), pp. 78-79.

ing innovation may have been carried out by the same person, but that was a chance coincidence which did not affect the validity of the distinction. Shaw Solo, however, considered that this definition of innovation as distinct from invention failed to account for the source of innovation.[143] Certainly in the late eighteenth century it had become common for patentees to combine the roles of inventor and businessman.

A patent could be a highly lucrative investment. An early example in the period under consideration here is that of Dollond's achromatic lens patent. It would appear that in 1765 Peter Dollond's profit margin was at least 200%, giving Dollond a minimum annual profit of £800. Successfully defending his patent in court had enhanced the value of the patented invention. Apparently, Peter Dollond substantially raised the price of his lenses once he had triumphed in court.[144] That a patent could be a valuable investment was pointed out by Moses Poole, who was a clerk in the patent office, in his testimony to the Select Committee on Patents in 1829: "I have known them to get £130,000 by a patent".[145] Those with a financial interest in a patent required that the validity of a patent would be sustained in court and that infringers could be deterred. This is illustrated by the legal actions brought by Boulton and Watt. As noted in chapter 1, Boulton was perfectly prepared to use the influence of his contacts to ensure the extension of their patent by a private Act of Parliament, but he was equally prepared to try to influence the court. Boulton is even reported as having dined with a judge shortly before a crucial hearing on Watt's patent.[146]

In this context, John Farey's comments on Watt's specification before the Select Committee 1829 make interesting reading. Farey considered:

"In allowing those heads to pass for a complete specification, a latitude was given to Mr. Watt in favour of his great services, which the courts have never allowed in any other case." As: "Those who wanted to practice the invention could not do it upon that specification."[147]

Nuvolari, who has recently carried out a study on the technical changes in steam power technology, points out that Watt wrote the patent specification in terms of "principles of action" without embodying these principles into any specific engine design. His analysis supports Farey's contention that Watt's specification was not the most complete of specifications. James Watt's 1769 patent specification was also very broad. Nuvolari observes that it covered not only any engine which used a separate condenser, but also all engines

143 Carolyn Shaw Solo, "Innovation in the Capitalist Process: A Critique of the Schumpterian Theory", *Quarterly Journal of Economics* 65, no. 3 August (1951), p. 421.
144 Sorrenson, "Dollond & Son's Pursuit of Achromaticity 1758-1759" (2001), fn 31 and 32, pp. 52-53.
145 *Select Committee Report 1829*, p. 86.
146 Hewish, "From Cromford to Chancery Lane: New Light on the Arkwright Patent Trials" (1987), p. 86.
147 *Select Committee Report 1829*, p. 32.

using steam, instead of atmospheric pressure as the 'working substance'. By maintaining that his invention covered the closed top cylinder and pistons pressed down by steam, it is clear that this would block any engine using steam as the driving agent.[148] It is indeed surprising that a specification drafted so broadly was not immediately set aside. This gives some reason to suspect that Boulton's lobbying may have been effective.

Nuvolari argues that Boulton and Watt actually used the courts as a weapon to scare off any real competition. The most serious competing design was that of Jonathan Hornblower. Jonathan Hornblower took out a patent in 1781 for a new pumping steam engine. In Hornblower's steam engine, the steam was expanded at atmospheric pressure consecutively into two cylinders, one larger than the other. It was the first compound design. Hornblower considered that Watt's patent was limited to the separate condenser, and as steam condensation took place in his engine in the lowest part of the second cylinder, he was convinced he was not infringing Watt's patent. Hornblower later realized that he could not improve his own engine without recourse to a separate condenser. It was for this reason that he applied to parliament for an extension to his patent. Nuvolari considers that it was due to Boulton's influence that parliament was not prepared to give Hornblower an extension. Consequently, Hornblower decided to use the separate condenser anyway, relying on defending this move by arguing the insufficiency of Watt's patent specification. Boulton and Watt's strategy for dealing with the threat of Jonathan Hornblower was to start a campaign of legal actions against those who were clearly infringing their patent. The first action was against Edward Bull. Bull's engine was essentially a simplified version of Watt's engine: it was worked without the beam, using the piston rods directly to work the pumps. The second was against Jonathan Hornblower's brother, Jabez Hornblower, and Maberley. Successful in both cases, the point had been made to the infringers. There would be no further courtroom clash between Boulton and Watt and Jonathan Hornblower.[149]

If Nuvolari is right to attribute this strategy to Boulton and Watt, they must have been reasonably confident of success. However, these proceedings were more risky than Nuvolari seems to have taken into account. It may well be the case that Bull's engine, from the technical perspective, was quite obviously an infringement of Watt's engine. Yet that would only be relevant if Watt's patent itself was held to be a valid patent. That was indeed the issue raised by Bull. The possibility was always there that Watt's patent would be set aside because of *legal* defects, for example that the specification was insufficient to instruct one skilled in the profession, it was claiming more than an improvement or that the patent was for a principle only. Nor did all the judges find in favour of Boulton and Watt in Bull's

---

148 Alessandro Nuvolari, *The Making of Steam Power Technology: a Study of Technical Change during the British Industrial Revolution*, Eindhoven 2004, p. 24, fn 34.

149 *Ibid.*, pp. 29-30, 102-103.

case. Heath considered that as the patent extended to all machinery build on the same principle, Watt had taken out a patent for more than he had specified and Buller argued that Watt was claiming the whole machine rather than an improvement to the steam engine.[150] Whether these two judges had succumbed to the pressure of the mine proprietors, for Watt was convinced that Buller and Heath were the ones "owned" by Cornwall and Devonshire, is a matter for speculation. Watt's patent was very broadly drafted in terms of "principles of action". Similarly speculative is whether the other judges, who did find in favour of Boulton and Watt, had been swayed by Boulton's extra judicial campaigning, whether indeed as Farey contended 'a latitude was given to Mr. Watt in favour of his great services'.

5.4 Summary

In the eighteenth century, the term 'monopoly' was tainted. The backlash against monopolistic abuse in the sixteenth and seventeenth century had been influential in forming public opinion. Monopolies were still popularly associated with the abuse of the royal prerogative by the Tudors and Stuarts. The perception of monopolies as 'odious', the adjective used by Coke to describe monopolies, had persisted.

Against this backdrop other factors came into play. Monopolies became even more suspect if they were considered to be contrary to the common law. By the eighteenth century, the predominant view seemed to be that monopolies had always been against the common law. It was also possible to interpret Natural law as being against monopolies, if monopolies were seen as violating the natural rights of mankind. There were also religious scruples to be taken into account. The common law, religion and morality appeared to be ranged against monopolies. If a monopoly for a new invention was considered in the light of these factors, rather than as a fair exchange for the patentee introducing something new and of value to the public, it is easy to see why some judges would have interpreted the patent grant strictly.

It is certainly not the case, however, that all judges viewed the grant of a patent for invention primarily in terms of a monopoly. There were those who chose to read the specification in the context of a contractual relationship between patentee and public. In this setting, it was possible to see the monopoly awarded by patent as a different sort of monopoly from those that had been declared void by the Statute of Monopolies. The monopoly was in return for disclosing a new invention, and the patentee would be rewarded by the monopoly in proportion to the usefulness of his invention. By the 1830s, the attitude of the courts to patent monopolies would become suppler, as these monopolies were placed

---

150 *Boulton and Watt v. Bull* 1795, 2 H. Black 483, 489-490.

in a utilitarian context rather than a religious or moral one. In the 1830s, the patentee as having a right, rather than a privilege, became more firmly embedded.

The social standing of inventors in general in the eighteenth century may have been another factor that affected the way in which patentees were treated. Genteel society had traditionally not esteemed inventors as highly as the authors of literary works. Inventors were often craftsmen, associated with industry and manufacture. Particularly those campaigning for perpetual copyright protection depicted inventors as little more than manual labourers. Their arguments found their way into the courtroom. The social status of inventors was also affected by religious considerations. The belief that intellectual creativity was a gift from God could colour the perception of the patent grant; the individual was simply God's vessel through which intellectual creativity was channelled for the benefit of the community, not for that individual's own benefit. For those who held such beliefs, the standing of those inventors who wished to patent their inventions, rather than make their discoveries freely available, would inevitably be diminished. As the eighteenth century progressed, a greater emphasis was being placed upon the individual and his own creative efforts rather than upon creativity as divine providence.

Nor should the influence of certain vested interests be disregarded. Vested interests could have a role to play in determining the sustainability of a patent monopoly. Manufacturers were prepared to oppose monopolies that got in their way not only by participating in private actions, but also by prompting the crown to bring *scire facias* proceedings to annul a patent. The stakes were equally high for patentees. As the eighteenth century progressed, patentees were more and more often businessmen as well as inventors. A patented invention could represent a substantial financial investment on the part of the inventor's backers. A lucrative patent would fail if it were rejected in court. To what extent judges were affected by these vested interests is difficult to say, but cases reveal that judges were certainly aware of the financial interests involved.

6   THE PATENT AS A FORM OF PERSONAL PROPERTY

As is clear from the preceding chapters, the terminology judges used to describe the legal nature of patents varied. There were judges who described the patent as a 'privilege' and others who spoke about patents in terms of 'rights'. Some judges considered patents primarily in terms of a grant of monopoly. There were other judges who analysed the patent in contractual terms, rather than as a monopoly. There was one other divisive issue lurking under the surface: the patent as a form of property. What becomes very apparent in the latter part of the eighteenth century is the lack of consensus within the judiciary as to the legal definition of property.

Parliament was not reticent in referring to patents in terms of property. Private Acts of Parliament were used to prolong a patent until Brougham's Act of 1835, which removed that competence to the Judicial Committee of the Privy Council. The language of the private Acts of Parliament is explicit: "the sole use and *property*" of the invention will be vested in the patentee. For example, in 1775 "the sole property of certain steam engines" was vested in James Watt; in 1776 "the sole use and property" of a certain composition of cement was vested in Liardet; in 1777 in Hartley for his method of securing buildings from fire and in1792 in Turner for producing a yellow colour.[1]

The common law approach to real property, based upon the feudal concept of tenure, had familiarised the legal profession with abstractions like the doctrine of estates in land. An estate did not refer to the land itself, but to a present or future temporal interest in the land. In principle, the way was open to construct similar legal abstractions within the realm of personal property, which could include copyright and patents for new inventions. Yet there was a difference between the abstraction of the estate in land and the abstraction of copyright or a patent. The estate in land clearly related to the land itself. Copyright and patents related to an economic interest rather than to a material thing. Copyright gave an author a right to prevent others from copying and selling his works. The right the patent gave was the right to prevent another from exploiting the patentee's invention for a specific period of time.

Patents and copyright did not conform, in the opinion of some judges, to the traditional, common law definition of what was to be understood as 'property'. If the patent and copyright granted a proprietary right, what constituted the object of this property? If the definition of property at common law was formulated in terms of rights relating to an

---

1   15 Geo. III c. 61, 16 Geo. III c. 29, 17 Geo. III c. 6, 32 Geo. III c. 73.

external thing, neither copyright nor patents seemed to fall within that definition. This led some judges to argue that copyright was not a species of property known to the common law, but it was a new right created by statute. Similarly, they argued that the patent right was unknown at common law. An inventor had no right to exclude others from copying and selling his invention without a patent, and that patent was dependent upon an act of the royal prerogative, not upon any common law right.

Was a patent a species of property at common law or was it an anomalous species of property created by the royal prerogative and regulated by statute? The issue may well have coloured how some judges saw the interests of the patentee, and this, in turn, would affect their reading of the patent specification. Furthermore, the legal discussion on what could be the object of property would have another indirect effect on the development of patent law. It slipped into the interpretation of the statutory term 'manufacture' and hence the determination of the validity of a patent.

6.1   The Patent Specification as a Contractual Relationship

Modern English law classifies patents as belonging to the law of property. It is all too easy to project that knowledge backwards to the eighteenth century and presume that it was a foregone conclusion that a patent gave a proprietary right rather than a personal right. Yet in the period covered in this study there were judges who looked at patents in terms of a bargain between the patentee and the public. Lord Eldon had explicitly placed the patent within a contractual setting, considering the patent as a bargain with the public and to be 'construed upon the same principle of good faith that regulated all other contracts'. It was Eldon's contractual interpretation of the patent specification which Godson considered to have been generally adopted by the time he wrote his treatise in 1823 (see chapter 4).

Analysing the patent in terms of contractual, reciprocal rights and obligations had its use. The contractual framework provided tools to enable judges to interpret the patent specification. Rather than determining the validity of a patent specification only according to a literal interpretation of its wording, its validity depended upon deciding whether the patentee had fulfilled his obligations. The patentee was under an obligation to disclose his invention fully and the description had to be sufficient to enable a skilled artisan to make the invention (see chapter 4). In return, the patentee had the sole right of working and making his invention for fourteen years. The right the public received was that the patentee's knowledge would enter the public domain at the end of the period of patent protection, and the obligation was not to thwart an inventor's legitimate expectation to make and sell his new invention in that period if the specification was sufficient and full disclosure had been made. The contractual approach offered a means of resolving an internal issue of patent law: how the validity of the patent specification should be determined. Although the contractual interpretation may have triumphed over the literal interpretation as a means of analysing the patent specification, the patent itself, as a legal entity, would be assigned to the category of property, not to the category of obligations.

Could the courts have opted to fit the patent within the common law of contract rather than as a distinct species of personal property? Modern practices did not always slot easily into the common law of contract. This was apparent when Blackstone attempted to accommodate the law regulating negotiable instruments within the general structure of the common law of contract. By seeing the payee as having property in the form of a chose in action, Blackstone was faced with the difficulty that a chose in action, according to the common law, could not be assigned. The application of that rule would defeat the purpose of negotiable instruments, and hence the negotiable instrument had to be seen as an exception. Mansfield, on the other hand, responded by emphasising the need to recognise these instruments as a distinct form of property governed by their usage in commerce.[2] There were other legal constructions where it was not immediately apparent as to whether a personal relationship or a proprietary right was the defining characteristic. Ibbetson points to the trust as a construction which straddled the boundary between rights *in rem* and rights *in personam* – it could be treated as a personal relationship between trustee and beneficiary or alternatively as a form of property right vested in the beneficiary. By the late seventeenth century, it had been determined that the proprietary dimension of the trust was uppermost.[3] As will be seen below, whether the patent was a form of personal property recognised at common law was controversial. However, there were also problems associated with treating the patent purely as a contractual, personal right rather than as a proprietary right.

By the mid-eighteenth century, there was not an all-embracing theoretical structure of a law of contract. As various historians have pointed out, this is reflected in the way Blackstone treats contracts in his *Commentaries*.[4] Nonetheless, as noted in chapter 4, by this time there were certain identifying features of contracts. There had to be agreement, consideration and the parties to the agreement were the ones bound by it. Yet a patent gave an absolute right: it was enforceable against persons generally without their previous consent. It is the hallmark of a proprietary right that it is a right enforceable against persons generally without their agreement. If a patent were to be seen as giving only a personal, contractual right, it would be a right enforceable against the particular person or persons who had entered into an agreement with the patentee.

Formally, the patent relationship was between the patentee and the crown, as the granting of a patent remained a prerogative act. However, in the eighteenth century courts,

2   Liebermann, *The province of legislation determined* (1989) pp. 106-108.
3   Ibbetson, *A Historical Introduction to the Law of Obligations* (1999), p. 206.
4   See for example, Oldham, *English Common Law in the age of Mansfield* (2004), pp. 83-84; Manchester, *A Modern Legal History of England and Wales 1750-1950* (1980), p. 265.

patents were treated *de facto* as giving rise to a relationship between the patentee and the public; the role of the crown was, in effect, to act as an agent on behalf of the public. For example, Lord Mansfield in *Liardet v. Johnson* 1778 was reported to have stated: "Hence the law requires as the price the patentee *should pay to the public* for his monopoly ... the fullest and most sufficient description of all the particulars on which the effect depends."[5] This is also the wording Bramah used in his description of the case in his letter to Eyre, C.J.[6] Buller, J. in *R v. Arkwright* 1785 acknowledged that his decision in that case "is of very great importance to the public upon the one hand, and to the individual who has the patent upon the other".[7] Early in the nineteenth century, in the case of *Harmar v. Playne* 1807, Lord Eldon stated the role of the crown as follows: "...where the crown on behalf of the public grants letters patent, the grantee, entering into a contract with the crown, the benefit of which contract the public are to have..."[8]

If the patent were to be formulated in those contractual terms, the crown appears to have been seen as the agent acting on behalf of the public at large. Applying the doctrine of agent and principal, this would place the crown as the agent and the public as the principal. As a contracting party, the public would owe a corresponding duty to the patentee's right. That would entail a very large number of persons. In itself, the numbers involved need not pose a problem. In the twentieth century, legal scholars, like Hohfeld and Honoré, rejected the numerical criterion as denoting whether a right was an absolute right or a relative right, an action *in rem* or *in personam*. Hohfeld argued that a right does not have to be a property right in order to bind third parties without their consent: for example a person has a right that another shall not publish a libellous statement about him and this right is not restricted to any particular person.[9] As Honoré points out:

> "I may enter into a contract with a very large number of persons...The associa-
> tion may contain all the members of a given society except myself. It just so
> happens that usually the parties to a contract are few."[10]

Even if it would be anachronistic to project the views of these more modern scholars back to the eighteenth century, the numerical factor need not have been an insurmountable

---

5   *Liardet v. Johnson* 1778, 1 CPC 37 [my italics]. According to Hulme, both Buller, for his book on trials at *nisi prius*, and Carpmael, for his reports, were using a pamphlet on the case produced by the defendant. Hulme (1902), p. 287.

6   Webster's fn (e), *Liardet v. Johnson* 1 WPC 54.

7   *R v. Arkwright* 1785, Arkwright (1785), p. 172.

8   *Harmar v. Playne* 1807, 1 CPC 257.

9   Wesley Newcomb Hohfeld, *Fundamental Legal Conceptions as applied in Judicial Reasoning*, Yale 1964, p. 85.

10 A.M. Honré, "Rights of Exclusion and Immunities Against Divesting", *Tulane Law Review* 34 (1959-1960), p. 454.

problem for eighteenth century lawyers. Legal fictions have always abounded in English law. They were acknowledged, and justified, by Blackstone in his *Commentaries*: "we are (it must be owned) obliged to have recourse to such arbitrary fictions and expedients."[11] It could have been argued that the public consisted of persons who could, in theory, be determined. That still left the problem of agreement. How could it be argued that there was an agreement between the patentee and all these members of the public?

There was a construction that could possibly have served as a legal fiction in this respect: the social contract. Mossoff argues that the idea of a social contract did have a role to play in patent law. It was the idea of the social contract that shifted the patent from being seen as a contract between the crown and the patentee to being one between the patentee and society. This fundamental shift in the law occurred at approximately the same time as the natural right theories of Grotius, Pufendorf and Locke became popular in England. In particular, Mossoff argues, it was the social contract idea which enabled some judges to interpret the patent specification as the inventor's consideration for his patent. By 1807 (the Chancery hearing of *Harmar v. Playne*), the reigning viewpoint was that a patent represented a social contract implemented by way of the specification. Of pivotal importance in this development, according to Mossoff, was John Locke's conception of the social contract. It was Locke's ideas that "permeated both the arguments and the terminology of judges adjudicating patent cases at the end of the eighteenth century". Mossoff must, however, concede the "glaring absence" of references to Locke in judicial opinions in the eighteenth century. A possible reason, he gives, is that Locke was a political theorist and not a legal philosopher.[12]

Locke's theories concerning the social contract cannot be entirely divorced from his political views. In the Second Treatise, Locke wanted to show that government is a trust; governments do not have absolute authority and may not violate the principles for which they were established. Men are at liberty "to resist the force of those, who without authority would impose anything upon them".[13] Yet Mossoff's argument that the lack of reference to Locke in judicial opinions in patent cases was because he was 'a political theorist and not a legal philosopher' would be stronger if Locke had never been referred to as an authority in argument. Blackstone, however, cites Locke as an authority on the acquisition of property by labour in his arguments as counsel in the copyright case of *Tonson v. Collins* 1762: "The right of occupancy is referred to this original, of bodily labour. Locke on government. part.2. c. 5."[14]

---

11   Blackstone, *Commentaries on the Laws of England* (1793), III, 266.
12   Adam Mossoff, "Rethinking the Development of Patents: An Intellectual History 1550-1800", *Hastings Law Journal* 52 (2001), pp. 1257-1258, 1292, 1300, 1315, 1317.
13   Locke, Second Treatise, XIX, 212.
14   *Tonson v. Collins* 1762 1 W. Black. 321-322.

It is possible that the concept of the social contract was of influence in the interpretation of the patent as a bargain between the patentee and the public and this, in turn, determined how the patent specification should be read. However, Mossoff quite possibly overestimates the significance of Locke's social contract theory in this respect. John Locke's idea of the social contract was not an imperative pre-condition to a contractual interpretation of the patent specification. Under the Tudors, and hence before the introduction of the patent specification and the requirement of disclosure, the recitals of the patent grant usually referred to the benefit to the public that was to be derived from the patentee's working of the invention (see chapter 4). The Statute of Monopolies 1624 had tied the patent grant to public policy in the sense that the grant could not be "contrary to the law, nor mischievous to the state, by raising prices of commodities at home, or hurt of trade, or generally inconvenient". By the time the patent specification had become standard, it was a relatively small step for the eighteenth century common law courts to think of the patent as a public matter, rather than as a private matter between the patentee and the person of the monarch.

Considering the patent in the light of a relationship between an individual and the state did not exclude the courts from applying, by analogy, the principles used to determine contractual disputes in private law to the interpretation of the patent specification. Although these contractual principles borrowed from civil actions may have provided a useful tool for interpreting the patent specification, it was quite a different matter for the courts to take that contractual analogy further and treat the patent grant itself as a contract between the public and the patentee. The patent grant was still an act of the royal prerogative. This was also reflected in the fact that a prosecution brought in the name of the crown was necessary for the formal revocation of the grant.

A contract required agreement between the parties. It was a stretch, even for a legal system accustomed to the use of legal fictions, to argue that the public had entered into an agreement with each individual patentee. The idea of the public as a contracting party with an author had been brought up in the copyright case of *Tonson v. Collins* 1762. It had been dismissed by Yates, when he acted as counsel for the defendant in that case:

> "Is this a contract between the public and the author, that none, but he, shall print these ideas? No: the public is not a corporation capable of contracting. There is no mutuality in the contract. The public cannot compel the author to furnish a sufficient number of copies."[15]

Although Lord Mansfield interrupted Yates' submission on several occasions to argue the point, he did not do so on this occasion. The idea of an implied contract involving the

---

15   *Tonson v. Collins* 1762 1 W. Black. 338.

public, this time between the booksellers and the public, was similarly dismissed by Lord Camden in the copyright case of *Donaldson v. Beckett* 1774:

> "I pass over the flimsy supposition of an implied contract between the bookseller who sells, and the public which buys the printed copy; it is a notion as unmeaning in itself as it is void of a legal foundation."[16]

In various respects, therefore, it was simpler for the law to treat the patent as an anomalous form of personal property rather than as a contract. There are instances of judges referring to patents in terms of property. In his summing up to the jury in *Arkwright v. Nightingale* 1785, Lord Loughborough had indirectly referred to patents as property when he pointed out that "nothing could be more essentially mischievous than that questions of *property* between A and B should ever be permitted to be decided upon considerations of public convenience or expediency".[17] Lord Ellenborough, in his summing up to the jury in *Huddart v. Grimshaw* 1803, used the term explicitly when he stated: "Gentlemen, this is *a species of property* highly important, as it respects the interests of the individual, and with him also the interests of the public."[18]

Placing the patent within a proprietary context may have accorded with an inclination in English law to gravitate towards proprietary rights rather than personal rights. The inclination is evident in the categorisation of incorporeal hereditaments as forms of property rather than as personal rights (see below). The importance of the proprietary right is indicated in the way English law treats contracts for the sale of goods. Ibbetson has traced the shift in sale of goods transactions from property to contract during the Middle Ages. In Europe, it moved from a model in which its primary function was perceived as the transfer of property to one which focused principally on the imposition of future obligations. Only in England did the medieval model of sale remain discernable. Unlike the Roman law distinction between contract and conveyance, English lawyers continued to treat a sale of goods as a unitary transaction in which the sale immediately passes ownership in the goods to the buyer. Although Ibbetson considers it would be wrong to overestimate the contrast between the English position and the rest of Europe in practical terms, he acknowledges that there was a clear difference at the conceptual level.[19] It is tempting to conclude that behind this different approach to the sale of goods contract, and the development of the trust in which proprietary rights rather than personal rights

---

16   *Donaldson v. Beckett* 1774, Cobbett (1813), col.1000.
17   *Arkwright v. Nightingale* 1785, 1 WPC 61 [my italics].
18   *Huddart v. Grimshaw* 1803, 1 CPC 225 [my italics].
19   Ibbetson, "From Property to Contract: The Transformation of Sale in the Middle Ages" (1992), pp. 1, 12-13.

became uppermost, the dominant tendency within the English legal profession was to focus upon proprietary rights rather than on obligations.

In this context, it is interesting to note that in his categorisation of English law in his *Commentaries*, Blackstone placed both copyright and patents in Book II, 'The Right of Things'. They both appeared in chapter 26, which was concerned with the title to personal property acquired by occupancy. Section (8) dealt with property "grounded on labour and invention": most of this section was devoted to copyright but the section ended with a reference to the privilege granted to an inventor of a new manufacture: "that a temporary property therein becomes vested in the king's patentee."[20]

6.2 THE ORGANISATION OF THE LAW OF PROPERTY AT COMMON LAW

The question of what was, and what was not, considered to be the object of property at common law gave rise to considerable disagreement in the eighteenth century courts. It will be argued below that the attitude of judges to the concept of property at common law was a factor which would affect not only how they conceived of the patent as a species of property but also their interpretation of the validity of the subject matter of the patent grant and the rights of patentees. Before examining these judicial debates, it is useful to outline the way in which the law of property was organised in the common law system at this time.

The historical development of the law of property in England meant that its organisation was quite different from that of civil law systems. In the civil law, the law of property has a uniform structure. While civil law systems acknowledge that property can be categorized as moveable or immovable, in theory the object of the property right does not play a role. It does not matter whether it is real property or personal property. There is a conceptual uniformity of property law because the law of property is founded upon the actions in Roman law (*actiones in rem*). The action to retrieve both forms of property in Roman law was the same: the *rei vindicatio*. In the civil law, the basic distinction is between property rights and personal rights: between absolute rights and relative rights. This has led to a division between property law on the one hand and the law of contract and tort on the other.[21] This systemisation is built upon the distinction in Roman law between *actiones in rem* and *actiones in personam*. In Roman law, there was a clear-cut division between *in rem* and *in personam*. An action *in rem* denoted a relationship between a person and a thing, and an action *in personam* a relationship between persons. A right *in rem* availed against persons generally, a right *in personam* against a particular person or particular

---

20 Blackstone, *Commentaries on the Laws of England* (1793), II, 407.
21 W.J. Zwalve, *C. Unikes Venema's Common Law & Civil Law*, Deventer 2000, pp. 96-97.

persons. Rights *in rem* were the subject matter of the law of property, rights *in personam* of the law of obligations.[22]

In the common law system, on the other hand, there is a major division within the law of property between real and personal property. The common law rules relating to personal property were separate from those relating to real property. It is only since the removal of many of these differences by legislation during the nineteenth and twentieth centuries that the distinction between real property and personal property has lost much of its former importance.[23] The distinction between the two property regimes affected such matters as the law of succession, the nature of the legal actions which could be instigated, and the legal concept of ownership.

6.2.1   The Categories of Real Property and Personal Property at Common Law

Blackstone sets out the distinction between real property and personal property in his *Commentaries*:

> "The object of dominion or property are things, as contradistinguished from persons: and things are by the laws of England distributed into two kinds; things real and thing personal. Things real are such as are permanent, fixed and immovable, which cannot be carried out of their place; as land and tenements: things personal are goods, money, and all other moveables; which may attend the owner's person wherever he thinks proper to go."[24]

However, real property was not confined purely to interests in land. As Blackstone pointed out in his *Commentaries*, real property included land, tenements or hereditaments. The terms tenements and hereditaments were broad terms. Tenements were not just houses and buildings, but extended in the legal sense of the word to such matters as offices and rent. Hereditament was an even broader term than tenements. For the purpose of succession, real property passed to the heir rather than to the executor. Hereditament referred to any property that could pass to an heir. Consequently, those rights which could be inherited, such as advowsons, franchises, peerages and offices, as well as chattels within the category of heirlooms, fell within the category of real property.[25] Advowsons, franchises, peerages and offices belonged to the category of incorporeal hereditaments together with

---

22   Barry Nicholas, *An Introduction to Roman Law*, Oxford 1988, pp. 100-101.
23   Halsbury, *Laws of England*, (4ᵗʰ edn.), London 1994, vol. 35, para. 1201, p. 723.
24   Blackstone, *Commentaries on the Laws of England* (1793), II, 16.
25   *Ibid.*, II, 16-17.

tithes, commons, ways, allowances or pensions, annuities and rents. An incorporeal hereditament was "not the thing corporate itself" but "something collateral thereto".[26]

All property rights that did not fall under the legal category of real property were deemed to fall under the category of personal property. Just as the category of real property extended beyond land and fixtures, so did the category of 'things personal' include more than things moveable. Blackstone explains in his *Commentaries* that the term 'chattels' was used to take into account this more extensive meaning. There are two sorts of chattels: chattels real and chattels personal. Real chattels are "interests issuing out of, or annexed to, real estates". For example, a lease for a term of years is a real chattel. It does not fall under the category of real property because its duration is limited to a certain time. It is this "precarious duration" that typifies things personal. Chattels personal are "properly and strictly speaking, things moveable". However, the property in these chattels personal may be either in possession, where a man has not only the right to enjoy the thing but actually has the enjoyment of it, or in action (to be recovered by a legal action), where a man only has a right to it without any occupation or enjoyment.[27]

6.2.2   The Legal Consequences of the Distinction

Whether property belonged to the category of real or personal property was significant. The law relating to land was tied to the system of feudalism, for the common law did not treat land as being the subject of absolute ownership. As all land was held by the crown, a tenant did not own the land itself but was said to hold an estate in the land. Estates were graded according to their duration. The law relating to personal property was not governed by the concepts of feudal tenancy. Indeed, the common law did not conceive of personal property in terms of successive interests or estates, or remainders or reversions.[28] Consequently the ownership of goods differed from that of land. This distinction between real property and personal property was reflected in the rules of succession. Real property passed directly to the heir on death whereas personal property passed to the deceased's executor for distribution. This was in marked contrast to old Roman law, which did not distinguish between real and personal property for the purpose of succession.

This was not the only distinction between the treatment of real and personal property at common law. The legal actions available depended upon this division of property. Real property rights were protected by real actions. A real action was one in which there was a remedy *in rem*: the court would allow a claimant to recover the specific property. Personal property, however, was called 'personal' because the remedy for infringement lay *in per-*

---

26   *Ibid.*, II, 20-21.
27   *Ibid.*, II, 384-389.
28   Halsbury, *Laws of England* (1994), para. 1227, p. 743.

sonam: the remedy was usually an action for damages. There were exceptions. An action of replevin would restore the possession of the personal chattel to the proper owner where goods had been taken unlawfully by way of distress; the goods could be restored pending trial. Detinue was an action whereby the original taking had been lawful, but the retaining of the property thereafter was unlawful. Detinue ordered the defendant to restore the goods to the plaintiff.[29]

Bracton, however, had come to the conclusion, in his legal treatise *De legibus et consuetudinibus Angliae*, written in the thirteenth century, that an action for a moveable thing was not a real action. At first sight, he noted, it looked as if it were an action *in rem* and *in personam*, since a specific thing was being claimed and the possessor was bound to restore that thing. However, by simply paying its value the defendant would be discharged from the obligation, whether the thing itself was in existence or not. Therefore, "in truth it will only be *in personam*".[30] The defendant could either restore the chattel or pay its price. Blackstone explains why damages were awarded instead of the restitution of the specific thing itself where the property at issue was personal property:

> "For things personal are looked upon by the law as of a nature so transitory and perishable, that it is for the most part impossible either to ascertain their identity, or to restore them in the same condition as when they came to the hands of the wrongful possessor… it therefore contents itself in general with restoring, not the thing itself, but a pecuniary equivalent to the party injured; by giving him a satisfaction in damages."[31]

Hence the distinction between *actiones in rem* and *actiones in personam* in Roman law did not entirely correspond to their usage in English law. The common law would never develop a proprietary action analogous to the Roman *vindicatio*.

6.3   THE OBJECT OF PROPERTY AT COMMON LAW

As will be seen below, whether the right of the inventor to exclude others from exploiting his invention was a species of property at common law or only a special species of property created by patent and regulated by statute was a controversial issue. If the patent were a form of property at common law, it would have to comply with the general rules of property set out in the common law. It was therefore necessary to determine what the common law laid down as the general, distinctive characteristics of property in order to see whether

---

29   Baker, *An Introduction to English Legal History* (2002), pp. 298, 390-391.
30   Bracton, f. 102 b (2:292 Thorne edition).
31   Blackstone, *Commentaries on the Laws of England* (1793), III, 146.

these applied to the patent. In trying to distinguish what were the hallmarks of property in the eighteenth century, two things become apparent: the doctrine was not coherent and the issue was deeply divisive.

6.3.1   *Blackstone's Definition of the Object of Property*

Blackstone states categorically in his *Commentaries* that: "The object of dominion or property are things, as contradistinguished from persons."[32] Property rights were: "those rights a man may acquire in and to such *external things* as are unconnected with his person." A property right gave "sole and despotic dominion which one man claims and exercises over the *external things* of the world, in total exclusion of the right of any other individual in the universe".[33] Hence, according to Blackstone, an incorporeal hereditament as a form of property, referred not to the thing itself, but it was "something collateral thereto".[34] Blackstone does not equate property with the external thing itself but refers to rights which a person may acquire "in and to" these external things. It would appear from Blackstone's description that a property right had to be related to a corporeal, "external thing".

This requirement seems to ignore the fact that not all forms of property that had long been condoned by the common law as property were clearly related to an external thing. This becomes apparent in Blackstone's attempt to subject the category of incorporeal hereditaments to a rational structure in his *Commentaries*. Blackstone distinguished corporeal and incorporeal as follows:

> "Corporeal consists of such as affect the senses; such as may be seen and handled by the body: incorporeal are not the object of sensation, can neither be seen nor handled, are creatures of the mind, and exist only in contemplation."[35]

Blackstone described incorporeal hereditaments as "a right issuing out of a thing corporate (whether real or personal) or concerning, or annexed to, or exercisable within, the same".[36] That would mean that each type of incorporeal hereditament could be traced back, and related to, a corporeal thing. In his description of the advowson, this is the line followed by Blackstone. He stresses that this right to present someone to a church benefice is not the same as the bodily possession of the church and its appendages. It is a right to give some other man a title to such bodily possession but the advowson "is the object of neither the sight, nor the touch". However, it "produces a visible, corporeal fruit, by entitling some

---

32 *Ibid.*, II, 16.
33 *Ibid.*, II, 1-2 [my italics].
34 *Ibid.*, II, 20.
35 *Ibid.*, II, 17.
36 *Ibid.*, II, 20.

clerk, whom the patron shall please to nominate, to enter and receive bodily possession of the lands and tenements of the church".[37] In this way, the 'incorporeal right' of the advowson was connected to the thing corporeal, the church property.

However, Blackstone acknowledged that: "*a condition*, the benefit of which may descend to a man from his ancestor, is also a hereditament."[38] An office is classed as an incorporeal hereditament, being "a right to exercise a public or private employment". This could be in the form of a public office, like a magistrate, or a private office, like a bailiff. A man could have an estate in an office. It could, for example be to him and his heirs, or for life or for a term of years.[39] A condition is not a thing. Therefore, a right connected to a condition cannot be said to be a right connected to a physical thing. In his description of offices as an incorporeal hereditament, Blackstone makes no attempt to link an office to a specific corporeal thing. Nonetheless, the common law recognised an office as incorporeal property, as a form of real property. It is but one indication that there was no coherent doctrine as to what the common law would see as the object of property, despite Blackstone's attempt to present the law on property as a rational system.

When Blackstone defined property rights as "those rights a man may acquire in and to such *external things* as are unconnected with his person", he was presumably giving what he considered to be the common law definition of property. It was, however, difficult for him to fit a right like copyright within the scope of that definition. If copyright was "a right issuing out of a thing corporate (whether real or personal) or concerning, or annexed to, or exercisable within, the same" how did that relate to an author's property if that property was in "the sentiments and the language" of a composition? Blackstone gives no definitive answer in his *Commentaries* as to whether copyright was a species of property recognised by the common law:

> " There is still another species of property, which (*if it subsists by the common law*) ...And this is the right, which an author may be supposed to have in his own original literary compositions." [40]

As will be seen below, it would seem that Blackstone's own opinion was that copyright was a form of property recognised at common law.

Blackstone's traditional definition of property sets out another characteristic of property: property rights have to be "rights that a man may *acquire*". There were various ways in which the title to property could be acquired, but if the object was a *res nullius*, the title to

---

37   *Ibid.*, II, 21-22.
38   *Ibid.*, II, 17 [my italics].
39   *Ibid.*, II, 36.
40   *Ibid.*, II, 405 [my italics].

it was acquired by occupancy. This required a man to take possession of it, thereby signifying that it had been removed from the communal domain. If the object to be occupied, however, was not a physical thing, this approach to the acquisition of property raised conceptual problems. There was a non-legal theory, which had filtered into legal circles, which offered a possible solution to the requirement of occupancy. In his Second Treatise, Locke had stated:

> "The **labour** of his body, and the *work* of his hands, we may say, are properly his. Whatsoever then he removes out of the state that nature hath provided, and left it in, he hath mixed his **labour** with, and joined to it something that is his own, and thereby makes it his *property*. It being by him removed from the common state nature hath placed it in, it hath by this **labour** something annexed to it, that excludes the common right of other men: for this **labour** being the unquestionable property of the **labour**er, no man but he can have a right to what that is once joined to, at least where there is enough, and as good, left in common for others."[41]

Locke's theory not only had to be taken out of the context of political philosophy and converted into a legal principle to be used for this purpose, the theory had to be extended to cover not just the labour of the body, but also the labour of the mind. In his *Commentaries*, Blackstone brings Locke's theory to the fore. If labours of the mind were forms of property recognised at common law, then Blackstone considered that the right of occupancy founded on personal labour was the most appropriate head of occupancy.[42]

6.3.2   *Judicial Debates on the Object of Property*

If eighteenth century judicial opinions are consulted, it becomes apparent that the legal nature of property was a divisive issue within the judiciary. There were judges who wished to cling to older definitions of property, whereas others considered that the definition of property should be adapted to the needs of the day. Those who preferred a traditional definition of property conceived of property in terms of rights related to and issuing out of something corporeal, visible and material. They argued that, as property was founded on occupancy, there had to be some physical thing which could be possessed or occupied. It was this physical thing to which a person's incorporeal property rights were attached. A thing without a physical existence could not be occupied and therefore it could not be the object of property, regardless of how much mental labour had been expended. Others

---

41 Locke, Second Treatise, V, 27.
42 Blackstone, *Commentaries on the Laws of England* (1793), II, 405.

argued that an object of property should be conceived of in terms of anything that had value or would provide a profit. The object of a proprietary right could be the profits derived from exercising the faculties of the mind. A man's labour, either of the body or of the intellect, could be a source of property and a means of occupation. These two competing lines of judicial reasoning would become explicit in the discussions on the nature of property in several high profile copyright cases.

One of the major proponents of a traditional, formalist approach to the object of property was Justice Yates. Yates argued that there could be no proprietary right if the object of that right was not a tangible thing. This was his standpoint not only as counsel in the copyright case *Tonson v. Collins* 1762, but also later as a judge of the King's Bench in another copyright case, *Millar v. Taylor* 1769. In *Tonson v. Collins*, Yates was adamant that for a thing to be given the status of property, to be classed by the law as a personal chattel:

> "It must be something, that may be seen, felt, given, delivered, lost or stolen, in order to constitute the subject of property."

Yates' definition of a personal chattel in that case extended only to material things. It excluded any form of incorporeal property. It earned him an interruption from Lord Mansfield who asked:

> "How would you steal an option, or the next turn of an advowson?"[43]

And a rebuke from Blackstone, counsel for the plaintiff in Tonson:

> "The principal pillar of Mr. Yates's argument rests upon his description of property. He considers it as having nothing for its subject, but what is substantial, palpable and visible. He has omitted the distinction, between corporeal and incorporeal rights; the latter of which are as much considered by the law, as the basis of property, as the former…The right of presenting to a church is not more visible or material, than the right of publishing a book. All these are mere potential rights, dormant and unnoticed, till opportunity calls them into act; and then they produce a visible fruit."[44]

However, in the Tonson case Blackstone had also manoeuvred himself into an awkward position. In Tonson, just as in his *Commentaries*, Blackstone attempted to link "incorporeal

---

43 *Tonson v. Collins* 1762, 1 W. Black. 338.
44 *Ibid.*, 340.

rights" (which in itself is a tautology as all rights are incorporeal) to an external thing: "a visible fruit". To be consistent, he had to make that link for copyright. It could be argued that the link is the paper upon which the sentiments appear. The problem Blackstone had, however, was that he had acknowledged that it was not the paper that was of value: the paper and print "are merely accidents, which serve as vehicles to convey that style and sentiment to a distance".[45] The value of the property is not in the paper, an 'accidental' external thing, but the style and sentiments of the composition.

Once again Blackstone was caught with one foot in two camps, just as he had been when he argued that judges did not create law but only applied it, while at the same time he had supported an equitable interpretation of statutes by judges (see chapter 2). Blackstone presented in his *Commentaries* a formalistic approach to property, using a definition of property which emphasised the materiality of property: rights in and to an external thing. Yet he argued in *Tonson v. Collins* 1762 that an author could have a property in something as intangible as the way in which that author had expressed his ideas. Blackstone found himself caught between his perpetual emphasis on relating an "incorporeal right" to some external thing and acknowledging that the external thing, in the case of copyright the paper, was not the source of the property right. Indeed, Blackstone had dismissed as absurd the Roman law which meant if one wrote a poem on another man's paper, the poem belonged to the owner of the paper, and not to the poet.[46] Blackstone was, of course, acting as counsel and not as judge in *Tonson v. Collins*. However, in his *Commentaries*, Blackstone states that the "identity of a literary composition consists entirely in the sentiment and the language".[47] Blackstone had also argued in *Tonson v. Collins* that copyright was not a new form of property made by statute but a form of property recognised by the common law.[48] This was a standpoint he would reiterate in *Donaldson v. Beckett* 1774, but this time in his capacity as a judge.[49]

The divisions within the judiciary on the subject of property became apparent when the Court of King's Bench heard *Millar v. Taylor* in 1769. In that case, Yates, now a judge of the King's Bench, set out a more detailed description of the legal concept of property than he had as counsel in *Tonson v. Collins* 1762, but the main principle remained the same:

---

45 *Ibid.*, 343.
46 *Ibid.*, 324.
47 Blackstone, *Commentaries on the Laws of England* (1793), II, 405.
48 *Tonson v. Collins* 1762, 1 W. Black 326.
49 *Donaldson v. Beckett* 1774, Cobbett, *Parliamentary History of England* (1813), col. 978.

"It is a well-known and established maxim (which I apprehend holds as true now, as it did 2000 years ago,) 'That nothing can be an object of property, which has not a corporeal substance.'"[50]

There may be different rights and distinct interests in the same subject, but "the *object* of them all, the *principal subject* to which they relate, or in which they enjoy, must be *corporeal*". This arose, according to Yates, from the necessary nature of all property. The object of it must be something visible. "I am speaking now of the *object* to which *all rights are confined*. There must be something *visible*; which has *bounds* to define it, and some *marks* to distinguish it."[51] Nothing could be an object of property that was not capable of distinguishable proprietary marks.

That was why, according to Yates, a right like copyright could not be a species of property at common law. Copyright was a right to bring an action against anyone who printed the author's work without his consent. If copyright was a species of property at common law, what was the object of property to which this right related? One of the arguments by those defending literary property was that the material thing to which the right related was the profit that could be gained. Yates rejected outright the idea that an object of property could be value. "Mere value does not constitute property." That fallacy arose from the equivocal use of the word 'property', which sometimes was used to denote the right of the person and sometimes the object itself. The rights of persons may be incorporeal. However the question was whether an object could be the object of a proprietary right if it did not have a corporeal substance. The answer to that was:

"No right can exist, without a substance to retain it, and to which it is confined."[52]

For the same reason, Yates dismissed the argument that the object of property could be intellectual ideas. Nothing could be the object of property that could not be appropriated. Some act of appropriation was necessary to take the thing out of being common and to show others that they must not use it. No possession could be taken, or any act of occupancy, with respect to mere intellectual ideas. "What distinguishing marks can a man fix upon a set of intellectual ideas, so as to call himself the proprietor of them?" Invention or labour, even if considerable, could not change the nature of things. Nor could invention or labour establish a right, where no private right could exist.[53] Yates rejected that property could be acquired by mental, as well as by bodily labour. This signified his disapproval of

---

50   *Millar v. Taylor* 1769, 4 Burr 2361.
51   *Ibid.*, 2361.
52   *Ibid.*, 2356, 2362.
53   *Ibid.*, 2357, 2366.

the use that had been made of Locke's theory on property by those seeking to justify literary property.[54] Nor did Yates accept that the object of property could be anything as ephemeral as an author's composition. How could an author have exclusive enjoyment of his composition if he had published it: "every sentiment in it made public, for ever."[55]

For Yates, value, ideas and composition could not be the objects of property at common law. With respect to copyright, that meant that the only property protected by the common law was the physical book itself. The book was the visible, tangible object of property from which the incorporeal property right of the author was derived. However, once the manuscript had been published, the property in the book was lost. It became the property of the purchaser: "Every purchaser of a book is the owner of it: and, as such, he had a right to make what use of it he pleases."[56] Hence copyright, Yates concluded, did not fall under any category of personal property known to the common law. It could not be classed as a chattel. It was in effect a mere right of action; a right *in personam*, not *in rem*. At common law, "the present action is a tort only".[57]

Yates' stance on the object of property, his formalist approach expressed in the case of *Millar v. Taylor*, brought him into open conflict with Lord Mansfield and other members of the King's Bench. Mansfield used Yates' style of analysis to show what he considered to be the shortcomings of Yates' approach to determining the object of property. In the debate on copyright, Yates had conceded that an author had a property in his sentiments prior to publication but after publication, when the author's sentiments were made common, the author lost his property in them. Mansfield argued that if it was admitted, as it had been, that an author had a right at common law to print "a set of intellectual ideas or modes of thinking, communicated in a set of words and sentences and modes of expression" then that was a right which was "equally detached from the manuscript, or any other physical existence whatsoever". Therefore, if an author had this property at common law before publication, the common law recognised an author's property in ideas communicated in a mode of expression. The publication of those ideas could not be a determining factor. Mansfield argued that the objections that had been made to this form of property after publication were the same as the objections which could be made to it before publication:

> "It is *incorporeal*: it relates to ideas detached from any *physical* existence. There are *no indicia*...The same string of questions may be asked, upon the copy before publication: Is it *real* or *personal*? Does it go to the *heir*, or to the *executor*? Being a right which can only be defended by action, is it, as a chose

---

54   For example, by Blackstone in *Tonson v. Collins* 1762, 1 W. Black 321-322.
55   *Millar v. Taylor* 1769, 4 Burr 2363.
56   *Ibid.*, 2364.
57   *Ibid.*, 2384-2386.

in action, *assignable*, or not? Can it be *forfeited*? Can it be taken in *execution*? Can it be *vested in the assignees* under a commission of bankruptcy?"[58]

It is, however, Aston, J. in the Millar case who is the most forthright in his rejection of the formalist approach to the object of property. Aston openly expresses his impatience with the existing written definitions of property:

> "I shall in the next place observe, that the written definitions of property, which have been taken notice of at the bar, are, in my opinion, very inadequate to the objects of property at this day. They are adapted, by the writers, to things in a primitive (not to say *imaginary*) state; when all things were in common; when the common right was to be *divested* by some act to render the thing privately and *exclusively* a man's own, which, before that act so done to separate and distinguish it, was as much *another's*."[59]

It was mistaken, argued Aston, to be looking back to determine what could be the object of property rather than looking forward, as by looking back to the origin of things sight was lost of the present state of the world:

> "Since those supposed times, therefore of universal communion, the objects of property have been much enlarged, by discovery, invention, and arts…The rules attending property must keep pace with its increase and improvement, and must be adapted to every case."[60]

Aston argued that not all objects of property could have been known to the common law at once and "many have been *disputed*, as not being objects of property at common law, which yet are *now established* to be such; as gunpowder etc".[61] Furthermore, if the rules of property were to keep pace with society, the objects of property set down in those old definitions had to be adjusted. Rights did not have to fasten onto some corporeal thing:

> "A DISTINGUISHABLE *existence* in the thing claimed as property; an ACTUAL VALUE in that thing *to the true owner*; are its *essentials*."[62]

---

58   *Ibid.*, 2396-2397.
59   *Ibid.*, 2338-2339.
60   *Ibid.*, 2339-2340.
61   *Ibid.*, 2344.
62   *Ibid.*, 2340.

Aston argued that the acquisition of property by occupancy had been relevant at one time. However, the concept of property was not static and as new forms of property were gradually introduced these older definitions "give a sort of property little superior to the legal idea of a beast-common". He cites Pufendorf in order to show that Pufendorf considered that distinct properties were not settled at the same time, nor by a single act but by successive degrees. Aston concluded that:

"The mode of obtaining property by occupancy has been abridged."[63]

Indeed, so impatient is Aston with the legal definitions of the object of property advanced at the bar that he refers to a quite different source, a philosophical book by William Wollaston, a well-known rationalist natural lawyer, called *The Religion of Nature Delineated*, which appeared in 1722. This allowed a broader definition:

"That a man may have property in his body, life, fame, labours and the like; and, in short, in anything that can be called his."[64]

The gulf between Yates' standpoint on the object and acquisition of property and that of Aston in the Millar case was huge.

The same lines of division appear in the copyright case of *Donaldson v. Beckett*, which was heard by the House of Lords in 1774. The opposing arguments were set out by Thurlow and Wedderburn who, once again, were acting as opposing counsel in a copyright case. Thurlow:

"Property, he said, was in his idea of a double nature, either original or derivable; it must be in itself corporeal, or derive its name from something of a corporeal nature; thence its relation to occupancy and possession."[65]

Whereas Wedderburn argued:

"The interpretation they [the appellants] had put upon the word 'property' was, that it implied something corporeal, tangible, and material. He begged leave to differ from this opinion, and to point out how common it was for terms to be misapplied as to their import. The word 'property' had, by the ablest writers, been called *jus utendi, fruendi, disponendi*; it was therefore evident that

---

63   *Ibid.*, 2339, (Aston cites his reference to Pufendorf as Lib. 4. c. 4 pa. 367, 6; pa. 377. 14).
64   *Ibid.*, 2338.
65   *Donaldson v. Beckett* 1774, Cobbett, *Parliamentary History of England* (1813), col. 968.

any idea, although it was incorporeal in itself, yet if it promised future profit to the inventor of it, was a property. And the latter word had, through inaccuracy, been used, as describing that, over which a possessor held an absolute reign, dominion, or power of disposal. The subject matter might be immaterial, and yet liable to be appropriated."

Wedderburn criticised the lawyers' way of describing property in terms of a divide between corporeal and incorporeal. He argued that the courts of law had admitted that matters incorporeal were matters of property, and the lawyers' division of it proved that matters not in occupancy or possession, were yet of value, and could be sold or given over, as in the cases of manors and advowsons, remainders, and reversions.[66] The positions adopted by Thurlow and Wedderburn were reflected in the opinions of several judges. Eyre, at that time baron of the Court of Exchequer stated:

"A right to appropriate ideas was a right to appropriate something so ethereal as to elude definition! so intellectual as not to fall within the limits of the human mind to describe with any tolerable degree of accuracy. Ideas, if convertible into objects of property, should bear some faint similitude to other objects of property; they did not bear any such similitude, they were altogether anomalous. They could not pass by descent to heirs; they were not liable to bequest; no characteristic marks remained whereby to ascertain them; and, were such incorporealities not subject to one of the conditions which constituted the very essence of property original or derivative; were such incorporealities liable to exclusive appropriation by any right founded in the common law?"[67]

Lord Camden similarly rejected Wedderburn's argument. Camden gave his opinion in Donaldson as a member of the House of Lords, but he had once served as Lord Chief Justice of Common Pleas and the Lord Chancellor in the Court of Chancery. He asked:

"what says the common law about the incorporeal ideas, and where does it prescribe a remedy for the recovery of them, independent of the materials to which they are affixed?... I hope judges will always copy the example, and never pretend to decide upon a claim of property, without attending to the old black letter of our law, without founding their judgment upon some solid written authority, preserved in their books, or in judicial records"[68]

---

66   *Ibid.*, col. 963-964.
67   *Ibid.*, col. 972 [my italics].
68   *Ibid.*, col. 997-999.

On the other hand, Ashhurst, J. considered that:

> "Every thing was property that was capable of being known or defined, capable of a separate enjoyment, and of value to the owner." [69]

6.4 The Patent as a Form of Personal Property

In the copyright cases of the eighteenth century, the judges had been forced to determine whether this item of personal property could be considered to be a species of property recognised at common law. That there was no judicial consensus on the matter is perhaps not surprising. Real property had traditionally been the focus of English law and it had generated abstract and complex legal constructions. Personal property, on the other hand, had received less attention.

Theoretically, as already noted, personal property in English law, unlike real property, was not tied to the concepts of feudal tenure which had shaped the development of the law of real property. However, it has been argued by Stein and Shand that it was this very heritage of feudalism which would enable the common law to designate such abstract rights as patents and copyright as personal property. Whereas the civil law tradition tends to identify ownership with the thing owned, and to limit its definition of things to moveable or immovable property as opposed to more abstract rights, the common law approach is different. Formed by the tenures of medieval feudalism, the common law has been more ready to analyse ownership in terms of bundles of rights, obligations and inter-personal relationships arising from the control and enjoyment of property. The common lawyer's understanding of property as a bundle of rights hence resulted in a flexibility which enabled the common law to accept, more easily than civil law systems, abstract rights like patents and copyright as forms of property.[70]

There is something to be said for this argument, as several examples illustrate. The doctrine of estates, as noted above, is based upon an abstract entity. An estate was not the land itself but a temporal interest in the land. A number of people could hold different estates in the same piece of land. An estate holder, who did not have present possession of the land but a future interest in it, could still sell that estate before the right to possession had arisen. He was the owner of a future interest in the land and that future interest was deemed property. Incorporeal hereditaments, like an advowson or an office, were similarly abstractions that were considered to be property. "Their existence", stated Blackstone, "is merely in idea and abstracted contemplation".[71] Such constructions as the estate and

---

69 *Ibid.*, col. 977.
70 Peter Stein and John Stand, *Legal Values in Western Society*, Edinburgh 1974, pp. 216-217.
71 Blackstone, *Commentaries on the Laws of England* (1793), II, 20.

incorporeal hereditaments demonstrate that an abstract legal approach to property was not alien to the eighteenth century common law mind.

This does not, however, imply the existence of any consistent doctrine by which more modern abstractions, like copyright and patent, could be fitted easily into the law of property. Nor does it imply that patents and copyrights would be accepted as forms of property at common law because the common law had, in the past, found a means to deal with rights to land that were distinct from the ownership or possession of land, or had treated such rights as a title or office as forms of property. A very public divide had opened up within the judiciary as to what was considered to be the object of property at common law. The judicial debates on property in the eighteenth century reveal that some judges rejected both the patent and copyright as forms of property recognised by the common law.

6.4.1   The Patent and Copyright: Species of Common Law Property?

The debate on property was played out in the literary property debates of the eighteenth century. Whether copyright was a form of property recognised at common law or whether it was a new sort of property created by statute was a major issue in these copyright cases because if copyright was only a form of property created by statute, the author only had protection for the fourteen-year period stated in the Statute of Anne 1709. If copyright was deemed to be a creation of the common law, and the Statute of Anne was interpreted as having simply supplemented the common law by setting out penalties for infringement, the author's rights did not expire at the end of the statutory period. With the statutory copyright period running out, the matter was of vital importance to the livelihood of the booksellers who held the copyright. Edward Christian, editor of Blackstone's *Commentaries*, observed:

> "Whether the productions of the mind could communicate a right of property or of exclusive enjoyment in reason and nature; and if such a moral right existed, whether it was recognised and supported by the common law of England; and whether the common law was intended to be restrained by the Statute of Queen Anne; are questions, upon which the learning and talents of the highest legal characters in this kingdom have been powerfully and zealously exerted."[72]

The question of whether an inventor had the right to exclude others from exploiting his invention at common law, however, was not addressed in patent cases. Patentees, unlike booksellers, had not challenged the duration of the statutory protection in open court.

---

72   *Ibid.*, II, 407 fn. (5).

Possibly this was because patentees could prolong the period of protection provided by the Statute of Monopolies 1624. Until Brougham's Act 1835 transferred the competence to the Judicial Committee of the Privy Council, and limited the period of extension to seven years, a patent could be extended by a private Act of Parliament, sometimes for a considerable period of time (see chapter 1).

Although not raised as a legal issue in court, there seems to have been agreement within the judiciary that, since the enactment of the Statute of Monopolies, an inventor could only protect his invention by patent and the duration of that patent protection was determined by the Statute of Monopolies. Grose, J. states this explicitly in *Hornblower v. Boulton and Watt* 1799:

> "The question then is, whether the patent be good in law, in other words, whether it be conformable to the statute of the 21 Jac. 1. c. 3. s. 6 under which the plaintiff or any party *can alone claim* the privilege of a monopoly."[73]

Similar comments regarding patents were made in the copyright cases. Ashhurst, J. considered that since the Statute of Monopolies, no questions could exist about mechanical inventions as since that Act no inventor could maintain an action without a patent. Aston, J. stated that with regard to mechanical instruments, the Statute of Monopolies had made it necessary for the inventors of them to seek security under a patent.[74] The Statute, by requiring inventors to seek protection by patent, had revoked any previous common law right that may have existed before 1624. The question was: had an inventor ever been able to protect his invention from piracy without a patent granted by the crown? Lord Camden, in *Donaldson v. Beckett*, dismissed the idea as absurd:

> "If there be such a right at common law, the crown is an usurper; but there is no such right at common law, which declares it a monopoly; no such action lies; resort must be had to the crown in all such cases."[75]

The copyright cases provide examples of judges arguing for and against the inventor's right to exclude others from using his invention as a common law species of property. Those who rejected copyright as a species of property at common law also rejected the patent as a species of property at common law. The rejection was based on the same line of reasoning: the common law required the object of property to which 'incorporeal rights' related to be a tangible, visible thing. Copyright as a form of property could not, therefore,

---

73 *Hornblower v. Boulton and Watt* 1799, 8 T.R. 99-100 [my italics].
74 *Donaldson v. Beckett* 1774, Cobbett, *Parliamentary History of England* (1813), col. 977, 981.
75 *Ibid.*, col. 999.

have its roots in the common law, but was the creation of statute. Similarly, an inventor had no rights without a patent grant from the crown, the requirements of which were regulated by statute.

In *Millar v. Taylor* 1769, Yates dealt with property dependent upon a prerogative grant by the crown. In the Millar case, one of the points raised had concerned the crown's sole right of publishing certain works, such as the Bible and Acts of Parliament. These works were printed under a patent from the crown by the Stationers Company. The grant was an act of the royal prerogative. As no other person was allowed to publish these works without the authority of the crown, the king was said to have a property in them. Yates pointed out:

> "This kind of property has always the additional distinction of prerogative property. The right is ground upon another foundation; and is founded on a distinction that can not exist in common property, and in the case of a subject."[76]

A patent for a new invention was also a grant of the royal prerogative. As the king's property was 'ground upon another foundation', it would seem from Yates' comment on prerogative patents for printing that a patent grant made by the crown for a new invention equally could not be seen as having the common law as its source. This was the opinion of Lord Camden (as noted above).

Yates in *Millar v. Taylor* stressed the similarities between the position of the author and that of the inventor. Copyright was not a form of property known at common law. The author was dependent on the Statute of Anne, which had created a new right:

> "The *legislature* indeed *may make a new* right. The statute of Queen Ann has vested a *new* right in authors, for a *limited* time: and *whilst* that right exists, they will be established in the possession of their property."[77]

Similarly, the inventor had no right without a patent:

> "but if the inventor has no patent for it, everyone may make it, and sell it."[78]

Yates argued that value was no more a mark of property with respect to an inventor's property than it was with respect to an author's property (giving the example of Harrison's time-piece and Thomson's 'Seasons').[79] A set of intellectual ideas could not be the object

---

76   *Millar v. Taylor* 1769, 4 Burr 2382.
77   *Ibid.*, 2386.
78   *Ibid.*, 2386.
79   *Ibid.*, 2387.

of an author's property nor could it be the object of an inventor's property. The only object of property to which copyright attached was the physical book. Once the book had been purchased, every purchaser of the book was the owner of it and had a right to make what use of it he pleased. Once an invention had been made known, it became common in the same way as the sentiments of an author became common after publication. The machine became the property of the purchaser, just as the book became the property of the purchaser: "it is the right of every purchaser of the instrument, to make what use of it he pleases."[80]

> "Both original inventions stand upon the same footing, in point of *property*; whether the case be *mechanical* or *literary*; whether it be *an epic poem*, or an *orrery*…if the inventor of the machine chooses to make a property of it, by selling the invention to an instrument maker, the invention will secure him a benefit. But when the invention is once made known to the world, it is laid open; it is a gift to the public… If the inventor has no patent, any person whatever may *copy* the invention and *sell* it."[81]

The inventor could argue for a perpetual monopoly by raising the very same points as an author, but the same rule applied: "no such property can exist, after the invention is published."[82] Copyright was not a species of property known to the common law, and neither was the patent.

Willes, J. in *Millar v. Taylor* disagreed with Yates with respect to an author's property but agreed with him as far as the inventor's rights were concerned. He agreed with Yates that once an author's book was sold to the public, free use could be made of all a book teaches. The knowledge provided by a book's content was, however, distinct from the literary composition, which remained the author's property. However, once an inventor had communicated his invention, it was free to all: "As by the communication of an invention in trade, manufacture, or machines, men are *taught the art or science*, they have a *right to use* it."[83] According to this reasoning, whatever property in his invention an inventor may have had at common law, it was lost once the invention was communicated.

This was a ratiocination which was, in principle, rejected by Mansfield with respect to copyright in the Millar case. Mansfield had considered it nonsensical that if an author had a property in his ideas at common law before they were communicated, an author could loose that property on communication. Mansfield does not make the comparison with an inventor in *Millar v. Taylor*, but it would seem that the same line of reasoning could be applied to an inventor. That would, at first, appear to be the tenor of Aston's opinion in

---

80   *Ibid.*, 2386.
81   *Ibid.*, 2386.
82   *Ibid.*, 2387.
83   *Ibid.*, 2331.

Millar. Aston, J. argued that without publication, the author's property was useless to its owner because it was without profit: "Publication therefore is the necessary act, and only means, to render this confessed property useful to mankind, and profitable to the owner." If this necessary act destroyed the original property, this would be harsh and unreasonable. However, Aston does not reach the same conclusion for inventors. Indeed, he considered mechanical invention to be of a very different nature:

> "And the difference consists in *this*, that the property of the maker of a *mechanical* engine is confined to that *individual thing*, which he has made; that the machine made in imitation or resemblance of it, is a *different work* in *substance, materials, labour* and *expense*, in which the maker of the original machine cannot claim any property, for it is *not his* but *only a resemblance* of his."[84]

The imitated machine was a new and different work, whereas a literary composition printed on paper belonging to someone else was still the same. The only property right an inventor had at common law was simply in the physical machine. He would have the right to exclude another from using his own machine without his consent, but not from using the know-how necessary to make that machine once the machine had been made public. As the inventor had no right at common law to protection beyond the individual machine that he had made, the patent right could not be a right recognised at common law. Apparently Aston had scant regard for the inventor's technical creativity, as something separate from the machine itself. Yet Aston had dismissed as absurd the suggestion that an author only had a property in the physical book, a property which he lost upon sale.[85]

Aston's judgment reflects the downplaying of the intellectual creativity of inventors which had been brought to the fore by those, like Warburton, who had been campaigning for perpetual copyright. To justify a different regime for authors, it was argued that the mental labour of an author was of a different order than that of an inventor (see paragraph 5.2.1). Furthermore, the emphasis here was placed on the "individual thing" that had been made by the inventor. In tracing the development of intellectual property law, Sherman and Bently point to the importance of the acceptance by the law that the scope of the property extended beyond the immediate form, beyond its first embodiment either in the form of a prototype or a manuscript. The protection of the invention would be the protection of its "pith and marrow".[86] It would appear, however, from the early copyright cases that judges were more inclined to see beyond this immediate form with respect to literary works than to inventions.

---

84 *Ibid.*, 2341, 2348-2349.
85 *Ibid.*, 2342.
86 Sherman and Bently, *The Making of Modern Intellectual Property Law: The British Experience 1760-1911* (1999), pp. 51, 55-56.

Very similar sentiments to those of Yates were expressed by Eyre, in *Donaldson v. Beckett* 1774:

> "On the whole, the baron contended, that a mechanic invention and a literary composition exactly agreed in point of similarity; the one therefore was no more entitled to be the object of common law property than the other; and as the common law was entirely silent with respect to what is called literary property, as ancient usage was against the supposition of such a property, and as no exclusive right of appropriating those other operations of the mind, which pass under the denomination of mechanical inventions, was vested in the inventor by common law, the baron, for these reasons, declared himself against the principle of admitting the author of a book, any more than the inventor of a piece of mechanism, to have a right at common law to the exclusive appropriation and sale of the same.[87]

There were judges who did not rule out the possibility that an inventor had had a proprietary right at common law prior to the Statute of Monopolies. Several examples of this opposing point of view may be found in *Donaldson v. Beckett*. Aston, J.:

> "With regard to mechanical instruments, because the Act against monopolies had rendered it necessary for the inventors of them to seek security under a patent, it could be no argument why in literary property there should be no common law right. He thought it would be more liberal to conclude, that previous to the monopoly statute, there existed a common law right, equally to an inventor of a machine and an author of a book."

And similarly Lord Chancellor Smythe in Donaldson:

> "As to mechanical inventions, he did not know that, previous to the Act of 21 James I, an action would not lie against the person who pirated an invention."[88]

Neither judge appears to have given any detailed reasoning: it 'was more liberal to conclude' that it was so or 'he did not know' that such an action could not have been possible was all the judges put forward. Furthermore, Aston's 'liberal' conclusion seems to be out of keeping with what he had maintained in *Millar v. Taylor*. There he had argued that there was a difference between a literary work and a mechanical invention. An inventor only

---

87 *Donaldson v. Beckett* 1774, Cobbett, *Parliamentary History of England* (1813), col. 974.
88 *Ibid.*, col. 981, 987.

had a property at common law in the individual thing that he had made and anyone would have the right to copy and sell it. In both instances cited here, the judges were of the opinion that the author's property was a species of property recognised at common law. It was strategic, therefore, to claim the same for the inventor. Camden would complain, in Donaldson, that when judges argued that an inventor had a right at common law, this contention had one purpose only and that was to support the claim that there was such a thing as literary property at common law.[89] He may well have had a ground for that opinion, at least with respect to Aston.

As noted above, Stein and Shand argue that it was the common lawyer's understanding of property as a bundle of rights that enabled the common law to accept abstract rights like patents and copyright as forms of property. Yet clearly there was no unanimity within the judiciary on whether copyright and patents were species of common law property. Furthermore, with respect to the development of copyright regulation, it should be pointed out that the House of Lords decided, in the copyright case of *Donaldson v. Beckett* 1774, that copyright did not exist at common law. With respect to patents for new inventions, there was a division of opinion within the judiciary as to whether there had ever been a right at common law for an inventor to exclude others from the use of his invention. Yet even the statements cited above, by Aston and Smythe in Donaldson, that the inventor might have had a common law right prior to the Statute of Monopolies, seem rather half-hearted. The judiciary was, however, unanimous in its agreement that whatever may have been the position of the inventor at common law prior to 1624, since the Statute of Monopolies an inventor only had protection for his invention by patent. Furthermore, as Willes, J. had pointed out in *Millar v. Taylor*, with respect to a patent all the conditions required by the Statute of Monopolies had to be observed.[90] The recognition of the patent as a form of property seems to have had more to do with the acceptance by the courts of a right dependent upon an act of the royal prerogative, regulated by a parliamentary statute and referred to in private Acts of Parliament as property, than with common law theories on 'bundles of rights'.

This does not imply, however, that the judicial debate on the legal origin of an inventor's claim was without significance. It might have affected how judges viewed the interests of the patentee. In the copyright cases, the issue of the moral rights of the author had been brought to the fore. This moral component was used in making the argument for and against copyright as a right known to the common law. Lord Mansfield, who argued that copyright was a common law species of property, placed the question of copyright within this moral context in *Millar v. Taylor*:

---

89   *Ibid.*, col. 999.
90   *Millar v. Taylor* 1769, 4 Burr 2323.

"The whole then must finally resolve in this question, 'Whether it is agreeable to natural principles, moral justice and fitness to allow him the copy, after publication, as well as before'."

"If it is agreeable to natural principles, to allow the copy after publication, I am warranted by the admission which allows it before publication, to say, 'This is common law.'"[91]

Aston too in Millar considered "the invasion of this sort of property is as much against every man's sense of it, as it is against natural reason and moral rectitude". As the common law was "founded on the law of nature and reason", why would the common law "be so narrow and illiberal" as not to protect such property? Hence "every principle of *reason, natural justice, morality* and *common law*" indicated that an author had the right to the copy of his work at common law.[92] It was an argument he repeated in *Donaldson v. Beckett*:

> "that our common law had its foundation in private justice, moral fitness, and public convenience; the natural rights, of every subject were protected by it, and there did not exist an argument which would amount to conviction that an author had not a natural right to the produce of his mental labours."[93]

Yates in Millar used the moral rectitude argument too, but to show that the lack of a moral justification for a perpetual monopoly for a product of the mind was another indication that copyright was not a species of property known to the common law. The law of personal property had its "grand foundation in *natural* law". While everyman was entitled to the fruits of his own labour, he should not expect these fruits to be eternal. That would be the injustice:

> "In *that* case, the injustice would lie on the side of the monopolist, who would thus *exclude all the rest* of mankind from enjoying their *natural and social rights*."[94]

The emphasis in all these arguments was placed on natural law and natural rights. The common law, to quote Aston, protected natural rights. If copyright were a species of property at common law that implied it was a natural right. If there was no difference between the position of an author and an inventor, and an author had a natural right, that implied that an inventor would also have a natural right in his invention. The natural law

---

91 *Ibid.*, 2399, 2400.
92 *Ibid.*, 2342-2343, 2354.
93 *Donaldson v. Beckett* 1774, Cobbett, *Parliamentary History of England* (1813), col. 980.
94 *Millar v. Taylor*, 2355, 2359-2360.

argument for inventors was used to effect in France in the eighteenth century. The premise that individuals had a natural right of property in their own ideas, that these ideas could not be used by others without some form of compensation, and that the state had a moral duty to enforce this exclusivity, became enshrined in the French patent law of 1791. However, the natural right in inventions theory was one that was far more pervasive on the continent than in England.[95]

If the patent right was not conceived of in terms of a natural right, this could help to explain why not all judges readily thought of a patentee as having a right rather than a privilege (see paragraph 5.2.3). In *Millar v. Taylor*, Yates had acknowledged that those who contributed to learning and science should be encouraged. Every man's labour should be "properly rewarded" but every reward had its proper bounds and a temporary monopoly was a sufficient reward. Hence, with respect to copyright, the whole basis of the author's protection was to encourage the author to write, as a benefit to the public. He was rewarded for this, but an author's claim was on public benevolence, by way of encouragement, but he had no "absolute coercive right".[96] What the author or inventor could claim was a *reward*, but a reward or a privilege, was something different from claiming a *right* to the legal protection of a composition or invention.

Deazley, in his history of copyright law, concluded that copyright in the eighteenth century was never simply concerned with the interests of the bookseller or the author, but was "primarily defined and justified in the interests of society and not the individual". The concern was for the encouragement and spread of education and the continued production of useful books. The common good was the organising principle of the system of copyright regulation.[97] This reasoning could similarly be applied to patents. There are indications that the interest of any individual patentee would weigh less heavily than the interests of the public.

When the subject matter of the invention was a labour-saving device, the courts had felt free to declare a patent for such an invention invalid because it was considered to be against the public interest. The courts had no qualms about preventing an inventor from reaping the benefit of his ingenuity and the Statute of Monopolies itself prohibited the legal protection of any invention which the courts would interpret as "generally inconvenient". Labour-saving devices became a valid subject matter of a patent in the latter part of the eighteenth century not because the law now recognised the inventor as having a right to reap the benefits of his invention, but because a supply of cheaper commodities could be considered to be even more in the public interest than the loss of employment in those

---

95 Dutton, *The patent system and inventive activity during the industrial revolution 1750-1852* (1984), pp. 17-18.
96 *Millar v. Taylor*, 2386, 2391-2392.
97 Ronan Deazley, *On the origin of the right to copy: charting the movement of copyright law in eighteenth century Britain (1695-1775)*, Oxford 2004, p. 226.

industries (see paragraph 3.3.3.1). Lord Mansfield in *Liardet v. Johnson* 1778 had warned the jury about extremes, the inventor should not be deprived of the benefit of his invention for the sake of the public, and Lord Loughborough had been clear that considerations of public convenience and expediency should not affect the determination of an action between two individuals (see paragraphs 4.2.4.3 and 3.3.3). Yet the weight of the public interest cannot be dismissed as a factor in judicial decision-making. It was also reflected in the approach of some judges to the specification: adherence to strict requirements for the disclosure of the invention seemed to have weighed more heavily than the protection of the patentee's invention from piracy.

The common good would remain a factor of influence in shaping patent law. However, there would be a shift away from an interpretation which pitched the public interest and the patentee's interests as competing interests. If the patentee's monopoly were seen as a different species of monopoly then, unlike the older 'odious' monopolies, it did not take away some right from the public which the public had previously enjoyed. The patentee's reward would simply be in proportion to the utility of the invention. Encouraging useful inventions would be in the interest of the public. This allowed the interests of the patentee to assume more weight: there could be a balance between the interests of the public and those of the patentee. This balance would be reflected in the way some judges would read the specification. Interpreting the specification in the context of a contract implied a recognition not only of obligations on the part of the patentee but also rights. In the eighteenth century, there had been judges who conceived of patents in term of giving rights but by the 1830s this mode of thought would become commonplace (see chapter 5).

6.4.2   *The Relationship between the Subject Matter of a Patent and the Object of Property*

At the same time that the judges were discussing what could be the object of property in copyright cases, judges were discussing what could be the subject matter of a patent in patent cases. What is remarkable is the similarity between these two discussions. Did the object of property at common law have to be a tangible, visible thing to which a person's rights were related or could anything that was of value constitute the object of property? Did the subject matter of a patent have to be a tangible, visible thing or could it be a thing of value, like a process or an effect? The division of opinions in patent cases concerning the interpretation of the statutory term 'manufacture' was similar to the division within the judiciary as to what could and what could not be the object of property at common law.

As noted above, some judges had argued that, at common law, the object of the author's property right was the physical book, and he lost this property upon sale. At common law, the object of the inventor's property right was his machine, and he lost this property upon sale. There were no residual rights in the composition or in the know-how of the invention. This had been Yates' stance in *Millar v. Taylor*. It was easy for this style of analysis to be adopted by some judges as a frame of reference to interpret the term 'manufacture' in the Statute of Monopolies.

The Statute of Monopolies gave to a patentee of a new invention the right to the "sole working or making of any manner of new manufactures". The question was, did 'manufacture' require a tangible object? If a judge considered that a proprietary right required a relationship with an external thing, it is possible that he implicitly conceived of a 'manufacture' in terms of a material thing to which the patent right was linked. The judge would naturally link the rights to exploit an invention awarded by the patent grant to the physical manifestation of that invention. If there was no physical invention as the subject of the patent grant, there was nothing to be protected by the law and therefore the patent grant was invalid.

If the judge construed property as being something that related to value, rather than rights pertaining to an 'external thing', then that flexibility may have made it easier for him to think that the subject matter protected by a patent could be a process, which had no material form. There would be an object of property even if the subject matter of the patent concerned only a method of making a thing, and not the thing itself, or even if the end result of that process was not a thing but an effect. The property right was not tied to the physical manifestation of a machine or chemical compound. The property laid in the future profit to be derived by the inventor from the right to exclude all others from using the patentee's process to produce that machine or compound.

What could and what could not be the subject matter of a patent was reviewed in some detail in *Boulton and Watt v. Bull* 1795. With respect to scientific principles, the judges agreed that an inventor could not patent his discovery of a scientific principle. These abstract principles had to be embodied, to take on some form which had been created by the inventor. In Buller's words, a principle had to have been "reduced into practice" and practice meant "the thing done or made, or in other words the manufacture which is invented". There had to be "some new production from those elements".[98] Just as it had been argued that ideas could not be the object of property in the copyright cases, scientific principles could not be the subject matter of a patent. Yates had drawn the comparison in *Millar v. Taylor*:

> "The inventor of the air-pump had certainly a property in the *machine* which he formed: but did he thereby gain a property in the *air*, which is common to all? Or did he gain the sole property in the *abstract principles* upon which he

---

98   *Boulton and Watt v. Bull* 1795, 2 H. Black 485-486.

constructed his machine? And yet these may be called the inventor's ideas, and as much his sole property as the ideas of an author."[99]

What is interesting in *Boulton and Watt v. Bull* is that Bull's counsel refers to this comparison made by Yates in *Millar v. Taylor* to fortify his interpretation of the word 'manufacture'. What Yates' was setting out in *Millar v. Taylor* was the rules of property at common law: what could and what could not be the object of property at common law. The link indicates that the issue of property was lurking under the surface of the discussion in patent cases on the meaning of the term 'manufacture'. If ideas could not be the object of property, ergo scientific principles could not be the subject matter of a patent. Yates had, according to Bull's counsel, made it clear that principles must be embodied to be the subject of a patent, as otherwise they are like the sentiments of an author.[100]

Although there was agreement that bare principles could not constitute the subject matter of a patent, what the case of *Boulton and Watt v. Bull* makes clear is that there was no judicial consensus as to whether a method could be the subject of a patent. In *Boulton and Watt v. Bull*, it was argued for the plaintiffs that a newly discovered method of producing an important effect came within the provisions of the Statute of Monopolies; that it was usual for patents to be granted "for the method of doing the thing, and not for the thing done".[101] Although the dispute on the patentability of a method ostensibly revolved around the interpretation of the meaning of the term 'manufacture' in the Statute of Monopolies, there is a strong parallel with the dispute within the judiciary on the object of property at common law.

The importance of a material substance as the subject matter of a patent underpins Heath, J.'s opinion in *Boulton and Watt v. Bull*. The term manufacture must be read as a vendible substance; if it is not a machine or a substance produced by a process it is not vendible.[102] Buller too had rejected in that case that a patent could be for a method; the method had to have resulted in "some new substance".[103] Their analysis comes very close

---

99 *Millar v. Taylor* 1769, 4 Burr 2357.
100 *Boulton and Watt v. Bull*, 2 H. Black 472. Bull's counsel gives as a reference 4 Burr 2361. If the defence counsel's reference is looked up, it will be seen that Yates does not make this analogy on page 2361. The reference to abstract principles appears on page 2357. Perhaps not too much significance must be drawn from this mistake. Possibly the defence counsel had a different version of Burrow's report from the standard one. Possibly, counsel was not quite as accurate as he should have been in his references, or possibly Henry Blackstone made a mistake in the page number when reporting this case, although the page cited for Eyre's reference to *Millar v. Taylor* in a footnote corresponds to the standard report page numbering. However, it is tempting to conclude that what the defence counsel had in the back of his mind was the issue of property, for that is what Yates does discuss on page 2361. Here Yates claims that nothing can be an object of property that does not have a corporeal substance (*Millar v. Taylor* 1769, 4 Burr 2361).
101 *Boulton and Watt v. Bull* 1795, 2 H. Black 467-468.
102 *Ibid.*, 482.
103 *Ibid.*, 486.

to Yates' definition of a personal chattel quoted above: "It must be something that may be seen, felt, given, delivered, lost or stolen, in order to constitute the subject of property." If the patentee only had rights with respect to the way in which a thing could be made, but no rights in the thing which resulted from that method, how could he be said, to use Blackstone's words, to have a right "in and to such *external things* as are unconnected with his person"?

Unlike the other judges in *Boulton and Watt v. Bull*, Eyre did not consider it necessary for the subject matter of a patent to be a material, visible thing. Giving Hartley's patent as an example, Eyre accepted that a method could be the subject matter of the patent right. Hartley's patent, which was for a method to prevent fire spreading in buildings, was not for a substance or a composition of things. It was, as Eyre readily conceded, for an effect: the absence of fire. Eyre quotes from Mansfield's opinion in *Millar v. Taylor* to emphasise his point that no physical manifestation is necessary:

"It must be, *for the method*; and I would say, in the very significant words of Lord *Mansfield* [4 Burr 2397] in the great case of the copyright, it must be for *method* detached from *all physical existence whatever*."[104]

That Eyre would highlight Mansfield's argument in that case is strange. Mansfield's position in *Millar v. Taylor* was contrary to Eyre's in *Donaldson v. Beckett*: Mansfield was for copyright as a common law right and Eyre was against it. Eyre's opinion in *Boulton and Watt v. Bull* seems inconsistent with his opinion in *Donaldson v. Beckett* 1774:

"The baron considered a book precisely upon the same footing with any other mechanical invention. In the case of mechanic inventions, ideas were in a manner embodied, *so as to render them tangible and visible*."[105]

In Donaldson, Eyre considered that "the question in fact was respecting a right to appropriate ideas"[106] and, as already noted, Eyre rejected that there was any such right at common law. However, in *Boulton and Watt v. Bull*, Eyre argued for the legitimacy of a method detached from all physical existence, for an idea that had not been embodied in a thing but was only discernable as an effect.

These two premises appear inconsistent. It could be argued that they were not. Eyre had said in *Donaldson v. Beckett* that the common law required a tangible object of property. Eyre had, therefore, emphatically rejected that the patent right was a right recognised by

---

104 *Ibid.*, 494.
105 *Donaldson v. Beckett* 1774, Cobbett, *Parliamentary History of England* (1813), col. 974 [my italics].
106 *Ibid.*, col. 972.

the common law (see paragraph 4.1 above). If the patent was a form of property that did not have its origins in the common law, then it was not bound by the rules of property laid down in the common law. It did not need to have as its object an external thing. This would be a rational argument, but whether it was Eyre's line of reasoning to justify a method as the subject matter of a patent is dubious. It is the reference to Lord Mansfield which gives grounds for doubt. Eyre refers to "the very significant words of Lord Mansfield". Lord Mansfield had been arguing for a common law right of property in a set of intellectual ideas, expressed in a certain mode, distinct from any physical manifestation. This seems to be the justification Eyre is giving for Hartley's patent.

The two statements are not inconsistent if the motivation for Eyre's opinion was not legal doctrine at all, but public utility. If copyright were a common law right, then an author or his assigns (the booksellers in the eighteenth century copyright cases) would have had a perpetual monopoly to print the works. Eyre was clearly against this perpetual monopoly. He points out in Donaldson that even if monopolies were allowable in some cases "the state had taken care to allow them only for a convenient time".[107] The point was made very explicitly by Lord Camden in the Donaldson case: "All our learning will be locked up in the hands of the Tonsons and the Lintons of the age, who will set what price upon it their avarice chooses."[108] In *Boulton and Watt v. Bull*, Eyre accepted an invention as the subject matter of a patent even if there was no tangible, physical substance to which the patentee's rights were related. What Eyre makes very clear in *Boulton and Watt v. Bull* was the importance of the common good. There was an advantage to the public by encouraging such useful inventions, whether these inventions had a tangible form or not: "The advantages to the public from improvements of this kind, are beyond all calculation important to a commercial country, and the ingenuity of artists who turn their thoughts to such improvements, is in itself deserving of encouragement."[109]

During the period under consideration, it would seem that patents for methods had become commonplace. Tindal, C.J., in the seminal case of *Crane v. Price* 1842, alluded to "the numerous instance of patents" which had already been granted for methods which allowed a substance to be produced in a more economical or beneficial way.[110] Some of these patents had even survived a legal action. For example, Hall had maintained his patent against Boot, despite the fact it was for "a method of improving every kind of lace or net". After the jury had returned its verdict in favour of the plaintiff, an application to show cause why a nonsuit should not be entered, as the invention was not a manufacture under the statute, was refused by Lord Chief Justice Abbott.[111] Derosne had also patented a

---

107 *Ibid.*, col. 973.
108 *Ibid.*, col. 1000.
109 *Boulton and Watt v. Bull* 1795, 2 H. Black 494.
110 *Crane v. Price* 1842, 134 ER 248.
111 *Hall v. Boot* 1822, 1 CPC 425, 430.

method, described in his patent specification as: "The invention consists in a means of discolouring syrups of every description, by the means of charcoal." Yet he would success-fully defend his patent in his infringement action against Fairie. Once he had amended the wording of his specification, which was still clearly for a process, the patent was not further questioned.[112]

As noted in chapter 3, *Crane v. Price* has been seen as the case that finally settled the debate as to whether a method could be the subject matter of a patent. In accepting a process as the subject matter of a patent, the judiciary no longer required that the term 'manufacture' should refer to a tangible, visible thing. It could refer to a set of ideas of how to make a thing or produce an effect of use to industry. The move was an early herald of the conditions for patentability which would be laid down more than a century later. The Patent Act 1977 required a new invention, which was an inventive step, capable of industrial application; an invention "capable of being made or used in any kind of industry".[113] What was significant was the linking of the invention to an industrial application, not that the invention itself was a physical thing. Recognising a process as the subject matter of a patent required a shift to recognising patent rights as relating to a thing of value rather than to a material thing. It mirrored a general trend in the development of property law to associate property rights with items of wealth, not just with a tangible thing. A paradigmatic shift in the definition of property was taking place. The old paradigm, grounded on the physi-cality of 'things', was being replaced by a new 'dephysicalised' paradigm grounded on value.[114] It was in the nineteenth century that '*intellectual* property', as a specific species of property, would come into its own right.

6.4.3   The Social Rise in Significance of Personal Property

In the eighteenth century, property was acknowledged as being at the very foundation of society. The legal protection of property had a purpose extending far beyond the protection of the rights of any individual. The protection of property was the protection of civil society itself. John Locke considered that the function of the state was to protect the natural rights of its citizens, primarily the right to property: "The great and chief end, therefore, of men's uniting into commonwealths, and putting themselves under government, is the preservation of their property."[115] The government of that community would ensure an ordered, peaceful society. This linking of social harmony with the protection of property was com-monplace. Blackstone in his *Commentaries* referred to the "innumerate tumults" that

---

112 *Derosne v. Fairie* 1835, 1 CPC 664, 698.
113 Patents Act 1977, 1 (1), 4 (1).
114 Nicole Graham, "Restoring the 'Real' to Real Property Law: A Return to Blackstone?", in *Blackstone and his Commentaries: Biography, Law, History*, (ed. Wilfred Prest), Oxford and Portland 2009, pp. 151-152.
115 Locke, Second Treatise, ix, 124.

would have arisen and the continual disturbance to "the good order of the world" if it were not for the institution and protection of property. "Necessity begat property; and in order to insure that property, recourse was had to civil society."[116] The need to preserve order had moulded, according to Yates, J. in *Millar v. Taylor* 1769, the basic rules of the law of property. It was why property must have distinguishing marks and be capable of occupation:

> "The principal *end* for which the first institution of property was established, was to preserve the *peace* of mankind; which could not exist in a *promiscuous scramble*. Therefore a moral obligation arose upon all, 'That none should *intrude* upon the *possession* of another'. But this obligation could only take place where the property was distinguishable; and every body knew that it was not open to another."[117]

Aston, J. considered that the type of society envisaged here by Yates was a primitive one, one in which it had been important to be able to separate and distinguish property from the commonality, because that property constituted the very necessities of life.[118] The implication was that the society of the eighteenth century was not the same sort of society.

The eighteenth century marked a period of transition in English society. A still predominantly agricultural society was becoming increasingly commercially orientated. Property as a social fact, Boorstin points out, was undergoing a striking metamorphosis: "Forces were at work which would eventually take the country away from the landowners and give it to the shopkeepers and their masters, the manufacturers."[119] In the eighteenth century there was a growing recognition of a distinction between two forms of property: landed and commercial. The landed interest drew its income from its estates. The commercial, 'moneyed', interest derived its income from a whole range of trading and manufacturing enterprises. Land was not synonymous with wealth, as some landed proprietors were struggling to survive, whereas some men in trade were very wealthy. If landed wealth was going to be challenged by major wealth derived from other sources of property this could alter the traditional balance of power. It has been argued that it was this fear which was behind the Land Qualification Act 1711. Parliament passed a bill which laid down substantial requirements of land ownership for both county and borough members. In their history of the House of Commons 1690-1715, Cruickshank et al point to an "almost obsessive anxiety" throughout that period shown by 'country' back-benchers concerning an alleged invasion of the House by the 'moneyed interest'. Yet when the Act was passed, it revealed that very few members were landless. The detailed research carried out by Cruickshank

---

116 Blackstone, *Commentaries on the Laws of England* (1793), II, 4, 8.
117 *Millar v. Taylor* 1769, 4 Burr 2365.
118 *Ibid.*, 2339.
119 Boorstin, *The Mysterious Science of the Law, An Essay on Blackstone's Commentaries* (1996), p. 167.

into the social backgrounds of the individual members of the House of Commons at the beginning of the eighteenth century reveals that it was still overwhelmingly an assembly of landed proprietors, although it was to some degree representative of the rising professional and business class of the later seventeenth century.[120]

At the mid-eighteenth century, it was still landed property that gave English society its elite and its structure. It provided the ruling elite at both the national and local level: the legislators and justices of the peace. Rosenheim argues that, although the legal system was more than a mere instrument of class rule, yet its ceremonial, its deference to precedent, its domination by figures of landed status and its increasingly protective attitude to property during the eighteenth century all made it, at the very least, congenial to landed interests.[121] Classical Marxist theorists have been blunter in their assessment of the role of the legal system: the law was an instrument of the ruling class and the law would uphold the interests of this dominant elite. The moneyed interest did not form the dominant elite in the latter part of the eighteenth century. If the law is an instrument to advance the interests of a dominant elite, it could be predicted that the courts would not be concerned with advancing the interests of patentees until their interests were more aligned with those of a dominant elite. The lack of elite status for those whose wealth was derived from the manufacturing sector would be reflected in the treatment of patentees.

As already noted in previous chapters, Dutton argued that the attitude of some judges towards patentees was "excessively hostile" and that there was an "early prejudice" against patents. It was in the 1830s that the courts began to show a more favourable attitude towards patentees. He linked this shift to the growing conviction within the judiciary that patents were good for the economy. In the 1830s, the manufacturing sector generated a far greater proportion of national income than before the Napoleonic wars. The structure of the economy was changing, and that change was in part caused by technological change. Factory production brought together the inventions of steam, iron and machinery and most of this change took place in the 1830s. In many ways, notes Dutton, the 1830s was a crucial decade in the British economy.[122] It is also in the 1830s that the very first, very modest stirrings of a shift in the distribution of power was taking place. The Great Reform Bill would be passed in 1832, which extended the franchise to £10 householders. Historians generally agree that this was not a radical change in the sense that it would be many years before there was a significant shift in the political power basis, but it did mark the beginning

---

120 Cruickshanks, Handley and Hayton, *The History of Parliament: The House of Commons 1690-1715* (2002), vol. I, pp. 263, 270.

121 James M. Rosenheim, *The Emergence of a Ruling Order: English Landed Society 1650-1750*, London 1998, p. 7.

122 Dutton, *The patent system and inventive activity during the industrial revolution 1750-1852* (1984), pp. 76-79, 176.

of the reform process: the Reform Act "opened the door on a new political world".[123] In this context, it is interesting to note that in the 1830s the patent specification was being more consistently interpreted in terms of contractual rights and obligations (see chapter 4). The patent had shifted from a privilege to a right. This would seem to indicate that there was possibly a correlation between a 'more favourable' attitude of the courts to patentees and the increased importance and wealth of industry, combined with the first slight crack in the bulwark of the landed elite's political power.

On the other hand, Blackstone, writing his *Commentaries* in the 1760s, had already detected a shift in the attitude of the courts to personal property:

> "Our ancient law-books, which are founded upon the feudal provisions, do not therefore often condescend to regulate this species of property…But of later years, since the introduction and extension of trade and commerce, which are entirely occupied in this species of property, and have greatly augmented its quantity and of course its value, we have learned to conceive different ideas of it. *Our courts now regard a man's personalty in a light nearly, if not quite, equal to his realty*: and have adopted a more enlarged and less technical mode of considering the one than the other; frequently drawn from the rules which they found already established by the Roman law wherever those rules appeared to be well-grounded and apposite to the case in question, but principally from reason and convenience, adapted to the circumstances of the times; preserving withal a due regard to ancient usages, and a certain feudal tincture, which is still to be found in some branches of personal property."[124]

He recognised that, as trade and industry gathered momentum, personal property was becoming a significant item of wealth and the courts were treating it as almost as important as real property. Yet in the 1760s, this shift in attitude by the courts could not be seen as a direct consequence of a weakening in the economic and political power base of the landed elite.

Long before it was apparent that there would be a major shift in economic and political power away from the landed elite, there always had been judges who acknowledged the importance of the commercial sector and the interests of the patentee. Several examples from the eighteenth century illustrate the point. As noted previously, Lord Mansfield had instructed the jury, in his address in the Liardet case 1778, to avoid extremes. A patentee should not be unnecessarily deprived of the benefits of his invention by the state. Lord

---

123 Eric J. Evans, *The forging of the modern state: early industrial Britain 1783-1870*, London and New York 1996, p. 229.
124 Blackstone, *Commentaries on the Laws of England* (1793), II, 385 [my italics].

Chief Justice Eyre had stressed the importance of commerce to the country and had even upheld the interests of those patentees whose inventions did not conform to the dominant judicial interpretation of the Statute of Monopolies. Lord Loughborough, in *Arkwright v. Nightingale*, had admonished those who tried to put the public interest before determining rights in a private law action. These opinions express concern for the interests of those in the manufacturing industry, for a sector of society that was not at that time part of the ruling elite. In patent cases, the judiciary simply did not act as one, homogenous block. There is no clear evidence that a concern with advancing the interests of the dominant landed elite had been a major factor influencing judicial decision-making in patent cases. Nor can it be concluded that the more liberal attitude of the courts to the patent in the 1830s was a reflection of the growing power of those in manufacturing.

6.5   SUMMARY

Although there were judges who interpreted the patent specification in terms of a contractual relationship, the patent as a legal entity was not treated as belonging to the law of obligations, but to the law of property. There were certain inherent conceptual difficulties in treating the patent right, which was to exclude others from exploiting the inventor's invention without his permission, as a purely contractual right. However, categorising the patent as a form of personal property was also problematic. There were judges who rejected the patent as a form of property recognised at common law.

A very clear split would emerge within the judiciary as to what could and what could not be the object of property at common law. It witnessed a clash between a formalistic approach to the concept of property, with its principles stemming from a previous era, and a teleological approach which advocated adapting the legal concept of property to the needs of the day. Judges who identified property in accordance with traditional maxims spoke of it in terms of rights relating to a tangible thing that could be marked out, occupied and possessed. Incorporeal property was a right issuing from and related to that tangible thing. Judges who preferred a more dynamic, pragmatic approach conceived of incorporeal property in terms of it being a thing of value rather than as rights only arising from a thing that had a material form.

The acceptance of a patent as a form of property had less to do with common law concepts of what could be the object of property, and more to do with the courts accepting the patent as an anomalous species of property which required an act of the royal prerogative and was regulated by statute. The majority of the judges, who gave an opinion in the copyright cases of the eighteenth century, considered that the inventor had had no right to exclude others from using his invention at common law. Once the invention was made public, everyone had the right to copy it. As the common law was associated with natural law, this implied that an inventor had no natural right to prevent others copying and selling his invention. This prompted some judges to interpret the patent grant primarily in terms of protecting the public interest, rather than protecting the patentee from piracy. A more balanced approach to the interests of the state and that of the patentee became discernable once the patent monopoly was placed within the context of utility: the reward for the invention was proportionate to its success on the market. In the 1830s, the idea that the patentee had a right, even if that right were dependent upon a patent, became more commonplace within the judiciary.

The debate that was taking place within the judiciary on the object of property at common law was mirrored in the debate that was taking place within the judiciary as to what could be the subject matter of a patent. The way in which judges would interpret the term 'manufacture' in the Statute of Monopolies may have been implicitly affected by their opinion on what could be the object of property at common law. From the comparisons made between the rights of authors and those of inventors in the copyright cases, it was apparent that some judges considered that only the individual physical machine could be the object of the inventor's property at common law. There could be no property in a set of ideas distinct from a physical manifestation. Judges who argued that the common law required a tangible thing as an object of property may have been more inclined to interpret the statutory term 'manufacture' as requiring a tangible, vendible article to be the subject of the patent grant. Judges who were prepared to conceive of property in terms of a thing of value may have been more inclined to accept a method as the subject matter of a patent. It may also have been the case that, for some judges, a pragmatic approach to the needs of the day had more to do with the determination of the validity of a patent than any legal doctrine.

In the eighteenth century, landed property provided the framework of society and the landed elite held the political power. Some commentators have argued that the law was an instrument to advance the interests of this dominant elite. This would predict that the law would look upon patentees more favourably when the industrial, moneyed interest became more important. In favour of this argument, it was in the 1830s that manufacturing became more significant to the British economy, the decade witnessed the first step in electoral reform and a more liberal interpretation of the patent specification became the dominant approach. On the other hand, in the eighteenth century the courts had recognised personal property as being almost as important as real property, there always had been judges who had balanced the interests of patentees against those of the state, and the judiciary had never acted as a block in patent cases. Although many patentees did not belong to the traditional landed elite, there is no conclusive evidence that advancing the interests of the dominant elite had been a determining factor in patent cases, nor that the more liberal attitude to patentees in the 1830s was determined by the first stirrings of a change in the structure of the elite. A shift in legal thinking was taking place with respect to the whole concept of property over this period.

7   From the Industrial Revolution to the Digital Revolution: The Software Challenge

In more recent times, innovations associated with computers have ushered in a new era of technology. This era has been christened the "Information Age", made possible by a so-called "digital revolution". This digital revolution depended upon the development of computer hardware together with the development of programs – the software to direct and control the hardware. A new form of technology now had to be processed through the patent system. Computer hardware was a tangible object; but what was software? Was software tangible or intangible? Was it patent eligible or was it not patent eligible? Judges would be called upon to determine the patentability of a new form of technology.

Software related inventions started to appear more often after the mid-twentieth century. This digital technology was very different from the mechanisation technology which characterised the inventions of the Industrial Revolution in the eighteenth century. It could be presumed that the issues confronting judges dealing with digital innovations would therefore be fundamentally different from the issues which confronted the judges dealing with mechanical innovations during the Industrial Revolution. It is argued here that such a presumption would be wrong. In the eighteenth century-early nineteenth century, the legal dispute concerned whether a process could be the subject matter of a patent. English law today recognises that a process may be the subject matter of a patent. Nonetheless, even today not all processes are patentable. English/European law excludes certain processes from patentability, for example, business methods are excluded. The legislation also excludes computer programs. If computer programs are seen as a method, as a form of process that directs a computer to perform certain tasks, then the debate on the patentable status of software has a place in the chronology of the history of legal debate on methods as the subject matter of a patent.

It is not the aim of this work to present an in-depth analysis of the legal issues associated with the patentability of software, but even a brief examination of the subject indicates a number of similarities between the reasoning of the judges hearing patent cases during the Industrial Revolution and the reasoning of the judges hearing patent disputes involving software. There is a surprising familiarity about the nature of the judicial debate on the patentability of software. Indeed, today's legal debates become clearer when they are placed within this historical perspective.

7.1   DEVELOPING A LEGAL CONCEPT OF SOFTWARE

Even in the last decade of the twentieth century the courts were still trying to determine the nature of software. In the English case of *St. Albans v. ICL* 1995-6, the High Court and then the Court of Appeal considered whether software was goods. In the High Court, Scott Baker, J. said that he did not wish it to be thought that his view was that software by itself was not goods. A program, he added *obiter*, "is not simply abstract information like information passed by word of mouth. Entering software alters the contents of the hardware". If he were called upon to decide he would probably hold that software was goods on the basis that if software was not goods he could not see what it could be "other than something to which no statutory rules applied".[1]

Sir Iain Glidewell in the Court of Appeal also expressed *obiter* an opinion upon the nature of a program. He acknowledged that he had found Scott Baker's description of a computer system helpful. A program was the instructions or commands that tell the hardware what to do. Glidewell considered that the program was an intangible, the disk the tangible, and it was necessary to make a distinction between the two. A disk was clearly goods for the purpose of the sale of goods legislation. But if a program on a disk was defective so that it could not instruct or enable a computer to carry out the intended purpose, would the seller or hirer of the disk be in breach of the terms as to satisfactory quality and fitness laid down in sale of goods legislation? In determining that question, Glidewell pointed out that there was no English precedent on the matter, nor had any reference been made to an authority in any common law jurisdiction. It appeared to him that if a disk was sold or hired by the computer manufacturer, but the program was defective, there would *prima facie* be a breach of the terms as to satisfactory quality and fitness for purpose implied by the Sale of Goods Act.[2] A computer program could apparently be classed as 'goods', and therefore fall within the ambit of sale of goods legislation, if the program was recorded on a tangible object, so-called 'hard media'.

In this reasoning, the underlying premise was that a computer program is intangible. A major reason for placing computer programs under the protection of the copyright regime had been that programs were seen primarily in terms of information; software was coded information. The expression of that coded information could be protected by copyright. As coded information, software was not a physical product. A rejection of a computer program as a 'product' appeared in the European Community Design Directive 1998. Article 1 (b) defined a product as 'any industrial or handicraft item', but it specifically excluded computer programs from the definition of product. There are those legal scholars who would disagree with the description of software as an intangible. De Mulder, Van

---

1   *St Albans v. ICL* [1995] FSR 686; 699.
2   [1997] F.S.R. 251; 264-265.

Noortwijk and Kleve have argued that software is not an intangible; its physical nature is apparent in its tangible magnetic patterns. If software were intangible, how could it make a machine work? Like goods it is deliverable, reproducible and of economic value.[3]

The attempts by the courts to determine the nature of a computer program would bring an old complaint voiced by the inventors of the Industrial Revolution back to the forefront: lawyers do not understand technology. This was the point of view consistently put forward by the witnesses testifying before the Select Committee on patents in 1829 (see paragraph 4.3). With respect to software, Leith has argued that the law has ignored the programmer's perspective; the way that a programmer sees a computer program is quite different from the way a judge might see a computer program.

> "To the programmer working on the design of a data object or a procedure, the task is tangible: the programmer views the objects he is dealing with as physical entities…The programmer is building a machine with the same mode of thinking as the eighteenth-century millwright John Rennie placing iron cogs and drive wheels in relationship to the power source at the Albion Mill."[4]

Eighteenth century judges struggled with the idea of a process separate from a product as a subject matter of a patent. Judges who disagreed with the patenting of methods argued that patenting a method was like trying to patent an idea. A method was rejected as having no material dimension; a patent required a 'manufacture' and that required a product in the form of a substance or a machine. The legal wrangling over the patentability of methods seems to persist. Computer related inventions have depended heavily on the 'computer' element; the machine, not the program, has been the subject of the patent. Leith points out that the physicality of the invention, its representation as a machine rather than program, was common in the early UK applications and central to the success of those applications. A physical machine had to be somewhere at the heart of the patented invention: "it was attempting to fit the new technology of software into an already-existing mental conception and the best-fitting conception was that of machine."[5]

7.2   THE PRESENT PATENT FRAMEWORK

The UK Patents Act 1977 laid down the following criteria for patentability in section 1:

---

3   P. Kleve, R. De Mulder and C. van Noortwijk, "The Amazing Diversity Framework of the Intellectual Property Rights Harmonisation", in *Globalisation and Harmonisation in Technology Law*. Accessible via RePub <http://hdl.handle.net/1765/8032>, pp. 5-6.
4   Philip Leith, *Software and Patents in Europe*, Cambridge 2007, p. 37.
5   *Ibid.*, pp. 17-18.

(1) A patent may be granted only for an invention in respect of which the following conditions are satisfied, that is to say

(a) the invention is new;

(b) it involves an inventive step;

(c) it is capable of industrial application

In accordance with Article 52(2) of the European Patent Convention (EPC) 1973, the Patents Act set down a number of inventions that were explicitly excluded. Section 1 (2) lists those inventions which will not be considered to be patent eligible:

(2) It is hereby declared that the following (among other things) are not inventions for the purposes of this Act, that is to say, anything which consists of—

(a) a discovery, scientific theory or mathematical method;

(b) a literary, dramatic, musical or artistic work or any other aesthetic creation whatsoever;

(c) a scheme, rule or method for performing a mental act, playing a game or doing business, or a program for a computer;

(d) the presentation of information;

but the foregoing provision shall prevent anything from being treated as an invention for the purposes of this Act only to the extent that a patent or application for a patent relates to that thing as such.

Computer programs were therefore explicitly excluded from patentability by the UK Patents Act 1977, which was modelled upon the EPC and designed to give effect to the EPC.[6] A proposal for a European Community directive on the patentability of what was termed 'computer-implemented inventions', which would have reflected a more flexible approach to software related inventions, was rejected by the European Parliament in 2005. The exclusion of computer programs in the amended versions of the UK Patents Act and the EPC was retained. The protection of computer programs has remained under the copyright regime, not the patent regime.

7.2.1   Software Patent Litigation

Given this specific exclusion, it would appear that the patent eligibility of software in England had been determined by legislation: it could not be patented. The UK Patents Act excluded computer programs from patentability, as did the EPC. However, the legal debate

---

6   Patents Act 1977 s.1 (2)(c); EPC 2000 Art. 52(2)(c).

on the patent eligibility of a computer program would prove to be far from over. Inventors often wanted to patent their software. Copyright protection was found wanting and insufficient. It would prohibit another from copying the original expression of the coded program, but it was often possible for a competitor to work around the copyrighted program. A programmer could implement a program's functionality in different ways, hence avoiding copyright. In the case of software related inventions, a patent on the other hand would give an exclusive right to apply the idea.

Software related inventions would become the subject of litigation both in the English courts and the Boards of Appeal of the European Patent Office (the EPO determined whether a European patent met the requirements of the EPC). The decisions of the Board are of influence upon the patent law of the UK courts; English courts have acknowledged that although they are not bound by the decisions of the Board of Appeal, the interpretation of the Patents Act should take its decisions into account.[7] The issue that confronted both the judges in the English courts and the experts in the Board was to determine when a computer program was only a computer program, and therefore excluded from patentability, and when a computer program was something more than just a computer program "as such" and not excluded from patentability.

7.2.2   The Role of the Judge

How vital would the role of the judges be in establishing a paradigm for the patentability of software related inventions? This study has stressed the importance of the role of the judges in the development of patent law during the early Industrial Revolution. In England in the eighteenth-early nineteenth century, to obtain a patent the inventor submitted a petition requesting a patent to one of the Secretaries of State. This petition would then be referred to the law officers of the crown. The task of the law officers was to be satisfied that the patent application did not infringe the Statute of Monopolies 1624. There was no system of examination of prior art and it was only rarely that an invention would be examined prior to the patent being granted. However, once all the necessary fees had been paid, the patent grant was usually a formality. Without any significant prior examination of a patent claim before registration, the first real examination of the validity of a patent was by the judges if a patentee sued for the infringement of his invention.

The law officers regularly granted patents for methods of use to industry. Whether a method was patent eligible was one of the key issues debated in the courts. If a patent was found invalid on the ground that it was for a process, because a process was deemed not to be a 'manufacture' under the Statute of Monopolies, that decision was not consistent

---

7   See for example *Gale's Application*, [1991] R.P.C. 305; 322, *Aerotel Ltd v. Telco Holdings Ltd*, [2007] R.P.C
7; 132.

with the practice of the law officers who granted the patents. This inconsistency was brought to the fore in *Boulton & Watt v. Bull* 1795 by Lord Chief Justice Eyre. Eyre was not in favour of the courts imposing a form of legal reasoning that would reject patents for methods and was apparently out of step with the practice of the law officers:

> "we may not shake the foundation upon which these patents stand. Probably I do not overrate it, when I state that two thirds, I believe I might say three fourths of all patents granted since the statute passed, are for *methods* of *operating* and of manufacturing, producing no new substances and employing no new machinery."[8]

He clearly considered that there was little justification for developing a paradigm of patent law in which patents for methods were rejected: "The advantages to the public from improvements of this kind, are beyond all calculation important to a commercial country."[9]

It may appear at first sight that an inconsistency between the types of patents issued by an authorised body and the statutory provisions on patentability would be less likely today, considering that the patent system has become one of examination rather than simple registration. Today, an application for a British patent can be made to the UK Intellectual Property Office or to the European Patent Office (EPO) for a European patent, which will be upheld in the United Kingdom. In either case, a patent is not granted before an examination of the application has taken place. The application must comply with the statutory requirements of the Patents Act and the EPC, and an examiner will carry out a search of prior art to determine the novelty of the invention. Given the exclusion of computer programs, it could be expected that patents for computer programs would not be granted either by the national UK Intellectual Property Office or the EPO. However, that would appear not to be the case. Many patents have been granted for software related inventions. The Comptroller of the British Office reported back in 2000 that over 15% of the patents it granted had a software element. The EPO has granted more than 20,000 software related patents.[10]

This situation seems to be not entirely dissimilar from that facing the judges of the eighteenth century. In the event of litigation, the eighteenth century judges had to decide whether they would uphold patents for methods that had already been granted. Some judges, like Eyre, considered that to do so was the appropriate response, particularly in the light of the perceived needs of a commercial society. Other judges, like Buller, refused to accept that such patents should be upheld. Their reading of the term 'manufacture' in

---

8   *Boulton and Watt v. Bull* 1795, 2 H. Black. 494-495.
9   *Ibid.*, 494.
10   Sherman and Bently, *Intellectual Property Law* (2009), p. 424, fn. 219.

the Statute of Monopolies excluded processes from patentability and hence the development of a legal paradigm for patents which would encompass patents for processes. Since the latter part of the twentieth century, judges have been called upon to decide the validity of various software related patent applications. Many such patents had apparently been granted. Like their predecessors, the judges would have to determine how flexible they were prepared to be in their interpretation of a statutory provision; in this case the interpretation as to what constituted a computer program "as such".

7.3   DETERMINING THE PATENTABILITY OF PROCESS INVENTIONS

In the eighteenth and early nineteenth century the relevant statutory criteria for patentability were found in Section VI of the Statute of Monopolies. The applicant for a patent had to be the first and true inventor of a new manufacture, and that invention had to be seen as not harmful to the state or generally inconvenient. In determining the validity of a patent, the judges had to reach a decision based upon these criteria: Who would be seen as the first inventor? When was an invention new? What did the word 'manufacture' mean? And when was an invention harmful to the state or generally inconvenient? It has been argued in this study that the interpretational style of individual judges, whether predominantly formalistic or predominantly purposive, would affect the way in which these terms would be interpreted. In particular, it was the meaning ascribed to the term 'manufacture' in the Statute of Monopolies which would bring diversity in judicial opinion to the fore. In the late twentieth-early twenty-first century, a legal debate on the patentability of software related inventions has taken place in the courts. A diversity of approach has come to the fore with respect to what constitutes a computer program 'as such'. Modern commentators refer to the controversy and legal confusion surrounding this issue.

7.3.1   Interpreting the Term 'Manufacture'

In the late eighteenth-early nineteenth century, judges were being called upon to determine whether the term 'manufacture' required some sort of physical product to be the subject matter of the patent, or whether the term also applied to a method as distinct from the product so produced. The matter was considered at length in the case of *Boulton & Watt v. Bull* 1795, one of the cases dealing with James Watt's patent for a steam engine (see chapter 3). It had been argued for the defendant in that case that there had been no infringement of Watt's patent as the patent was not valid; there had been no new mechanical invention by Watt. Watt had, after all, described his invention in the specification as a "*method* of lessening the consumption of steam and consequently fuel in fire engines". It had long been known that steam had an expansive power and was condensed by cold. What was new was the application of those principles. That was not the subject of a patent.[11]

Eyre, L.C.J., was the only judge in that case who was openly prepared to interpret the term 'manufacture' to include processes. Eyre stated that the validity of these patents had to rest, as a point of law, upon the same foundation as that of Hartley's patent. Hartley's patent (an invention consisting of placing iron plates to prevent the spread of fire) produced no substance at all: it was for a method "detached from *all physical existence whatever*". Eyre considered this patent to have been "very properly granted" to the inventor. He pointed out that there were many patents for new methods where "the sole merit and the only effect produced was the saving of time and expense, which lowered the price of the article and therefore introduced it into more general use". As for the interpretation of the term 'manufacture': "Now I think these methods may be said to be new manufactures, in one of the common acceptations of the word, as we speak of manufactory of glass or any other thing of that kind."[12]

In *Boulton & Watt v. Bull*, Justice Buller, who found against Boulton and Watt, rejected the patentability of a method: "I think it is impossible to support a patent for a method only, without having carried it into effect and produced some new substance." "When the thing is done or produced, then it becomes the manufacture which is the proper subject of a patent."[13] Like Justice Heath, Buller considered that mechanical and chemical discoveries could only be described as manufactures if the patent was for a new, physical article so produced.

The wording of an early seventeenth century statute would raise various interpretational issues for the courts in the late eighteenth-early nineteenth century. The Statute of Monopolies 1624 had been drafted in response to the concerns of an earlier era when whole industries, rather than specific techniques, had been the subject of patent protection. Inventions had become more technical since the early seventeenth century.[14] Rather than coming out clearly for an interpretation of 'manufacture' that would include a process, a certain amount of judicial sidestepping appears from the cases after 1795. If the patent included a material component in the form of instruments that had been built to put the method into effect, then these instruments could be seen as the 'manufacture' even if they were only relevant to carrying out a method.

In the nineteenth century, there would be a *de facto* recognition by the courts of process patents. A 'manufacture' could be a new process to be carried out by known implements, acting on known substances and producing a known substance, but producing it more

---

11 *Boulton and Watt v. Bull* 1795, 2 H. Black. 470-471.

12 *Ibid.*, 493-494.

13 *Ibid.*, pp. 485-487.

14 Van Zijl Smit, *The Social Creation of a Legal Reality: A Study of the Emergence and Acceptance of the British Patent System as a Legal Instrument for the Control of New Technology* (1981), p. 90.

cheaply or efficiently. The term 'manufacture' would no longer be read as requiring the subject matter of the patent to be a material thing, such as a new chemical compound or a machine. In the 1820s and 30s, patents that were for a new combination of well-known materials were being accepted.[15] In practice, this signified the rejection of the older legal interpretation of the term 'manufacture'. That approach was endorsed by Tindal, L.C.J. in *Crane v. Price* 1842 and his judgment has been seen as finally settling the law on this point.

7.3.2 The Interpretation of a Computer Program 'as such'

Today's English judges no longer interpret the Statute of Monopolies, but they must still interpret a patent statute: the Patents Act 1977. Each statute brings to the fore its own interpretational difficulties for judges. Given a paucity of case law on the interpretation of the term 'manufacture', English judges in the eighteenth century had to develop the legal concept of what constituted a 'manufacture'. The UK Patents Act 1977, like the EPC Article 52(2), also contained a major conceptual legal problem. Section 1(2) listed things excluded from patentability. However, the provision would only prevent a thing being treated as a patentable invention "to the extent that a patent or application for a patent relates to that thing *as such*". Therefore, only a computer program "as such" was excluded from patentability.[16]

With such recent technology, there were no long established precedents setting out when a computer program was more than a computer program "as such". The judges were faced with a paucity of case law, as had been the lot of their eighteenth century predecessors. Once again the development of the law would depend upon the interpretational style and frames of reference of the judiciary. And once again there would be disagreements within the judiciary. Contradictory reasoning appeared within the ranks of the English judiciary and between the English courts and the Boards of Appeal of the EPO.

The review of *Gale's Application*, heard in the Patents Court and then in the Court of Appeal 1990-1991, is illustrative of the different approaches to the determination of a computer program 'as such' within the English courts. Gale had developed an improved method for calculating the square root of a number by using a computer. The instructions had been put into the electronic circuitry of a read-only memory unit (ROM). Gale's application for a patent was denied by the examiner in the Patent Office on the grounds that the invention was no more than a computer program and therefore excluded from patentability. Gale argued that the invention should not be disqualified because it related to a new technical product.

---

15 A whole list of such cases were summed up by Tindal, L.C.J in *Crane v. Price* 1842, 1 WPC 409-410.
16 [my italics].

In his judgment Aldous, J. (in the Patent Court) reviewed the earlier cases of *Merill Lynch's Application* 1988 and *Genentech Inc's Patent* 1989. The construction of section 1(2) of the Patents Act had first been considered by Falconer, J. in the case of *Merill Lynch's Application*. Falconer, J. had reasoned that the words "only to the extent that" in section 1(2) meant that there could not be a patentable invention if the inventive step resided in the computer program itself, but if some technical effect was achieved by the computer operating according to the program and such effect was novel and inventive, a claim to that practical end was patentable. This interpretation would be termed the 'contribution approach' because the question was whether the inventive step resided only in the contribution of excluded matter; if it did then the Article 52(2) exclusion would apply.

Aldous pointed out that Falconer's approach had been disputed by the Court of Appeal in the *Genentech* case. Purchas, L.J. was of the opinion that Falconer's interpretation was incorrect. Purchas had a different interpretation of "the plain and ordinary interpretation to be given to the words 'only to the extent that' in conjunction with 'relates to that thing as such'". For Purchas, the exclusions set out in section 1(2) meant that a disqualified matter could form the basis of a patentable invention only if it was applied in a technique or process incorporated in a product. Dillon, L.J. had a similar construction. Applying the judgments of Purchas and Dillon to the case before him, Aldous concluded that the fact that the inventive step was a program would not disqualify the invention from being patentable provided the invention claimed was the practical application of the program as applied as a technique or a process or incorporated into a product. He pointed out that it was this construction which had been upheld by the Court of Appeal hearing of the *Merill Lynch's Application* in 1989. The Court of Appeal in that hearing had also drawn upon the decision of the Board of Appeal in the *Vicom* case. The Board of Appeal had stated in that case that the "technical contribution" made by the invention to the known art was decisive. A technical contribution would make a computer program more than a computer program *per se.*[17] Aldous argued that Gale's ROM was different from a disk as it was more than just a carrier of a program. It was a new technical product, "a manufactured article having circuit connections which enables the program to be operated". He accordingly allowed Gales's appeal.[18]

In the Court of Appeal hearing of *Gale's Application*, however, the Court reached a different conclusion. It considered that Gale's claim was in substance a claim for a computer program. The instructions of that program neither represented a technical process outside the computer nor a solution to a technical problem within the computer. Nicholls L.J., who gave the leading judgment in the case, defined a computer program as:

---

17 *Vicom Systems Incorporated's Application* 1987, (Decision T208/84) OJ EPO 14.
18 *Gale's Application* [1991] R.P.C. 305; 311-317.

"essentially a series of instructions capable of being followed by a cpu [central processing unit] to produce a desired result. The instructions as such are not patentable. This is not surprising. A computer is an apparatus which operates, within its capacity, in response to instructions…Thus writing a fresh set of instructions for use in a computer in particular circumstances or for particular purposes cannot in itself be regarded as an invention."[19]

Those instructions, he said, were not patentable but computer instructions could represent a technical process with the aid of a computer. In such cases, following the decision of the Board in the *Vicom* case, the process would not be barred from patentability simply because a computer program had been used if there was a 'technical contribution'. He considered that Gale's program simply made a more efficient use of a computer's resources, but the instructions did not embody a technical process that existed outside of the computer. Nor could it be argued that the program solved a 'technical' problem within the computer, as was argued in *IBM Corp/ computer related invention* case heard by the Board of Appeal in 1990. With respect to this last point, he did however add: "I confess to having difficulty in identifying clearly the boundary line between what is and what is not a technical problem for this purpose."[20]

Parker, L.J. agreed with Nicholls, but added a judgment of his own, partly because he was sensitive to the fact that their judgment reversed the judgment of Aldous, J., a judge from the Patent Court "who is very experienced in patent matters". He also confessed that he found the question at issue of considerable difficulty. The focus of Parker's approach was on the wording of section 1 (2). He pointed out that the opening words of the sub-section were "anything which consists of" and how the patent application related to the excluded subject matters "as such". The issue was therefore whether Gale's application "consists of" any of the listed matters and, if so, did it relate to the listed matters "as such". That the matter was far from self-evident was acknowledged by Parker: "In the course of the argument it appeared to me from time to time that the contentions in favour of patentability should be accepted in preference to those against." However, he parted company with Aldous, J. with respect to the distinction that judge had made between hardware and software, which he considered to be "counter to authority".[21] Finally, Sir Nicholas Browne-Wilson V.C. gave his judgment, indorsing the view of Nicholls. The mere incorporation of a program in a ROM did not alter its nature: it remained a computer program.[22] What the reasoning of the Court of Appeal in this case signified was that even if the computer program represented a process which was an inventive step, it was not

---

19   *Gale's Application,* 324.
20   *Ibid.,* 327-328.
21   *Ibid.,* 328-331.
22   *Ibid.,* 333.

patentable unless it produced a technical effect either on a process which was not itself a computing process or on the operation of the computer itself.

Fujitsu Ltd's Application was for a computer programmed to represent crystal structures. In Fujitsu Ltd's Application, heard by the Court of Appeal in 1997, reference was made to Gale's Application, as decided in the Court of Appeal, as a precedent. Aldous, L.J. now sitting as a judge in the Court of Appeal, acknowledged in Fujitsu Ltd's Application that the Court of Appeal had found his decision in Gale's Application to be wrong and that it was both convenient and right to strip away, as a confusing irrelevance, the fact that the claim was for 'hardware'.[23] Aldous, L.J. brought to the fore the decision of the Technical Board in Vicom, highlighting the point made in that case that in deciding the patentability of a software related invention, the critical point was whether the invention made a technical contribution. With respect to the Fujitsu Ltd's Application: "Clearly the whole operation revolves around the computer program and the question for decision is whether there is a technical contribution so that it cannot be said that the invention consists of a computer program as such."[24] Aldous was of the opinion that what was concerned here was no more than a computer program. The other judges agreed, Roch, L.J. noting: "In my opinion, what the appellants have done here is no more than to produce, brilliant though it may be, a new computer program. The invention may be new but as it is no more than a computer program it is not patentable."[25]

The decision of the Board of Appeal in the Vicom case had played an important role in the English courts in their interpretation of a computer program "as such". Computer programs would be held to be patentable provided that the program, when run on a computer, produced a technical effect which was more than simply the result of running a program on a computer and that it made a substantive technical contribution. However, within a few years of the hearing of Fujitsu Ltd's Application, a difference in interpretation would open up between the English courts and the Boards of Appeal.

By the time the Court of Appeal heard Aerotel Ltd v. Telco Holdings Ltd in 2006 (an action brought for the infringement of Aerotel's patent related to a method of making a telephone call using pre-payments), the Court was able to observe that a whole range of approaches had been adopted over the years both by the EPO and national courts. Two of these approaches were the so-called 'technical effect approach' and the 'any hardware' approach. The first approach asked whether the invention as defined in the claim made a technical contribution to the art; if not it was excluded. This was the approach in Gale and Fujitsu, and the approach of the English courts was similar to that adopted by the EPO Boards of Appeal in Vicom, IBM/Text processing and IBM/Data processing network (except

---

23 Fujitsu Ltd's Application, [1997] R.P.C. 608; 618.
24 Ibid., 615, 618.
25 Ibid., 621.

the English courts added the rider that a contribution that consisted solely of excluded matter would not count as a technical contribution). The latter approach, the 'any hardware' approach asked whether the claim involved the use of or was to a piece of hardware; if yes, the exclusion did not apply. This approach had been taken by the Boards of Appeal in a trio of cases: the *Pension Benefits, Hitachi* and *Microsoft/Data transfer* cases, although this trio of cases demonstrated variations within the 'any hardware' approach.[26]

In giving the judgment of the Court of Appeal in the *Aerotel* case, Jacob, L.J acknowledged the need to place "great weight" upon the decisions of the Boards of Appeal but he was critical of the "state of conflict" which had emerged between the Board's old approach evidenced in the *Vicom* decision and its new approach in the more recent cases like *Hitachi*. Jacob considered that this change in course by the Board was based upon an incorrect interpretation of what the EPC had meant by the term 'computer program'. A narrow interpretation of the term saw a computer program as a set of instructions, as an abstract thing, although these instructions could be written down on a piece of paper. A wider view of the term was that the term covered also the instructions on some form of media (such as a disk or hard drive) which caused the computer to execute the program; in other words a program that works. The earlier Board of Appeal decisions and the decisions of the English Court of Appeal clearly took the latter view of a computer program; the trio of decisions reached by the Board in more recent cases indicated the former view. Jacob, expressing the view of the Court of Appeal, considered that this narrow reading of the term 'computer program' was wrong. The exclusion in the EPC was meant to cover not just an abstract series of instructions but also a working program, otherwise the exclusion was without real content.[27] As the Court was bound by its own precedent, it would follow the decisions of *Merill Lynch, Gale* and *Fujitsu*: the technical effect approach with the rider.

The patentability status of software related inventions had become increasingly confused. In *Astron Clinica Ltd v. Comptroller-General of Patents, Designs and Trade Marks*, heard in the Patents Court in 2008, Kitchin, J. reviewed this history of conflicting interpretations. Kitchin rejected the idea that in the *Aerotel* case the Court of Appeal was saying that all computer programs were necessarily excluded. The Court had stated that the computer program exclusion in Article 52 EPC was not limited to abstract instructions, but included programs on storage media. The consideration was expressly limited to the meaning of 'computer program' in Article 52, before the "as such" qualification was taken into account. Kitchin, J.:

"I do not detect anything in the reasoning of the Court of Appeal which suggests that all computer programs are necessarily excluded...But the criticism is

---

26 *Aerotel Ltd v. Telco Holdings Ltd*, [2007] R.P.C 7; 131-132.
27 *Ibid.*, 132-133.

directed at the 'any hardware will do' approach and the return to form over substance with the drawing of a distinction between a program as a set of instructions and a program on a carrier." [28]

This 'any hardware will do approach' had been developed a stage further in the most recent of the trio of cases heard by the Board: the *Microsoft/Data transfer* case 2006. In that case the Board had held that the method was implemented in a computer and this amounted to technical means sufficient to escape the prohibition in Article 52. Kitchin: "In short, the Board appears to have found that any program on a carrier has a technical character and so escapes the prohibition in Article 52, following Hitachi." [29]

The court in the *Aerotel* appeal had already rejected this 'any hardware will do' interpretation that had emerged in the trio of cases heard by the Board. Giving the judgment of the Court of Appeal in the *Macrossan* application (the second patent application appeal heard by that court at the time of the *Aerotel* appeal), Jacob L.J. addressed this growing gulf between the interpretation of the English courts and that of the Boards of the EPO. Encouraged by the British comptroller of patents, the Court ventured to suggest that the President of the EPO could find it helpful to put certain questions to the Enlarged Board of Appeal. One question that the Court specifically proposed to put forward was: is an operative computer program loaded onto a medium such as a chip or hard drive of a computer excluded by Article 52(2) unless it produces a technical effect; if so what is meant by 'technical effect'? [30]

When a claim could avoid exclusion under Article 52(2)(c) EPC was indeed one of the questions which would be referred by the President of the European Patent Office to the Enlarged Board of Appeal in 2008. According to the older line of Board decisions, technical character was established if the claimed subject matter presented some "technical effect". The more recent line of decisions seemed to indicate that the simple inclusion of 'by a processor' or 'in a memory unit' in a method claim would avoid the exclusion. Which of these two approaches was the correct approach? [31] Having deliberated upon the referral, the Enlarged Board of Appeal gave its answer in 2010. The Enlarged Board considered that it could not develop the law in the same way as the Boards of Appeal, because it did not have to decide on the facts of pending appeals, but only in specific instances and in the context of points of law referred to it under Article 112(1) EPC. That article permitted a presidential referral where two Boards of Appeal had given different decisions on the same question. The Enlarged Board pointed out that the term 'different decisions' was an

---

28 *Astron Clinica Ltd v. Comptroller-General of Patents, Designs and Trade Marks*, [2008] R.P.C. 14; 352-355.
29 *Ibid.*, 350-351.
30 *Aerotel Ltd v. Telco Holdings Ltd*, [2007] R.P.C 7; 141.
31 Fabian Edlund, 'Software Related Inventions at the Enlarged Board of Appeals', 92 (2010) *Journal Patent and Trademark Office Society*, p. 131.

undefined legal term. It was of the opinion that legal development as such could not form the basis for a referral; changes of direction in legal development were a normal part of judicial activity and there was no need to speak of different decisions within the meaning of Article 112(1)(b) simply because of departures from earlier practice. Not even a radical shift in jurisprudence would necessarily be construed as 'different decisions' within the meaning of Article 112(1)(b). The Enlarged Board therefore concluded that the referral by the President of the EPO was inadmissible.[32]

In *Aerotel Ltd v. Telco Holdings Ltd* in 2006, Jacob, L.J. had noted that "there has been some political pressure on Europe to remove or reduce the categories of non-inventions." Colin Birss, appearing as counsel for the comptroller-general in that case, had suggested that part of that pressure had come from the fact that the agreement on Trade Related Intellectual Property Rights (TRIPS) 1994 did not have the same explicit categories of non-invention as the EPC.[33] One country in particular appeared to adopt a wide approach to the concept of patentability: the United States. That the English courts were keenly aware of this rift between the English position with respect to computer programs (one which was more stringent than the approach adopted in the trio of EPO Board decisions) and the position in the United States appears from the *Aerotel* appeal. In that case, Jacob, L.J. devoted part of the judgment of the court to the approach to the patentability of computer programs in the United States.[34]

The US Patent Act of 1793 was drafted by Thomas Jefferson. Under that Act, statutory subject matter was defined as "any new and useful art, machine, manufacture, or composition of matter, or any new or useful improvement [thereof]". In 1952, when the patent laws were codified, Congress replaced the word 'art' with the word 'process'.[35] Case law would determine that the laws of nature, physical phenomena and abstract ideas could not be patented.[36] A restrictive reading of the term 'process' had the potential to limit the scope of patent protection for information-intensive processes, such as software. But would any process be within the statute as long as it had a practical application? The Court in *Diamond v. Chakrabarty* 1980 had announced, after all, that Congress had intended statutory subject matter to include "anything under the sun that is made by man".[37] Or, as the US Patent and Trademark Office argued, did the historical meaning of the term 'process' demonstrate that "only technological and industrial processes are patent-eligible".[38]

In the United States, there is no equivalent of Article 52(2) EPC. In the 1970s and 80s, the American courts were called upon to determine whether computer programs were

---

32   *Programs for computers* (G3/08), [2010] E.P.O.R. 36; 361, 376.
33   *Aerotel Ltd v. Telco Holdings Ltd* [2007] R.P.C. 7; 129.
34   *Ibid.*, 128-129.
35   Patent Act, 35 U.S.C.A. Section 101.
36   Listed in *Diamond v. Diehr*, 450 U.S (1981).
37   *Diamond v. Chakrabarty* (1980), 447 US 303, 309.
38   Brief for the Respondent at 16, *Bilski v. Kappos*, No. 08-964 (U.S. 25 September 2009).

patentable in such cases as *Gottschalk v. Benson* 1972, *Parker v. Flook* 1978, *In re Freeman* 1978, *In re Walter* 1980. Given the exclusion from patent eligibility of laws of nature and abstract ideas, where was the line between a computer program and a non-patentable mathematical algorithm? *Diamond v. Diehr* 1981 marked a milestone when the US Supreme Court held that the software, which enabled a process for constantly measuring the temperature of a mould for raw, synthetic rubber by feeding the temperature measurements into a computer, was patentable. The Supreme Court stated: "industrial processes such as this are the types which have historically been eligible to receive the protection of our patent law". The court noted that its conclusion was not altered by "the fact that, in several steps of the process, a mathematical equation and a programmed digital computer are used".[39] In *Aerotel Ltd v. Telco Holdings Ltd* 2006, Jacob, L.J. cited the decision of the US Court of Appeals for the Federal Circuit in *Re Alappat* 1994: that computer programs were patentable.[40] In *Aerotel*, Jacob, L.J. considered that pressure was being put upon patent offices by people applying for patents for what were arguably computer programs or business methods because in the United States it was possible for people to have patents for these subject matters.[41]

The decision in *Re Alappat* 1994 was not quite as clear cut as depicted by the Court of Appeal in its judgment in *Aerotel*. *Re Alappat* was heard *en banc* and the bench was sharply divided. Judge Rich, who gave the opinion of the majority, stopped short of claiming that a computer program by itself (one not tied to a specific apparatus, such as a digital computer) could be patentable. He stated in the *Alappat* case:

> "such programming creates a new machine because a general purpose computer in effect becomes a special purpose computer once it is programmed to perform particular functions pursuant to instructions from program software."[42]

The emphasis was still on the computer, the machine. The court found that the patentee's invention, an improved display screen, was a machine. An invention involving a mathematical algorithm was patentable because Alappat had used the algorithm to achieve a "useful, concrete and tangible result" i.e., a smooth curve on an electronic display.[43] Nonetheless, as commentators have pointed out, the concurring opinions of Judges Newman and Radar in *Alappat* have indicated that the Federal Circuit Court was distinctly leaning towards a broader recognition that computer programs, standing alone, would constitute

---

39 *Diamond v. Diehr*, 450 U.S. at 184-5, (1981).
40 *Re Alappat*, (1994) 33 F. 3d 1526, 31 U.S.P.O. 2nd 1545.
41 *Aerotel Ltd v. Telco Holdings Ltd* [2007] R.P.C. 7; 129.
42 *Re Alappat*, 33 F. 3d 1526; 1545.
43 *Ibid.*, 1541-1544.

patentable subject matter.[44] A few years later in *State Street Bank & Trust Co v. Signature Financial Group* 1998, the Federal Circuit Court would cite *Alappat* as a precedent for the decision that the mathematical algorithm exclusion from patentability only applied when a patent recited an abstract idea, one which was not, from a practical standpoint, 'useful'. Patent protection would extend to an invention that applied an algorithm in a useful way to yield a concrete and tangible result. In *State Street* the Court concluded that the subject matter of the patent was a machine and it did produce a useful, concrete and tangible result, even if that useful result was expressed in numbers, such as price, profit, percentage, cost or loss.[45]

In order to have an invention protected by patent, must an invention involve some sort of machinery or apparatus? Or does a method have to result in some sort of physical transformation of something? The answer to that was "Yes", according to the Federal Circuit Court in the recent case of *Bilski v. Kappos*. The case concerned a business method to manage consumption risk costs. Bilski's claim did not involve the use of a computer, but while it was not written as a software claim, it has been argued that the judicial opinions expressed in the case could impact on the patentability of software: "The software baby, in other words, should not be thrown out with the business method bathwater."[46]

In the Federal Circuit hearing of *Bilski v. Kappos*, the court concluded that the test of patent eligibility for a process was whether it was tied to a machine or transformed a particular article into a different state or thing.[47] The subject of patentability was discussed at length and the case produced five different opinions. Judge Dyk wrote a separate concurring opinion, in which he considered Bilski's claim within a historical context, arguing that the claim was not consistent with the types of claims historically recognised by the patent system, and would not have been a manufacture under the old English Statute of Monopolies 1624. Judge Newman disagreed with the majority reasoning, arguing that earlier US Supreme Court decisions had made it clear that the law should not freeze process patents to old technologies.[48] On appeal, the decision of the US Supreme Court in 2010 confirmed the rejection of Bilski's claim, but it also rejected the Federal Circuit Court's machine or transformation test as the sole test of patent eligibility.[49]*Bilski v. Kappos* exposed major divisions within the US judiciary concerning patent eligibility for software related inventions.

---

44 See, for example, C. Mark Kittredge, 'The Federal Circuit and non-patentable subject matter under Re Alappat and In Re Warmerdam', 11 (1995) *Santa Clara Computer & High Tech Law Journal*, pp. 261, 264.
45 *State Street Bank & Trust Co v. Signature Financial Group* (1998), 149 F.3d 1368; 1373, 1375.
46 Andrei Iancu and Peter Gratzinger, 'Machines and Transformations: The Past, Present, and Future Patentability of Software', *Northwestern Journal of Technology and Intellectual Property*, vol. 8, nr. 2, (Spring 2010), pp. 248, 274.
47 *Bilski v. Kappos*, 545 F.3d, at 954.
48 *Ibid.*, 966-976, 997.
49 *Bilski v. Kappos*, 130 S.Ct. 3218.

7.3.3   *Comparing the Interpretation of 'Manufacture' and a Computer Program 'as such'*

In reviewing the history of the decisions by the English courts and the Boards of Appeal of the EPO on the patentability of computer programs, Justice Kitchin in his judgment in the *Astron* case had drawn attention to the EPO Board of Appeal case *IBM/Computer Program Product.*[50] In reaching its decision in the *IBM/Computer Program Product* case, he considered that the Board:

> "was clearly influenced by the apparent illogicality of allowing claims to a suitably programmed computer and to the method performed by the computer so programmed but not to the program itself."[51]

It is contended here that this is the crux of the problem in the determination of the patentability of software related inventions. As Sherman and Bently point out, how could the fact that computer related inventions are an essential form of technology be reconciled with the fact that computer programs as such are explicitly excluded from the scope of protection? The physical model of the invention was being used in English courts to determine whether a patent fell within the scope of section 1(2).[52] Was the exclusion of computer programs "as such" misguided; had the legislators based this exclusion upon a lack of understanding of the new technology involved? Even if this was the personal opinion of the judges of the Boards, the Boards could not openly flout the exclusion. But if the Boards did consider that to exclude the program itself was illogical, this 'illogicality' arguably resulted in the EPO's 'any hardware will do' approach.

This 'any hardware will do' approach has a parallel in the approach to process patents by English courts in the eighteenth-early nineteenth century. At that time, the underlying question was whether it was illogical to exclude from patentability a method that was clearly of great value to commerce and industry simply because the term 'manufacture' was being generally interpreted as referring to a material product. In determining whether a method fell within the ambit of the term 'manufacture', the approach that would be adopted by the English courts in the course of the Industrial Revolution could be termed the 'any instrument will do' approach. During the early phase of the Industrial Revolution only a few judges were prepared openly to treat the term 'manufacture' as covering a method separate from a product. Nonetheless, there was a way for judges to sanction a patent that was essentially for a method; by accepting any instrument produced that was necessary for the method to be carried out as being the manufacture.

---

50 *IBM/Computer Program Product* T1173/97, [1999]).J. E.P.O. 609.
51 *Astron Clinica Ltd v. Comptroller-General of Patents, Designs and Trade Marks*, [2008] R.P.C. 14; 345.
52 Sherman and Bently, *Intellectual Property Law* (2009), pp. 409, 414.

In *R v. Wheeler* 1819, which involved a patent described to be for "a new or improved method of drying and preparing malt", Abbott, L.C.J had not been prepared to assert categorically that a method could be the object of a patent (see paragraph 3.3.2.2). He did accept, however, that the term 'manufacture' could "mean an engine or instrument, or some part of an engine or instrument, to be employed, either in the making of some previously known article, or in some other useful purpose, as a stocking-frame, or a steam engine for raising water from mines". In this analysis, the patent claim did not have to relate to an end product; any 'hardware' invented in order to carry out a method would satisfy the criterion of 'manufacture'. An instrument that had been made that was only relevant to a method would allow that method to be patentable. Using this line of reasoning, Abbott considered that Watt's patent for a new method of lessening the consumption of steam and fuel in engines was patentable; Watt's specification described certain parts to be used in the construction of these engines. However, there did have to be something that could pass as 'hardware', something of a material nature. Wheeler's patent would fail in the Court of King's Bench because there did not appear to Abbott to be any new instruments to carry out the method.[53]

By the end of the 1830s, the English courts would have in practice accepted that a method, as separate from the thing so produced, could be the subject matter of a patent. Arguably, the Boards of the EPO have been treading that path; in effect accepting the patentability of any computer program in a workable form. In *Aerotel Ltd v. Telco Holdings Ltd* 2006, the Court of Appeal firmly dismissed the suggestion that Pumfrey, J. had been of the view that the English court should incline towards patentability in the case of computer programs. Pumfrey, J. had said in the case of Sarl's patent:

> "I am anxious that these exclusions are not given too wide a scope. All modern industry depends upon programmed computers, and one must be astute not to defeat patents on the ground that the subject matter is excluded under Article 52 unless the invention lies in the excluded subject matter as such."[54]

There is something of a purposive approach here, and the words are certainly reminiscent of those of Eyre, L.C.J in *Boulton & Watt v. Bull*. In that case Eyre considered modern industry to depend upon inventions like Watt's steam engine: "The advantages to the public from improvements of this kind, are beyond all calculation important to a commercial country." This was a reason for Eyre to accept a method as a manufacture, even where that method had no physical component. Although in *Aerotel* the Court of Appeal did not read Justice Pumfrey's words as encouraging the English courts to incline towards the

---

53   *R v. Wheeler* 1819, 106 ER. 396.
54   *Inpro Licensing Sarl's Patent* (Application for revocation by Research in Motion Ltd) [2006] R.P.C. 20; 187.

patentability of computer programs, Jacob, L.J was certainly aware of the financial significance of determining the right approach: "Billions (euros, pounds or dollars) turn on it."[55]

Leith sees the root of the problem in the attempt both by the English courts and the Board to fit new technology within the patent system as a form of old technology, rather than accept that it was actually a whole new and radical technology of its own. The approach of the courts was based upon nineteenth century notions of a machine, not the manner in which a programmer saw this new machine. "Such legal fictions led to contradictions at the heart of the patent examination system – to protect one artefact by basing it upon the metaphor of a different artefact must lead to problems – which are difficult to uphold and thus we had *Vicom* and the later Board of Appeal decisions."[56]

Pinning the patentability of a computer program to some form of material object or some technical effect beyond simply running on a computer is very reminiscent of the reasoning of the majority of the eighteenth century judges in patent cases. For those judges, the subject matter of a patent had to be a vendible, material object, or at the very least it had to be physical instruments or parts to enable a method to be carried out. Of interest, given the decisions on computer programs both in Europe and the United States, is that when the English courts did *de facto* come to accept the validity of process patents in the early nineteenth century, the subject matter of those patents was linked either to some sort of apparatus or to some sort of physical transformation (see chapter 3). For example, in *Hullett v. Hague* 1831, Abbott (Lord Tenterden) acknowledged in his judgment that the patent was "in substance, an invention of a process for the more rapid crystallization and for the evaporation of fluids at comparatively low temperatures".[57] This was achieved by means of a coil of pipes perforated with small holes. The apparatus, the coil of pipes, was relevant only to a method but this was not seen as undermining the patent. It was 'hardware'. Derosne's patent was for a method of filtering syrup of sugar through a filter to act with charcoal. It took the colour out of the sugar and hence transformed the sugar; it brought about a physical transformation. It is possible that today's judges have retained that frame of reference to deal with a form of technology of a very different nature.

7.4   The Attitude to Monopolies

Perhaps one clue to the approach to computer programs adopted by the English courts can be found in the attitude of the judges to the monopoly granted by the patent. There is an indication of a query regarding the value of a monopoly for a computer program in the judgment of the court in *Aerotel Ltd v. Telco Holdings Ltd* 2006. Jacob, L.J. noting the

---

55   *Aerotel Ltd v. Telco Holdings Ltd* [2007] R.P.C. 7; 131.
56   Leith, *Software and Patents in Europe* (2007), pp. 30-31, 37-38.
57   *Hullet v. Hague* 1831, 109 ER 1183.

pressure put upon patent offices by applicants wishing to patent computer programs, because people had been able to obtain patents for this subject matter in the United States, described this as: "An arms race in which the weapons are patents has set in." The comparison between patents and weapons is an interesting one. Why the judge chose that comparison must remain a matter for speculation, but the tone of his comment would seem to indicate that the judge saw this as a negative development. Commenting on this pressure from applicants to obtain patents for excluded categories, Jacob observed dryly: "Just as with arms, merely because people want them is not sufficient reason for giving them."[58]

Jacob then observed that despite the fact that such patents had been granted for some time in the United States, it was far from certain that it had been a 'Good Thing'. The patent system had a price:

> "That price (what economists call 'transaction costs') is paid in a host of ways: the costs of patenting, the impediment to competition, the compliance cost of ensuring non-infringement, the cost of uncertainty, litigation costs and so on. There is, so far as we know, no really hard empirical data showing that the liberalisation of what is patentable in the USA has resulted in a *greater* rate of innovation or investment in the excluded categories. Innovation in computer programs, for instance, proceeded at an immense speed for years before anyone thought of granting patents for them as such."[59]

The patent monopoly remains controversial. With respect to computer programs, this came very much to the fore when a proposal for a directive of the European Parliament and Council on the patentability of computer implemented inventions appeared in 2002. In a report commissioned by the European Parliament on the desirability of EU level legislation for software patents, the report authors noted that while disclosing inventions may serve as a source of inspiration and information to subsequent inventors, by creating exclusive rights patents could cause economic monopolies with negative effects for potential competitors and for society as a whole. In considering whether Europe should follow the example of the United States, the authors also pointed to the serious concerns that the negative effect of these new types of patents could be stronger than those of 'traditional' patents. They concluded that there was no firm data to prove that software patents provided any benefit to society; neither was there firm evidence of the opposite. They did however consider that the granting of "trivial" patents was an urgent issue that needed to be addressed and that patent inflation was a fundamental problem particularly with regard

---

58   *Aerotel Ltd v. Telco Holdings Ltd* [2007] R.P.C. 7; 130.
59   *Ibid.*, 130.

to software related patents.[60] In some quarters there has been open hostility to the adoption of a more American approach to the patentability of computer programs. The open source community in Europe has campaigned against any moves which it sees as increasing the protection given to software.[61] The failure of the proposal for an EU directive on the patentability of computer implemented inventions was hailed as a victory by those against software patents.

The monopoly on an invention imposed by the grant of patent was an issue that concerned the judiciary back in the Industrial Revolution. There was a division of opinion within the judiciary. The word 'monopoly' had a negative connotation in the eighteenth century, associated as it still was with earlier instances of abuse of the royal prerogative. Lord Kenyon was well known for his dislike of monopolies and inventors complained that Kenyon failed to distinguish between monopolies on existing commodities and monopolies on new inventions, although no rights previously enjoyed by the public were taken away by the patent on the new invention (see paragraph 5.1.3). Lord Mansfield seems to have adopted an attitude to monopolies for new inventions more in keeping with the opinion expressed by Adam Smith. Smith did not like monopolies but considered that monopolies for new inventions were "harmless enough", given that if the invention were poor so would be the reward to the inventor, but if it were a good invention both the inventor and society could profit from it (see paragraph 5.1.2). By the 1830s, it was this latter approach to monopolies for new inventions which would predominate in the courts.

Judicial attitudes to patent monopolies swing. This was pointed out by Salmon, L.J who considered that "from 1883 until after the end of the [Second World War], the courts tended to regard patent monopolies with some disfavour as being generally contrary to the public interest". Giving his opinion in a case in 1972, Salmon considered that the climate of opinion had changed and "the modern tendency of the courts has been to regard patent claims with considerably more favour than before".[62] There seems to be something of a cyclical pattern in judicial attitudes to patents. At present, there is resistance by the English courts to embrace the Board's wider interpretation of what constitutes a computer program "as such". Whether this resistance is connected to a disposition towards formalism by the majority of the bench in the interpretation of the Patents Act and the EPC or from a feeling of caution with respect to whether a more flexible approach to awarding monopolies for software would be in the public interest is a question that cannot be answered conclusively.

---

60 Reinier Bakels and P. Bernt Hugenholtz, *The patentability of computer programs: discussion of European-level legislation in the field of patents for software*, working paper JURI 107 EN, European Parliament 2002, pp. 5, 43-44.

61 For example, the organisation EuroLinux campaigns for open source software in Europe and against European software patenting.

62 *Ethyl Corporation's Patent*, [1972] R.P.C. 169; 193.

7.5   LEGAL UNCERTAINTY

Throughout the late eighteenth-early nineteenth century, there was considerable legal uncertainty as to whether a patent for a process would be upheld in court. If the court considered that the subject matter of the patent was a material product, even if the specification had described the invention to be a method, the patent would not fail for that reason alone. Instruments necessary to carry out the method could also be seen as products, and hence falling within the dominant interpretation of the term 'manufacture' in the Statute of Monopolies. There were few judges who openly argued that the term 'manufacture' encompassed a method, separate from the thing so produced. As noted above, one such judge was Eyre, L.C. J. Although legal commentators like Collier and Godson considered that Eyre was mistaken, Eyre's endorsement of a method even without any new physical component, contributed to the lack of legal certainty with respect to the interpretation of the term 'manufacture'. In the early nineteenth century, it would be Eyre's approach that would be successful. However, whereas Eyre had accepted as patentable a method "detached from all physical existence whatever", the methods the courts deemed to be the valid subject matter of a patent involved either some sort of instrument or the physical transformation of a thing.

A similar lack of legal certainty now surrounds the term computer program 'as such'. Does a computer program 'as such' only refer to a set of instructions which could simply be written down on paper? Or does the term 'as such' also extend to a computer program on some form of media; a program in a working form which causes the computer to carry out the program? In trying to interpret the exclusions in Article 52 EPC, the basis of section 1(2) of the UK Patents Act, Jacob, L.J. in the *Aerotel* case commented that the excluded categories seemed to be the "result of various compromises" and "that there was no indication of any intention as to how the categories should be construed – either restrictively or widely". Looking at the preparatory work for the EPC, he concluded:

> "What was done was to formulate the language of each of the categories independently of one another, add the 'as such' rider to all of them and leave it to the EPO and European patent judges to work out the detail."[63]

There has been an ensuing conflict between the 'technical effect' approach and the 'any hardware' approach, the first approach reflecting an earlier period in the decision-making of the Boards of Appeal. The English courts have argued for the retention of that earlier, more restrictive interpretational approach, being of the opinion that the 'any hardware' approach will make the exclusion of computer programs meaningless; any working program

---

63   *Aerotel Ltd v. Telco Holdings Ltd* [2007] R.P.C. 7; 127.

will be patentable. The earlier and the later approaches of the Board are inconsistent, but the Enlarged Board was not prepared to see these approaches as reflecting contradictory 'different decisions' but only in the light of legal development. It is hard to know where the Enlarged Board would draw a line between 'a radical shift in jurisprudence' and 'different decisions'. It is argued in this study that the *de facto* decision of the English courts in the 1830s to treat the term 'manufacture' as encompassing not just a product but also a method, separate from the product so produced, did not represent a simple progression in legal development, but a straightforward rejection of an earlier dominant approach to the interpretation of the term 'manufacture'. It is submitted here that the recent decisions of the Boards are more obviously explained as a rejection of an earlier approach than as a form of linear legal development.

In the courts, at least, a computer program has been regarded as intangible. The reasoning is not always convincing. In making a distinction between the narrow view of a computer program as a set of instructions and a wider view of a computer program as an operable program on some form of media, the Court in *Aerotel* described the set of instructions as "an *abstract thing* albeit they could be written down on a piece of paper".[64] This raises the question of whether a set of instructions that is sufficiently concrete that it can be written down, containing instructions that can be protected by copyright, and can be used to implement the running of a program on a computer is an abstraction.

The courts wrestled with the concept of intangible property during the Industrial Revolution; the patent as a form of property did not fit within the traditional definition of property at common law. Some judges argued that at common law an inventor only had a property in the individual thing that he had made; the inventor had no right at common law to exclude others from copying and selling it because the know-how was not a form of property recognised at common law. The object of property at common law had to be a tangible, visible thing to which a person's rights were related. The patent was therefore an anomalous form of property created by statute. However, other judges disputed this restrictive interpretation of the concept of property at common law; anything that was of value could constitute the object of property. The division of opinion in patent cases concerning the interpretation of the statutory term 'manufacture' was similar to this division within the judiciary as to what could and what could not be the object of property at common law. Did the subject matter of a patent have to be a tangible, visible thing or could it be a thing simply represented in terms of its value, like a process or an effect (see paragraph 6.4.2)? Even when a process was found to be a valid subject of a patent, the process either involved an apparatus or instrument of some kind or some form of physical transformation of an item. Arguably, the discussions on the nature of a computer program

---

64   *Ibid.*, 133 [my italics].

indicate that the courts still tend to approach the question of patentability from this perspective.

In developing a legal paradigm for patents applicable to digital technology, there has
been an emphasis on some form of physicality to make that computer program more than
a computer program 'as such'. Depending on the approach, this could be in the form of
any hardware or in the form of a technical contribution beyond simply running on a
computer. Even in the United States, the Court of Appeals for the Federal Circuit in the
Bilski case followed a machine or transformation test as the test of patent eligibility, although
this would later be rejected by the US Supreme Court as the sole test of patent eligibility.
The wide approach in the United States to interpreting a useful computer program as more
than an abstract mathematical algorithm and the wide approach of the Boards inherent
in the 'any hardware' approach may indicate that the exclusion of a computer program
'as such' has had its longest time. A 'manufacture' would eventually be interpreted, in
practice, as including a method separate from a product so produced. The teleological,
purposive approach would triumph over a more formalistic approach to the interpretation
of the term 'manufacture'. As Lord Mansfield stated: "as the usages of society alter, the law
must adapt itself to the various situations of mankind."[65] Similarly, with respect to the
interpretation of a computer program 'as such', a teleological, purposive approach may
triumph over a more formalistic, restrictive approach (represented currently by the EPO
Board of Appeal and the English Court of Appeal respectively). If it does, the exclusion of
a computer program 'as such' may indeed in practice become meaningless. Software has
become a valuable item. Some software now costs more than the hardware upon which it
runs. Hardware, Leith observes, is becoming of less value to the market than it was in the
period in which the EPC was drafted. One commentator has predicted: "The time will
come when manufacturers will give away computers so as to be able to sell software."[66]

During the Industrial Revolution, the meaning of the term 'manufacture' shifted as an
older generation of judges was replaced by a younger generation more familiar with the
needs of a rapidly industrialising society. The judges who were deciding upon computer
programs 'as such' in the 1970s were not brought up with digital technology. That generation is giving way to a generation of judges more familiar with digital technology and the
workings of the Information Age. It will be interesting to see whether, or to what extent,
the meaning of the term computer program 'as such' will shift in the English courts.

---

65   *Johnson v. Spiller* (1784) 3 Doug 373.
66   Leith, *Software and Patents in Europe* (2007), p. 39, fn. 1. The prediction cited by Leith is from H. Aiken.

7.6 Summary

An invention in the form of a process continues to pose problems for the judicial determination of patentability. The nature of the technology has changed since the era of the Industrial Revolution, but the problem persists, albeit in a different form. In the late eighteenth century, judges were divided as to whether a process could be the subject matter of a patent at all. The debate ushered in a period of legal uncertainty. There was a transition phase in which a compromise was reached: instruments used for the process could be seen as the 'manufacture', for the purpose of satisfying the conditions of the Statute of Monopolies, even though these instruments were only relevant to a method. It would only be in the nineteenth century that the courts *de facto* accepted that patent protection could extend to a process, as separate from the thing so produced.

Today, it is still the case that not all processes are patentable. Computer technology has posed a problem for the courts. It is the computer program that directs and controls the computer hardware; the program is the process by which certain tasks may be carried out on the computer. Under the UK Patents Act and the EPC, however, a computer program 'as such' is excluded from patentability. The determination of the boundaries of patentability for computer programs is still in the process of development, as differences in approach have opened up between the English courts and the Boards of Appeal of the European Patent Office in their interpretation of the excluded categories. The English courts have adopted the earlier approach of the EPO's Board of Appeal: to be patentable, a computer program must have a technical effect beyond simply running on a computer. In recent decisions of the Board, however, a computer program has been seen as patentable simply by being on a carrier: the so-called "any hardware will do" approach to the patentability of computer programs. There are parallels to be drawn here between the development of the term 'manufacture' as a legal term in the eighteenth-early nineteenth century and the development of the way in which a computer program 'as such' is being interpreted.

In the late eighteenth-early nineteenth century, there had been few patent disputes and patent law was not a familiar legal domain to the judges of the late eighteenth century. The judges had to come to terms with the industrialisation of society, as their society was undergoing what would be a profound change. The society of the late twentieth-early twenty-first century has also undergone a profound change, as it has shifted from the industrial age to the information age. It is possible that judges today are similarly caught on the cusp, as were their predecessors in the eighteenth century. A computer program 'as such' may be the new 'manufacture' issue. It is tempting to conclude that in some ways the judicial debates on patent law today are not very different from those of the late eighteenth-early nineteenth century.

8   Conclusion

In the 1750s, patent law was an unfamiliar area of law for the judges of the common law courts. It was only in this decade that the Privy Council ceded jurisdiction to the common law courts in patent validity cases. There was no well-developed body of law available to the common law courts: precedents were scarce. The only statutory enactment relevant to patents at this time was the Statute of Monopolies 1624, which contained one short section on the requirements for patents for new inventions and was already more than a hundred years old. This left the early structuring of patent law in the hands of the eighteenth century judges of the common law courts.

This study set out to examine what factors influenced judicial decision-making in patent cases and how these factors affected the development of patent law in the common law courts in the period 1750s to the 1830s. Certain factors in particular emerged as clearly significant: the interpretational style adopted by an individual judge, a judge's attitude to the monopoly awarded by a grant of patent and his view on the patent as a species of property. In the 1830s, a clear shift in the judicial interpretation of patents becomes discernable. A new paradigm was emerging, as an older way of looking at patents for new inventions was giving way to one more in keeping with the requirements of an industrial economy.

8.1   Factors Affecting Judicial Decision-Making in Patent Cases

It has been contended in various studies that judicial decision-making in patent cases was affected by the dislike of the courts for patents. As noted in chapter 2, Holdsworth, Dutton and MacLeod have all suggested that judges were generally 'hostile' or 'prejudiced' towards patents at certain points of time. It is considered in this study that non-legal factors may have influenced judicial decision-making. Character, educational background, personal experience and beliefs could contribute to the frames of reference through which the facts of a case were viewed. However, the use of such essentially emotive terminology as 'hostility' and 'prejudice' causes analytical problems. The terms are imprecise, dependent upon subjective norms. Placing judicial attitudes to patents within a construct of such vague concepts as hostility and prejudice may help to explain why this so-called judicial hostility ceased at the end of the eighteenth century according to Holdsworth, but only in the 1830s according to Dutton.

As pejorative labels, the terms 'hostility' and 'prejudice' also imply a measure of ill will on the part of the judge: that the judge was not open to the merits of the case. Lord Kenyon had openly admitted in *Hornblower v. Boulton and Watt* 1799 that he was not one who favoured patents. He also had a certain reputation among patentees for setting aside a patent on the slightest technicality. This is not, however, evidence in itself that he was 'hostile' to patents; that his personal distaste dictated the use of spurious technicalities to upset a patent. In the high profile case of *Hornblower v. Boulton and Watt* 1799, Kenyon found for the patentees, although some other members of the bench had not. Another example of a judge who was prepared to set aside a patent on a technicality was Lord Ellenborough. Lord Ellenborough was the judge who had found the patents in *Bainbridge v. Wigley* 1810 and *R v. Metcalf* 1817 void because of grammatical irregularities. Yet Ellenborough would, for example, find for the patentee in *Harmar v. Playne* 1809, despite Lord Eldon's condemnation of the patent specification in the Chancery hearing of that case. Neither of these judges, therefore, appears to have been relentlessly against patentees.

As pointed out in chapter 4, several members of the bench acknowledged that a restrictive and mechanistic interpretation had characterised the approach of some judges in patent disputes. Lord Eldon, speaking in 1815, expressed the opinion that patentees "were rather hardly dealt by". In 1831, Abbott expressed a similar opinion: "I think a great deal too much critical acumen has been applied to the construction of patents, as if the object was to defeat and not sustain them." Yet even where a mechanistic, restrictive interpretation of a patent is evident, this does not necessarily imply that all judges who adopted that interpretation were hostile to or prejudiced against patentees in particular. A judge who adopted a strict, literal approach with respect to patents may very well have adopted that approach in other areas of law. It may have been the style of interpretation he generally adopted. Care should be taken, therefore, not to label all restrictive interpretations of patents as signs of hostility or prejudice.

8.1.1   The Interpretational Style of Judges

Formalism was the approach advocated by the legal treatises popular in the eighteenth century. Judges were warned by such writers as Bacon, Hale and Blackstone that their task was *jus dicere* not *jus dare*. An observation made by Blackstone in his *Commentaries* also suggests that a restrictive interpretational style would be dominant within the rank and file of the legal profession in the eighteenth century because of the nature of legal education at that time. Until Blackstone became the first professor of common law at Oxford in 1758, instruction in the common law was the province of the Inns of Court, not the university. The common law was taught during a period of apprenticeship. The result was, according to Blackstone:

"If practice be the whole he is taught, practice must also be the whole he will ever know…the least variation from established precedents will totally distract and bewilder him…; he must never aspire to form, and seldom expect to comprehend, any arguments drawn a priori, from the spirit of the laws and the natural foundations of justice."

Blackstone's message was contradictory. While advocating a formalist approach for judges, he at the same time expected a judge to be able to use his own discernment to determine such matters as whether a precedent was plainly absurd, and could be ignored, and what should be understood to be the spirit, if not the wording, of a statute.

It is argued in this study that in practice, the task of a judge is always creative, although there are bounds to that creativity. Where those bounds are drawn depends to some extent upon an individual judge's conception of his role. In the eighteenth century, there were judges who believed their role was to apply the black-letter of the law and others who were clearly prepared to look at the purpose of a law within a contemporary social context. A split between judges who prefer a formalist approach and those who are prepared to adjust the law to the circumstances of the day seems to be embedded within the judiciary. As Allen pointed out: "some judges will always play safe and some will be astute to mitigate the *rigor juris* in accordance with common sense, justice and social requirements." Lord Kenyon was an example of the former, Lord Mansfield an example of the latter. If the attitude of judges to patents is viewed in the light of this split, a rather different picture emerges, as the following examples illustrate.

As noted in paragraph 2.3.2, Lord Kenyon had explicitly rejected a creative approach to judicial interpretation: it was not for judges "to change the law so as to adapt it to the fashions of the times". Kenyon apparently had a reputation as a formalist judge in general. Campbell, admittedly not a great admirer of Kenyon, described Kenyon as a "mere formalist". Of Kenyon's influence over King's Bench, Campbell remarked:

"And from the stout resistance which then continued to be offered in Westminster Hall to all attempts to relieve the administration of justice from wretched technicalities, Lord Chief Justice Kenyon was long hailed as the Restorer of the rigid doctrines to be deduced from the Year Books."

Campbell's observation, even if not entirely impartial, is of interest in the light of the observation by Blackstone on the education of lawyers cited above (and in paragraph 2.3.1). Kenyon had not received a university education. Although all lawyers had to learn the common law during an apprenticeship at the Inns of Court, Kenyon's entire further education had been of the practical variety provided by the Inns of Court. It is possible that Kenyon's rather restrictive interpretational style illustrates Blackstone's point.

Nor was Lord Ellenborough's eye for technicalities restricted to patent specifications. As noted in chapter 4, Ellenborough was quite prepared to find against a party on a technicality in other areas of law too. He had a general reputation for severity and a tendency to suspect fraud. There are no obvious grounds to suppose he was singling out patents for special treatment. Yates, J., in the copyright case of *Millar v. Taylor* 1769, rejected the patent as a right at common law. The patent, along with copyright, was not a right at common law: copyright owed its origins to a statute and a patent was an act of the royal prerogative regulated by statute. That deduction was based upon a formalistic, traditional concept of the object of property at common law. He exhibited the same formalism, a clinging to precedent whether antiquated or otherwise, in *Perrin v. Blake* 1769, which was a case dealing with an entirely different area of law. The subject matter of *Perrin v. Blake* was a plantation bequeathed in a will (see paragraphs 2.3 and paragraph 3. 3.2.3).

Lord Mansfield, on the other hand, is known as a judge who was prepared to adjust the law to what he conceived to be the needs of the day. With respect to commercial matters, Mansfield had insisted that these matters fell within the ambit of the separate system of rules known as the law merchant. By applying the law merchant to commercial matters, Mansfield had been able to adopt a more flexible approach, enabling him to take into account the needs and opinions of the merchant community. If Lord Mansfield's rulings in patent cases are examined, they reveal a high rate of nonsuits and nominal damage awards. This may be the reason why some commentators have contended that he was against patents. He has been accused of putting the patent first and foremost in the light of a monopoly and of using the patent specification as a blunt instrument to void patents (see paragraph 4.2.4.3).

However, his attitude to patents also reveals a flexible approach, attuned to the needs of a manufacturing community. When it became apparent that the old law, which did not allow a patent for an improvement, meant withholding legal protection from many of the important technological advances of the time, Mansfield would see no reason to abide by an antiquated precedent (Bircot's case). Allowing improvements and additions to be the subject matter of a patent marked an enormous step forward for patentees. Similarly, if it had become more practical for an inventor to disclose that invention in a patent specification rather than to be under an obligation to work the invention and supervise the training of apprentices in return for his patent, then Mansfield would hold that the purpose of the patent specification was the instruction of the public and the older form of consideration would disappear. Nor would it appear that Mansfield was implacably set against monopolies for new inventions (see paragraph 4.2.4.3 and below).

Where more familiar legal issues were concerned, the split between a formalist and a teleological approach would be less discernable. Even though the reasoning of the judges may have been different, the outcome would often be the same. There would be what Scholten described as an 'intuitive' perception as to where the boundaries of the legally acceptable were fixed. An all too obvious attempt by a judge to change those traditional boundaries would, however, expose the division. The division in interpretational style would also become conspicuous where a new area of law was concerned: patent law. In the eighteenth century, patent validity cases were new to the common law courts and the boundaries of orthodoxy had yet to become established. Decisions in patent disputes would at first be more individualistic, more dependent upon an individual judge's interpretational style. In the period under consideration in this study, patent law was subject to the pull and push within the judiciary of a formalist, 'play safe', approach to patent law and a pragmatic, teleological approach.

This push and pull effect is illustrated in the differing ways in which the terms of the Statute of Monopolies were read (see chapter 3). It is apparent in the interpretation of the term 'manufacture' in the Statute of Monopolies. The formalist approach would emerge in a more literal, or historical, interpretation. If the term 'manufacture' in the Statute was taken literally, as a thing made by the hands of man, a 'thing' had to have been made. This was the interpretation of manufacture used by Kenyon in *Hornblower v. Boulton and Watt* 1799: "something made by the hands of man". It excluded a method from being seen as a 'manufacture' for the purpose of the Statute. Kenyon accepted Watt's patent not because he thought it was for a method, but because he thought it was for "an engine or machine, composed of material parts, which are to produce the effects described". His emphasis on the materiality of the invention comes to the fore more particularly in the report of the case in *The Times*. The historical approach was also used to reinforce an interpretation which required a 'thing' to have been made. The term 'manufacture' should be interpreted by looking back at what it meant at the time the Statute of Monopolies was passed and not by adjusting it to any personal concepts of the needs of contemporary trade and industry. This approach is illustrated by Heath, J. in *Boulton and Watt v. Bull* 1795 (see paragraph 3. 3.2.2).

On the other hand, a judge adopting a purposeful or teleological approach would simply recognise that many patents were granted for methods of use to industry and consider it imprudent to disturb a practice which seemed to be beneficial to the country. Several judges would explicitly argue that the term 'manufacture' did cover a method: notable in this respect are Eyre, C.J. and Lord Eldon. Another, less explicit, means of validating patents for methods was to consider the instruments that had been made in order to carry out the method to be the 'manufacture' required by the Statute. It would seem from *R v. Wheeler* 1819 that it had become accepted to uphold a patent for a method if physical instruments necessary to carry out the method had been made, even though these physical instruments were only pertinent to a patent for a method, not to a patent for a new substance. These two conflicting interpretational approaches to the term 'manufacture' would long make it unclear whether the statutory term 'manufacture' covered a method.

The same split between a literal and a purposeful approach appeared in the interpretation of the patent specification. The literal approach mandated that the patent specification should be read strictly according to its wording and grammar. A teleological approach allowed it be read primarily in terms of the purpose of the specification: whether the description of the invention given in the specification was clear and sufficient to enable one skilled in the craft to make the invention. Minor shortcomings would be fatal to the patent in the first approach, but not necessarily in the latter approach. Again these two conflicting approaches to the patent specification are evident in case reports. For example, Buller argued in *Turner v. Winter* 1787 that it was appropriate to set aside a patent for a 'slight defect' in the specification and Dallas in *Campion v. Benyon* 1821 stressed the importance of the grammatical component of the specification. On the other hand, other judges considered that the patentee had fulfilled his duty of disclosure if he had, in good faith, adequately communicated the nature of the invention. This was the approach adopted by Lord Eldon in *Cartwright v. Amatt* 1800 and Lord Lyndhurst in *Sturtz v. De la Rue* 1828.

There may also have been another factor which contributed to whether the patent specification was read literally, as a text to be analysed grammatically, or as a set of technical instructions. Understanding the technical description of an invention could be quite demanding for a judge. Focusing on the patent specification as a legal text, rather than as a set of practical technical instructions, allowed the judge to approach the specification on more familiar ground. The frames of reference of the legal profession were different from those of scientists and engineers. As noted in paragraph 4.3, that a judge read the specification in a different way from the way in which an engineer would read the specification was a point raised before the Select Committee on Patents in 1829.

By placing the confusion and uncertainty, which was rife in the early phase of the development of patent law, within a context of judicial hostility and prejudice, Dutton neglects the underlying cause of that confusion and uncertainty: the division within the judiciary along formalist or teleological lines. Different interpretational styles within the judiciary would mean that certain factors would weigh more heavily with one judge than with another. A restrictive, formalist approach to the interpretation of the Statute of Monopolies or the patent specification is not in itself evidence of either hostility or prejudice towards patents.

8.1.2   The Attitude of Judges to the Monopoly Granted by Patent

However, the way in which the patent specification would be read was clearly connected to another factor of importance in judicial decision-making in this period: the attitude of the judge to the monopoly granted by a patent for a new invention. In the eighteenth century, the word 'monopoly' could still conjure up examples of the more extreme abuses of the royal prerogative in former times. Since Coke's time, the common law had been said to be against monopolies. The Statute of Monopolies allowed certain exceptions to the general prohibition on monopolies, including the monopoly awarded by a grant of patent for a new invention, but those exceptions had to comply with the conditions laid down in the Statute.

A judge was more likely to have adopted a restrictive approach to the patent specification if the monopoly awarded by patent was not seen as a different species of monopoly from such monopolistic practices as forestalling, engrossing and regrating. Although also statutory offences until the latter part of the eighteenth century, these monopolistic practices were seen as originally common law offences which related to basic foodstuffs. If the common law, seen by many judges as an expression of natural reason and justice, had prohibited these monopolistic practices, it could be argued that the duty of the courts was to protect the public from the avarice of unscrupulous businessmen. Failure to make the distinction between older species of monopoly on existing commodities and a monopoly for a new invention brought the monopoly for a new invention within this moral, protectionist frame of reference. The task of the judge seen from within this frame of reference was to be alert to any attempt by the patentee to obtain a patent on wrongful grounds or renegade on his obligation to disclose his invention to the public. It justified reading the patent specification strictly and the slightest suggestion that the patent specification failed to describe the real nature of the invention would be sufficient to have the patent set aside.

On the other hand, if a patent monopoly for a new invention was considered not to have taken away from the public any rights that existed before the exploitation of the new invention, the way was open to view the patent within a very different context: that of social utility. The monopoly for a new invention did not hinder the public. If the new invention were no good, it would simply fail but if the invention was good, then both the public and the inventor could reap the benefits. It was a monopoly that was, to use Adam Smith's description, 'harmless' (see paragraph 5.1.2). In a context in which the patent did not grant a 'pernicious' monopoly, it became far more acceptable to view the patent as awarding a right to the patentee. The patent specification could be read in terms of rights and duties, as if the grant were a contract between the patentee and the public. If the patentee had fulfilled his duty to disclose his invention in a way clearly understandable to one skilled in the craft, he had a right to his monopoly. It was a right which should not be undermined simply because of minor defects in the patent specification.

Several case reports dealt with in chapter 4 indicate splits along these lines. Counsel in *Harmar v. Playne* 1807 had argued before Lord Eldon that both Mansfield and Buller saw patents primarily in the light of a monopoly, whereas Eldon conceived of the patent specification in terms of a bargain with the public. Counsel's implication is that the 'light of a monopoly' carried with it a negative connotation for these two judges. The newspaper reports and the trial notes of *Liardet v. Johnson* 1778 indicate that his argument may have been unfounded with respect to Mansfield. It would seem from his directions to the jury in *Liardet v. Johnson* 1778 that Mansfield was not troubled by a temporary monopoly being offered to a patentee as an 'inducement' to encourage inventions of benefit to society. However, it is possible that Buller's strict reading of patent specifications was at least to some extent influenced by the awarding of a monopoly. In *Turner v. Winter* 1787, Buller stressed that he had a "strong bias" in favour of a patentee who had made a fair disclosure, but he also stated that "where the discovery is not fully made, the court ought to look with a very watchful eye to prevent any imposition on the public". (See paragraph 4.2.4.2). That "imposition" could only be a reference to the granting of a monopoly to the patentee. Apparently the imposition was so significant that "a very watchful eye" was justified.

Lord Kenyon's attitude to the monopoly awarded by a patent certainly seems to have been connected to his moral sense of a duty imposed by the law to protect the more vulnerable sections of the public. This duty was made explicit by Kenyon in the engrossing and forestalling cases of *R v. Waddington* and *R v. Rusby* 1800. As pointed out in chapter 5, one of the complaints made against Kenyon was that he did not see the monopoly granted by patent as a different species of monopoly (paragraph 5.1.3). An indication for the legitimacy of that complaint is the comment Kenyon made in the Hornblower case. Kenyon was clearly concerned that a patent would be the cause of "great oppression" on "inferior mechanics by those who are more opulent". In *The Times* version of the report, the great oppression seems to cover a greater group than 'inferior mechanics', as it speaks of "a great deal of oppression of the lower orders of men from Patents".

8.1.3 The Attitude of Judges to the Patent as a Form of Property

There was another factor which may have influenced judicial decision-making: the legal nature of the patent as a form of personal property. Although the patent specification was analysed by some judges in terms of a contract between the patentee and the public, the patent itself seems to have been treated as a species of property rather than as a personal right. In his *Commentaries*, Blackstone had placed both copyright and patents in Book II, 'The Right of Things', referring to patents as a grant of "a temporary property" (see paragraph 6.1). However, the concept of property at common law may have affected not only whether a judge saw the patentee as having a right rather than a privilege, but also the interpretation of the term 'manufacture' in the Statute of Monopolies.

If the patent was not seen as a form of property at common law, but as an anomalous species of property created by an act of the royal prerogative as regulated by statute, the patentee did not have a right at common law to prevent others copying and making his invention. As noted above, the common law was associated with concepts of natural reason and justice. A right at common law suggests a right with a foundation in natural reason and justice. It was of a different moral order than a temporary right granted by the crown. Furthermore, the wording of that royal grant did not refer to a right; the grant awarded a 'privilege'. Regarding the monopoly awarded by patent as a privilege and not as a right may have encouraged some judges to consider the interests of the public to be more significant than those of any individual patentee. It was an approach that Lord Loughborough had brought to the fore and condemned in *Arkwright v. Nightingale* 1785: matters of public interest should not affect the determination of property in a patent dispute between two private individuals (paragraph 3.3.3).

The traditional concept of property at common law required that the object of property was a thing. A very clear division within the judiciary would emerge in the copyright cases of the eighteenth century on this point. Those judges who preferred a traditional, formalist approach considered that property arose in the form of a right derived from a relationship with a physical thing. Other judges, however, considered that anything which was of value, as a source of profit, could give a property right, as long as it could be distinguished. It was not dependent upon any specific material manifestation.

For the inventor, the traditional approach meant that his property right at common law was confined to the physical machine or substance he had produced. Once that was sold, the property right in that machine or substance was transferred to the purchaser. In this approach, there was said to be no property at common law in intellectual ideas, and hence no right which would prevent another copying and making that machine or substance once it was in the trade. The property right extended no further than the thing made. Although it is clear from the eighteenth century copyright cases that there were judges who saw the author's literary composition as the property, not the physical book in which that mode of expression appeared, this distinction does not seem to have been made so readily with respect to inventions. The imitated machine was seen by these judges as a new and different work, unlike a literary composition which remained the same regardless of whether it was printed on paper belonging to someone else. Whatever property in his invention an inventor may have had at common law, it was apparently seen as lost once the invention was communicated (see paragraph 6.4.1).

At the same time as these discussions on the nature of property were taking place in copyright cases, a discussion was taking place in patent cases as to the meaning of the term 'manufacture' in the Statute of Monopolies. Did the subject matter of a patent have to be a material thing? If a judge considered that a proprietary right required a relationship with an external thing, it is possible that he transferred that line of reasoning to patent law. If a patent was seen as the property right issuing from the 'manufacture', that would require the 'manufacture' to be a material thing. It would exclude a method from being a subject matter of a patent. If there was no physical invention as the subject matter of the patent grant, no machinery or substance, there was no 'manufacture'. As there was nothing to be protected by the law, the patent grant was therefore void.

8.2 THE SHIFT IN JUDICIAL INTERPRETATION IN THE 1830S

The decade of the 1830s is brought to the fore by Dutton as a watershed: "from the mid-1830s the law, as applied by the courts became both more certain and more favourable for patentees." (See paragraph 4.2.4.4). His statistical analysis of patent cases showed that in the 1830s more cases were now found in favour of the patentee than in any previous period. It is in this decade that a change can be discerned in the structuring of patent law. The literal, strict interpretation of both the Statute of Monopolies and the patent specification gives way to a less restrictive and mechanistic approach.

8.2.1   The Shift in Interpretation of the Statute of Monopolies 1624

With respect to the Statute of Monopolies, the interpretation of the term 'true and first inventor' appears to have remained the same in the 1830s as in the eighteenth century. In *Lewis v. Marling* 1829, it was still being held that the true and first inventor need not be the creative force behind the invention; an 'inventor' could be the first to bring an invention known elsewhere into use in Britain. From counsel's argument in *Crane v. Price*, it would appear that the importer as inventor was still good law in 1842. However, it is clear that the way in which other terms in the Statute were being interpreted in the 1830s was not the same as in the 1750s.

By the 1830s, what was, and what was not, considered by judges to fall under the heading of 'generally inconvenient' had changed. Any mechanisation which could reduce labour had been condemned in the seventeenth century as a violation of the proviso set down in the Statute of Monopolies, that a patent should not be 'generally inconvenient'. Already in the latter part of the eighteenth century, a swing was taking place. Labour-saving devices were no longer automatically seen as harmful to the state, as was apparent from the case of *R v. Arkwright* 1785. By the 1830s, increased efficiency was being recognised by the courts as an important aspect of a new invention.

Of particular interest to this study is the change in the interpretation of the term 'new manufacture'. In the early eighteenth century, an addition or improvement was not considered to be a proper subject matter for a patent, as it was not seen as a 'new manufacture'. The authority was the precedent laid down in Bircot's case. After *Morris v. Bramson* in 1776, the courts had accepted an addition or improvement as a new manufacture, as long as a clear distinction was drawn by the patentee between his addition or improvement and the original invention. In the nineteenth century, what was understood to constitute a 'manufacture' would change. The dominant judicial opinion in the eighteenth century was that the term 'manufacture' required the subject matter of the patent to be a material thing, such as a new substance or a machine. A method as such could not be the subject matter of a patent. Yet many patents were granted for methods. The subject matter of this type of patent could be a new process to be carried out by known implements, acting on known substances and producing a known substance, but producing it more cheaply or efficiently. In the 1820s and 30s, various cases established that there could be a patent for a new combination of well-known materials. Examples are Hall's patent for singeing off superfluous fibres, Russell's patent for a process of welding tubes (in this case without using a known implement, the mandrel), Derosne's patent for refining sugar and Cornish and Sievier's patent for a new combination of known materials to make an elastic cloth.

A change in a process which enabled a product to be made more efficiently or more economically had been implicitly accepted by these judges as constituting the 'manufacture'. The apparent acceptance of various patents for methods by the courts in this period cannot be labelled simply as a further refinement in interpretation. It was in effect a rejection of a former interpretation of the term, which required a patent to be for a material thing. The rejection of the older view of 'manufacture' marked a radical change of direction. It was no less significant than the rejection in the eighteenth century of a precedent which had stated that an improvement could not be the subject matter of a patent. A method as a subject matter of a patent was endorsed by Tindal, C.J. in *Crane v. Price* 1842 and this case has been seen as finally settling the law on this point.

Lokin argued that the text of a law can only remain the same because the interpretation of that text will have changed over time. The law is an empty shell: the judge does not find the law, it is the judge who gives the law its meaning (see paragraph 2.1.2). There is much to be said in favour of that argument, but the judge is not entirely at liberty to interpret a text at will. It must fit within the boundaries of a community's legal order at any one point in time. The interpretation of the Statute of Monopolies illustrates this point. When Eyre, C.J. announced in *Boulton and Watt v. Bull* 1795 that a method could be the subject matter of a patent, he made explicit a different approach to the interpretation of the legal concept of 'manufacture'. It was one that recognised that the granting of patents for methods had become commonplace in the society of his day and that these inventions were important to a commercial nation.

Patent law was relatively new and requiring a 'manufacture' to be a material thing had not the force of traditional authorities behind it. Eyre's disagreement with the other members of the bench on this point was not comparable, therefore, to the reaction encountered by Mansfield when, in *Perrin v. Blake* 1769, he had rejected the old rule in Shelley's case. Nonetheless, Eyre was openly deviating from what appears to have been the dominant judicial approach to the interpretation of the term 'manufacture' in the Statute of Monopolies at that time. At first, Eyre's opinion was treated as a minority opinion. As noted in paragraph 3.3.2.1, Collier, in his 1803 treatise, considered that it had since been decided that a patent for a method would be void. Godson in his 1823 treatise was far less emphatic on the point, observing that whether a method could be the subject of a patent was not entirely clear. He did, however, remark that the doctrine of Eyre, C.J. has long been doubted. Given the lack of authoritative precedents on the issue, the judiciary could not totally discount Eyre's opinion. It would take some time before the law on this point would be settled. When it was finally settled, it was Eyre's opinion that prevailed.

This response by the legal community to a new interpretation of a legal concept is similar to that observed by Kuhn in a scientific community when a new theory is announced. The intervening period, between the announcement of the new theory and its acceptance, marks a period of insecurity. When confronted with an anomaly, the response of scientists is to devise numerous articulations and ad hoc modifications of their theory in order to eliminate any apparent conflict. The transfer of allegiance from paradigm to paradigm is a conversion experience that cannot be forced. The transposition is made as a new generation grows up that is familiar with the new theory (see paragraph 2.3). After Eyre's announcement that a method could be the subject matter of a patent, there followed a period of legal uncertainty. The more traditionally minded judges remained adamant that a method could not be the subject matter of a patent. Some judges tried to find ways to eliminate the conflict by viewing any new instruments developed to carry out a process as the 'manufacture'. Lord Eldon was one of the older generation of judges who appears to have accepted the different approach to the term 'manufacture', despite Campbell's assertion that Eldon was a formalist. In *Hill v. Thompson* 1817, Eldon stated there could be a valid patent "for a new combination of materials previously in use for the same purpose, or for a new method of applying such materials". It was an endorsement of Eyre's opinion given some twenty years earlier. By the time Tindal, C.J. gave his opinion in *Crane v. Price* 1842 that the courts had already, *de facto*, recognised that a patent could be for a method, members of a new generation of judges had been taking their places in the senior courts. This generation was more familiar with patents and a society in which manufacturing was of increasing importance. That made it easier for the shift in patent law to take place.

The judicial interpretation of the Statute of Monopolies seems to buck the trend sketched by Vogenauer. Vogenauer describes the period from the Year Books to 1830 as the period of equitable construction of statutes: a statute should be construed according to its spirit, rather than according to the literal wording of the enactment. The literal interpretation of statutes, already discernable in the late eighteenth century, would become the dominant form of interpretation from 1830. However, in the eighteenth century, the dominant interpretation of the Statute of Monopolies seems to have been literal and historical, particularly with respect to the term 'manufacture'. 'Manufacture' was mainly read as requiring a thing made by the hands of man, and hence excluding a method. In the early years of the nineteenth century it would seem that methods were being implicitly accepted by the courts as the subject matter of a patent. It would be in *Crane v. Price* 1842, a case heard later than the 1830 watershed delineated by Vogenauer as ushering in the period of literal interpretation, that Tindal would in effect formalise the practice of the courts. The 'spirit' of the statute seems to have triumphed over the literal interpretation.

8.2.2   *The Shift in the Interpretation of the Patent Specification*

In the 1830s, a shift in the way the patent specification was being interpreted also became apparent. Mansfield had warned the jury, back in 1778, that extremes should be avoided. The inventor should not be deprived of the benefit of his invention for the sake of the public, nor should an inventor receive a monopoly that was not warranted (paragraph 4.2.4.3). However, the strict interpretation of the patent specification advocated by Buller in *Turner v. Winter* 1787, by which a patent could be set aside for 'slight defects', was long considered to be good law. Dallas, J., in *Hill v. Thompson* in 1818, cited Buller's words in *Turner v. Winter* as an authority on this point (see paragraph 4.2.4).

The strict interpretation of the patent specification would be resisted in the Court of King's Bench under Abbott in the 1820s. In the 1830s, it would become commonplace for the courts to read the patent specification within a contractual context: the patent specification represented a bargain between the patentee and the public. The consideration for the monopoly awarded by the state to the patentee was that the patentee must disclose the nature of his invention in such a way that another skilled in the craft could make the invention. Minor defects would not invalidate the patent, if they did not impede an understanding of the invention by such a person and would allow that person to make the invention as advantageously as the patentee had made the invention himself.

This more balanced approach to the interests of both parties was summed up by Alderson, B. in *Russell v. Cowley* 1834:

> "we ought not to be understood to deprive people of advantages which their own ingenuity and talents entitle them to receive; we ought to give them a fair and candid construction, certainly not by any means being astute to pick holes in their specifications."

Adopting an approach which accepted the patent specification as essentially a scientific document, its purpose being to describe the invention and to give instructions to others skilled in the craft to make that invention, marked a departure from reading the patent specification as first and foremost a text to be subjected to a strict syntactical analysis. Placing more emphasis on the technical nature of the document opened the way for the evidence of expert witnesses to become more significant. The high status of an expert witness may have been a factor influencing some judges' opinions.

By placing the patent specification within a contractual framework, the implication was that both the patentee and the public had rights and duties. This shifted the position of the patentee: the patentee had a right, not simply a privilege granted as a reward. The move away from seeing the patent as a privilege granted in public law by the state to a *de facto* private right of a novel kind, is brought to the fore by Van Zijl Smit (see paragraph 5.2.3). The transition from privilege to right is admirably illustrated by the quotation from Alderson above: "their own ingenuity and talents *entitle* them to receive." Although there were judges who had referred to patentees as having 'rights' in the eighteenth century, the idea of entitlement becomes far more prevalent in the 1830s. The way in which the patent specification was interpreted would be affected by acknowledging that the patentee had a right to a monopoly, if his invention had been disclosed in a sufficient and reasonable manner. This shift is reflected in Godson's remark in the 1832 supplement to his treatise: "It is worthy of observation that the tide has turned in favour of patentees, and that the judges of the present day make every reasonable intendment in favour of the patentee."

8.2.3   The Causes of the Shift in the 1830s

There was no straightforward progression in the judicial interpretation of the Statute of Monopolies and the patent specification from the 1750s to the 1830s. There always had been interpretational diversity within the judiciary. There were judges who preferred a literal, formalist approach to interpretation and judges who had sought to interpret patent law within a contemporary social context. However, by the 1830s, certain older forms of interpretation were being rejected. The once more predominant view of what constituted a 'manufacture' was being phased out, as was the strict, literal approach to the interpretation of a patent specification.

Dutton argued that this shift in the interpretation of the Statute and the patent specification took place in the 1830s because "the early prejudice against patents" had given way: "Judges' attitude to patents changed because they now accepted that inventions led to prosperity and economic growth." (See paragraph 5.1.2) It has been argued in this study that placing judicial attitudes to patents within a framework of prejudice and hostility hinders an objective analysis. However, a change in attitude to the monopoly awarded by the patent is certainly a factor. Viewed in terms of utility, the monopoly for a successful, useful new invention did not seem to be an imposition on the public; it was harmless. A monopoly which stimulated inventors to produce inventions that increased trade and industry, and made more and better commodities available to the public at a lower price was beneficial to both the patentee and the public. A poor invention would simply fail.

Such a reading of the patent meant that the heavy emphasis which had been given by some judges in the past to protecting the interests of the public, as compared to protecting the interests of the patentee, appeared unnecessary. The stringent measures mandated by Buller's 'watchful eye' function were not required of the court.

The change in the structuring of patent law was a response to a society in which manufacturing and industry were gradually growing in importance. A shift in the attitude of the judiciary towards patents in the 1830s was no doubt assisted by a younger generation of lawyers becoming judges, a generation who were more familiar with patents for inventions as an aspect of everyday commercial life. However, the changes taking place in patent law must also be fitted within the framework of the broader legal developments taking place during the period covered by this study. In the mid-eighteenth century, the concept of personal property was demanding the attention of the courts. Land had long been the focus of English property law. By the time Blackstone was writing his *Commentaries* in the 1760s, personal property was increasing in importance and that increased importance was being recognised by the courts. According to Blackstone, the courts were now regarding a man's personal property "in a light nearly, if not quite, equal to his realty". (See paragraph 6.4.3)

There would be disagreements within the legal community as to what was, and what was not, property. These disagreements were triggered by litigation concerning more modern forms of commercial practice. The law of negotiable instruments is one such example. As noted in paragraph 6.1, Lieberman pointed to the contrast in attitudes between Blackstone and Mansfield with respect to negotiable instruments. Blackstone was apparently trying to accommodate the law regulating negotiable instruments within the general structure of the common law of contract, while Mansfield responded by emphasising the need to recognise these instruments as a distinct form of property governed by their usage in commerce. Copyright is another example. Yates, J. considered copyright to be the creation of statute, but not a form of property recognised by the common law. Whereas some judges, like Yates, argued that the common law of property required a proprietary right to issue from a physical thing, others were prepared to conceive of property in terms of a thing of value separate from a physical manifestation.

The development of patent law must also be viewed in the light of that whole discussion on the nature of property. Whether judges considered that inventions were good for the economy, that the monopoly granted by patent could stimulate trade and commerce, was not the only factor contributing to a more liberal interpretation of the Statute of Monopolies and the patent specification in the 1830s. Accepting a process as the subject matter of the patent reflected the shift which was taking place in judicial reasoning. The legal definition of property was moving away from an older concept of property, as a right issuing from a physical thing, to seeing property in terms of economic interests enforceable against third parties. The legal definition of property was becoming broader and more abstract.

When the courts in the 1830s began to uphold the validity of patents granted for a process more consistently, the legal protection given to the patentee was becoming more clearly detached from a right subsisting in a physical thing. The value of an invention was not any specific machine or substance, but the know-how that enabled that machine or substance to be made. The value was in the ingenuity, the intellectual creativity, which made the machine, or substance or effect possible. It marked an important step towards seeing the patent as a form of 'intellectual property'.

8.3 Concluding Remarks

The question of what can, and what cannot, be the subject of patent protection is a recurring one, as technical innovations force judges to reappraise and redefine the matter of patentability. In the period under consideration here, the Statute of Monopolies provided the criteria for patentability: the invention had to be 'any manner of new manufactures', not already in use within the realm, nor contrary to the law, mischievous to the state or generally inconvenient. By the end of this period, a 'manufacture' could be not only the product made, but a process to make a product. Patent protection had in effect been given by the courts to processes, separate from a patent for a product. At present, the main patent statute in English law is The Patents Act 1977. It provides patent protection for products and processes which comply with four basic requirements: the invention is novel, involves an inventive step, is capable of industrial application and has not been excluded in section 1 (2) or (3). Yet the matter of what is patentable still appears to be far from settled.

This is illustrated by the legal discussions which have arisen concerning one of the items that was specifically excluded from patentability in this Act: a program for a computer. New questions have been presented for the determination of the courts. Is a computer program in the form of software a 'thing', regardless of whether it is on a disk (as it has tangible patterns of a magnetic or other nature and can be copied)? Or could a computer program be patented if that program was embodied in hardware? Or why would a computer program not be patentable if the program functioned as part of an essentially technical process (patentable in the same way as other processes that were capable of industrial application)? This latter question is of particular interest here, given the struggle to accept the patentability of a process which characterised the period of this study. It is tempting to conclude that although these questions relate to an advance from a different sort of revolution – the digital revolution rather than the Industrial Revolution – some of the issues raised are in essence similar to those which confronted the judges of the eighteenth and early nineteenth century.

Appendix 1

The Statute of Monopolies 1624

C A P. III.

An Act concerning Monopolies and Difpenfations of Penal Laws, and the Forfeitures thereof.

'FOrafmuch as your moft excellent Majefty, in your Royal Judgment, and of your blefled Difpofition *Monopolies, &c.*
' to the Weal and Quiet of your Subjects, did in the Year of our Lord God one thoufand fix hun- *contrary to the*
' dren and ten, publifh in Print to the whole Realm, and to all Pofterity, That all Grants and Monopo- *Laws of the Realm.*
' lies, and of the Benefit of any Penal Laws, or of Power to difpenfe with the Law, or to compound for *All Monopolies,*
' the Forfeiture, are contrary to your Majefty's Laws, which your Majefty's Declaration is truly confonant *&c. fhall be void.*
' and agreeable to the ancient and fundamental Laws of this your Realm : (2) And whereas your Majefty *3 Inft. 181,*
' was further gracioufly pleafed, exprefly to command, that no Suitor fhould prefume to move your *182, 183.*
' Majefty for Matters of that Nature; (3) yet neverthelefs upon Mifinformations, and untrue Pretences *1 Haw. P. C.*
' of publick Good, many fuch Grants have been unduly obtained, and unlawfully put in Execution, to *P. 230 & fequent.*
' the great Grievance and Inconvenience of your Majefty's Subjects, contrary to the Laws of this your
' Realm, and contrary to your Majefty's moft Royal and Blefled Intention fo publifhed as aforefaid :'
(4) For avoiding whereof, and preventing of the like in Time to come, May it pleafe your excellent
Majefty, at the humble Suit of the Lords Spiritual and Temporal, and the Commons, in this prefent
Parliament affembled, That it may be declared and enacted; (5) and be it declared and enacted by
Authority of this prefent Parliament, That all Monopolies, and all Commiffions, Grants, Licences,
Charters and Letters Patents heretofore made or granted, or hereafter to be made or granted, to any
Perfon or Perfons, Bodies Politick or Corporate whatfoever, of or for the fole Buying, Selling, Making,
Working or Ufing of any Thing within this Realm, or the Dominion of *Wales*, (6) or of any other
Monopolies, or of Power, Liberty or Faculty, to difpenfe with any others, or to give Licence or Toleration to do, ufe or exercife any Thing againft the Tenor or Purport of any Law or Statute; (7) or to
give or make any Warrant for any fuch Difpenfation, Licence or Toleration to be had or made: or to
agree or compound with any others for any Penalty or Forfeitures limited by any Statute; or of any
Grant or Promife of the Benefit, Profit or Commodity of any Forfeiture, Penalty or Sum of Money,
that is or fhall be due by any Statute, before Judgment thereupon had; (8) and all Proclamations, Inhibitions, Reftraints, Warrants of Affiftants, and all other Matters and Things whatfoever, any way
tending to the Inftituting, Erecting, Strengthening, Furthering or Countenancing of the fame or any
of them; (9) are altogether contrary to the Laws of this Realm, and fo are, and fhall be utterly void and *3 Mod. 131.*
of none Effect, and in no wife to be put in Ure or Execution.

II. And be it further declared and enacted by the Authority aforefaid, That all Monopolies, and all *Monopolies, &c.*
fuch Commiffions, Grants, Licences, Charters, Letters Patents, Proclamations, Inhibitions, Reftraints, *fhall be tried by*
Warrants of Affiftance, and all other Matters and Things tending as aforefaid, and the Force and Vali- *the Common*
dity of them and of every of them, ought to be and fhall be for ever hereafter examined, heard, tried and *Laws of this Realm.*
determined by and according to the Common Laws of this Realm, and not otherwife.

III. And be it further enacted by the Authority aforefaid, That all Perfon and Perfons, Bodies Politick *All Perfons dif-*
and Corporate whatfoever, which now are or hereafter fhall be, fhall ftand and be difabled and uncapable *abled to ufe Mo-*
nopolies, &c.

to have, use, exercise or put in Ure any Monopoly, or any such Commiffion, Grant, Licence, Charter, Letters Patents, Proclamation, Inhibition, Reftraint, Warrant of Affiftance, or other Matter or Thing tending as aforefaid, or any Liberty, Power or Faculty, grounded or pretended to be grounded upon them or any of them.

The Party grieved by Pretext of a Monopoly, &c. fhall recover treble Damages and double Cofts. IV. And be it further enacted by the Authority aforefaid, That if any Perfon or Perfons at any Time after the End of forty Days next after the End of this prefent Seffion of Parliament, fhall be hindred, grieved, difturbed or difquieted, or his or their Goods or Chattels any way feized, attached, diftrained, taken, carried away or detained, by Occafion or Pretext of any Monopoly, or of any fuch Commiffion, Grant, Licence, Power, Liberty, Faculty, Letters Patents, Proclamation, Inhibition, Reftraint, Warrant of Affiftance, or other Matter or Thing tending as aforefaid, and will fue to be relieved in or for any of the Premiffes; That then and in every fuch Cafe, the fame Perfon and Perfons fhall and may have his and their Remedy for the fame at the Common Law, by any Action or Actions to be grounded upon this Statute; the fame Action and Actions to be heard and determined in the Courts of King's Bench, Common Pleas and Exchequer or in any of them, againft him or them by whom he or they fhall be fo hindred, grieved, difturbed or difquieted, or againft him or them by whom his or their Goods or Chattels fhall be fo feized, attached, diftrained, taken, carried away or detained; (2) wherein all and every fuch Perfon and Perfons which fhall be fo hindred, grieved, difturbed or difquieted, or whofe Goods or Chattels fhall be fo feized, attached, diftrained, taken, carried away or detained, fhall recover three Times fo much as the Damages which he or they fuftained by means or occafion of being fo hindred, grieved, difturbed or difquieted, or by means of having his or their Goods or Chattels feized, attached, diftrained, taken, carried away or detained, and double Cofts; (3) and in fuch Suits, or for the Staying or Delaying thereof, no Effoin, Protection, Wager of Law, Aid Prayer, Privilege, Injunction or Order of Reftraint, fhall be in any wife prayed, granted, admitted or allowed, nor any more than one Imparlance:

He that delayeth an Action grounded upon this Statute incurs a Praemunire. **16 R. 2. c. 5.** (4) And if any Perfon or Perfons fhall, after Notice given, that the Action depending is grounded upon this Statute, caufe or procure any Action at the Common Law, grounded upon this Statute, to be ftayed or delayed before Judgment, by colour or means of any Order, Warrant, Power or Authofity, fave only of the Court wherein fuch Action as aforefaid fhall be brought and depending, or after Judgment had upon fuch Action, fhall caufe or procure the Execution of or upon any fuch Judgment to be ftayed or delayed by colour or means of any Order, Warrant, Power or Authority, fave only by Writ of Error or Attaint; That then the faid Perfon and Perfons fo offending fhall incur and fuftain the Pains, Penalties and Forfeitures, ordained and provided by the Statute of Provifion and *Praemunire* made in the fixteenth Year of the Reign of King *Richard* the Second.

Letters Patents to ufe new Manufactures, faved. V. Provided neverthelefs, and be it declared and enacted, That any Declaration before mentioned fhall not extend to any Letters Patents and Grants of Privilege for the Term of one and twenty Years or under, heretofore made, of the fole Working or Making of any Manner of new Manufacture within this Realm, to the firft and true Inventor or Inventors of fuch Manufactures, which others at the Time of the Making of fuch Letters Patents and Grants did not ufe, fo they be not contrary to the Law, nor mifchievous to the State, by raifing of the Prices of Commodities at home, or Hurt of Trade, or generally inconvenient, but that the fame fhall be of fuch Force as they were or fhould be, if this Act had not been made, and of none other: (2) And if the fame were made for more than one and twenty Years, That then the fame for the Term of one and twenty Years only, to be accounted from the Date of the firft Letters Patents and Grants thereof made, fhall be of fuch Force as they were or fhould have been, if the fame had been made but for Term of one and twenty Years only, and as if this Act had never been had or made, and of none other.

VI. Provided alfo, and be it declared and enacted, That any Declaration before-mentioned fhall not extend to any Letters Patents and Grants of Privilege for the Term of fourteen Years or under, hereafter to be made, of the fole Working or Making of any manner of new Manufactures within this Realm, to the true and firft Inventor and Inventors of fuch Manufactures, which others at the Time of Making fuch Letters Patents and Grants fhall not ufe, fo as alfo they be not contrary to the Law, nor mifchievous to the State, by raifing Prices of Commodities at home, or Hurt of Trade, or generally inconvenient: The faid fourteen Years to be accounted from the Date of the firft Letters Patents, or Grant of fuch Privilege hereafter to be made, but that the fame fhall be of fuch Force as they fhould be, if this Act had never been made, and of none other.

VII. Provided alfo, and it is hereby further intended, declared and enacted by Authority aforefaid, That this Act or any Thing therein contained fhall not in any wife extend, or be prejudicial to any Grant or Privilege, Power or Authority whatfoever heretofore made, granted, allowed or confirmed by any Act of Parliament now in force, fo long as the fame fhall fo continue in force.

Warrants granted to Juftices, faved. VIII. Provided alfo, That this Act fhall not extend to any Warrant or Privy Seal, made or directed or to be made or directed by his Majefty, his Heirs or Succeffors, to the Juftices of the Courts of the King's Bench or Common Pleas, and Barons of the Exchequer, Juftices of Affize, Juftices of *Oyer and Terminer* and Gaol-delivery, Juftices of the Peace, and other Juftices for the Time being, having Power to hear and determine Offences done againft any Penal Statute, to compound for the Forfeitures of any Penal Statute, depending in Suit and Queftion before them or any of them refpectively, after Plea pleaded by the Party Defendant.

Charters granted to Corporations, faved. Inft. 185. IX. Provided alfo, and it is hereby further intended, declared and enacted, That this Act or any Thing therein contained fhall not in any wife extend or be prejudicial unto the City of *London*, or to any City, Borough or Town Corporate within this Realm, for or concerning any Grants, Charters or Letters Patents, to them or any of them made or granted, or for or concerning any Cuftom or Cuftoms ufed by or within them or any of them; (2) or unto any Corporations, Companies or Fellowfhips of any Art, Trade, Oc-

3

A. D. 1623.   Anno vicefimo primo JACOBI I.   C. 3.   93

Occupation or Myftery, or to any Companies or Societies of Merchants within this Realm, erected for the
Maintenance, Enlargement, or ordering of any Trade of Merchandize; (3) but that the fame Charters,
Cuftoms, Corporations, Companies, Fellowfhips and Societies and their Liberties, Privileges, Powers
and Immunities, fhall be and continue of fuch Force and Effect as they were before the Making of this
Act, and of none other; any Thing before in this Act contained to the contrary in any wife notwith-
ftanding.

X. Provided alfo, and be it enacted, That this Act, or any Declaration, Provifion, Difablement, Pe- *Letters Patents.*
nalty, Forfeiture, or other Thing before-mentioned, fhall not extend to any Letters Patents or Grants *that concern*
of Privilege heretofore made, or hereafter to be made, of, for or concerning Printing, (2) nor to any *Printing, Salt-*
Commiffion, Grant or Letters Patents heretofore made, or hereafter to be made, of, for or concerning *petre, Gun-*
the Digging, Making or Compounding of Salt-petre or Gunpowder, or the Cafting or Making of Ord- *powder, great*
nance, or Shot for Ordnance, (3) nor to any Grant or Letters Patents heretofore made, or hereafter *Ordnance, Shot,*
to be made, of any Office or Offices heretofore erected, made or ordained, and now in Being, and put *or Offices,*
in Execution, other than fuch Offices as have been decried by any his Majefty's Proclamation or Procla- *faved.*
mations : (4) But that all and every the fame Grants, Commiffions and Letters Patents, and all other
Matters and Things tending to the Maintaining, Strengthning and Furtherance of the fame, or any of
them, fhall be and remain of the like Force and Effect, and no other, and as free from the Declarations,
Provifions, Penalties and Forfeitures contained in this Act, as if this Act had never been had nor made,
and not otherwife.

XI. Provided alfo, and be it enacted, That this Act, or any Declaration, Provifion, Difablement, Pe- *This Act fhall*
nalty, Forfeiture, or other Thing before-mentioned, fhall not extend to any Commiffion, Grant, Let- *not extend to*
ters Patents or Privilege heretofore made, or hereafter to be made, of, for or concerning the Digging, *Commiffions for*
Compounding or Making of Allum or Allum Mines, but that all and every the fame Commiffions, *Allum Mines.*
Grants, Letters Patents and Privileges fhall be and remain of the like Force and Effect, and no other,
and as free from the Declarations, Provifions, Penalties and Forfeitures contained in this Act, as if this
Act had never been had nor made, and not otherwife.

XII. Provided alfo, and be it enacted, That this Act, or any Declaration, Provifion, Penalty, For- *Nor to the Li-*
feiture, or other Thing before-mentioned, fhall not extend or be prejudicial to any Ufe, Cuftom, Pre- *berties of New-*
fcription, Franchife, Freedom, Jurifdiction, Immunity, Liberty or Privilege, heretofore claimed, ufed or *caftle upon*
enjoyed by the Governors and Stewards, and Brethren of the Fellowfhip of the Hoaft-men of the Town *Tyne, nor to Li-*
of Newcaftle upon Tyne, or by the ancient Fellowfhip, Guild or Fraternity, commonly called Hoaft-men, *ing Taverns,*
(2) for or concerning the Selling, Carrying, Lading, Difpofing, Shipping, Venting or Trading of or
for any Sea-coals, Stone-coals or Pit-coals, forth or out of the Haven and River of Tyne; or to any
Grant made by the faid Governor and Stewards, and Brethren of the Fellowfhip of the faid Hoaft-men,
to the late Queen Elizabeth, of any Duty or Sum of Money to be paid for or in refpect of any fuch
Coals as aforefaid ; (3) nor to any Grants, Letters Patents or Commiffion, heretofore granted, or hereafter to be granted, of, for or concerning the Licencing of the Keeping of any Tavern or Taverns; or
felling, uttering or retailing of Wines to be drunk or fpent in the Manfion Houfe or Houfes, or other
Place in the Tenure or Occupation of the Party or Parties fo felling or uttering the fame ; or for or concerning the Making of any Compofitions for fuch Licences, fo as the Benefit of fuch Compofitions be
referved and applied to and for the Ufe of his Majefty, his Heirs or Succeffors, and not to the private Ufe
of any other Perfon or Perfons.

XIII. Provided alfo, and be it enacted, That this Act, or any Declaration, Provifion, Penalty, For- *Nor to Letters*
feiture, or other Thing before-mentioned, fhall not extend or be prejudicial to a Grant or Privilege for *Patents granted*
or concerning the Making of Glafs, by his Majefty's Letters Patents under the Great Seal of England, *to Sir Robert*
bearing Date the two and twentieth Day of May in the one and twentieth Year of his Majefty's Reign *Manfel, Kot.*
of England, made and granted to Sir Robert Manfel Knight, Vice-Admiral of England : (2) Nor to a *or to James*
Grant or Letters Patents bearing Date the twelfth Day of June in the thirtieth Year of his Majefty's *Maxewell, Efq;*
Reign of England, made to James Maxewell Efquire, concerning the Tranfportation of Calves Skins :
(3) But that the faid feveral Letters Patents laft mentioned fhall be and remain of the like Force and Effect,
and as free from the Declarations, Provifions, Penalties and Forfeitures before-mentioned, as if this Act
had never been had nor made, and not otherwife.

XIV. Provided alfo, and be it decl red and enacted, That this Act, or any Declaration, Provifion, *Nor to thofe*
Penalty, Forfeiture or other Thing before-mentioned, fhall not extend or be prejudicial to a Grant or *granted to Abra-*
Privilege for or concerning the Making of Smalt, by his Majefty's Letters Patents under the Great Seal *ham Baker, cr.*
of England, bearing Date the fixteenth Day of February in the fixteenth Year of his Majefty's Reign of *Edward Lord*
England, made or granted to Abraham Baker : (2) Nor to a Grant or Privilege, for or concerning the *Dudley.*
Melting of Iron Ewer, and of Making the fame into Caft-works or Bars with Sea-coals or Pit-coals,
by his Majefty's Letters Patents under the Great Seal of England, bearing Date the twentieth Day of
February in the nineteenth Year of his Majefty's Reign of England, made or granted to Edward Lord
Dudley; (3) but that the fame feveral Letters Patents and Grants fhall be and remain of the like Force
and Effect, and as free from the Declarations, Provifions, Penalties and Forfeitures before-mentioned, as
if this Act had never been had nor made, and not otherwife.

C A P.

Source: *The statutes at large, from Magna Charta, to the end of the last Parliament 1761*, volume 3 (London: 1768-70): British Library document.

Appendix 2

The Chief Justices, Chief Barons and Lord Chancellors 1750s-1830s

Chief Barons of the Court of Exchequer	Chief Justices of the Court of Common Pleas	Chief Justices of the Court of King's Bench	Chancellors of the High Court of Chancery
1742: Sir Thomas Parker	1737: Sir John Willes	1737: Sir William Lee	1737: Philip Yorke, Lord Hardwicke
1772: Sir Sydney Smythe	1762: Charles Pratt, Lord Camden	1754: Sir Dudley Ryder	1757: Robert Henley, Lord Northington
1777: Sir John Skinner	1766: Sir John Wilmot	1756: William Murray, Lord Mansfield	1766: Charles Pratt, Lord Camden
1787: Sir James Eyre	1771: Sir William De Grey	1788: Lloyd Kenyon, Lord Kenyon	1771: Henry Bathurst, Lord Apsley
1793: Sir Archibald Macdonald	1780: Alexander Wedderburn, Lord Loughborough	1802: Edward Law, Lord Ellenborough	1778: Edward Thurlow, Lord Thurlow
1813: Sir Vicary Gibbs	1793: Sir James Eyre	1818: Charles Abbott, Lord Tenterden	1793: Alexander Wedderburn, Lord Loughborough
1814: Sir Alexander Thomson	1799: John Scott, Lord Eldon	1832-1850: Thomas Denman, Lord Denman	1801: John Scott, Lord Eldon
1817: Sir Richard Richards	1801: Richard Pepper Arden, Lord Alvanley		1806: Thomas Erskine, Lord Erskine
1824: Sir William Alexander	1804: Sir James Mansfield		1807: John Scott, Lord Eldon
1831: John Copley, Lord Lyndhurst	1814: Sir Vicary Gibbs		1827: John Copley, Lord Lyndhurst
1834-1844: Sir James Scarlett, Lord Abinger	1818: Sir Robert Dallas		1830: Henry Brougham, Lord Brougham
	1824: Robert Gifford, Lord Gifford		1834: John Copley, Lord Lyndhurst
	1824: Sir William Best		1836-1841: Charles Pepys, Lord Cottenman
	1829-1846: Sir Nicholas Conyngham Tindal		

In the above table, a listing is given of the heads of the courts of Common Pleas, Exchequer, King's Bench and Chancery from the mid-eighteenth century to the early nineteenth century. As can be seen from that listing, the length of tenancy in office in any one court could vary considerably. For example, Lord Mansfield remained in office as Chief Justice of the Court of King's Bench for thirty-two years whereas Sir Vicary Gibbs was only Chief Baron of the Court of Exchequer for less than three months before moving to the Court of Common Pleas. As the example of Sir Vicary Gibbs shows, it was not unusual for chief judges to transfer from one court to another. Sir James Eyre went from Chief Baron of the Court of Exchequer to Chief Justice of Common Pleas; Lord Lyndhurst left the Court of Chancery for the Exchequer, only to return to the position of Chancellor several years later; Lord Camden went from Chief Justice of Common Pleas to Lord Chancellor, as did Lord Eldon. As these examples illustrate, transferring from a common law court to a court of equity was not exceptional.

The Chief Justices and Chief Barons of the senior courts sat with three puisne judges. Although some of these puisne judges long remained in the panel of the same court, for example William Ashhurst of King's Bench sat there for thirty years, these puisne judges could also transfer from court to court. Examples of such transfers are Joseph Yates's departure from King's Bench to Common Pleas in 1770, which was possibly triggered by his dissenting opinion;[1] Francis Buller, whom Mansfield had hoped would be his successor, left King's Bench for Common Pleas in 1794 and William Blackstone, after a very brief period in King's Bench, was to make his judicial career in the Court of Common Pleas.

---

1   Fifoot speaks of Yates "as nursing a grievance": *Lord Mansfield,* Oxford 1977, p. 47, but Holdsworth in *A History of English Law* vol. XII, dismisses Junius's assertion that Mansfield had shown resentment, as there was no evidence to support a reading that the move was occasioned by personal feelings, pp. 482-483.

Bibliography

A.Z, *A New Essay on Divine Providence*, London 1755.

Adams, John, and Averley, Gwen, "The Patent Specification: The Role of Liardet v Johnson", *Journal of Legal History*, vol. 7 (1986), pp. 156-177.

Allen, C.K., *Law in the Making*, Oxford 1978.

Anon, *A Law Grammar; or, an Introduction to the Theory and Practice of English Jurisprudence*, London 1791.

Arkwright, Richard, *The Trial of a Cause instituted by Richard Pepper Arden, Esq*, London 1785.

Ashton, T.S., *The Industrial Revolution 1760-1830*, Oxford 1968.

Bacon, Francis, *The philosophical Works of Francis Bacon, Baron of Verulam, methodized, and made English, from the Originals... In three Volumes, by Peter Shaw*, vol. 1, London 1733.

Bacon, Francis, *Essays moral, economical, and political*, London 1798.

Bailey, N., *An Universal Etymological English Dictionary*, Edinburgh 1800.

Bakels, R. and Hugenholtz, P. Bernt, *The patentability of computer programs: discussion of European-level legislation in the field of patents for software*, working paper JURI 107 EN, European Parliament 2002.

Baker, J. H., *An Introduction to English Legal History*, London 2002.

Bentham, Jeremy, *A Manual of Political Economy*, edited by Bowring, vol. 3 Edinburgh 1843.

Bentham, Jeremy, *The Theory of Legislation, translated from the French of Etienne Dumont by Richard Hildreth*, Oceana Publications 1975.

Bentham, Jeremy, *A Comment on the Commentaries and A fragment on Government*, edited by J.H. Burns and H.L.A. Hart, London 1977.

Besselink, Leonard F.M., *Keeping Faith: a Study of Grotius' Doctrine of Natural Law* (Unpublished Ph.D. thesis), Florence 1988.

Birks, Peter (ed.), *Oxford English Law: English Private Law*, vol. 1 Oxford 2000.

Blackstone, Henry, *Reports of Cases argued and determined in the Courts of Common Pleas and Exchequer from 1788-1791*, in 2 vols., London 1791-1796.

Blackstone, William, *Reports of Cases determined in the several Courts of Westminster-Hall, from 1746 to 1779*, in 2 vols., London 1781.

Blackstone, William, *Commentaries on the Laws of England*, (12th ed.), London 1793.

Boehm, Klaus, *The British Patent System I*, Cambridge 1967.

Boorstin, Daniel J., *The Mysterious Science of the Law, An Essay on Blackstone's Commentaries*, Chicago 1996.

Boucher, David and Kelly, Paul (eds.), *The Social Contract from Hobbes to Rawls*, London 1994.

Bramah, Joseph, "The petition and case of Joseph Bramah, of Piccadilly, engineer, inventor of the patent locks for the security of life and property", London 1798.

Brewer, John, and Staves, Susan (eds.), *Early Modern Conceptions of Property*, London 1995.

Brown, Josiah, *Reports of Cases, upon Appeals and Writs of Error, in the High Court of Parliament: from the Year 1701, to the Year 1779*, London 1779-1783.

Buckle, Stephen, *Natural Law and the Theory of Property: Grotius to Hume*, Oxford 1991.

Buller, Francis, *An Introduction to the Law relative to Trials at nisi prius*, (5th ed.), London 1790.

Burns, Richard, *A new Law Dictionary: intended for general use, as well as for Gentlemen of the Profession*, vol. 2, London 1792.

Burrow, James, *Reports of Cases argued and adjudged in the Court of King's Bench during the Time of Lord Mansfield's presiding from 1756-1772*, in 5 vols., London 1790.

Campbell, John, *The Lives of the Chief Justices of England*, London 1874.

Carey Miller, David L. and Zimmermann Reinhard (eds.), *The Civilian Tradition and Scots Law*, Berlin 1997.

Carpmael, William, *Law Reports of Patent Cases*, in 3 vols., London 1843.

Cheshire, Fifoot, and Furmston, *Law of Contract*, London 2001.

Cobbett, William, *Parliamentary History of England*, vol. 17, London 1813.

Coke, Edward, *Institutes of the Laws of England*,
    The Third Part of the Institutes, London, 1797.
    The Fourth Part of the Institutes, London, 1797.

Collier, John Dyer, *An Essay on Patents for new Inventions*, London 1803.

Cowper, Henry, *Reports of Cases adjudged in the Court of King's Bench*, in 2 vols., London 1800.

Cruickshanks, Eveline, Handley, Stuart, and Hayton, D.W., *The History of Parliament: The House of Commons 1690-1715*, Cambridge 2002.

Daniel, W.T.S., *The History and Origins of the Law Reports*, London 1884.

Davenport, A.N., *James Watt and the Patent System*, The British Library 1989.

Davies, D. Seaborne, "The Early History of the Patent Specification", *Law Quarterly Review* 50 (1934), pp. 86-109.

Davies, John, *A Collection of the Most Important Cases respecting Patents of Invention*, London 1816.

Dawson, John P., "The Privy Council and Private Law in the Tudor and Stuart Periods", *Michigan Law Review* 48, No. 4 (1950), pp. 393-428.

De Roover, Raymond, "Monopoly Theory Prior to Adam Smith: A Revision", *The Quarterly Journal of Economics* 65, no. 4 (1951), pp. 492-524.

Deazley, Ronan, "The Myth of Copyright at Common Law", *Cambridge Law Journal* 62, (2003), pp. 106-133.

Deazley, Ronan, *On the origin of the right to copy: charting the movement of copyright law in eighteenth century Britain (1695-1775)*, Oxford 2004.

Dent, Chris, "Patent Policy in Early Modern England: Jobs, Trade and Regulation", *Legal History* vol. 10 (2006), pp. 71-95.

Douglas, Sylvester, *Reports of Cases argued and determined in the Court of King's Bench*, in 4 vols., London 1790.

Duman, Daniel, *The Judicial Bench in England 1727-1875: The Reshaping of a Professional Elite*, London Royal Historical Society 1982.

Durnford, Charles and East, Edward, *Term reports in the Court of King's Bench: from…39th George III to …40th George III…* in 8 vols., London 1794-1802.

Dutton, H.I., *The patent system and inventive activity during the industrial revolution 1750-1852*, Manchester 1984.

Edlund, Fabian, "Software Related Inventions at the Enlarged Board of Appeals", 92 (2010) *Journal Patent and Trademark Office Society*, pp. 131-134.

Edwards, John, *Theologia Reformata: or the Body and Substance of the Christian Religion, comprised in Distinct Discourses*, vol. 2 London 1713.

Espinasse, Isaac, *A Digest of the Law of Actions and Trials at nisi prius*, (3rd ed.), vol. 2, London 1798.

Eure, Samson, *Trials per pais: or, the law of England concerning juries by nisi prius, &c*, London 1766.

Evans, Eric J., *The forging of the modern state: early industrial Britain 1783-1870*, London 1996.

Fifoot, C.H.S., *Lord Mansfield*, Oxford 1977.

Forbes, William, *The Institutes of the Law of Scotland*, vol. 2, Edinburgh 1722-1730.

Fox, Harold G., *Monopolies and Patents: a Study of the History and Future of the Patent Monopoly*, Toronto 1947.

Gentleman of the Middle Temple, *Readings upon the Statute Law*, vol. IV, 1723-1725.

Getz, L., "History of the Patentee's Obligations in Great Britain", *Journal of the Patent Office Society* 46 (1964), pp. 62-81.

Girdler, J.S, *Observations on the pernicious consequences of forestalling, regrating and ingrossing*, London 1800.

Godson, Richard, *A Practical Treatise on the Law of Patents for Inventions and of Copyright*, London 1823.

Godson, Richard, *Supplement to A Practical Treatise on the Law of Patents for Invention*, London 1832.

Graham, Nicole, "Restoring the 'Real' to Real Property Law: A Return to Blackstone?", in Wilfred Prest (ed.), *Blackstone and his Commentaries: Biography, Law, History*, Oxford and Portland 2009, pp. 151-163

Graziadei, Michele, "Changing Images of the Law in XIX Century Legal Thought (The Continental Impulse)", in Mathias Reiman (ed.), *The Reception of Continental Ideas in the Common Law World 1820-1920*, Berlin 1993, pp 115-163.

Grotius, Hugo, *The Rights of War and Peace*, vol. 2, London 1715.

Haakonssen, Knud, *The Science of a Legislator: the Natural Jurisprudence of David Hume and Adam Smith*, Cambridge 1981.

Hale, Matthew, *The History of the Common Law of England*, Chicago 1971.

Halsbury, *Laws of England*, (4th ed.), vol. 35, London 1994.

Hargrave, Francis, *An Argument in Defence of Literary Property*, London 1774.

Hargrave, Francis, *A Collection of Tracts relative to the Laws of England*, Dublin 1787.

Hargrave, Francis, *Collectanea Juridica*, London 1791.

Harris, J.W., *Law and Legal Science: An Inquiry into the Concepts Legal Rule and Legal System*, Oxford 1979.

Hart, H.L.A., *Essays on Bentham: Studies in Jurisprudence and Political Theory*, Oxford 1982.

Hartendorp, R.C., *Praktisch gesproken: Alledaagse Civiel Rechtspleging als praktische Oordeelsvorming*, Rotterdam 2008.

Hay, Douglas, article: "Kenyon, Lloyd", in *Oxford Dictionary of National Biography*, at <www.oxforddnb.com> (15431).

Hayward, Peter, *Hayward's Patent Cases 1600-1883*, Abingdon, Oxon 1987.

Heward, Edmund, *Lord Mansfield*, Chichester and London, 1979.

Hewish, John, "From Cromford to Chancery Lane: New Light on the Arkwright Patent Trials", *Technology and Culture* 28 (1987), pp. 80-86

Hills, Richard L., *Power in the Industrial Revolution*, Manchester 1970.

Hochstrasser, T.J., *Natural Law Theories in the Early Enlightenment*, Cambridge 2000.

Hohfeld, Wesley Newcomb, *Fundamental Legal Conceptions as applied in Judicial Reasoning*, Yale 1964.

Holdsworth, William, *A History of English Law*, London 1964.

Holliday, John, *The Life of William late Earl of Mansfield*, London 1797.

Holmes, Oliver Wendell, *The Common Law*, Chicago 1881/2000.

Honoré, A.M., "Rights of Exclusion and Immunities against Divesting", *Tulane Law Review* 34 (1959-1960) pp. 453-468.

Honoré, A.M., "Ownership", in A.G. Guest (ed.), *Oxford Essays in Jurisprudence*, Oxford 1961, pp. 107-147.

Hulme, E., "The History of the Patent System under the Prerogative and at Common Law", *Law Quarterly Review* 12 (1896) pp. 141-154.

Hulme, E., "On the Consideration of the Patent Grant Past and Present", *Law Quarterly Review* 13 (1897) pp. 313-318.

Hulme, E., "The History of the Patent System under the Prerogative and at Common Law: A Sequel", *Law Quarterly Review* 16 (1900), pp. 44-56.

Hulme, E., "On the History of Patent Law in the Seventeenth and Eighteenth Centuries", *Law Quarterly Review* 18 (1902), pp. 280-288.

Hulme, E., "Privy Council Law and Practice of Letters Patent for Invention from the Restoration to 1794", *Law Quarterly Review* 33 (1917), pp. 63-75 and 180-195.

Huntingford, George, *Twelve Discourses on Different Subjects*, vol. 2, London 1795.

Iancu Andrei and Gratzinger, Peter, "Machines and Transformations: The Past, Present, and Future Patentability of Software", *Northwestern Journal of Technology and Intellectual Property*, vol. 8, nr. 2, (Spring 2010), pp. 247-274

Ibbetson, D.J., "From Property to Contract: The Transformation of Sale in the Middle Ages", *The Journal of Legal History* 13 (1992) pp. 1-22.

Ibbetson, D.J., *A Historical Introduction to the Law of Obligations*, Oxford 1999.

Ibbetson, D.J., "Natural Law and Common Law", *Edinburgh Law Review* 5 (2001) pp. 4-20.

Jacob, Giles, *A New Law Dictionary*, London 1782.

Jacob, Giles, *The Law Dictionary: Explaining the Rise, Progress and Present State of the English Law*, vol. 1, London 1797.

Jones, P.M., "Industrial Enlightenment in Practice: Visitors to the Soho Manufactory 1765-1820", *Midland History Journal*, University of Birmingham vol. 33, 1 Spring (2008) pp. 71-96.

Keeton, George W., and Schwarzenberger, Georg, (eds.), *Jeremy Bentham and the law: a symposium*, London 1948.

Kleve, P., Noortwijk, C. and De Mulder, R., "The Amazing Diversity Framework of the Intellectual Property Rights Harmonisation", in Brockdorff et al., (Eds.), *Globalisation and Harmonisation in Technology Law*, proceedings 21th Bileta conference, 15 pp., Bileta: Malta. Accessible via RePub <http://hdl.handle.net/1765/8032>.

Kenrick, W., *An Address to the Artists and Manufacturers of Great Britain; respecting an Application to Parliament for the farther Encouragement of new Discoveries and Inventions in the useful Arts*, London 1774.

Kittredge, C. Mark, "The Federal Circuit and non-patentable subject matter under Re Alappat and In Re Warmerdam", 11 *Santa Clara Computer & High Tech Law Journal*, 1995, pp. 261-268.

Kuhn, Thomas S., *The Structures of Scientific Revolutions*, Chicago 1996.

Lambert, Shelia, *Bills and Acts: Legislative Procedure in Eighteenth-Century England*, Cambridge 1971.

Langbein, John H., "Blackstone on Judging", in Wilfred Prest (ed.), *Blackstone and his Commentaries: Biography, Law, History*, Oxford and Portland 2009, pp. 65-77.

Leith, Philip, *Software and Patents in Europe*, Cambridge 2007.

Lemmings, David, *Professors of the Law: Barristers and English Legal Culture in the Eighteenth Century*, Oxford 2000.

Lieberman, David, "Blackstone's science of legislation", *Journal of British Studies* 27 (1988), pp. 117-149.

Lieberman, David, *The province of legislation determined*, Cambridge 1989.

Lieberman, David, "Property, Commerce and the Common Law: Attitudes to Legal Change in the Eighteenth Century", in Brewer, John and Staves, Susan (eds.), *Early Modern Conceptions of Property*, London 1995, pp. 144-158.

Locke, John, *Two Treatise of Government*, Cambridge 1988.

Lokin, J.H.A, *Tekst en Uitleg*, Groningen 1994.

MacLeod, Christine, *Inventing the Industrial Revolution: the English patent system, 1660-1800*, Cambridge 1988.

Malloy, Robin Paul, and Evensky, Jerry, (eds.), *Adam Smith and the Philosophy of Law and Economics*, Dordrecht 1994.

Manchester, A.H., *A Modern Legal History of England and Wales 1750-1950*, London 1980.

McCoubrey, Hilaire, and White, Nigel D., *Textbook on Jurisprudence*, London 1996.

Meijers, E.M., *Verzamelde Privaatrechtelijke Opstellen: Derde Deel Verbintenissenrecht*, Leiden 1955.

Mingay, G.E., *English landed Society in the eighteenth century*, London 1963.

Mokyr, Joel, "The Industrial Revolution and the economic history of technology: Lessons from the British experience 1760-1850", *Quarterly Review of Economics and Finance* 41 (2001), pp. 295-311.

Mossoff, Adam, "Rethinking the Development of Patents: An Intellectual History 1550-1800", *Hastings Law Journal*, 52 (2001) pp. 1255-1322

Munzer, Stephen R., *A theory of property*, Cambridge 1990.

Musson, A.E., and Robinson, Eric, *Science and Technology in the Industrial Revolution*, Manchester 1969.

Nicholas, Barry, *An Introduction to Roman Law*, Oxford 1988.

Nuvolari, Alessandro, *The Making of Steam Power Technology: a Study of Technical Change during the British Industrial Revolution*, Eindhoven 2004.

Oldham, James, "Eighteenth-Century Judges' Notes: how they explain, correct and enhance the Reports", *American Journal of Legal History* 31 (1987) pp. 9-42.

Oldham, James, "Law Reporting in the London Newspapers, 1756-1786", *American Journal of Legal History* 31 (1987) pp. 177-206.

Oldham, James, *The Mansfield Manuscripts and the growth of English law in the eighteenth century*, London 1992.

Oldham, James, *English Common Law in the age of Mansfield*, Chapel Hill and London 2004.

Owen, W., *The Method of Proceeding in Order to Obtain a Private Act of Parliament*, London 1767.

Parekh, Bhikhu, (ed.), *Jeremy Bentham: Critical Assessments*, vol. 111, *Law and Politics*, London 1993.

Parliament, *Report from the Select Committee on the Law relative to Patents for Inventions 1829*, Parliamentary papers, 1829, III.

Plucknett, Theodore F.T., *A Concise History of the Common Law*, London 1956.

Popper, Karl R., *Objective Knowledge: an evolutionary Approach*, Oxford 1974.

Popper, Karl R., and Eccles, John C., *The Self and its Brain*, London and New York 1977.

Posner, Richard A., *Law and Legal Theory in England and America*, Oxford 1996.

Postema, Gerald J., *Bentham and the Common Law Tradition*, Oxford 1986.

Prager, Frank D., "Standards of Patentable Invention from 1474 to 1952", *University of Chicago Law Review* 20 (1952) pp. 69-95.

Pufendorf, Samuel, *The Law of Nature and Nations*, London 1749.

Rajan, Raghuram G., and Zingales, Luigi, *The Emergence of Strong Property Rights: Speculations from History*, NBER Working Paper Series, nr. 9478, 2003.

Rede, Leman Thomas, *Strictures on the Lives and Characters of the most eminent Lâwyers of the present Day: including, among other celebrated names, those of the Lord Chancellor, and the twelve judges*, London 1790.

Reich, Charles A., "The New Property", *Yale Law Journal* 73 (1964), pp. 733-787.

Robinson, Eric, "Matthew Boulton and the Art of Parliamentary Lobbying", *The Historical Journal*, vol. 7, no. 2 (1964) pp. 209-229.

Robinson, Eric, and McKie, Douglas, (eds.), *Partners in Science: James Watt & Joseph Black*, London 1970.

Rosenheim, James M., *The Emergence of a Ruling Order: English Landed Society 1650-1750*, London 1998.

Ruttan, Vernon W., "Usher and Schumpeter on Invention, Innovation, and Technological Change", *Quarterly Journal of Economics* 73 (1959), pp. 596-606.

Scholten, Paul, *Asser's Handleiding tot de Beoefening van het Nederlands Burgerlijk Recht: Algemeen Deel*, derde druk, Zwolle 1974.

Shaw Solo, Carolyn, "Innovation in the Capitalist Process: A Critique of the Schumperterian Theory", *Quarterly Journal of Economics* 65 (1951), pp. 417-428.

Sherman, Brad, and Bently, Lionel, *The Making of Modern Intellectual Property Law: The British Experience 1760-1911*, Cambridge 1999.

Sherman, Brad, and Bently, Lionel, *Intellectual Property Law*, Oxford 2009.

Simpson, A.W.B., *Legal theory and legal history: essays on the common law*, London 1987.

Smith, Adam, *An inquiry into the nature and causes of the wealth of nations*, Cannan online edition, London, 1776.

Smith, Adam, *Lectures on Jurisprudence*, reprint of Oxford University Press 1978 edition, Indianapolis 1982.

Society of Gentlemen of the Middle Temple, *The Counsellor's Magazine; or a Complete Law Library for barristers etc*, London 1796.

Sorrenson, Richard, "Dollond & Son's Pursuit of Achromaticity 1758-1789", *History of Science* xxxix (2001), pp. 31-55.

Stein, Peter, *Regulae iuris: from juristic rules to legal maxims*, Edinburgh 1966.

Stein, Peter, *Legal Evolution: the story of an idea*, Cambridge 1980.

Stein, Peter, *Roman Law in European History*, Cambridge 1999.

Stein, Peter, and Shand, John, *Legal Values in Western Society*, Edinburgh 1974.

Sullivan, Richard J., "The Revolution of Ideas: Widespread Patenting and Invention during the English Industrial Revolution", *Journal of Economic History* 50 (1990), pp. 349-362.

Tawney, R.H., *Religion and the rise of capitalism*, New York 1947.

The Mechanics Magazine, Museum, Register, Journal and Gazette:
"Cochrane v Braithwaite", 19 (1833) at 253-254.
"Barton's improved metallic pistons", 22 (1834-5) at 38-39.

Thompson, F.M.L., *Gentrification and the Enterprise Culture: Britain 1780-1980*, Oxford 2001.

Toynbee, A., *Lectures on the Industrial Revolution of the Eighteenth Century in England*, London 1916.

Trebilcock, M.J., *The common law of restraint of trade: a legal and economic analysis*, Toronto 1986.

Twining, William, (ed.), *Legal Theory and Common Law*, Oxford 1986.

Van den Bergh, G.C.J.J., *Eigendom: grepen uit de geschiedenis van een omstreden begrip*, Deventer 1988.

Van Dulken, Stephen, *British Patents of Invention 1617-1977: A Guide for Researchers*, British Library 1999.

Van Maanen, G.E., and Walt, van der A.J., (eds.), *Property Law on the Threshold of the 21st Century*, Antwerp-Apeldoorn 1996.

Van Zijl Smit, Dirk, *The Social Creation of a Legal Reality: A Study of the Emergence and Acceptance of the British Patent System as a Legal Instrument for the Control of New Technology* (unpublished Ph.D. thesis), Edinburgh 1981.

Vinogradoff, Paul, *Common Sense in Law*, New Jersey 2006/1914.

Vogenauer, Stefan, *Die Auslegung von Gesetzen in England und auf dem Kontinent*, Tübingen 2001.

Vogenauer, Stefan, "Statutory Interpretation", in Jan Smits (ed.), *Elgar Encyclopedia of Comparative Law*, Cheltenham 2006, pp. 677-688

Warburton, William, "A Letter from an Author to a Member of Parliament", in *The Works of the Right Reverend William Warburton*, vol. 12, London 1811.

Watt, James, Boulton Matthew, *Boulton & Watt Papers*, edited by the Cornwall Record Office, available at <www.cornish-mining.org.uk>.

Webster, Thomas, *Reports and Notes of cases on Letters Patent for Inventions,* in 2 vols., London 1844.

Westerman, Pauline C., *The disintegration of natural law theory: Aquinas to Finnis*, Leiden 1998.

Wooddeson, Richard, *A systematical view of the laws of England; as treated of in a course of Vinerian lectures, read at Oxford, during a series of years, commencing in Michaelmas Term, 1777*, vol. 2, London 1792-1793.

Zwalve, W.J, *C. Uniken Venema's Common Law & Civil Law*, Deventer 2000.

Index

CURRICULUM VITAE

Before coming to the Netherlands in 1980, Helen Gubby studied history and law in England. While at the University of Nottingham, where she received her bachelor's degree in medieval and modern history, she was awarded the Cooper Prize for History. Having decided to become a barrister, she became a member of Gray's Inn and was given an entrance award and later a training award by the Inn. She was called to the Bar in 1978.

Once in the Netherlands, she worked as a legal editor and translator, as well as giving in-house courses on English legal terminology to Dutch law firms, the legal departments of Dutch companies and for the Dutch Ministry of Foreign Affairs. In 1993, she also became a lecturer in the Law Faculty of the Erasmus University, teaching English legal terminology to Dutch and international law students. After working as an advocate for a Dutch law firm, she decided to return to the university. She now not only teaches in the Law Faculty, but also teaches business law to international business administration students and general management students in the Rotterdam School of Management of the Erasmus University. She did not, however, forget her love of history and received a master's degree in history from the University of Leiden in 1991. In 2011 she received her Ph.D. in legal history from the Erasmus School of Law.

Helen Gubby's publications reflect her history and law background. She has written several textbooks on English legal terminology (*English legal terminology: legal concepts in language* 2011, which is now in its third edition, and *Practical legal English: legal terminology* 2006), co-authored a number of articles on computers and law (including *Sentencing by computer: an experiment*, Oslo, Universitetsforlaget, 1982 and "Legal decision making by computer: an experiment in sentencing", *Computer/Law Journal*, 1983) and more recently on patents ("Taking patents seriously", *International Law and Trade*, and *International Journal of Intellectual Property Management*, vol. 2, 2007). For a number of years, she also wrote articles on current events in England for a Dutch daily newspaper.